Habermas and Literature

Habermas and Literature

The Public Sphere and the Social Imaginary

Geoff Boucher

BLOOMSBURY ACADEMIC
NEW YORK • LONDON • OXFORD • NEW DELHI • SYDNEY

BLOOMSBURY ACADEMIC
Bloomsbury Publishing Inc
1385 Broadway, New York, NY 10018, USA
50 Bedford Square, London, WC1B 3DP, UK
29 Earlsfort Terrace, Dublin 2, Ireland

BLOOMSBURY, BLOOMSBURY ACADEMIC and the Diana logo are trademarks of
Bloomsbury Publishing Plc

First published in the United States of America 2021
This paperback edition published 2023

Copyright © Geoff Boucher, 2021

For legal purposes the Acknowledgements on p. vi constitute an extension
of this copyright page.

Cover design by Eleanor Rose
Courtesy Galerie Thaddaeus Ropac, London · Paris · Salzburg © Anselm Kiefer /
VG Bildkunst, Bonn 2020
Photo: Johansen Krause

All rights reserved. No part of this publication may be reproduced or transmitted
in any form or by any means, electronic or mechanical, including photocopying,
recording, or any information storage or retrieval system, without prior
permission in writing from the publishers.

Bloomsbury Publishing Inc does not have any control over, or responsibility for, any
third-party websites referred to or in this book. All internet addresses given in
this book were correct at the time of going to press. The author and publisher
regret any inconvenience caused if addresses have changed or sites have
ceased to exist, but can accept no responsibility for any such changes.

Whilst every effort has been made to locate copyright holders the publishers
would be grateful to hear from any person(s) not here acknowledged.

Library of Congress Control Number: 2021935673

ISBN: HB: 978-1-5013-4405-3
PB: 978-1-5013-6977-3
ePDF: 978-1-5013-4407-7
eBook: 978-1-5013-4406-0

Typeset by Deanta Global Publishing Services, Chennai India

To find out more about our authors and books visit www.bloomsbury.com and
sign up for our newsletters.

CONTENTS

Acknowledgements vi
List of abbreviations vii

Introduction 1

1 Adorno's social philosophy 13

2 Adorno's aesthetic theory 35

3 Habermasian social theory 59

4 The literary discourse of modernity 85

5 The nature of literary critique 111

6 Silenced needs, hidden desires 137

7 Habermas and the Devil: A communicative reading of *Doctor Faustus* 159

8 Imaginative disclosure and literary identification 187

9 Literary visions and the social imaginary 211

10 The phoenix and the serpent: J. K. Rowling's Harry Potter series 231

References 255
Index 270

ACKNOWLEDGEMENTS

Some parts of this book rework or reuse previously published material. Parts of the Introduction appeared as 'Habermas and Literature: The Public Sphere and the Social Imaginary', *Berlin Journal of Critical Theory*: 1 (1): 33–60. Chapter 1, on Adorno's social philosophy, and Chapter 3, on Habermas's social theory, extensively rework material originally published in *Understanding Marxism* (Durham: Acumen; 2012). Chapter 3, on Adorno's aesthetic theory, reuses some material from *Adorno Reframed* (London: IB Tauris; 2012), together with new material, in an entirely different context. The original sketch for Chapter 5, on literary critique, first appeared as 'The Politics of Aesthetic Affect – A Reconstruction of Habermas's Art Theory', *Parrhesia: A Journal of Critical Philosophy* (13): 62–78. Some sections of Chapter 7, on Mann's *Doctor Faustus*, were initially published in 'Adorno and the Magic Square: Schönberg and Stravinsky in Thomas Mann's *Doctor Faustus*', in Amirhosein Khandijazi (ed), *Reading Adorno: The Endless Road* (London; New York: Palgrave Macmillan), pp. 183–211. An early sketch for the chapter on literary disclosures, Chapter 8, was published as '"A Cataclysm of Truth from the Crisis of Falsehood": Reading Habermas on Calvino', *Parrhesia: A Journal of Critical Philosophy* (22): 22–37. I develop a different theoretical line now, but think the reading of Calvino remains valid. Finally, a section of Chapter 9, on social imaginaries, reworks material published in 'Ultimate Questions: Habermas on Philosophy and Religion', *Philosophical Inquiry* 41 (1): 50–62. I am grateful to the editors of some of these publications for the relevant permissions and note that the others have contractual or creative commons reuse licenses. I would like to acknowledge my deep gratitude to Frauke Hoffmann, for her assistance with this book, and the ongoing inspiration that she provides.

ABBREVIATIONS

References given to English translation ( ) and then German original [ ] as follows: (PDM: 121 [148]).

AT   Theodor Adorno, *Aesthetic Theory*, trans. Robert Hullot-Kentor (London: Continuum & The Althone Press; 2002 [1970]). Theodor Adorno, *Gesammelte Schriften, Band 7: Ästhetische Theorie*, (Frankfurt-am-Main: Suhrkamp; 1997 [1970]).

DoE   Theodor Adorno and Max Horkheimer, *Dialectic of Enlightenment: Philosophical Fragments*, ed. Gunzelin Schmid Noerr, trans. Edmund Jephcott (Stanford: Stanford University Press; 2012 [1947]). Theodor Adorno und Max Horkheimer, *Theodor Adorno, Gesammelte Schriften, Band 3: Dialektik der Aufklärung, Philosophische Fragmente* (Frankfurt-am-Main: Suhrkamp; 1997 [1947]).

KHI   Jürgen Habermas, *Knowledge and Human Interests*, trans. Jeremy Shapiro Boston: Beacon Press; 2002 [1968]). Jürgen Habermas, *Erkenntnis und Interesse. Mit einem neuen Nachwort* (Frankfurt-am-Main: Suhrkamp; 1973 [1968]).

PDM   Jürgen Habermas, *The Philosophical Discourse of Modernity: Twelve Lectures*, trans. Fredrick Lawrence (Cambridge: Polity Press; 1987 [1985]). Jürgen Habermas, *Der philosophische Diskurs der Moderne: Zwölf Vorlesungen* (Frankfurt-am-Main: Suhrkamp; 1985).

TCA1   Jürgen Habermas, *The Theory of Communicative Action, Volume 1: Reason and the Rationalisation of Society*, trans. Thomas McCarthy (Boston: Beacon Press; 1984 [1981]). Jürgen Habermas, *Theorie des kommunikativen Handelns, Band 1: Handlungsrationalität und gesellschaftliche Rationalisierung* (Frankfurt-am-Main: Suhrkamp; 1990 [1981]).

TCA2   Jürgen Habermas, *The Theory of Communicative Action, Volume 2. System and Lifeworld*, trans. Thomas McCarthy

(Boston: Beacon Press; 1987 [1981]). Jürgen Habermas, *Theorie des kommunikativen Handelns, Band 2: Zur Kritik der funktionalistischen Vernunft* (Frankfurt-am-Main: Suhrkamp; 1995 [1981]).

STPS   Jürgen Habermas, *The Structural Transformation of the Public Sphere: An Inquiry into a Category of Bourgeois Society*, trans. Thomas Burger (Cambridge, MA; MIT Press; 1991 [1962]). Jürgen Habermas, *Strukturwandel der Öffentlichkeit. Untersuchungen zu einer Kategorie der bürgerlichen Gesellschaft* (Frankfurt-am-Main: Suhrkamp; 1990 [1962]).

DF   Thomas Mann, *Doctor Faustus: The Life of the German Composer Adrian Leverkühn as Told by a Friend*, trans. John E. Woods (New York: Vintage; 1997 [1947]). Thomas Mann, *Doktor Faustus: Das Leben des deutschen Tonsetzers Adrian Leverkühn, erzählt von einem Freunde* (Berlin: Fischer; 1975 [1947]).

HPS 1–7   J. K. Rowling, *Harry Potter and the Philosopher's Stone* (London: Bloomsbury; 2014 [1997]) [1], *Harry Potter and the Chamber of Secrets* (London: Bloomsbury; 2014 [1998]) [2], *Harry Potter and the Prisoner of Azkaban* (London: Bloomsbury; 2014 [1999]) [3], *Harry Potter and the Goblet of Fire* (London: Bloomsbury; 2014 [2000]) [4], *Harry Potter and the Order of the Phoenix* (London: Bloomsbury; 2014 [2003]) [5], *Harry Potter and the Half-Blood Prince* (London: Bloomsbury; 2014 [2005]) [6], *Harry Potter and the Deathly Hallows* (London: Bloomsbury; 2014 [2007]) [7].

Introduction

We live on a planet of slums that is hurtling towards ecological catastrophe. The current pandemic, whose causal matrix includes deforestation and urbanization, is the first global environmental event to affect all humanity at once, but it will not be the last. Already, the polarized response to the pandemic, marked by the rise of authoritarian populism and the denial of reason, indicates that we are moving into an extremely dangerous conjuncture. This development compounds the resurgence of fundamentalist religion and the emergence into global prominence of highly successful forms of authoritarian state capitalism. Meanwhile, almost a billion people live in poverty, while billions more are effectively locked out of meaningful access to sustainable prosperity, by entrenched forms of social inequality. This is social unreason, on a global scale. There is every possibility that emancipatory social forces will have to engage in a desperate struggle this century to defend democracy and transform society, while mitigating climate change. Against this disastrous background, what earthly justification can there be for studying literature?

There are standard answers to this question. The salutary answer is: literature illuminates our humanity, thereby guiding the encounter with technology and institutions onto a path of release and reconciliation. The militant answer is: literature is a site of struggle, where utopian representations power ideological world views. The one sees literature as an instrument for moral instruction. The other sees it as a weapon of liberation, an implement for winning hegemony. Both agree that it is a tool. But literature is not (just) a tool. It is (also) a form of communication. The peculiarly indirect kind of communication that literature is has special, emancipatory effects. These effects are awakened – not manipulated – in the reader by its imaginative properties. Modern literature is a sort of laboratory experiment that suggests new structures of feeling and maps these onto the social world and the natural environment. These literary conjectures are supported by a refreshment of meaning-potentials that renders eloquent a different subjectivity. Literary communication incompletely sketches an imaginary world whose resemblance to the real world depends on reader response. Its aesthetic structures bind its worldly relevance to an innovative presentation of an integrated, new experience. The text therefore invites the reader to a vicarious experience, through active reception and imaginative participation. Readership communities then discuss the meaning of this imaginative world and its significance for society, or readers find themselves transformed by the literary journey. When literature has an emancipatory effect, it triggers public debate about the impact of society on the individual, or it catalyses the restructuring of the personality in ways that promote openness, inclusiveness and engagement.

Literature, in short, is a contributor to social reason. It sparks productive social debates. It catalyses transformations in subjectivity. Accordingly, this book will *not* be giving the routine replies to the 'why literature?' question. In particular, this book is neither utopian nor relativist. Hope, not utopianism, is the basic motivation for emancipatory struggle. Hope is based on the wish for a better world, but it is correctible in light of reality, for hopes can fail. This book is informed by that corrigible, fallible, desire. Partly for that reason, it is not a relativist book. I do not accept the false dichotomy of absolute truth or fashionable relativism. It is to escape this impasse in contemporary continental philosophy and literary theory that I have turned to the concept of intersubjectivity. Reason is social, and it unmasks social unreason. I think the vast bulk of social suffering is caused by unreasonable structural inequalities that are protected by ideological distortions. Indeed, the main cause of today's right-wing assault on reason is that – just as in the 1930s – there are only two ways to defend structural inequality once it starts to lose rational legitimacy: deny reason and/or resort to force. Reason is emancipatory: it exposes these distortions, points towards equality and provides an alternative to coercion.

Habermas and modernity

Enter Jürgen Habermas. But I had better stop right there. Introducing Habermas to English-speaking literary studies is a bit like introducing the Devil. Habermas is a partisan of enlightenment and a defender of democracy. For many, perhaps most, the first rhymes with European apologies for colonial domination. The second sounds like a meliorist politics restricted to 'actually existing democracy'. It is reasonable to be suspicious of such things. On my reading, however, Habermas is neither of them. I wondered for a long time how best to *show* this. My solution is to approach Habermas through his mentor, Theodor Adorno. The classical Frankfurt School in general and Adorno in particular are reasonably well understood in literary studies. Accordingly, I am going to reconstruct the Habermasian position on literature as a communicative rethinking of Adorno's aesthetics, framing this in terms of Habermas's communicative reformulation of Adorno's social philosophy. Against this background, by showing how and why Habermas communicatively reframes Adorno, I aim to make the kinds of position that the communicative approach unlocks intelligible and plausible.

Beginning from his reconstruction of historical materialism, in his work on communication and the evolution of society, Habermas has focused on retrieving the insights of the classical Frankfurt School. The Habermasian version of Critical Theory retains its emancipatory thrust. Indeed, he prolongs this into a communicative critique of modern alienation that condemns the bourgeois implementation of the modern project. After the political experience of Stalinism and the discrediting of teleological philosophies of history, however, it is no longer possible to assume the fundamental correctness of an unreconstructed Marxism. The classical critique of alienation unfolded as a 'single existential judgment' on how capitalism deserves to perish (Horkheimer 1982: 227). Today, this must take the form of a set of radical initiatives within a theory of social complexity and democratic politics. Guided by the practical intention of advising the struggles for liberation of suffering humanity, the Habermasian version of Critical Theory develops proposals for discourse ethics, deliberative democracy, the progressive reconstruction of the public sphere and the extension and deepening of modern moral autonomy. In his diagnosis of the social pathologies of the modern world – the problems of domination and nihilism, or alienation and meaninglessness – as generated within runaway capitalism and bureaucracy, Habermas clearly extends Adorno's critique of instrumental rationality. However, Habermas's condemnation of the 'colonization of the lifeworld by the system' happens within a reframing of the classical problematic, after the introduction of communicative interaction into historical materialism. By introducing the concept of communicative reason as an alternative to instrumental rationality, Habermas avoids the need to search for an exotic 'Other of Reason' in aesthetics (Adorno), religion (Horkheimer) or the libido (Marcuse). Additionally, Habermas rehabilitates the materialist interpretation of humanity's metabolism with nature. He rejects the Romantic notion that labour, rather than structural oppression, is the source of domination. For Habermas, an interdisciplinary, materialist research programme, one that aims at an emancipatory Critical Theory with a practical intent, must seek to unite the critique of domination with the question of a meaningful existence, in the context of a focus on human suffering. It is for this reason that he has vigorously proclaimed himself 'the last Marxist', someone 'fiercely determined to defend [historical materialism] as a still-meaningful enterprise' (Habermas 1992b: 464, 69).

Habermas's best-known work in the English-speaking world, *The Structural Transformation of the Public Sphere* [1962], illustrates the subtle interplay of identity and difference between Habermasian social theory and Adorno's negative dialectics. In *Structural Transformation*, Habermas insists, with Adorno, that the moral, political and cultural ideals based around autonomy that characterize the modern world are a fit critical standard against which to measure the bourgeoisie's failure to implement its own ideals. Hence Habermas's valorization of the inaugural moment of the public sphere in the aftermath of the democratic revolution, and of the Enlightenment's struggle against religious obscurantism and aristocratic anti-egalitarianism. Perhaps startlingly, *Structural Transformation* accepts the historical narrative of Adorno's and Horkheimer's *Dialectic of Enlightenment*, that the rise of the culture industry and the integration of state and economy have led to the atrophy of democratic politics and the manipulation of modern subjectivity. So grave is this transformation of the democratic revolution that it stands on the threshold of abandonment of negative liberty and moral autonomy. Habermas describes it as a 're-feudalization' of public life, equivalent to the demise of liberalism detected by Adorno. Yet the total effect of the work is the diametrical opposite to Adorno's elegiac *Negative Dialectics*, with its lamentation for the eclipse of reason and the elimination of the individual. The reason is not difficult to find: instead of a tragic paradox gnawing fatally at the heart of enlightenment, Habermas identifies an ongoing struggle between proponents of democracy and autonomy, and the forces of capitalism and bureaucracy.

With exemplary consistency and moral vision, Habermas's entire work represents an effort to bring German philosophy, beginning with Critical Theory itself, into the light of the democratic revolution of modernity. That means bringing it out from the darkness of Romantic celebrations of irrationality, and the counter-revolution's condemnations of the Enlightenment. The historical experience of fascist dictatorship demonstrates with clarity the falsity of the denunciation of parliamentary democracy and human rights, as a mere façade for capitalist domination. Meanwhile, the ideological sustenance provided to Nazism by Romantic philosophy illustrates the dangers of seeking freedom through alternatives to reason and through rejections of dialogue. Habermas's retrieval of democratic theory for progressive ends has a strong normative component that is nowhere more evident than in his willingness to debate with all parties. His social theory, including his political philosophy, moral theory and concept of communication, has developed through (often critical) dialogue with other thinkers in Critical Theory, such as Karl-Otto Apel, Axel Honneth, Albrecht Wellmer, Nancy Fraser, Seyla Benhabib and Thomas McCarthy. Furthermore, Habermas has debated thinkers outside Critical Theory, such as Jacques Derrida, John Rawls, Richard Rorty, Hans-Georg Gadamer, Nikolas Luhmann and Joseph Ratzinger, in philosophical exchanges often marked by reconsideration. Habermas's philosophical style, emphasizing the provisionality of claims and the revisable character of his own positions in light of objections from interlocutors, is deliberately the opposite of currents in German thought whose monological revelations of 'Being' and 'Truth' had a deeply irrationalist and authoritarian core. Habermas's 'post-metaphysical thinking' participates in a broad movement that has decisively shifted the centre of gravity of social philosophy in a progressive direction. In the period of the post-war reconstruction of global order, Habermas provided a crucial direction for Critical Theory, with a critique of the welfare state as merely a postponement of crisis tendencies, rather than a fundamental resolution of social antagonisms. As the post-war settlement has been replaced with a form of deregulated capitalism, Habermasian Critical Theory has turned to problems of post-national politics in the European Union. This has included analysis of the rights of refugees, the future of secularized societies, the role the media in society and the Western military interventions following the terrorist attacks of 11 September 2001.

Habermas and literature

Perhaps not surprisingly, in light of the current break-up of post-structuralist-influenced critical orthodoxies in literary studies, there is growing interest in the topic of 'Habermas and literature' (Colclasure 2010; Duvenage 2003; Hengen-Fox 2012: 235–54; Ingram 1991: 67–103; Kompridis 2006; Koppe 2004; Mcmahon 2011: 155–75). On the one hand, Habermas's concepts of the public sphere, communicative reason, deliberative democracy and discourse ethics have had an enormous influence in the humanities and beyond. On the other hand, there is increasing dissatisfaction with post-structuralist influenced theories that are mired in relativism, and there is broad interest in the approach of Frankfurt School Critical Theory to literature and culture (Jarvis 1998; Zuidervaart 1991). Although Habermas has written about the cultural role of literature and about literary works, however, he has not systematically articulated a literary-critical method as a component of either communicative reason or post-metaphysical thinking. Nonetheless, proposals for a communicative understanding of literary works focused on active reception and on the role of the ordinary reader in public debates on literature have significantly advanced the project of a Habermasian literary criticism (Eberly 2000; Hengen-Fox 2017). These link up with a growing perception in literary studies that critical practices involving monological versions of the hermeneutics of suspicion need to be rethought, and supplemented by approaches drawn from the hermeneutics of retrieval (Felski and Anker 2017; Felski 2015). Accordingly, the current book is synthetic in its intention, bringing Habermasian concepts and categories into contact with aesthetic and cultural theories in and around the Frankfurt School, and beyond.

The fundamental aim of this project is to understand how literature contributes to the cultural frameworks supporting social democratization now, which may perhaps support a democratic socialism, in the future. The central claims that the project advances, inspired by Habermas, are that literature contributes to the rationality of cultural and social processes, through catalysing debates in the public sphere, and that literature performs a key role in the formation of modern social imaginaries. But this book is 'Habermasian', or, better, oriented by a communicative perspective, rather than an explication of Habermas. On the one hand, the last thing that literary studies needs is another 'name brand' literary theory. On the other hand, in many places, I disagree with Habermas entirely. The central one concerns the main substance of this book. Although Habermas affirms the validity of modern literature in his celebrated defence of modernity, the position of the literary work is actually theoretically ambivalent within the architecture of Habermasian philosophy. The problematic status of aesthetics in Habermasian theory has been noticed by many commentators and intensively discussed within critical-theoretical circles (Duvenage 2003; Ingram 1991; Kompridis 2006; Wellmer 1991: 1–35). In effect, Habermas vacillates, initially locating aesthetic critique as a development of the expressive dimension within communicative reason, but subsequently proposing an opposition between communicative reason and artistic disclosure. (In the Frankfurt School tradition around Habermas and cothinkers, 'critique' does not just mean critical demystification. Rational argumentation in the space of public debate is what is known as 'critique', while the holistic presentation of imaginative visions is described as 'disclosure'.) In this context, it can be argued that Habermas presents two different, mutually exclusive models of the literary work: critique versus disclosure. I disagree. They are not mutually exclusive. I think they can be reconciled.

Specifically, what I am going to suggest here extends the proposal of Pieter Duvenage for the 'reciprocity of critique and disclosure', the idea that the specialized analysis of truth claims works side-by-side with the imaginative refreshment of language and perception (Duvenage 2003: 137–41). I am claiming, then, that literature triggers processes of critique and disclosure, and that these modalities of reception are related to (but not reducible to) the hermeneutics of suspicion and the hermeneutics of retrieval (Ricoeur 1970: 32), respectively. Through provoking public debate – especially in the form of professional and citizen literary criticism – literature generates arguments about the meaning and significance of works, and about their literary value and implications for life, arguments that ultimately have to do with the cultural interpretation of human needs. But through stimulating imaginative transportation, literary works also galvanize transformations in the life histories of individuals, providing fresh perceptions and new feelings, along with a renovation of language and the transformation of socially dominant images.

From the communicative perspective, then, literary works have 'two faces' – discursive intervention in the public sphere and personal integration of imaginative disclosures – that depend upon two modalities of literary reception: critique and identification. It is crucial to notice that these two faces of literature are not simply dimensions of the text, but are at the same time attitudes taken in reception. Following reception aesthetics, the literary text is actively constructed in the act of reading through the reader's imaginative concretization of its schematic hints, so that the literary work only emerges as the result of the reader's participation in the process of meaning-making. Critique and disclosure are what happens next, rather than 'things' lodged in the text, for readers may spark public debates about the significance of a work – critique – or imaginatively identify with meanings and incorporate these into their life histories – disclosure. Rather than a detailed reading of a literary text at this point, perhaps it would be better to refer briefly to a striking image that communicates this point with precision.

Anselm Kiefer's *The Secret Life of Plants* (2001) helps to focus these themes of the reciprocity of critique and disclosure, aesthetic communication and active reception, in a powerful visual enigma. The book-like objects in this extended series (one of which is reproduced on the cover of this book) are at once intrusively public, in their vast size, and completely private, in their seemingly hermetic resistance to everyday communication. Their apparently oblique relationship to their titular subject provokes conjecture and dialogue, while the imagery of constellations invites the viewer to freely project possible relationships and enter into visionary identification with the potentials unlocked by the work. Kiefer's gigantic codex is a work of oil paint on lead plates, where many of the indentations and markings on the surface of the metal leaves have been inscribed with alphanumeric sequences, some of which have been connected by lines and assigned names, reminiscent of constellations. These identifying sequences might be star designations from a stellar catalogue, for instance, or inmate numbers from a concentration camp, as in Kiefer's earlier sequence *Sternenlager*, 'star camp'. But they may also evoke the idea of a register of citizens, because the notion of a secret life of plants, in connection with monstrous books, is reminiscent of Kiefer's *Leviathan*. There, a census of chickpeas happens in a huge leaden archive, contrasting the fragility of persons, or souls, with the crushing mechanism of the state, and I wonder whether the surface indentations in *Secret Life* were in fact made by shutting the sheets on some flora. Finally, the heavenly connotations of a book of stars resonate with Kiefer's own meditation practice of Merkabah Kabbalah and its notions of mystical ascent. Finally, of course, every viewer finds themselves inscribed in the work through their participation in releasing its truth-potential, something which at once highlights their personal vulnerability and catalyses their intervention in the public space of reception.

In this book, I explain the first face of literature, the way that literary works intervene in the public sphere through catalysing forms of critique, by developing and extending Habermas's position on communicative reason.

The central proposition defended here is that autonomous literature is a sort of laboratory experiment with new feelings, desires, beliefs and needs. This has the potential to unlock, through critical debate, authentic new forms of self-realization. The second face of modern literature is its ability to affect the personality structures of individuals through identification. The integration of narrative arcs and social ideals into individual life histories transforms subjectivity. I explore the debates on imaginative world-disclosure in this context and then turn to the notion of the social imaginary, as a specific component of the lifeworld's horizon of expectations that is articulated narratively.

The plan for this book, then, is as follows. In Chapter 1, I present Adorno's social philosophy, focused on *Dialectic of Enlightenment* and associated texts, before discussing Habermas's criticism of the classical framework. In Chapter 2, I explicate Adorno's aesthetic theory, noticing its role in Adorno's social philosophy as well as its specifically musical and literary claims. Then, in Chapter 3, I turn to Habermas's communicative reframing of Adorno, in the social theory presented in his work on legitimation crises and communicative action, as well as his position on the public sphere. Against this background, in Chapter 4, I clarify Habermas's discussion of aesthetics in terms of what I describe as the 'literary discourse of modernity', something that parallels his better-known concept of a philosophical discourse of modernity.

In the next section of the book, I discuss literature and critique, that is, the way that literary texts catalyse critical debates that affect public discourse. In Chapter 5, I explore the nature of literary critique, building up a communicative model of the literary text and its critical reception by systematically reconstructing Habermas's position in his *Theory of Communicative Action*. In Chapter 6, I deepen this by returning to Habermas's incomplete encounter with psychoanalysis, proposing that literature and criticism uncover hidden desires and silenced needs, thereby exploring the subjective world in depth. Chapter 7 tests the resulting position against Thomas Mann's *Doctor Faustus*, which provides an opportunity to contrast the communicative interpretation with Adorno-inspired readings, clarifying what difference a Habermasian approach might make to literary critique.

In the final section of the book, I discuss literary disclosures. In Chapter 8, I argue that a 'disclosure' is what readers call the vision presented by a literary work, when they identify with it after being imaginatively transported by reading. In Chapter 9, I turn to the social effects of literary disclosure, proposing that literature plays an important role in the formation of modern social imaginaries, in relation to the articulation of what a culture regards as human flourishing. Chapter 10 explores 'reading for the vision', the communicative hermeneutics of retrieval, in relation to J. K. Rowling's *Harry Potter* series.

About this book

In the work of Habermas, literature acts as a placemarker for every non-pragmatic aesthetic medium. This is motivated by considerations that are historical – in the rise of the public sphere – and systematic – because of literature's special relation to language. Conversely, Habermas also often speaks about 'art' (*Kunst*), especially when discussing modern culture in terms of expert specializations in 'science, law and art', but his examples are almost exclusively literary (Adorno does the same thing, but his paradigm is music). It is beyond the scope of this book to discuss the complex relations between legitimate aesthetic generalizations and medium-specific considerations across all of the arts, but it is important to note that literature is not the 'queen of the media'. In the contemporary corporatization of the public sphere, cinema and television are being gradually supplanted by information and computer technology–mediated aesthetic forms (e.g. games), while the global reading public (now often happening through electronic books and even hypertext fictions) grows absolutely while declining relatively. It is no part of the logic of this book to argue that literature is disproportionately important because it is 'better' (e.g. more complex, conceptual, experimental or more linguistic, communicative or intersubjective), for it is neither better nor more important. My inquiry is into what literature potentially does, if and when it is read. Habermas makes answers to that particularly available, because of the way that his linguistic theory of communicative intersubjectivity intersects with this linguistic aesthetic medium.

Against this background, I intend to restrict the scope of literature somewhat. Throughout his book, by 'literature', I shall mean narrative fictions. Unfortunately, because I would need to introduce certain qualifications or specifications that would excessively burden this book, I cannot discuss drama and poetry, graphic novels and hypertext fictions. I also speak only of *modern* literature, for the characteristics of fairy tale and folk tales, medieval legends and ancient novels, are located in a different sociocultural matrix. However, modern literature (roughly, after 1600 ACE) is not restricted to literary modernism (the period style of interwar experimental literature). The term 'literature' is intended descriptively rather than evaluatively – it means story books, not great works – but, recognizing that some literature is culturally conformist, I sometimes discuss specifically emancipatory literature. My decisions regarding examples – *Doctor Faustus* and *Harry Potter* – are guided by the idea that emancipatory literature is a cultural intervention that sparks debate or transforms subjectivity. This is a synthesis of twentieth-century debates between 'commitment' and 'experimentation', which perhaps sits closer to the former than the later. Certainly, the communicative position that I propose emphatically rejects 'political migration', the idea that somehow experimental literature is politically revolutionary simply because it is aesthetically innovative, which is not only Adorno's key thesis but also the guiding star for most continental philosophy.

It is important to keep in mind that the Frankfurt School uses the nomenclature of German Idealism to describe the dimensions of reason, as well as the difference between conventional 'ethical' values and reflective 'moral' principles. (In the English-speaking world this nomenclature is generally the other way around.) When they refer to theoretical reason, practical reason and aesthetic judgement, Frankfurt School thinkers are speaking about the cognitive, normative and expressive dimensions of rationality, through the lens of Kant's three critiques. Their employment of the distinction between moral principle and ethical life is Hegelian, for Hegel contrasted the rational formalism of Kantian morality with the substantive values and customary norms constitutive of ethical life. By 'moral' and 'moral principles' or 'moral reasoning', then, is meant reflection on practical reason and its evaluative standards, in deontological or consequentialist reasoning about the validity of practical maxims (rules governing practical action). The Kantian moral law – 'do your duty; you can, because you must!' – and the universality test – 'act in such a way that the maxim guiding your action always takes other agents as ends, and not as means, of your action' – are examples of a conception of morality, as meta-ethical reflection. By contrast, by 'ethical', and 'ethical life' or 'values', is meant the traditional and historical framework of mutual recognition that has evolved in a society. I discuss recognition frameworks further in Chapter 9.

In this book, I often employ the expression 'motivations and orientations'. Habermas generally describes motivations as 'need-interpretations' (*Bedürfnisdispositionen* – 'dispositions-towards-needs') and sometimes as 'cultural meanings', expressions which are best read as 'need plus its symbolizations'. I discuss the content of the term 'need' in the context of psychoanalysis in Chapter 6. From the Habermasian perspective that I reconstruct, the concept of an individual motivation synthesizes a personal need with its public symbolization, as an intersubjectively recognizable request to the other, or demand for action, which is capable of consensual satisfaction. Motivations are rational just in case argumentative warrants can be provided for their intersubjective symbolization as based in shared meanings, and irrational when such warrants cannot be produced; motivations are pathological when, excepting for states of declared hostility or legitimate coercion, their fulfilment is non-consensual. When personal needs can be intersubjectively generalized in a potentially context-transcending way, they are candidates for a civilization's interpretation of 'human needs', or general interests, with the proviso that because there is an irreducible interpretive component, these cannot claim to be entirely culture-independent.

The concept of orientations refers to the ensemble of teleological values, normative principles and social attitudes that individuals use, in flexible and situated ways, to develop goals for action. Practical orientations are specified within the reigning form of ethical life, or framework of mutual recognition, and the ends of practical action are typically the teleological values that prevail in it. Following contemporary reconstructions of mutual recognition, it is possible to suggest that ethical life consists of a set of reciprocal expectations governing right conduct that include mutual respect and mutual esteem. These principles are codified into both formal regulations and informal expectations, such as rights (mutual respect) and status (mutual esteem), and arranged around a substantive conception of the highest good, for instance, human flourishing through individual self-realization. As explained in Chapter 3, Habermas is most concerned with the distinction between 'conventional' and 'post-conventional' orientations to practical action, but orientations are not exclusively directed towards practical ends, for they can also concern scientific inquiry and cultural meanings. Importantly, post-conventional moral orientations are impossible without a 'post-traditional' reflexivity towards hitherto 'traditional' motivations.

Finally, a note on Habermas in relation to the synthesis of social theory with Lacanian psychoanalysis, especially in the work of Slavoj Žižek, which I have discussed extensively in the last decade in my other books. The problem with the theories of ideology that have arisen in the wake of Althusser's Structural Marxism, such as the one developed by Žižek, is that they aim to enrich a functionalist social theory by adding a critical hermeneutics of culture. But instead of considering these as two different perspectives on society, 'system' and 'lifeworld', as Habermas does, thinkers such as Žižek try to graft hermeneutics directly onto the torso of functionalism, by locating subjectivity, symbolization and conventions in the functional slot marked 'ideology'. The result is a radical inflation of the category of ideology, combined with a social theory that lacks functional specificity. Habermas showed me how to avoid this problem. *Habermas and Literature*, which implements some of the things I have learnt from studying the Frankfurt School, is the result of this research. To write it, I have had to inhabit the communicative perspective from the inside; I was not capable of simultaneously developing a critical dialogue between Žižek and Habermas, while exploring Habermasian social and cultural theory, and applying it to a new domain. The retrieval of post-Althusserian theory in light of the communicative perspective is a project that remains to be completed.

1

Adorno's social philosophy

Although Adorno is not the sole influence on Habermas, the theory of communicative action is presented as a response to the impasses of Adorno's social philosophy and aesthetic theory (TCA1: 345–96 [414–75]). Accordingly, I intend to present the key motifs of Habermasian social philosophy and aesthetic theory as a communicative reframing of Adorno's core insights. Habermas reformulates Adorno's critique of instrumental rationality as the problem of the 'colonization' of everyday life by system imperatives originating in the economy and the state. The inspiration for Habermas's celebrated concept of communicative reason springs from Adorno's search for an alternative to instrumental rationality. The result of Adorno's enquiry, his conception of aesthetic mimesis, is rethought by Habermas in terms of a communicative aesthetics that locates art and literature within an intersubjective framework. The effect of Habermas's communicative rethinking of Adorno's social philosophy is a break with the bleak pessimism of Adorno's notion of the 'administered society'. It is also a democratization of the relation between progressive literature and the readership community, for Habermas rejects what he describes as the 'strategy of hibernation' of hermetic forms of modernism. Yet the Habermasian position is a prolongation, rather than a rejection, of Adorno's effort to develop a Critical Theory of society with an emancipatory practical intent.

The concept of a dialectic of enlightenment is central to Habermas and Adorno, but they have entirely different conceptions of what this means. It is reasonable to say that Adorno's (and Horkheimer's) controversial and provocative *Dialectic of Enlightenment* is the definitive work of classical Frankfurt School Marxism. The social philosophy and aesthetic theory that emerges from *Dialectic of Enlightenment* is the basis for Adorno's subsequent *Negative Dialectics* (1966) and *Aesthetic Theory* (1970). Not surprisingly, that seminal text is the main object of Habermas's criticisms of

Adorno as well as the starting point for Habermas's democratic retrieval, in his celebrated *The Structural Transformation of the Public Sphere* (1962). Furthermore, in many respects, *The Theory of Communicative Action* (1981) is Habermas's effort to rewrite *Dialectic of Enlightenment* in intersubjective and post-metaphysical terms, after the linguistic turn. Accordingly, I intend to concentrate on the way that *Dialectic of Enlightenment* sets up a whole line of thinking about literature and society, so as to clarify why I think that Habermas has a dialectical relation to Adorno. But I will be doing it a little bit differently.

The standard Habermasian presentation of the relation between the theory of communicative action and Adorno involves the idea of a paradigm shift from the 'philosophy of the subject' to communicative intersubjectivity (PDM: 106–30 [130–58]). Had it been stated in this form, however, Adorno would not have accepted this characterization of his position. Adorno certainly would have represented his own thinking as part of a critique of the philosophy of the subject, centred on a repetition, with two differences, of the Hegelian critique of Kant. The basic Hegelian strategy is to locate the 'transcendental subject' of Kantian philosophy in its social environment and show that this site evolves according to a dialectical logic of historical development. Dialectical reinscription inserts the (now merely quasi-transcendental) subject into the intersubjective network of social conventions and customary norms that Hegel describes as 'ethical life'. Now for the two twists. The first is the historical materialist reading of ethical life as itself merely the superstructural reflection of forms of political economy centred on the labour process. This locates the subject, grasped in materialist terms through the concept of labour as the human metabolism with nature, in an ascending sequences of historical stages in the dialectic of forces and relations of production. The second is the psychoanalytic interpretation of the subject as a material ego that is the result of a formative process of socialization. In its maturation process, the ego must traverse a series of potential vicissitudes in coping with instinctual impulses, by successfully developing its reality principle, social conscience and socially acceptable love objects. Both of these twists to the Hegelian dialectic radically de-transcendentalize the subject and re-locate the material ego in social and historical processes that depend on the human relation to nature.

The problem is that the Hegelian critique of Kant only partly succeeds, because it displaces the locus of the transcendental subject from the individual, as its empirical bearer, to the world spirit (Hegel) or the human species (Marx). In the Hegelian Marxism of Georg Lukács, this problem is intensely visible, as the claim that the proletariat is a collective subject whose world-constituting destiny is inscribed in the historical teleology of the forces of production. How then to retain the critical insights into historical development (Hegel), social alienation (Marx) and commodity reification (Lukács), without relapse into historical teleology and a transcendental meta-subject? In many respects, this is the fundamental question that *Dialectic of Enlightenment* sets out to answer, and a key part of its response is to propose that the Freudian twist makes the Hegelian dialectic divergent, not convergent. The ascent of the productive forces is a descent into repression, so that enlightenment culminates in totalitarianism, not emancipation, because barbaric irrationalism, not socialist revolution, breaks forth in protest against the 'renunciation of instinctual satisfaction' demanded by a civilization founded on domination. This is what Adorno means by a 'dialectic of enlightenment'.

Habermas's basic argument is that Adorno generates an inverted Hegelianism, a Hegelianism of disaster, not progress, because he lacks access to the conceptual framework of communicative intersubjectivity. The plan for the chapter, then, is to trace out the genesis of Adorno's dialectic of enlightenment, beginning from the Frankfurt School's initial alternative to the Lukácsian theory of commodity reification. After looking at the Frankfurt School's research programme of 'Critical Theory', and Adorno's role within that, the chapter then turns to the School's two initial breaks with Hegelian Marxism. The first is the critique of labour, as the source of 'instrumental reason', and its implications for the Hegelian-Marxist concept of the subject. The second is the turn to Freudian psychoanalysis and its implications for the Hegelian-Marxist philosophy of history. Then, the chapter looks at Adorno's (and Horkheimer's) provisional summary of the philosophical results of this investigation, in *Dialectic of Enlightenment*. After analysing Adorno's underlying philosophical anthropology, I return to the Habermasian critique of Adorno. In conclusion, I show how Habermas resumes Adorno's project from within a different conceptual framework.

Reification: Alienation plus rationalization

According to Habermas, the trajectory of Frankfurt School Marxism, or Critical Theory, including Adorno's work, is significantly inflected by the problematic of reification developed in Lukács's *History and Class Consciousness* (1921) (TCA1: 366 [490]). Lukács's brilliant synthesis of Marx's critique of alienation with Weber's notion of rationalization, in 'the reifying effects of the dominant commodity form' (Lukács 1971: 84), defines the starting point for Adorno's critical social theory (Buck-Morss 1977: 27; Claussen 2008: 83–5; Held 1980: 22–3; Jarvis 1998: 8–9; Jay 1973: 42). In fact, the entire notion of a 'dialectic of enlightenment', in which enlightenment reverses into mystification, and emancipation twists around into domination, is unimaginable without Lukács's discovery that rationality might sometimes reinforce, rather than dissolve, alienation.

Arguably, Critical Theory represents an effort to dialectically transcend the problems inherent in Lukács's totalizing integration of social philosophy and aesthetic theory, while extending and deepening the critique of reification (Rose 2014: 35–62).

Lukács adds Weber to Marx – as do Adorno and Habermas. Marx's critique of commodity fetishism, the way that 'a definite social relation between men that assumes, in their eyes, the fantastic form of a relation between things', when mediated by exchange value (Marx 1963: 72), is the origin of the concept of reification (*Verdinglichung* – petrifaction). Commodity fetishism and capitalist alienation are the same thing, and, in a society dominated by commodity production, Lukács proposes, instrumental calculations and logical consistency dominate social action. Enter Weber. For Weber, the modern world is formed through a new type of 'formal rationality', which abstracts the calculable form of rational procedures from the substantive goals of social action (Weber 1968: 84–5). What Weber calls 'purposive rationality' involves instrumental calculations of the most efficient means to (potentially irrational) goals, while reflection on the goals of action happens in 'value rationality', the submission of reason's ends to procedural formalism. This focus on calculation, Lukács argues, 'leads to the destruction of every image of the whole', that is, to the de-totalization of theoretical consciousness and the practical fragmentation of human activity (Lukács 1971: 103). Accordingly, the central conceptual contrast in dialectical theory is between sociocultural fragmentation and revolutionary totalization (Lukács 1971: 27).

According to Lukács, in line with the Hegelian conception of totality, the commodity is the 'universal category of society as a whole', a 'central structural problem' whose 'consequences are able to influence the *total* . . . life of society' (Lukács 1971: 86, 84). Hegelian dialectics focuses on 'a conception of the subject which can be thought of as the conscious creator of the totality of content' (Lukács 1971: 122), that is, an active subject who consciously creates the world and at the same time transforms themselves (Lukács 1971: 128). Lukács maintains that Hegel idealistically reified this agent of totalization into the 'world spirit', but Marx's discovery indicates that the proletariat is the 'identical subject-object of history' (Lukács 1971: 206). Confident about the Marxist version of historical teleology, Lukács boldly announces that commodity reification is therefore the last major contradiction of world history. According to Lukács, with 'the entry of the proletariat into history', at last a 'historical situation has arisen in which . . . the unity of theory and practice becomes possible' (Lukács 1971: 3).

Initially, then, Lukács argued that the practical totalization proposed by the vanguard party of the revolutionary proletariat was the antidote to reification, but with the retreat of the revolutionary tide, Lukács turned to the historical novel as the agent of a conceptual totalization. Lukács suggests that, irrespective of the politics of the author, the aesthetic programme of the historical novel demands the representation of an entire social formation, consisting of historical agents, social relations and material institutions (Lukács 1962). Through the selection of socially typical representative characters, the novelist reconstructs the total internally related network of social practices that constitutes an historical world, not just as a set of reified appearances (experiential fragments constrained by social location), but also as an essential process (social relations based in material production). Accordingly, the realist novel provides a figuration of the historical process itself, locating class agents in the rise and fall of modes of production. At the same time, the novel presents human universality but in a way that speaks to the reader about individual experience and communicates a revolutionary injunction: 'you must change your life!' (Lukács 1963: 645). In the late work of Lukács, therefore, the historical novel itself becomes loaded up with the messianic expectation of a unification of theory and practice. Literature is regarded as a revolutionary totalization that involves world-constituting creative praxis, acting as a placemarker for a now-quiescent proletariat.

Although insightful, the concept of reification secretes a problematic metaphysics. The Hegelian cumulative series of historical stages of 'consciousness in the progress of freedom' – in its Marxist acceptation as an ascending sequence of modes of production – is not the only ballast hidden in the reification problematic. Alongside historical teleology, Hegelian dialectics also relies on the concept of society as an expressive totality, that is, on the theory that all social structures (economic, political, juridical, ideological) are merely expressions of a single 'principal contradiction' that determines the particular historical stage. Finally, Hegelian dialectics depends on a 'subject of history', a social macrosubject such as the proletariat, supposed to be the agent of revolutionary transformation. In Lukács's formulation of reification, these three aspects of Hegelian dialectics – historical teleology, expressive totality and social macrosubject – are inscribed with particular force.

Adorno and Horkheimer had their doubts. Adorno vehemently rejected the notion of a historical subject capable of generating the natural environment and the social totality (Adorno 1973: 22–4, 189–92; Jay 1977: 147–74). Horkheimer agreed (Abromeit 2011: 121). Accordingly, the programmatic documents of the Institute for Social Research, under the directorship of Max Horkheimer, describe the critique of reification in terms of the ubiquity of 'calculation' and 'equivalence'. Despite refusing his terminology, however, their synthesis of Marx and Weber is without question an extension and development of the problematic inaugurated by Lukács (Buck-Morss 1977; Rose 2014).

Instrumental reason: Reification plus repression

Frankfurt School Marxism, then, or 'Critical Theory' (Horkheimer 1982: 188–252), deliberately diverges from the Hegelian-Marxist formulations of

Lukács in some crucial respects. The most significant of these is that Adorno and Horkheimer add Freud to Marx and Weber, thus combining repression with reification in the single figure of 'instrumental reason'. But the importance of that innovation only emerges clearly against the background of the other three – the development of an interdisciplinary materialism, the critique of labour as inherently alienated and 'sympathy for the devil' of counter-Enlightenment philosophy.

To provide an alternative to the expressive totality generated by Hegelian Marxism, it was necessary for Adorno and Horkheimer to develop an interdisciplinary theory capable of grasping social complexity. In Horkheimer's inaugural lecture (1931), and in subsequent programmatic documents (1937), this innovation in historical materialism was prudently described as Critical Theory, rather than as Marxism (Horkheimer 1982: 188–252). The Institute's survival in a hostile academic and political environment was not the only consideration motivating Horkheimer's euphemism, however, for the dialectical methodology of Critical Theory differs from Lukácsian totalization in major respects.

For Lukács, the crisis tendencies of capitalism are a direct expression of the principal contradiction of the social formation: in an economic collapse, 'the true structure of society appears' (Lukács 1971: 101). Consequently, although Marxist theory is constantly evolving in light of historical developments, a single homogenous theoretical medium (Marxist method and its empirical findings) suffices to describe bourgeois society (Lukács 1971: 1–26).

By contrast, anticipating contemporary theories of social complexity, Frankfurt School Marxism took into consideration the relative autonomy of the functional structures of capitalist society. For the Frankfurt School, society is a complex arrangement of relatively autonomous social institutions, involving the economy, the state (including both law and politics), cultural apparatuses – and the family. It therefore acknowledges the need for discipline-specific inquiry into the fields of economics, politics, jurisprudence and culture. Yet, although each set of social institutions has its own evolutionary dynamic and social conflicts, their interaction is mediated by what Adorno calls 'the principle of equivalence' (Adorno 1973: 178).

To grasp this complexity requires a critique of the bourgeois disciplines in materialist terms, by historicizing their categories of inquiry (in accordance with the history of their objects), before integrating these conclusions into a complex totality. The implication is that Horkheimer's proposal for methodological totalization of the research findings of an interdisciplinary materialism replaces the 'category of totality as the bearer in theory of the principle of revolution' (Lukács). This recasts the problem of transcending conceptual reification as a question of the dialectical integration of disciplinary specializations (Horkheimer 1982: 199–205). Historical materialism becomes a method for the dialectical integration of relatively autonomous domains, rather than a total unification of theory and practice in a 'philosophy of praxis'.

The second aspect of Adorno's and Horkheimer's reformulation of the reification problematic decisively distances the Frankfurt School from Hegelian Marxism. Lukács thought that the labour process originated in creative self-expression, which was only subsequently denatured by rationalization and commodification. By contrast, for Adorno and Horkheimer, the purposive rationality involved in labour is the root of reification. Where Lukács regarded revolutionary totalization as the solution to sociocultural fragmentation under capitalism, Adorno and Horkheimer considered capitalist society to be a seamless totality constituted by universal equivalence. Adorno's and Horkheimer's reading of Weber suggested to them that the success-oriented manipulation of raw materials, based on calculations of efficiency and effectiveness, is deployed in the service of the self-preservative instinct and expresses a desire for the mastery of nature (DoE: 28–9 [42–3], 42–3 [61–2]). Labour as instrumental action, as purposive rationality formalized into means-ends calculations, is the origin of domination, not liberation, and it is rationally systematic as well as systematically reifying. Thus, where Lukács saw cultural fragmentation awaiting revolutionary totalization, Adorno and Horkheimer register a rational totality of seamless domination, one that has virtually extinguished any spark of revolt.

Finally, when Lukács considers the post-Enlightenment trajectory of bourgeois philosophy after German Idealism, he sees a history of the increasing 'destruction of reason', proceeding necessarily as the intellectual reflex of the growing irrationality of capitalism in decay (Lukács 1980). By contrast, Adorno and Horkheimer discover in the Romantic reactionaries, the anti-Enlightenment philosophers that they call the 'dark writers of the bourgeoisie', the evidence of a desperate search for lost substance amidst an increasingly formalized, but empty, world. For Adorno and Horkheimer, then, the Romantic critique of Enlightenment was just as valid as the Enlightenment's critique of the aristocratic and religious reaction against the democratic revolutions (DoE: 71 [97]).

In particular, Horkheimer and Adorno focus on the problem of existential meaningfulness, through prolonged engagement with the Romantic critique of the Enlightenment. Their dialectical appropriation of the figures they called the 'dark writers of the bourgeoisie' – especially the Marquis De Sade, Schopenhauer and Nietzsche – is integrated into a synthesis of Marx and Weber that is inflected by a reading of Freud. But Marx, Weber and Freud are interpreted as the critique of formal rationality, while Schopenhauer, De Sade and Nietzsche are grasped as testifying to the return of the repressed substance, which Adorno and Horkheimer equate with nature (DoE: 74 [101]). The dark writers of the bourgeoisie can mercilessly expose the truth of enlightenment because they are the ambassadors of the revolt of nature.

The dialectic of Enlightenment

I am now in a position to describe Adorno's and Horkheimer's analysis of instrumental reason, outlined in their extraordinarily influential book, which will make it possible to explain how Habermas modifies their critique. Under the sign of the critique of instrumental reason, its master argument lends a Freudian twist, with a Romantic inflection, to the analysis of reification.

Developed in exile in California during the bleakest moments of the twentieth century, between the Battle of Stalingrad and the Liberation of France, the work was revised after the discovery of Auschwitz and in light of the emergence of the Cold War. Where socialist thinkers in the interwar period had posed the historical alternatives of 'socialism or barbarism' to the anti-fascist movements on the Continent, Adorno and Horkheimer now believed that they were confronted by a spectacle of universally regnant barbarism, with communist, fascist and democratic variants. In short, Adorno and Horkheimer set themselves the task of explaining 'why humanity, instead of entering a truly human state, is sinking into a new kind of barbarism' that arms itself with the weaponry of enlightenment (DoE: xiv [1]). 'Enlightenment', they write, 'aimed at liberating human beings from fear and installing them as masters [of nature]. Yet the wholly enlightened earth is radiant with triumphant calamity' (DoE: 1 [9]). The tendency towards the functional integration of a managed economy, state bureaucracy and the culture industries that they detect, together with a gravitation towards dictatorship and persecution, is the result of a formally rational society that has entirely lost contact with substantive reason. Instrumental rationality, then, is the explanation for why 'enlightenment reverts to myth', for enlightenment means the full deployment of instrumental rationality as a social principle.

Dialectic of Enlightenment is an extraordinarily enigmatic book, one whose central motifs are cryptic and paradoxical – 'enlightenment reverts to myth' – and whose project involves deliberate aporia, rather than the Hegelian dialectical resolution of historical contradictions that its designers constantly allude to. Their description, not just of the bourgeois Enlightenment in Western Europe, but of the process of enlightenment grasped in Weberian terms as rationalization, is sweepingly negative. 'The system which enlightenment aims for', they claim, 'is the form of knowledge which most ably deals with the facts, most effectively assists the subject in mastering nature' (DoE: 65 [90]). But Enlightenment as global domination over nature, they warn, turns against the thinking subject (DoE: 28–9 [39–40]). That is because, aside from the estrangement which transforms the natural environment into raw materials for instrumental manipulation, the human being is a part of nature who must therefore repress her or his own nature, and alienate himself or herself from fellow men and women. In other words, enlightenment is alienation in the Marxist sense. Additionally, enlightenment is rationalization in the Weberian sense. 'For the Enlightenment', they assert, 'only what can be encompassed by unity has the status of an existent or an event; its ideal is the system from which everything and anything follows' (DoE: 4 [12]). Systematization of knowledge means 'the connection of all parts in conformity with a single principle', which means, the logical subsumption of particulars under universal categories in determining judgement (DoE: 63 [88]). Enlightened human beings have replaced meaning by calculation, the concept by the formula. This results in a radical shrinking of the world, since 'for the enlightenment, anything which does not conform to the standard of calculability and utility must be viewed with suspicion' (DoE: 3 [11]). The reason is that 'the system's principles are those of self-preservation', and so 'enlightenment is mythical fear radicalised' (DoE: 65, 11 [90, 22]). 'Enlightenment is totalitarian', they conclude, 'as only a system can be' (DoE: 4, 18 [12, 29]).

Interpreting the emergence of fascism as a 'revolt of nature', in both *Dialectic of Enlightenment* and *Eclipse of Reason* Adorno and Horkheimer add a Freudian dimension to their synthesis of Marx and Weber (Adorno and Horkheimer 2002: 152; Horkheimer 1974: 122). The fascistic return of repressed of nature involves delight in causing suffering, not a return to innocence, because the mechanism of repression depends on superego guilt (DoE: 74 [101–2]). To the authors, fascist barbarism, as reactionary modernism, as combination of technological rationality with atavistic collectivism, seemed like the eclipse of any prospect of a substantively reasonable society, behind the black sun of formal rationality gone wild. The result is a risky build-up of impressionistic connections between the subjective reason of the modern period, instrumental rationality as reification plus repression, and fascist politics as a 'satanic synthesis of nature and reason' (Horkheimer 1974: 123).

Under the sign of the triumph of instrumental rationality, then, Adorno and Horkheimer inflate Critical Theory's analysis of the incipiently totalitarian character of the interwar political conjuncture into a global diagnosis of the nature of the historical epoch of late capitalism. It is important to recognize that this is not an isolated work that reflects a moment of historical despair, but is rather the mature statement of a position with a clear internal logic, which is expressed in the surrounding penumbra of works alongside it. These works include Horkheimer's *The Eclipse of Reason* (1947), Adorno's *Philosophy of Modern Music* (1947) and *Minima Moralia* (1951), and Adorno's and Horkheimer's sections of *The Authoritarian Personality* (1951). Adorno and Horkheimer do gesture in the direction of the Hegelian critique of Kant, which would set dialectical reason against formal logic and the categories of the understanding (TCA1: 372–4 [498–501]). But the Lukácsian route, which relies on a dialectical supersession of the Kantian antinomies in the unification made possible by labour praxis, is ultimately barred to them. The effect is to create a scission between the Marxian narrative of historical progress and a Freudian narrative of increasing repression, whose final dialectical turn is the 'revolt of nature' in the twisted form of totalitarian domination.

The dialectical critique of Kant

Now, the key to the architecture of *Dialectic of Enlightenment* is that its chapter structure reflects Adorno's and Horkheimer's version of Lukács's analysis of the antinomies of bourgeois thought (Lukács 1971: 110–49). Kant is regarded as the central figure in the Enlightenment because moral autonomy is central to bourgeois society. For that reason, the structure of the work corresponds to Kant's three critiques, in a metacritique of theoretical reason ('Odysseus and Enlightenment': cognitive), practical reason ('Juliette and Enlightenment': normative) and aesthetic judgement ('The Culture Industry': aesthetic). Instrumental reason is grasped as technological manipulation, means-end calculations of efficiency and effectiveness, moral formalism, indifferent to ethical ends, and the logical subsumption of particular data under universal principles. In each instance, the central thesis is that enlightenment dialectically reverts to its opposite, because of an insoluble contradiction. Scientific cognition, by separating formula and fact from quality and process, transforms into nominalism, the positivist 'myth of the given', which reifies the products of processes into variables in equations. Moral formalism, by abstracting the coherence of maxims from the goodness of ends, arrives at a perverse inversion of substantive humaneness, in which 'anything goes', provided that it is logically consistent. Aesthetic rationalization, by reducing cultured judgement to stereotypical responses to calculated arrangements, transforms reflective judgement into determining judgement, the subsumption of particulars under the universal. In the fourth chapter, on anti-Semitism, Freud provides the missing fourth critique of the inevitable transformation of liberalism into fascism, and autonomy into submission.

Metacritique of theoretical (cognitive) reason and social labour

Against this background, in the chapter on Odysseus, Adorno and Horkheimer locate theoretical reason in the social context of labour practices, as informed by the scientific-technical accomplishments of historical societies. They propose that 'the enthronement of the means as the end, which in late capitalism takes on the character of overt madness, is already detectible in the earliest history of subjectivity', precisely in the instrumental rationality that shapes labour practice as teleological action (DoE: 43 [62]). There is, in other words, no hope that labour provides the model for a way out of the dialectic of enlightenment. Instead, labour is the model for instrumental reason. Not only does labour depend on the instrumental calculations of efficiency and effectiveness, but it is dynamized by instinctual self-preservation and motivated by considerations of usefulness (DoE: 22–3 [35–6]). Having identified labour as the prodrome of reification rather than the locus of emancipation, Adorno and Horkheimer project the characteristics of alienated labour under capitalism backwards onto the entirety of history, by means of the claim that 'Odysseus is . . . the prototype of the bourgeois individual' (DoE: 35 [47]).

The social context of theoretical reason in labour practice is not exhausted by anthropological generalities, for there is also a specifically historical aspect. Archival research indicates that Adorno and Horkheimer accept the 'state capitalist' hypothesis of Friedrich Pollock, which proposes the emergence of a crisis-free, rationally planned social formation with democratic and totalitarian (fascist and soviet) variants (Abromeit 2011: 394–424, esp., 05; Noerr 2002: 217–47). According to Pollock, constant state intervention in the economy and regulation of labour markets, together with aggressive programmes of imperialist expansion and the creation of vast military industries, mean that the crisis potentials of capitalism have been suppressed, replaced by rational planning (Pollock 1985: 71–94). Pollock's position certainly influenced Adorno's and Horkheimer's formulation in *Dialectic of Enlightenment* that 'it is no longer the objective laws of the market which govern the actions of industrialists and drive humanity toward catastrophe' (Adorno and Horkheimer 2002: 30). In 'Reflections on Class Theory' (1942), Adorno cites Pollock as the authority for the claim that class relations are mediated under state capitalism by planning agencies and corporate boardrooms, rather than by the blind processes of the unregulated market (Adorno 2003: 93–110). In 'The Authoritarian State' (1942), Horkheimer goes further than Pollock in proposing that 'state capitalism', which is 'the authoritarian state of the present', manages to 'do away with the market [entirely] and [thereby] hypostatize the crisis'. The implication is not only that state capitalism (i.e. fascism) is the same as integral (i.e. Soviet) socialism, because these are the totalitarian forms of the post-liberal historical epoch, but also that restriction to 'economic-technical considerations' reduces democratic variants to pseudo-alternatives (Horkheimer 1973: 4, 8, 14–15). Adorno's and Horkheimer's contribution to the fusion of economics and politics described by Pollock, then, is to supplement this with an account of the integration of culture and the personality into what Adorno eventually calls the 'administered world' (Adorno 1987: 44).

Metacritique of practical (normative) reason and moral formalism

In the next chapter Adorno's and Horkheimer's provocative combination of 'Kant with Sade' anticipates subsequent psychoanalytic discussions of formal morality and the superego command of moral conscience, but it suffers from a significant defect. Adorno and Horkheimer think that Kantian deontological moral reasoning – the testing of practical maxims in light of their universal applicability – is consistent with totalitarian conceptions of the nature of ethical life. This is supported by Adorno's conviction that the 'damaged life' of the modern individual is mainly mutilated by a moral formalism that extirpates natural sympathy (Adorno 2005a: 78–80).

Against this background, the chapter on 'Sade's Juliette, or, Enlightenment Morality' essays a polemical demolition of bourgeois ethical life on grounds that the prevailing moral formalism, caused by the Enlightenment, has resulted in nihilism. Two criticisms are advanced in support of this contention. The first is that moral formalism is consistent with any ends of practical reason whatsoever. Moral formalism tests the logical consistency of a practical maxim, not its substantive humanity. According to Adorno and Horkheimer, the will-to-power of the Nietzschean superman 'is no less despotic than [Kant's] categorical imperative' (DoE: 90 [123]). The second is that the resulting corrosion of substantive conceptions of human flourishing leads bourgeois society to eventually arrive at the conclusion that ethical substance is the problem. A nihilistic vacuum forms in the wake of the Enlightenment's destruction of traditional and historical ethical life: 'the special architectonic structure of the Kantian system, like the gymnasts' pyramids in Sade's orgies . . . prefigures the organization, devoid of any substantial goals, which was to encompass the whole of life' (DoE: 69 [95]). Reading De Sade together with Nietzsche, Adorno and Horkheimer propose that reason, having reduced nature to raw material and society to positive facts, is capable of systematizing any cruelty or perversion (DoE: 74–9 [102–6]).

> The dark writers of the bourgeoisie, unlike its apologists, did not seek to avert the consequences of the Enlightenment with harmonistic doctrines. They did not pretend that formalistic reason had a closer affinity to morality than to immorality. While the light-bringing writers protected the indissoluble alliance of reason and atrocity, bourgeois society and power, by denying that alliance, the bearers of darker messages pitilessly expressed the shocking truth. (DoE: 92 [126])

On this interpretation, the reading of Kant with Sade is the centrepiece of *Dialectic of Enlightenment*. The argument is that formal morality is consistent with substantive immorality, because it involves the imposition of logical consistency on arbitrary contents. The choice of Sade to demonstrate this thesis is motivated by the idea that the Enlightenment superego is sadistic in its excessive enforcement of the rules, while the modern ego is masochistic in its submission to the superegoic repression of nature. Accordingly, the Enlightenment is not only 'totalitarian' but also 'sadistic' in its 'lethal desire' [*tödliche Liebe*] (DoE: 89 [121]).

Metacritique of aesthetic judgement and culture industry

In the chapter on the culture industry, Adorno and Horkheimer situate aesthetic judgement in the context of the industrialization of culture and the emergence of state propaganda. The culture industry thesis involves the proposition that the penetration of commodification and rationalization throughout society results in the assimilation of bourgeois culture and socialization patterns to the fusion of economics and politics characteristic of the authoritarian state. The adaptation of cultural forms to social reality happens because artworks, which are inherently purposeless, are turned towards the function of entertainment and recruited into the process of social reproduction, as forms of escape after work (DoE: 112–15 [149–52]). The conversion of useless artworks into useful culture by the leisure industries involves the routinization of audience response, attained through stereotypical contents and repetitious forms, which decisively subordinates the material of the artwork to instrumental calculations (DoE: 107–11 [145–9]). The formal abstraction involved in the commodification of art, its inclusion within circuits of exchange value, is completed with the real subsumption of cultural labour into processes framed by the abstractions of value and the quantification of labour power. The real subsumption of cultural labour to the industrial conditions of the entertainment corporations means the substitution of forms of pseudo-individuation, such as brand differentiation and the star system, for the autonomous process by which the artwork legislates its own forms based on its core concerns (DoE: 102–10 [134–44]). 'As the demand for the marketability of art becomes total, a shift in the inner economic composition of cultural commodities is becoming apparent', Adorno and Horkheimer conclude. 'In adapting itself entirely to need, the work of art defrauds human beings in advance of liberation from the principle of utility' (DoE: 128 [167]).

Adorno and Horkheimer's descriptive claim about the culture industry, therefore, is not a complaint about the rise of entertainment corporations or the decline of artisanal methods in artistic labour, but a thesis about the *standardization* of cultural forms and the consequent *trivialization* of aesthetic content. Instead of the anticipation of human happiness that is to be expected from free creativity, the products of the culture industry promote instant gratification, based on the infantile regression that results from identification with successful aggression or sexual conquest (DoE: 120–5 [159–64]).

The authoritarian personality and the repression of nature

Adorno's synthesis of Marx and Weber is only completed with the Freudian category of repression, for the alienation detected by the critique of instrumental reason includes the suppression of human nature. In a celebrated passage from DoE, the authors propose that 'humanity had to inflict terrible injuries on itself before the self – the identical, purpose-directed, masculine character of human beings – was created, and something of this process is repeated in every childhood' (DoE: 26 [40]). Conversely, Adorno maintains that Freud's instinct theory is the social-theoretical centre of gravity of psychoanalysis, for the concept of repression implies a natural limit to social adaptation (Adorno 1967b: 86–8). Despite his endorsement of the concept of the instincts, however, Adorno's perspective is consistent with libido theory. He speaks of aggression and sexuality, not the late Freudian speculative principles of Eros and Thanatos. Adorno once declared that 'in psychoanalysis, nothing is true except the exaggerations' (Adorno 2005b: 78). But for Adorno, included under the category of veracity is the bulk of psychoanalytic theory. He accepts the developmental account of the Oedipus Complex, the psychoanalytic theory of the defence mechanisms and the connection between neurotic failures of repression and symptom formation. These categories are central to Adorno's interpretation of fascism, because only a theory of irrational motivations could explain the peculiar combination of submissive and destructive orientations visible what he called the 'authoritarian personality'.

Horkheimer described fascism as a 'satanic synthesis of reason and nature', the 'revolt of natural man' against social alienation (Horkheimer 1974: 83), twisted into the diabolical form of a delight in transgression. Instrumental rationality and moral formalism then provide fascism with the possibility of combining rational means with perverse ends, placing this in the service of domination. Adorno grasps the authoritarian personality in psychoanalytic terms as the thesis of a latently sadomasochistic character underlying the personality structure of the modern individual. Adorno's notion of fascism as a 'rebellion of nature' is therefore best grasped in the Freudian context proposed to the Institute for Social research by Erich Fromm, who draws conclusions cognate to Freud's *Civilization and Its Discontents* (1930). Freud proposed that the advance of civilization was necessarily accompanied by the increasing 'renunciation of instinctual satisfactions', that is, constant incrementation in repression (S. Freud 1930: 57–146). Fromm's critique of Freud involves historicization of psychoanalytic anthropology and its material contextualization in economic and familial structures, but Fromm's social psychology is in complete agreement with the thrust of Freud's argument (Fromm 1991). For Fromm, generalizing beyond Freud, oedipal arrangements centred on the strict father and the distant mother, sustained by the economic and marital structures of society, promote subservience to authority and aggression towards unconventionality. 'Since the term sado-masochistic is associated with ideas of perversion and neurosis, I prefer to speak instead of the sado-masochistic character, especially when not the neurotic but the normal person is meant' (Fromm 1994: 162). According to Fromm, then, the normal person has an underlying sadomasochistic character by virtue of bourgeois socialization, but this normally manifests as modern conformity, rather than the reactionary modernism of fascist rebellion.

Adorno elaborates on Fromm by proposing that the formation of the culture industry and the administration of social reproduction imply increasing corporate influence and state control over the process of socialization and the dynamics of the family. The demand of the culture industries for unconditional adjustment to social norms results in the imposition on the individual of 'something truly heteronomous and alien to the ego', a ferocious superego, which represents 'blindly, unconsciously internalised social coercion' (Adorno 1973: 272). In summaries of the research conducted by the Institute in the interwar and post-war periods, Adorno proposed that a severe superego resulted in moral masochism, a submissive identification with authority figures involving guilt and anxiety about following social rules. In *Dialectic of Enlightenment*, Adorno and Horkheimer suggest that the superego's sadistic hostility to the masochistic ego eventually becomes intolerable, whereupon the ego defends itself by means of the primitive defence of the projection outwards of libidinally inflected aggression. It turns out that the authoritarian personality, in which extreme superegoic sadism combined with moral formalism results in a gravitation towards fascist politics, merely represents the extreme end of a continuum of personality types characterized by a new heteronomy.

> [The authoritarian personality] follows the 'classic' psychoanalytic pattern involving a sadomasochistic resolution of the Oedipus complex, [as] pointed out by Erich Fromm under the title of the 'sadomasochistic' character. According to Max Horkheimer's theory . . . in order to achieve 'internalization' of social control which never gives as much to the individual as it takes, the latter's attitude towards authority and its psychological agency, the superego, assumes an irrational aspect. The subject achieves his own social adjustment only by taking pleasure in obedience and subordination. This brings into play the sadomasochistic

impulse structure both as a condition and as a result of social adjustment. In our form of society, sadistic as well as masochistic tendencies actually find gratification. The pattern for the translation of such gratifications into character traits is a specific resolution of the Oedipus complex which defines the formation of the syndrome here in question. Love for the mother, in its primary form, comes under a severe taboo. The resulting hatred against the father is transformed by reaction-formation into love. This transformation leads to a particular kind of superego . . . . In the psychodynamics of the 'authoritarian character', part of the preceding aggressiveness is absorbed and turned into masochism, while another part is left over as sadism, which seeks an outlet in those with whom the subject does not identify himself: ultimately the outgroup. (Adorno et al. 2019: 759)

The underlying logic of this construction of the authoritarian personality is clearly exhibited in Horkheimer's major statement on Critical Theory and anti-Semitism, 'The Jews and Europe' (1939), which articulates the background to the anti-Semitism chapter of *Dialectic of Enlightenment*. The central thesis is that 'the totalitarian order differs from its bourgeois predecessor only in that it has lost its inhibitions', or, in other words, 'fascism is the truth of modern society' (Horkheimer 1989: 78). Correlatively, the authoritarian personality is the characteristic subjectivity of the bourgeois epoch. Consequently, just as the administered society is latently totalitarian in democratic, fascist and communist variants, so too, the modern individual is latently both authoritarian and submissive to authority, and always potentially prejudiced.

Aesthetic mimesis as the antidote to instrumental rationality

For Adorno, the antidote to instrumental rationality and its gravitation towards the authoritarian personality and totalitarian society is aesthetic mimesis, by which Adorno means a relation to the world as well as a property of artworks. Aesthetic mimesis involves the spontaneous expressiveness of human beings and a natural capacity for sympathy, as well as a response to natural and artistic beauty, and a kind of absorption in aesthetic experience. The key to the manifold qualities of aesthetic mimesis is the anthropological thesis at the heart of *Dialectic of Enlightenment*. If the primal history of subjectivity reveals that the self-preservative instinct focused on the ego is the basis for instrumental rationality, then discovery of an alternative involves finding a kind of thinking that is not instrumental and not based in the ego. For Adorno, this alternative is aesthetic mimesis, illustrated by the companion text to *Dialectic of Enlightenment*, his *Philosophy of Modern Music* (1949), but only theorized fully in the posthumous *Aesthetic Theory* (1970). In *Aesthetic Theory* Adorno announces his project by stating that 'Kant's aesthetics is the antithesis of Freud's theory of art as wish-fulfilment' (AT: 9–14 [16–25]). The discussion that follows suggests that aesthetic mimesis is the result of a dialectical synthesis of the contradiction between Kant and Freud.

Where for Freud, art is linked to sublimation, for Adorno this is problematic, not only because Adorno thinks that sublimation involves affirmation, not negation, but also because sublimation happens through the ego. In *Minima Moralia*, Adorno suggests that Freud 'vacillates' between criticism of instinctual renunciation as repression and celebration of it as sublimation (Adorno 2005a: 60). Although sublimation captures a dynamic aspect of mimesis, 'if art has psychoanalytic roots, then they are the roots of fantasy, in the fantasy of omnipotence . . . includ[ing] the wish to bring about a better world' (AT: 9 [16]). Freud's wish-fulfilment theory of art is a better guide than Kant's notion of disinterested pleasure, but Kant better grasps the 'thorniness of artworks', their antithetical relation to the ego (AT: 12 [21]). The significance of art is not 'exhausted in the psychological performance of gaining mastery over instinctual renunciation', but instead involves reflexive judgements. Unlike determining judgements, which subsume particulars under universal rules and are the model for instrumental rationality, reflexive determinations invent new universals for exemplary instances, 'without a concept' (AT: 94 [167]). Adorno's claim for art, that 'contrary to the Kantian and Freudian interpretation of art, artworks imply in themselves a relation between interest and its renunciation' (AT: 12 [21]), flows from its links to the id and its refusal of the concept. Aesthetic mimesis originates in wish-fulfilment, but terminates, not in world mastery, but in a relinquishment of the ego that opens the subject to thinking the non-identical.

Yvonne Sherrat's reconstruction of 'Adorno's positive dialectic' in his aesthetic theory precisely summarizes the core idea:

> We have seen that in absorption the 'loss of the self' means that the conceptual faculties of the mind are not deployed at all . . . . In fact, the loss of the Subject's conceptual faculties entails a loss of involvement of that part of the self that is the ego. This loss of involvement of the ego includes not only its loss in instinctual terms but also its loss in structural terms . . . . Therefore, it is the boundary around the self that is lost. . . . Adorno describes this connection between the loss of the two roles of the ego when he depicts 'the weakness of *thought* in the face of natural beauty' as being 'a weakness of the *subject*' . . . . [But] it only consists of a loss of the ego. It retains the aspects of the self that are associated with the id. here, Adorno differs from Freud because for Freud the loss of the ego would have to entail a regression. For Adorno this is not the case . . . because the id for Adorno is like the ego for Freud . . . . Adorno describes this loss of separation as resulting in an 'immersion' of the Subject into

the work of art.... This Adorno claims is a deeply pleasurable experience
.... It involves a momentary unification with the work of art. (Sherratt 2002: 166–7)

Adorno describes this unification variously as absorption, immersion and the shudder of contact with absolute otherness. Indeed, Adorno thinks that 'the artwork ... is the plenipotentiary of ... the thing in-itself', which in Freudian terms would be the id (AT: 63 [112]). Richard Bernstein describes this in terms of a dialectic of concept and intuition (Bernstein 1992: 188–224), leading up to an ethical philosophy of non-identity based the role of reflective judgement in 'processual activities of concept formation' (Bernstein 2001: 308, 30–70). But I do not think that Adorno is considering a kind of material inference – or substantive thinking – through the category of aesthetic mimesis. Bernstein's interpretation strikes me as a fascinating post-Adornian alternative to Habermas (Bernstein 1995: 136–58), rather than an explication of Adorno's position.

As Joel Whitebook has demonstrated in considerable detail, the implication of Adorno's mimesis is that he opposes a kind of 'id psychology' to the ego's manipulative orientation to the world (Whitebook 1995: 119–64). Indeed, as Sherrat implies, Adorno's position is perilously close to an affirmation of magical thinking and infantile regression as the basis of aesthetic absorption. That should be read in conjunction with the claim in *Dialectic of Enlightenment* that in enlightenment thinking, 'mimetic, mythical, and metaphysical forms of behaviour were successively regarded as stages of world history' (DoE: 24 [37]). Mimesis, as the unconscious wish governed by the pleasure principle, is here the repressed, while myth and metaphysics are symptoms, the return of the repressed through the formation of a compromise between reason and desire. 'My claim is that a theory of sublimation', Whitebook concludes, '... as a fully embodied integration of the ego with the drives, could have assisted Adorno'. But instead, 'because he equates sublimation with pacified social conformity, and because the important contemporary works of art are, by their nature, neither pacified nor socially desirable in any conventional sense, Adorno is led to reject the notion of sublimation' (Whitebook 1995: 258, 61). The exclusion of sublimation and the embrace of the id entails a fundamental dilemma. Adorno's aesthetic theory and negative dialectics must performatively enact the aestheticization of reason, indeed, the exclusion of the concept for the 'constellation', if they are to remain true to thinking the non-identical under these stipulations.

Habermas's critique of Adorno

The original perspective of the Frankfurt School, reminiscent of the young Marx, was to accuse capitalist society of a failure to realize the modern ideals of autonomy and democracy, clearly visible in the revolutionary inauguration of the bourgeois epoch. In mature capitalist society, as these ideals receded before the political realities of maintaining class domination, high bourgeois culture preserved, albeit in a somewhat apologetic form, the ideal of a free reconciliation of particular and general. The morally autonomous individual and the democratic political citizen remained the norm for the socialization of the bourgeois ego, even though that individual found themselves increasingly alienated from society. The moment that the superstructures were engulfed by the disaster of an ascendant instrumental reason, then, the critical standards inherent in moral reason and reflective judgement began to disintegrate. The total integration of production and reproduction, distribution and consumption, social roles and personality types, political economy and cultural industry, results in what Horkheimer calls the 'eclipse of reason' (Horkheimer 1974). But with that, critical reason, which was to have insisted on a social transformation in line with the unrealized ideal of freedom, begins to implicate itself in the process of domination. Meanwhile, aesthetic mimesis goes to ground in difficult works, in order to avoid the fate of bourgeois art as 'affirmative culture' (Marcuse 1968: 65–98), or its routinization and trivialization by the culture industry. Critique retreats in the direction of aphoristic interventions into localized manifestations of a global irrationality, that is, into a 'philosophy in fragments' that mordantly documents the logic of disintegration inherent in a self-contradictory rational domination.

Against this background, Habermas makes two main criticisms of Adorno. In *The Theory of Communicative Action*, Habermas proposes that Adorno's and Horkheimer's dialectic of enlightenment develops a monolithic conception of society, one whose only outside is the 'revolt of nature' (TCA1: 366–99 [490–535]; TCA2: 378–83 [556–63]). Adorno and Horkheimer 'consider the rationalisation of the world to be . . . complete, and thus they need a conceptual apparatus that will allow them nothing less than to denounce the whole as the untrue' (TCA1: 378 [556]). Seeking to explicate the revolt of nature by retrieving it from anti-Enlightenment Romanticism and the anti-democratic counter-revolution – the 'dark writers of the bourgeoisie' – tilts them towards a reading of Freud inflected by Romanticism. That provides Adorno and Horkheimer with philosophical anthropology capable of delivering a sweepingly critical negation of modernity. Disastrously, the cost is reliance on a metaphysics of natural substance, according to which the original, animistic relation of the human being to the world is retrieved through absorption in aesthetic mimesis. The quest for an 'Other of Reason' leads Adorno in particular towards an 'extravagant' conception of the non-identical, one that is resistant to intersubjectively accessible articulation, because it is framed as the opposite of theoretical conceptuality (Habermas 1982: 13–30). Habermas concludes:

> Horkheimer and Adorno are also guided by the idea of reconciliation; but they would rather renounce entirely any explication of it than fall into a metaphysics of reconciliation . . . . The critique of instrumental reason conceptualised as negative dialectics renounces its theoretical claim while operating with the means of theory. (TCA1: 386–7 [519–20])

In *Philosophical Discourse*, Habermas reformulates this criticism of the administered society as a monolithic totality, in relation to Adorno's *Negative Dialectics* and *Aesthetic Theory*, by following up the suggestion that Adorno engages in a logical fallacy. It is the search for a non-violent synthesis that would think the non-identical without resorting to theory, which connects the *aporia* of negative dialectics to the category of mimesis in the aesthetic theory. Adorno, he maintains, 'remained faithful to [the] philosophical impulse [of *Dialectic of Enlightenment*] and never deviated from the paradoxical structure of thinking through its totalising critique' (PDM: 119–20 [145]). Indeed:

> Adorno's negative dialectics reads like a continuing explanation of why we have to circle around within a performative contradiction and indeed even remain there; of why only the insistent, relentless unfolding of this paradox opens up the prospect of that magically invoked 'mindfulness of nature in the subject in whose fulfilment the unacknowledged truth of all culture lies hidden'. (PDM: 119–20 [145] DoE cited)

The problem with the total critique of reason by means of reason itself is that the accusations hurled against reason rebound onto the critique, which, to remain consistent, must engage in an aestheticization of rationality.

I indicated in the beginning of this chapter that Adorno's most likely rejoinder would have been to reference the Hegelian critique of Kant, the logic of which forces Hegel to introduce contradiction into the field of reason. Hegel's thinking involves a distinction between dialectical Reason and the positivistic Understanding, which seems to be what is at stake in the difference between Adorno's negative dialectics and instrumental rationality. Accordingly, Adorno might reply that the total critique of instrumental rationality by means of dialectical Reason is perfectly legitimate, provided that logical contradictions are accepted as reasonable.

Habermas thinks this defence fails. For unlike Lukács or Marcuse, who keep Hegel clear of the shot and danger of reification by reading him as an anticipation of Marx (Lukács 1975; Marcuse 1999), Adorno and Horkheimer explicitly implicate Hegelian logic in the 'totalitarianism' of enlightenment.

> With the concept of determinate negation Hegel gave prominence to an element which distinguishes enlightenment from the positivist decay to

which he consigned it. However, by finally postulating the known result of the whole process of negation, totality in the system and in history, as the absolute, he violated the prohibition and himself succumbed to mythology . . . . For enlightenment is totalitarian, as only a system can be. (DoE: 18 [30])

Not even the standard distinction between (true) dialectical method and (false) monolithic system survives this condemnation, because method itself is the pre-eminent bearer of enlightenment rationalization. According to Habermas, that means that '*Dialectic of Enlightenment* owes more to Nietzsche than just the strategy of an ideology critique turned against itself' (PDM: 121 [148]). Nietzsche 'devalues the truth of assertive statements and the rightness of normative ones, by reducing validity and invalidity to positive and negative value judgements' (PDM: 123 [149]). Then, Nietzsche assimilates value judgements to expressions of the will so that, for instance, to contradict only has the sense of wanting to be different. The fusion of reason with power that results deprives critique of any normative standard by which to judge whether a form of life promotes or mutilates human flourishing. Confronted with this problem, Adorno and Horkheimer, rather than advocating a return to archaic impulses, as Nietzsche did, decide to simply remain within the frame of performative contradiction.

Habermas maintains that the keystone to an alternative to the quest for the 'Other of Reason' is to begin from communicative intersubjectivity, rather than the contradictory starting point of 'using the use the strength of the subject to break through the fallacy of constitutive subjectivity' (Adorno 1973: xx). Instead of a theory of society as a monolithic totality, Habermas proposes a concept of social complexity that includes the possibility for meaningful democratic will-formation, as well as acknowledging that modern societies do have totalitarian potentials. Meanwhile, to support the democratic potentials of modernity, Habermas develops a polyvocal concept of communicative reason, while reframing instrumental rationality as 'functional reason', the logic of invasive systems. Finally, rather than aesthetic mimesis as opposed to reason, Habermas develops a concept of expressive-aesthetic rationality within communicative action, and it is to the elements of Adorno on art that are preserved in Habermas's critical engagement that I now want to turn.

2

Adorno's aesthetic theory

The clue to Adorno's aesthetic theory is the notion of political migration – the claim that 'politics has migrated into autonomous art, and nowhere more so than where art appears to be politically dead' (Adorno 2007a: 194). All of the connections between Adorno's social theory and his celebrated defence of modernist dissonance, with its focus on difficult art, are contained in this claim. What has migrated is the locus of resistance to domination, formerly represented by the revolutionary proletariat's potential for inaugurating a new society. Today, art inherits the paradoxical position of being a social antithesis located at the heart of society, because the artwork, as the plenipotentiary of aesthetic mimesis, is the ambassador of a future creative praxis. But just as the victory of the proletariat heralds its dissolution into a classless society, the utopia implied by the avant-garde involves an aestheticization of society. Accordingly, the 'realization of philosophy', meaning, the actualization of the dialectical social programme, entails the end of art, termination of the decline of art in the epoch of capitalist decay (AT: 32–3 [57]).

Adorno's entirely classical schema is then complicated by the philosophy of history implied by the dialectic of enlightenment and the critique of instrumental reason. The organic totality of the classical artwork, whose harmony between general and particular allegorized the balance between social universal and individual particularity, represented a prolegomenon to the socialist vision, an 'anticipation of reconciliation'. The divergent dialectic of prosperity and happiness, based in the link between deepening reification and increasing repression, combined with the failure of socialist revolutions, means the indefinite postponement of any utopian prospects. Capitalism enters its epoch of decay, with the consequence that both philosophy and art begin exhibit symptoms of irrationalism and morbidity, but with Adorno's modernist twist. The classical homophonic symphony, bourgeois realism and lyric poetry are implicated in the catastrophe, by virtue of the culture industry, which transforms them into formulae. The political alternatives of socialism or barbarism confront the art world and the republic of letters, as the decision between two forms of modernist dissonance – rationalism or authenticity. Both lament the decline of the qualitative, the eclipse of the individual, the subsumption of the particular under the universal, but only one of them has progressive implications. Perhaps counter-intuitively, it is aesthetic rationalism, which, like the proletariat, presses dialectically forward through the process of reification and repression, refusing the allure of the turn backwards to a reactionary vitalism.

For Adorno, the artwork is inhabited by an antagonism between social labour, qua instrumental rationality, and aesthetic mimesis. That dialectic imbues art with a tragic dimension, in which spontaneous expression is formed by rationalized techniques into advanced aesthetic materials, at the cost of a further annexation of the mimetic terrain by reification. The situation is dire. Utility is the problem. So too is communication. Social labour produces use values which have an exchange value; the rationalization and commodification of art also means its recruitment into social functions, such as distinction and entertainment. 'For a society in which art no longer has a place and which is pathological in all its reactions to it, art fragments, on the one hand, into a reified, hardened cultural possession, and, on the other hand, into a source of pleasure that the customer pockets' (AT: 15 [30]). But art's autonomy is its liberation from the principle of utility, its ability to communicate mimetically and evoke a peculiar combination of thinking and feeling. This results in contradiction. 'The dual nature of artworks as autonomous structures and social phenomena results in oscillating criteria: autonomous works provoke the verdict of social indifference . . . ; conversely, works that make socially univocal discursive judgments thereby negate art as well as themselves' (AT: 248 [369]). Autonomous artworks must not only refuse functionality but also must 'rid themselves of any communicative means that would make them accessible to the public' (AT: 243 [362]). Accordingly, the politics of political migration is a politics of the refusal of utility – the atelic work – that is also resistance to decipherment – the hermetic work.

Habermas describes Adorno's advocacy of atelic hermeticism as a 'strategy of hibernation' that borders on political quietism. In this chapter, I intend to exhibit the Adornian positions that justify Habermas's criticism while clarifying those Adornian intuitions which Habermas prolongs, rather than refuses. My strategy follows the same line as the discussion of Adorno's social theory. The formative moment for Adorno's mature positions is the cluster of works around *Dialectic of Enlightenment*, especially Adorno's *Philosophy of Modern Music*, which was written simultaneously. When Adorno speaks about 'artworks', his primary reference is to music, but this is complemented by some key essays on literature from the same period. In discussing Adorno on music I am guided by Max Paddison's extensive reconstruction of Adornian musical theory (Paddison 1993), while in thinking about literature, I follow the detailed discussion presented by Peter Hohendahl (Hohendahl 1997).[1] Both Paddison and Hohendahl argue that Adorno's history of aesthetics, guided by his philosophy of history, is the key to his specific readings, and that these follow a logic of exemplification or illustration. Adorno's essays on music are structured around a contrast between the progressive and reactionary modernisms of Arnold Schönberg and Igor Stravinsky, respectively, which provides the cornerstone illustration of Adorno's general thesis on aesthetic mimesis in the modern world. This is supported by a contrast in the literary field, developed at the same time as the music essays, between Stefan Georg and Heinrich Heine, which, although it deals with the Romantic precursors to modernism, follows the same logic as the Schönberg/Stravinsky opposition. This clarifies Adorno's positions on Franz Kafka and (later) Samuel Beckett, discussion of which concludes the chapter.

Creative praxis and artistic monads

According to Gillian Rose, 'the central thesis of [Adorno's] sociology of art is that there is a contradiction between the forces and the relations of production in the realm of culture' (Rose 2014: 119). This is particularly insightful, because it clarifies what is otherwise unintelligible, namely, why, although Adorno thinks that instrumental rationality is the key problem in the administered world, he also thinks that aesthetic rationalization is politically progressive. The contradiction between instrumental rationality and aesthetic mimesis, constituted by its location in the division of labour, represents a transposition of the dialectics of the social relations and productive forces (as described by Marx) into the heart of the artwork.

Adorno's interpretation of the artwork as the social antithesis of society is supported by his description of modernist art – especially modern music – as a constellation of 'monads' strewn in the void of universal equivalence (AT: 321–2 [476–7]). The autonomous artwork is a Leibnizian monad – a closed

---

[1] I have also been guided by the following: Albrecht Wellmer's essays on Adorno's aesthetic theory Wellmer, *The Persistence of Modernity: Essays on Aesthetics, Ethics and Postmodernism*; Simon Jarvis on the literary aspects of Adorno's work Jarvis, *Adorno: A Critical Introduction*; the deconstruction-influenced reading of Adorno on literature by Ulrich Plass. Ulrich Plass (2012) and the historically oriented reconstruction of this by Nortbert Bolz. Norbert Bolz (1979). Shierry Weber Nicholson was valuable on Adorno's late work Sherry Weber-Nicholsen (1997); Lambert Zuidervaart's brilliant and sympathetic reconstruction of *Aesthetic Theory* also highlights the continuities with Adorno's interwar thinking Zuidervaart, *Adorno's Aesthetic Theory: The Redemption of Illusion*; and Yvonne Sherrat's insightful notion of Adorno's positive dialectic of aesthetic absorption guided my understanding of aesthetic mimesis Yvonne Sherratt (2002).

microcosm that nonetheless is inscribed with the logic of the macrocosm – because its hermetic, hieroglyphic quality is precisely the signature of its social location. Accordingly, as a monad, the artwork is at once entirely autarchic and completely unique, because its autonomy consists in its individuated self-legislation of the relations between materials and technique, content and form. At the same time, it is an expression of the social totality generated within the division of labour under capitalism, which commodifies it by assigning it an exchange value despite its uselessness. Artworks are thus those microcosms (aesthetic universes) that express the contradictions of the macrocosm (the social totality). It is crucial to realize that, for Adorno, this stamps autonomous artworks with the social contradictions of capitalist society, irrespective of authorship and theme.

Although Adorno believes that the proletariat is a conservative force, in Marxian fashion, he positions art in a revolutionary role at the heart of the contradictions of capitalism. For Adorno, although autonomous art is commodified, unlike the standardized commercial products of the culture industry, it is not structured as a useful item. Unlike alienated labour performed through instrumental rationality in the normal workplace, the formation of the artwork requires creative praxis, which brings aesthetic mimesis into operation. Aesthetic mimesis, for Adorno, means the imitation of nature through impractical things – pure play – whereas social labour means the transformation of nature into practical items intended for commercial exchange. Because it is playfully produced to express individuality, the autonomous artwork is hermetic, since this sort of practice is quite literally unintelligible in a market society. The autonomous artwork is therefore a special commodity – it is the commodity that expresses the self-consciousness of social labour, the last reservoir of creative praxis in an alienated world (AT: 246–9 [367–8]). As Zuidervaart states, 'in the apparent absence of a revolutionary proletariat and a critical public, Adorno's philosophy is driven to discover how spontaneity in authentic modern art can encourage transformative praxis' (Zuidervaart 1991: 108).

'Artworks are', says Adorno, 'the plenipotentiaries of things that are no longer distorted by exchange, profit, and the false needs of a degraded humanity' (AT: 227 [338]). Autonomous art, by its existence, protests against reification. Its combination of human creativity with a labour process is the opposite of routinization and domination. Its combination of mental with manual labour is the opposite of the mutilating separation of these forms of activity in the social division of labour. Accordingly, art is the antithesis of society because it represents the possibility of creative praxis, something that inherently anticipates utopian reconciliation (AT: 8 [21]). In agreement with Kant's idea of art as 'deliberate uselessness', Adorno maintains that 'insofar as a social function can be predicated for artworks, it is their functionlessness' (AT: 227 [338]). Indeed, under conditions where intellectual culture has been included in the division of labour and industrialized, with results of standardization and homogenization, the independence and individuality of the artwork is an act of defiance. 'Art keeps itself alive through its force of resistance', Adorno suggests, which springs from its combination of social dysfunctionality and aesthetic autonomy (AT: 226 [337]).

In an almost totally reified society, autonomous art has become the last refuge of that creative praxis which points beyond alienated labour. It is therefore also the final retreat of the expressive subject under conditions where full individuality cannot be achieved in society. Yet despite the transformative potential of autonomous art, were art to attempt to directly exhibit a world characterized by non-alienated human creativity, this would lead immediately to falsification. This is not only because aesthetic practices continue to be part of the social division of labour, but also because the society itself has not yet been transformed from a state of unfreedom to a condition of freedom. Art therefore has what Adorno calls a 'double character', as both autonomous structure and social phenomenon – it is 'both more and less than praxis' (AT: 241, 248 [359, 369]). Autonomous art is at once a form of creative praxis that is the antithesis of social reification, and something powerless to alter the mutilated practices enmeshed in the social division of alienated labour. Radical artworks must therefore remain true to the contradiction that constitutes them, by simultaneously both preserving and negating the artistic promise of human happiness. Adorno thinks that the only way that this can happen is through aesthetic dissonance.

Authenticity versus rationalization

Adorno's aesthetic theory is located within the philosophy of history proposed in *Dialectic of Enlightenment* and ratified in *Negative Dialectics*. Because of the generalization of the principle of equivalence, there is a divergent evolution between quantitative and qualitative, universal and particular, society and individual. The antagonism between individual and social is caused by the dissolution of the qualitatively specific in quantitative generalizations, a process which subordinates particular distinctness to universal formalizations. The result is a tendency towards the replacement of the autonomous subject, or bourgeois individual, by a new kind of heteronomous conformist. Modern music and literature expresses this tendency through the homogenization of aesthetic parts within the coercive whole of a false harmony (or literary closure). Only the rebellion of the parts against the affirmative whole, in modernist dissonance (or literary openness), resists the pseudo-totality announced by the culture industry as the allegory of the administered world.

Especially in *Philosophy of Modern Music*, Adorno explores the social antagonism expressed in modernist dissonance against the conceptual background of an opposition between rationalization and authenticity.

His underlying position is based on the selection of extreme points on the historical and aesthetic continuum to illustrate a general process. This is the diachronic rise and decay of high bourgeois forms, followed by the emergence of a synchronic antagonism between progressive and reactionary modernisms. In his sociology of music, Adorno sets forth the historical sequence and contemporary bifurcation that – behind the scenes – determines his signature interpretation of Schönberg and Stravinsky. In his interpretations of literature, Adorno is focused on the moment of the Romantic protest that precedes the emergence of literary modernism. Subsequently, Adorno also produced readings of the progressive modernism of Kafka and Beckett, while his literary equivalent to Stravinsky is Stefan George.

Adorno and Horkheimer suggest that the word combines concept and image, in a way which implies that the rationalized conventionality of the linguistic symbol has a mimetic semantics, based in visual or audial resemblances, as its underside. 'As the hieroglyphs attest', they write, 'the word originally had a pictorial function. This function was transferred to myths. They, like magic rites, refer to the repetitive cycle of nature' (DoE: 12 [23]). In terms of Peircean semiotics, Adorno thinks that the word combines the conceptuality possible through conventional symbols, with the representation possible through motivated icons. Accordingly, 'in the case of the rational, the identity principle reigns supreme, with the mimetic it is not, strictly speaking, the principle of differentiation but that of similarity that wins out' (Müller and Gillespie 2009: 98). Therefore in lyrical expression, akin to music in this respect, the mimetic element predominates, whereas in narrative representation, the conceptual element coordinates literary mimesis through causal sequencing. Consequently, as frequent use of Schönberg as a compass indicates, in the field of lyric poetry, Adorno's approach to musical problems is transposed directly onto his interpretation of literary works.

According to Adorno, the literary and musical rebellion of the particular represents a struggle for expressive individuation that bifurcates into two diametrically opposed tendencies in modernism. The writer or composer can develop new means for the expression of qualitative distinctness by gaining an improved mastery over their medium, which unlocks socially suppressed complexes of feeling and perception at the cost of enduring the process of rationalization. Rationally driven revolutions in artistic technique and new understandings of the aesthetic medium create a radical field of self-expression, capable of registering the distress of the individual, protesting the lack of freedom and depicting the crushing of personality. Alternatively, the writer can seek to defend traditional forms of qualitative distinctness that are on the point of elimination by quantitative generalizations. This is done by means of a regression in literary or musical technique that aims at the 'vitality' of a more 'primordial' experience, and at the inclusion of extra-aesthetic reality, through the direct incorporation of non-diegetic or non-musical elements in literary pastiche or acoustic icons. The quest for 'authenticity' rejects literariness for an expressive return to the origins of feelings and insights, in primitivism and nativism.

Adorno's assignment of a progressive valence to aesthetic rationalization resonates with Marx's historical dialectics, in which antagonistic development simultaneously involves completed domination and potential liberation. The crisis tendencies latent in a social contradiction should be analysed from the perspective of the historically necessary satisfaction of the social preconditions for successful socialist revolution. Improvements in technical mastery over the presumed naturalness of language or music have the temporary effect of deepening and extending the capacity of individuals to articulate their feelings and insights. It also allegorizes a further development of social individuation, although the failure of revolution may mean that these fragile discoveries are soon surrendered to the advance of reification. By contrast, the recovery of authenticity through the rejection of rationalization in effect seeks to protect a narrow form of individuality, by clinging to forms of articulation that have been historically superseded. Despite certain affinities to Heidegger's project of the 'recollection of Being' (Habermas 1984: 385), then, Adorno's defence of the artwork's thinking about nature leads in the opposite political direction. This is because Adorno insists that cultural irrationalism ultimately involves a drastic foreshortening of the possibilities for individuation that are unlocked by the tragic dialectic of enlightenment.

Avant-garde rupture and artistic truth

For Adorno, an aesthetic breakthrough realigns the entire front in an artistic medium while providing the highest historically possible figuration of philosophical truth. The logic of avant-garde shockwaves is completely dependent on the claim that 'Hegel's theory of the movement of the concept has its legitimacy in aesthetics' (AT: 351 [521]). The specific link between socio-historical reality and artistic truth is the principle of individuation, which provides Adorno's bridge between aesthetics and society. 'Aesthetics moves within the medium of universal concepts even in the face of the radically nominalist situation of art and in spite of the utopia of the particular that aesthetics prizes along with art' (AT: 350 [520]). Because autonomous art provides 'insight into the life of the [social] universal in the midst of aesthetic particularisation', even though 'art dreams the absolutely monadological', the social totality is inscribed in its structure of individuation (AT: 351 [521]).

The effect of this thesis is to make aesthetic rupture and artistic truth coextensive. On the one hand, 'every work is the mortal enemy of the other' (AT: 211 [314]). That means every now and again, along comes a work that sweeps all of the others into their graves. On the other hand, a work is true, not by virtue of some special representation of social reality, but because it represents something special in society. That something involves individuation, via a triple-decker dialectic between material and technique, content and form, import and impact. Each of the first of these is connected to aesthetic mimesis and the productive forces, and each of the second of these is connected to instrumental rationality and the social relations of production.

Material and technique

Adorno has a demanding conception of artistic progress that depends upon the idea of artistic breakthroughs defining the level of advance of the aesthetic materials. For Adorno, technique involves the mastery of these advanced materials, and can be defined as 'all the artistic procedures that form the material and allow themselves to be guided by it' (AT: 213 [317]). As the latter part of that definition suggests, the concept of technique is complex, because Adorno thinks that technique is not entirely external to the material, but arises from a confrontation with the expressive possibilities latent in it. Specifically, technique is a determinate negation of the material, which means, colloquially, it is a set of historically conditioned procedures for doing something different with the material. Most importantly, technique is a response to the objective problem that advanced material poses.

Content and form

According to Adorno, the dialectic of material and technique gives rise to the dialectic of content and form. The historical material confronts the modernist artist as an ensemble of exhausted genres, conventions and devices. Only radical technical innovation can accomplish a renovation of the historical material, and this is deposited in the work as decisively new content. Yet the content, which arises from artistic mimesis, that is, the effort to imitate something in the world, must be aesthetically formed, and this is crucial, because form differentiates art from potentially useful things. 'Art', Adorno maintains, 'is [only] released from the empirical world by its formal consistency' (AT: 138 [209]). If mimesis is spontaneous imitative behaviour that is natural to human beings, consistency belongs to rational thinking and therefore to the dialectic of enlightenment. Thus, for Adorno, the opposition between mimetic content and aesthetic form creates the artistic continuum lying between authenticity and rationalization.

Import and impact

Adorno claims that 'the truth content of artworks is the objective solution to the enigma posed by each and every one . . . [which] can only be achieved by philosophical reflection' (AT: 128 [195]). Adorno's conception of truth-content as conveyed by the mute particularity of modernist artworks and unfolded by philosophical reflection is twofold, because it connects to social reconciliation and to artistic progress. The key is Hegel, for whom art is the highest expression, in the medium of figuration, of the historical development of the consciousness of freedom in an epoch. But art, because it is figuration, cannot itself disclose the truth it tells about the social evolution of an expanded and deepened understanding of freedom, without becoming conceptual discourse, i.e. philosophy. *All* modernist artworks speak of the strangulation of creative praxis by alienated labour and the totalitarian history that this implies, but only *some* raise this to the level of explicit thematization, in the context of artistic breakthrough. *Each* of them requires the mediation of philosophical aesthetics to release this truth-content from artistic particularity into propositional discourse.

Historical dialectics of musical material

In *Philosophy of Modern Music* Adorno believed it was legitimate to speak of a work as exhibiting the 'single' technically 'correct solution' to an expressive problematic defining an entire medium (Adorno 2007b: 26). This approach influences Adorno's theoretical reconstruction of musical history, which engages with Weber's sociological analysis of the rationalization of music (Paddison 1993). In *The Rational and Social Foundations of Music* (1921), Weber proposes that the harmonic ratios governing the various ancient and medieval scales have a nature-like quality that, because they can be mathematically calculated, are particularly susceptible to rationalization. Weber describes this as 'the drive toward rationality, that is, the submission of an area of experience to calculable rules' and argues that 'this drive to reduce artistic creativity to the form of a calculable procedure based on comprehensible principles appears above all in music' (Weber 1958: xxii). He suggests that the process of rationalization that results in the classical sonata form, begun in the Renaissance, is completed by about 1850, but that the existence of major seventh and minor ninth chords attests to a nature-like residue within the musical material. Describing the Romantic employment of these chords as a response to classical music that seeks a kind of return to nature, Weber maintains that 'these kinds of triads are *real revolutionaries* when compared with the harmonically divided fifths' (Weber 1958: 6). Nonetheless, as Adorno notes, for Weber, the Romantic revolution is ultimately futile, so that the introduction of dissonance merely represents an exception that confirms the rules governing rationalization (Adorno 2007b: 52).

Adorno's conception of the historical dialectics of aesthetic material consists of a Hegelian-Marxist re-description of the social process that drives the rationalization of music as interpreted by Weber. 'The most progressive level of technical procedures designs tasks', Adorno concludes, 'before which traditional sounds reveal themselves as impotent clichés' (Adorno 2007b: 24–5). Accordingly, although Adorno accepts the notion that the Romantic revolt is doomed to fail, he interprets revolutionary dissonance as a protest of the alienated individual as well as a rebellion of nature. Because art is a struggle for individuation through qualitative distinctness, it expresses the struggle of the individual in society, and Adorno locates this within the dialectics of alienation. Furthermore, his avant-garde conception of the relation between compositions, as competitive, even adversarial, springs from the Hegelian concept of objectification (*Entäusserung*). According to Hegel, the externalization of a conception in the transformation of an object results in a petrified objectivity that confronts the subject as an alien reality. Consequently, Adorno proposes that, for a composer today, the tonal arrangements of the homophonic sonata have become exhausted, even 'cacophonous', so that only the 'real revolutionaries', the dissonant intervals, preserve any interest.

Adorno tracks the trajectory of the homophonic sonata form and its ossification into affirmative culture through analyses of individual figures as well as a work on the sociology of music that resumes this sequence in a descriptive form. The classical sonata, developed by Handel (1685–1759) and completed by Haydn (1732–1809), but already subverted by Mozart (1756–91), represents an emancipation of music from its religious functions (Adorno 1976). Adorno proposes that compositionally, the idea of 'motivic development', the repetition-with-alterations of a distinct musical figure or sound phrase, emerges at this stage (Adorno 1976: 208). During the Enlightenment, there is a gradual synthesis of details and whole in the period of classical bourgeois art, which culminates in the middle of the nineteenth century with reconciled, balanced works. Beethoven (1770–1827), in particular, 'is the musical prototype of the revolutionary bourgeoisie', whose work is the paradigm of 'a music that has escaped from its social tutelage and is aesthetically fully autonomous' (Adorno 1976: 209). Not only is music liberated from sacral functions and, therefore, institutionally autonomous, but the musical material is emancipated from subservience to purposes of entertainment or ceremony, so that its aesthetic autonomy consists in it providing itself with an 'autarchic motivational context' (Adorno 1976: 209). Beethoven achieves this through the systematic development of a motif so that it eventually returns upon itself, as if it had in the first place been generated through the formal necessity of the composition, thus enclosing all of the parts of the work within the charmed circle of a self-generating whole (Adorno 2002: 162–80). This musical form not only expresses the social reality of the autonomous individual, as a self-legislating rational being, but its harmonious balance of parts and whole, or organic totality, also reflects a fleeting reconciliation of this individual to the social totality. Adorno links Beethoven's organic musical totalities to the intellectual reconciliation of the particular and universal in Hegelian philosophy, arguing that they both express the same historical moment (Adorno 2002: 162–80). More generally, Adorno connects motivic development in the secular sonata with the principle of autonomous individuation, because it is the expression of a highly individual fragment that, through its quasi-logical permutations, legislates the form of the work (Adorno 1967a: 133–47).

Classicism, Romanticism, modernism

In this section, I want to summarize the historical dialectics of musical material, before turning to the specifically literary variant in the next section. Adorno correlates Beethoven's musical development with the shift in capitalist society that happened after the failed democratic revolutions of 1848, after which, Adorno argues, following Marx, the revolutionary role of the bourgeoisie ceased, as it became evident that capitalism was based on exploitation of the labouring classes (Adorno 1976). The politically liberal, autonomous individual is alienated from the objective socio-historical context, which begins to confront him or her as resistant to the realization of individuality. From the 1850s onwards, confronted by increasing reification, the individual protects their autonomy through a turn inwards from alienated objectivity to free subjectivity. In late Romanticism, subjective freedom protests the breakdown of the harmonious reconciliation of universal and particular, objective and subjective, social and individual, whole and parts. Adorno's justifiably famous articles on 'Late Style in Beethoven' and 'Alienated Masterpiece: The *Missa Solemnis*', together with the recently translated book draft, *Beethoven: The Philosophy of Music*, interpret Beethoven's final work in this light. Both the *Missa Solemnis* and the *Appassionata* illustrate the proposition that 'in the history of art, the late works are the catastrophes' (Adorno 2002: 567), for they are characterized by an 'expressionlessness' indicative of deep alienation. Likewise, Adorno maintains that Brahms:

> bears the mark of bourgeois society's individualistic phase indisputably enough to have become a platitude. In Beethoven, the category of totality still preserves a picture of the right society; in Brahms it fades into a self-sufficiently aesthetic principle for the organisation of private feelings. (Adorno 1976: 63–4)

Brahms intensified Beethoven's quest for formal structure in the direction of a strict (i.e. formalized) style, while integrating certain Romantic developments, but Schumann marks the point where Romanticism became a set of exhausted conventions, celebrating an individuality that no longer existed (i.e. affirmative culture) (Adorno 1999: 111). As Max Paddison points out, on Adorno's interpretation, a divergence between the affirmative culture of the symphony orchestra and the popular culture of the light opera sets in and drives a post-Romantic effort to retrieve musical relevance, at the cost of the disintegration of the highly rationalized musical material (Paddison 1993: 218–78). The line running from Berlioz (1803–69) through to Wagner exemplifies the introduction of heterogeneous material – fairground bells, trumpet flourishes, industrial horns and so forth – into the musical texture.

Adorno interprets the Wagnerian 'total work' as an inversion of Brahms: Wagner's project is the total mastery of the musical material through strict integration of all parts, but this is achieved through the incorporation of non-homophonic elements – external sound elements, directly incorporated or musically mimicked – into the structure, thereby disintegrating its organic wholeness. There is no doubt that Wagner engages in a progressive rationalization of the technical structure of the musical material, involving motivic and harmonic construction, refinement of orchestral technique and evolution of new instruments, the manipulation of time and the integration of music with drama. Yet Adorno thinks that Wagner's technical progress is deployed in the service of expressive reaction, specifically, that Wagner seeks to make the artwork so seamless that it appears natural (Adorno 1981: 82–97). This implies a conservative desire to recover a 'natural', authentic form of life as an enchanted alternative to the modern world, one that, because 'natural', is overpowering and monolithic (Adorno 1981: 91). On Adorno's interpretation, like the sorcerer's apprentice, this transforms cultural materials into a second nature that then dominates the wielder:

> The parable of the man who dominates nature only to relapse into a state of natural bondage gains an historical dimension in the action of [Wagner's opera] *The Ring*: with the victory of the bourgeoisie, the idea that society is like a natural process, something 'fated' is reaffirmed. (Adorno 1981: 137–8)

The twentieth-century revolution of atonal music frees the composer from the restriction of the chromatic scale (i.e. the selection of eight notes from the twelve semitones of the classical major and minor scales). Where classical music has to content itself with a highly limited number of tonal combinations, the modernist composer is no longer constrained by the demands of vertical harmony or tonal melody. Yet this emancipation itself becomes, in keeping with the tragic dialectic that Adorno detects in the development of musical material, a fresh cage:

> With the liberation of musical material, there arose the possibility of mastering it technically. It is as if music had thrown off that last alleged

force of nature which its subject matter exercises upon it, and would now be able to assume command over this subject matter freely, consciously and openly. The composer has emancipated himself along with his sounds. . . . [But] a system by which music dominates nature results. . . . The conscious disposition over the material of nature is two-sided: the emancipation of the human being from the musical force of nature and the subjection of nature to human purposes. At the same time, however, this technique further approaches the ideal of mastery as domination . . . Music, in its surrender to historical dialectics, has played its role in this process. Twelve-tone technique is truly the fate of music. It enchains music by liberating it. The subject dominates music through the rationality of the system, only in order to succumb to the rational system itself. . . . From the procedures which broke the blind domination of tonal material there evolves a second blind nature by means of this regulatory system. (Adorno 2007b: 39, 47, 49–50)

According to Adorno's dialectical theory – an extension of his idea of the dialectic of enlightenment – every composer confronts the historical state of the musical material (i.e. the achievements of their predecessors) as an alien objectivity. Their technical accomplishments deposit in their wake a systematization of music as a rationally mastered field, one that verges on the reduction of musicality to mathematical formulae. This mastery of the musical material, achieved through rationality, yields a new expressivity only at the cost of a further systematization of the musical material. Thus, the vice of rationalization closes ever tighter around each successive generation of composers.

Historical dialectics of literary material

Adorno's dialectics of literary material follows the same trajectory as that followed by his sociology of music, tracing out the historical contours of the reification of language. For Adorno, lyric poetry is the pre-eminent literary form in modernity – a song of individuality that seeks to rediscover expressive language at the same time as encountering a reconciled world. It is evident to Adorno that the 'lyric is a subjective expression of a social antagonism' that is particular to the world of bourgeois individualism (Adorno 2019: 66). This locates the dialectics of expression and/as objectification within the dynamic of reification and eventually captures it within the gravity well of the rise of the culture industry.

On the one side, 'lyric expression, having escaped from the weight of material existence, evokes the image of a life free from the coercion of reigning practices, of utility, of the relentless pressures of self-preservation' (Adorno 2019: 61). This implies a protest against the social conditions of an alienated society, typically expressed through the imaginative encounter with a vision of natural spontaneity. For this reason, lyric poetry characteristically dramatizes dialectic of alienation and de-alienation, for 'the "I" whose voice is heard in the lyric is an "I" that defines and expresses itself as something opposed to the collective . . . [and] nature' (Adorno 2019: 62). The song of the individual becomes a humanization of nature and society, for 'it is only through humanization that nature is to be restored the rights that human domination took from it' (Adorno 2019: 62).

On the other side, expression as humanization simultaneously requires the presence and absence of poetic conventions, the negation of prosaic communication through form and the return of spontaneous speech without artifice. Adorno thinks that 'the highest lyric works are those in which the subject, with no remaining trace of mere matter, sounds forth in language until language itself acquires a voice' (Adorno 2019: 64). But 'at the same time, language remains the medium of concepts, remains that which establishes an inescapable relationship to the universal and to society' (Adorno 2019: 64). Hence, 'the paradox specific to the lyric work, a subjectivity that turns into objectivity, is tied to the priority of linguistic form in the lyric; it is that priority from which the primacy of language in literature in general . . . is derived' (Adorno 2019: 64).

Against this conceptual background, Adorno sketches the rise of modern lyric poetry through Joseph Freiherr von Eichendorf (1788–1857) (Adorno 2019: 74–95) and Friedrich Hölderlin (1770–1843) (Adorno 2019: 376–412). Despite Eichendorf's conservative nostalgia for an aristocratic tradition, the modernity in his poetry is visible in its surrender to the music of speech, which 'raises a mute objection to the poetic subject, a sacrifice to the impulses of language' (Adorno 2019: 83). If Eichendorf exemplifies the linguistic pole of Adorno's theory of literary materials, Hölderlin illustrates its conceptual pole, with his 'paratactic' thinking through poetic images. Here, Hölderlin is paradigmatic for the paradoxical claims of aesthetic mimesis, in which 'the paratactic revolt against synthesis attains its limit in the synthetic function of language' (Adorno 2019: 399). In Heinrich Heine (1797–1856) (Adorno 2019: 96–101), by contrast, Adorno finds that the Romantic celebration of the individual against the calculating society of the Enlightenment leads to an incorporation of heterogeneous materials. Adorno's complicated and only partly successful essay seeks to defend Heine – a Jewish socialist – from subsequent Nazi vilification while at the same time situating his work as an anticipation of regressive surrender to the culture industry (Hohendahl 1997: 105–18; Plass 2012: 115–22).

Adorno's literary Beethoven is Johann Wolfgang von Goethe (1749–1832) (Adorno 2019: 123–31 and 415–29). In his essay on the classical status of Goethe, Adorno proposes that the epic poem *Iphigenia in Tauris* (1786) both expresses a mature subjectivity and represents the apex of bourgeois literary reflection. Its constitutive contradiction is the knowledge that enlightenment, represented through the harmonious totality of the work, allegorizing the reconciliation of the individual and society, is intrinsically linked to barbarism and mythology. Humaneness, the theme of the work, is enmeshed in exchange, the motif governing Iphigenia's fate, which denatures reciprocity and exposes the 'dark secret of the [French] revolution' (Adorno 2019: 422). Adorno therefore reads the opposition between Greek and foreigners in the work as a projection of the social antagonisms of bourgeois society onto the ancient world (Adorno 2019: 219). He then interprets the mythology in the work as a fraudulent, bourgeois vision of reconciliation without revolution, through a religious supplement to liberal individualism (Adorno 2019: 426, 28–9). The temporization with domination implicit in this perspective is registered formally in the tension between the sculpted iambs of the Greeks and the natural flow of the Scythian king Thoas (Adorno 2019: 420). Substantively, the problem is that stylization in language, which was to express proportionality, becomes the representative of order, which merely dominates nature, yet spontaneity, whose apotheosis is the speech of madness, unravels the tapestry of liberal individuality (Adorno 2019: 420, 26). 'The reconciliation of the subject with something that evades it', Adorno concludes, 'a reconciliation with which language is burdened, the substitution of form for a content antagonistic to the subject, is already fully visible in *Iphigenie*'. Accordingly, 'With *Iphigenie* begins language's development into an objectifying moment, a development that culminates in Flaubert and Baudelaire' (Adorno 2019: 420).

In the Romantic protest of Baudelaire in particular, the reification of language is explicitly thematized as the struggle of the expressive individual against a prosaic modernity characterized by commodity culture. 'Baudelaire's work ... did not stop with the sufferings of the individual but chose the modern itself, as the anti-lyrical pure and simple, for its theme and struck a poetic spark in it by dint of a heroically stylized language' (Adorno 2019: 65). At least, unlike Rainer Maria Rilke (1875–1926) (Adorno 2019: 112–13, 443), Baudelaire did not surrender to the aesthetic betrayal of the populist integration of heterogeneous material and submission to entertainment value. Yet already in Baudelaire, the intrinsic paradox of modern lyric intensifies towards the destruction of form, expressing the tension between the ironic self-negation of a desperate subjectivity and the expressive impulse to explode individuality completely.

Schönberg and progress

Now I want to examine the opposition between rationalization and authenticity. The best place to start is Adorno's music theory, because here it receives its clearest and most emblematic formulation. The progressive pole of the antagonism within modernist music is the pole of rationalization emblematized by Schönberg. In line with the notion that externalization becomes objectification, which turns into alienation, according to Adorno the situation that Schönberg confronts is the cultural exhaustion of the homophonic sonata form (Adorno 2007b: 25). Schönberg's response to the exhaustion of classicism and the failure of Romanticism is to reintroduce dissonant, nature-like, intervals back into the musical material, but through the strictest possible rationalization of technique. Adorno's crypto-Marxist interpretation of material and technique as aesthetic placeholders for the dialectic of productive forces and social relations means that he regards this as progressive, but fatal. 'The technical procedures of composition', Adorno writes, 'which make music into a picture of repressive society, are more advanced than the procedures of mass production which march beyond modern music . . . serving repressive society' (Adorno 2007b: 84). The twelve-tone row procedure of musical 'serialism', or 'dodecaphonic composition', makes possible a breakthrough from the Romantic subversion of classicism into a dissonant and dissident atonality. Initially, the dodecaphonic procedure is a preliminary preparation of the musical material rather than a compositional rule, for it consists in the arbitrary selection of a sequence of notes, or tone row, which then forms the basis for a non-chromatic scale. Adorno criticizes Webern, for instance, for the conflation of technique with composition, for his work is 'bad serialism', merely 'schemata of the rows translated into notes', where the preparation of the material has usurped the process of composition and become a sterile formula (Adorno 2007b: 81).

For Adorno, Schönberg's technical innovation improves the rationality of music, breaking with the supposed naturalness of the harmonic scales and thereby extending technical control to the 'irrational' dissonances generated beyond them. But his significance as a composer depends on the way that Schönberg uses this innovation to make music capable of expressing contemporary alienation. Effectively, Adorno reads Schönberg as a prolongation of the Romantic protest that expresses the lonely suffering of the modern individual, trying to communicate across an 'abyss of silence which marks the boundaries of its isolation', but with atonal rather than tonal means (Adorno 2007b: 29, 88). Adorno's discussion of Schönberg's *Erwartung* is an excellent example of this reading of the work as a dramatization of the distress of frigidity or impotence, brought on by Romantic fiasco in a context of loneliness and anguish. The work consists in expressive 'gestures of shock resembling bodily convulsions . . . and a crystalline standstill of the human being' possessed by anxiety (Adorno 2007b: 30). Adorno concludes:

> The subject of modern music, upon which the music itself presents a case study, is the emancipated, isolated, concrete subject of the late bourgeois era. This concrete subjectivity, and the material which it so radically

and thoroughly shapes, supplies Schönberg with the canon of aesthetic objectification. (Adorno 2007b: 41)

It is in relation to this interpretation of the combination of critical potential and tragic dialectic in the work of Schönberg, for instance, or Beckett, that Adorno's late lamentation about the 'neutralization of culture' assumes its full meaning. The neutralization of culture is the suspension of the dialectical process that happens within advanced art. Adorno's critique of that dialectic involves probing the potential for serial preparation to become transformed into a rigid convention whose mathematical rigour becomes the means for a new suppression of expressive individuality. The compositional rule set by Schönberg for his own work was that all twelve arbitrarily selected tones of a tone row must sound (in whatever order) before the next bracket (a combination from the same selection) could be constructed. The mathematical field of permutations and combinations is the logical reference for this procedure, with the rule applied both 'horizontally', in the temporal sequence of tones, and 'vertically', in the construction of chords, and the threat that logical deduction might usurp creative spontaneity is very real. Each bar represents the exhaustion of the tonal row that is its 'scale', and the whole composition represents the total saturation of the logical space of possibilities for the permutation and combination of these tonal elements. The alienation of the expressive subject in its objectified externalization of subjectivity is completed by the automatism of a procedure that inexorably tends to transform the methodical preparation of the material into a compositional rule that shrinks potentials for feeling and meaning even as it provides new means of expression.

> The abstractness not only of these rules, but of their substratum as well, has its origin in the fact that the historical subject is able to achieve agreement with the historical element of the material only in the region of the most general definitions. . . . Only in the mathematical determination through the row do the compositional will and the claim to continual permutation, which appears historically in the material of the chromatic scale – that is to say, the resistance to the repetition of tones – concur in the total musical domination of nature as the thorough organisation of material. It is this abstract reconciliation which, in the final analysis, places in opposition to the subject the self-contained system of rules in the subjugated material as an alienated, hostile and dominating power. This degrades the subject, making it a slave of the material, as of an empty concept of rules, at that moment in which the subject completely subdues the material, indenturing it to its mathematical logic. . . . For in twelve-tone technique, the rationality of the material. . . asserts itself blindly over the will of the subjects, triumphing thereby as irrationality. (Adorno 2007b: 87)

Adorno's analysis of this dialectical process of opening and closing expressive possibilities is subtle, suggestive of a sort of process of squeezing, where rationalization wrings irrational residues from the subject, transforms them into expressive possibilities through technical innovation, only to leave the subject wrung out, empty and hollow. For new expressive possibilities to be won, the subject must be squeezed even harder in the next round. For Adorno, the total consistency of Schönberg's music becomes an iron cage for the expressive subject, who finds itself rationally dominated by the musical material it had sought to rationally dominate. This is the process of 'enchaining music by unchaining it', through liberation as domination.

Stravinsky and regression

Stravinsky's mature, affirmative neoclassicism is the dialectical opposite to Schönberg's modernist negativity. Surprisingly, Adorno also regards Stravinsky's initial period of experimentation as anti-modernist positivity. Schönberg defends expressive subjectivity by exploring the suffering individual on the threshold of annihilation. By contrast, Stravinsky adapts to an alienated objectivity, seeking the 'authenticity' of the primitive collective, or conforming to the second nature of a reified culture. In either case, the intention is the opposite of Schönberg, whose innovations expose the conventional character of musical language. Stravinsky, on Adorno's interpretation, is searching for a music that is inevitable and eternal because it is as immutable as nature.

Adorno's polemic against Stravinsky sometimes seems forced, and several critics have challenged basic aspects of his critique in *Philosophy of Modern Music*. Based on criticisms presented by Carl Dahlhaus and Peter Bürger, Max Paddison argues that Adorno's dialectical portrait of Stravinsky is something of a return to his original strategy of locating the composer as distributed across several cultural tendencies and therefore as divided against himself (Paddison 1993, 2003). James Marsh contests Adorno's reading of Stravinsky's experimental period, arguing that it is difficult to differentiate Stravinsky's unorthodox rhythmic and instrumental variations from Schönberg's experiments with tonality, at least on formal grounds (Marsh 1983).

The basic difficulty with Adorno's critique of Stravinsky, then, is as follows. It seems intuitively plausible to align neoclassical restoration of musical traditions and tonal harmonies with resignation to social objectivity and therefore with political 'restoration'. But Adorno simultaneously insists that experimental works such as *The Rites of Spring* (1913) and *Petrushka* (1911) are central evidence for Stravinsky's reactionary formal tendencies and regressive thematic content. How can it be so?

Bracketing the descriptive accuracy of Adorno's commentary, I believe that his critique of Stravinsky is logically consistent with an opposition between expressive subjectivity (Schönberg) and reified objectivity (Stravinsky), and consists of three indictments: formal, thematic and psychodynamic. In formal terms, Stravinsky is accused of surrendering aesthetic autonomy to the external legislation imposed by society. The result is the opposite of Schönberg's self-legislating musical forms, namely, the formal decomposition of music through its fragmentation or its ritualization. In thematic terms, it is alleged that Stravinsky promotes identification with atavistic re-enchantment whose role as affirmative culture is evident in the use of pastiche and reliance on premodern myth. The absence of irony in Stravinsky's cultural citations, for Adorno, indicates an abdication of subjectivity that neoclassical objectivity completely confirms. Finally, in psychodynamic terms, Stravinsky is charged with infantile regression of a schizophrenic character, based on an effort to disintegrate the mature ego.

Adorno's interpretation of Stravinsky's work as involving formal decomposition and aesthetic heteronomy is best grasped as a prolongation of Adorno's indictment against Wagner. Formal decomposition happens because Stravinsky concentrates on efforts to demonstrate the power of music through shock and awe, especially through percussive effects. These percussive effects mean that rhythm becomes an external envelope, a 'heterogeneous alienated progression', representing the pseudo-objectivity of the collective as a social fact that literally beats time for the subject (Adorno 2007b: 144). The arbitrary juxtaposition of musical elements forms an eclectic combinatory to which decorative inclusions from popular culture are added. For Adorno, '*Petrushka* – neo-Impressionistic in style – is pieced together from innumerable artistic fragments, from the minutely detailed whirring of the fairground down to the mocking imitation of all music rejected by official culture' (Adorno 2007b: 104). In a semiotic sense, these are musical icons – acoustic images that resemble the referent – as opposed to musical signs – arbitrary symbols with a conventional designation.

Adorno then interprets the motivic content of Stravinsky's work as involving the thematic of collective supremacy and the erasure of the individual. Adorno is aware of the experimental aspects of Stravinsky's work, but he thinks that these are merely pressed into the service of the formulation of a new sacrificial myth. Stravinsky's quest for naturalness resonates with Heidegger's notion of authenticity, something that quickly leads to primitivism and hostility to autonomy. Adorno's analyses of *Petrushka* and *Rites* emphasize the music siding with the mocking or deadly collective. Again and again, in *Philosophy of Modern Music*, Adorno returns to the evidently traumatic sacrificial scene in *Rites of Spring*, where the music endorses the collectivity against the individual (Adorno 2007b: 106–8). The atavistic return to the orgiastic rites of the spring festival is here connected with human sacrifice in a dark myth of that is incipiently fascist.

In Schönberg, everything is based on that lonely subjectivity which withdraws into itself.... In Stravinsky's case, subjectivity assumes the character of a sacrifice, but – and this is where he sneers at the tradition of humanistic art – the music does not identify with the victim, but rather with the destructive element.... Both [*Petrouchka* and *Rite*] have a common nucleus: the anti-humanistic sacrifice to the collective – sacrifice without tragedy, made not in the name of a renewed image of man, but only in the blind affirmation of a situation recognised by the victim. (Adorno 2007b: 103–7)

Consequently, the music (and the jerking, spasmodic dance that accompanies it) mimes the disintegration of the bourgeois ego into schizoid states, as infantile regression prompted by destructive aggression results not in a return to childhood happiness, but in a state of agonized disturbance. Finally, therefore, Adorno's interprets Stravinsky's work as involving infantile regression and schizophrenic disintegration. He maintains that 'there is hardly a schizophrenic mechanism—as defined in psychoanalysis by Otto Fenichel—which does not find [in Stravinsky] a highly valid equivalent. The negative objectivity of the work of art recalls in itself the phenomenon of... de-personalization' (Adorno 2007b: 127). Adorno thinks that Stravinsky's *Rites of Spring* indicates a return to archaic instincts of sexuality and aggression that belongs to the hypostatization of inner nature. Meanwhile, *Orpheus* indicates resignation to the second nature of a reified society as an 'immutable fact', something that indicates the disintegration of the autonomous ego.

Stefan George and authenticity

For Adorno, then, Stravinsky deploys the techniques of modernism against the intentionality of the alienated subject, seeking to recover authentic expression by regression to the primitive, infantile and collective. Instead of bringing alienation to self-consciousness and actively seeking reconciliation, intellectual regression accepts alienation and seeks compensation in collective rituals, something with frightening political implications in the 1930s. Rather than developing the musical material through rational construction, aesthetic regression merely raids the existing repertoire of techniques in search of overpowering effects, revealing an accommodation to popularity. Instead of disclosing perceptions and feelings through wringing new expressive possibilities from the rationalized materials, emotional regression rejects the complexity of adult desires for the simplicity of infantile reactions. The simple expedient of eliminating lonely individuality and replacing it with collectivist conformity preserves the modernist sensibility without modern anxiety. Stravinsky's use of folkloric and neoclassical elements in this context appears to Adorno as an aesthetic pastiche lacking any critical dimension, animated by deep nostalgia for a premodern community.

Turning to the literary field, Adorno interprets the modernist lyric poetry of Stefan George (1868–1933) (Adorno 2019: 437–50) as ambivalent, based on the idea of a mid-career pivot from rationalization to authenticity. In the context of discussing Schönberg's musical adaptations of George's poetry, his early work is saluted by Adorno as 'kindred in spirit' to 'Schönberg's compositions' (Adorno 2019: 441). George's initial impulse is a neoromantic 'yearning for beauty', in a prosaic world where the sentimental ornamentation of affirmative culture's decay into the culture industry has clogged language with clichés (Adorno 2019: 443). George's exorcism of ornamentation results in an extraordinary brevity of language and a breaking of traditional lyric form, resulting in a 'cryptogram of the urge . . . to wrest nature from what is absolutely artifactual' (Adorno 2019: 448). Like Schönberg, Adorno comments that 'the melancholy of [George], whom philistine heartiness likes to accuse of coldness, finds an expression of hollowness that is more despairing than a full-toned one could be' (Adorno 2019: 444).

But then George, under the influence of Nietzsche, develops a poetic programme of abstraction and compression, and renounces neoromantic yearning for the will-to-power. Adorno interprets the period from George's 'secret Germany' (1922) to the 'new empire' (1928 – *Das neue Reich*) as a self-destructive rejection of the quest for a poetry of sympathetic feeling. Instead, Georges turns to a different feeling – destructiveness – in search of an authenticity that might explode modern artifice entirely.

> George's violent will reaches even into the works that are intended to be purely lyrical. The lack of congruence between wilful intervention and the semblance of relaxed spontaneous language is so ubiquitous that it confirms [the] suspicion that there is hardly a poem by George in which violence is not manifested in self-destructive form. George, the man who demanded the perfection of the poem with a forcefulness previously unknown in Germany . . . [now] wreak[ed] havoc with what had come before, subjecting something utterly spontaneous to the will. (Adorno 2019: 439–40)

Like Stravinsky's early work, then, George's late work essays a destruction of aesthetic form in the service of a psychologically regressive and politically reactionary disintegration of the individual. Instead of protesting the impending eclipse of the individual, George (like Stravinsky) orients towards its replacement by forms of authentic collectivity, characterized by a folkloric primitivism with authoritarian overtones (Adorno 2019: 438).

By contrast with George, Adorno interprets the work of Franz Kafka (1883–1924) (Adorno 1967a: 245–71), especially *The Trial* (1925), as a progressive modernist encounter with reified fragmentation and the elimination of the subject. Kafka's modernism is regarded by Adorno in the same light as Schönberg's experimentation (Adorno 1967a: 254) – as (1) an exposure of the conventionality of representation and (2) as a howl of protest against the liquidation of the subject. Adorno does acknowledge that music is in general expressive while narrative is in general representational – hence, his preference for lyric poetry rather than narrative fiction – but he thinks that 'Kafka . . . follows the expressionist impulse further than any but the most radical of the poets' (Adorno 1967a: 261). Equally importantly, Adorno recognizes that Kafka's representation of the disintegration of the subject and his serialization of literary form involve the complete regression of subjectivity and the total reification of objectivity (Adorno 1967a: 255, 62). But rather than inviting the accusations levelled at Stravinsky, Adorno thinks that 'Kafka's hermetic memoranda contain the social genesis of schizophrenia' (Adorno 1967a: 255).

For Adorno, 'Kafka seeks salvation in the incorporation of the powers of the adversary – the subject seeks to break the spell of reification by reifying itself' (Adorno 1967a: 270). If psychoanalysis convicts civilization and explodes the transcendental subject then so too does Kafka. Kafka's demolition of the psychic integrity of the individual indicts society for its infliction of neurosis upon the person and exhibits this disintegration 'brought to a standstill' (Adorno 1967a: 253). Autarchic subjectivity annexes objective reality only to become a thing in its own world: 'the thinglike becomes a graphic sign; his spellbound figures do not determine their actions, but rather behave as if each had fallen into a magnetic field' (Adorno 1967a: 262). That is particularly true of depersonalization in sexuality, where the extended family as archaic collective disposes over couplings without reference to individual desire (Adorno 1967a: 263). In short, the world represented by Kafka, including its regressiveness, is akin to that of National Socialism's totalitarian society, while Kafka's expressionism is a denunciation of everything that exists (Adorno 1967a: 259, 61).

Beckett and rationalization

According to Adorno, Samuel Beckett is a literary prolongation of the impulse in Kafka, but also (somewhat confusingly) a combination of Schönberg and Stravinsky.

> Beckett converges with the newest musical tendencies by combining aspects of Stravinsky's radical past—the oppressive stasis of disintegrating continuity—with the most advanced expressive and constructive means from the Schönberg school. (Adorno 2019: 261)

In his analysis of Beckett's *Endgame* (1957), Adorno interprets Beckett through three main lenses. First, he locates Beckett in historical and intellectual context, in what might be called post-historical existentialism. Second, Adorno proposes that the play dramatizes the end of metaphysical meaning, as consequence of reification. Third, he suggests that this is the endpoint of rationalization, in a meta-theatrical reflection on the exhaustion of drama. It is crucial to note that although Adorno contextualizes the play within the problem of 'art after Auschwitz', as in *Dialectic of Enlightenment*, the concentration camps and the mechanized battlefields are regarded by him as realizations of an epochal historical tendency. For Adorno:

> after the Second World War, everything is destroyed, even resurrected culture, without knowing it; humanity vegetates along, crawling, after events which even the survivors cannot really survive. . . . [But] the condition presented in the play is nothing other than that in which 'there is no more nature'. . . the complete reification of the world . . . permanent catastrophe . . . in which nature has been extinguished. (Adorno 2019: 240)

Adorno's Marxist reading of Hegel is prominent in his interpretation of Beckett's 'existentialist' drama. The master–slave dialectic, decoded by Marxism as the dialectic of class struggle, has arrived at a 'standstill', where determinate negation is impossible. Accordingly, no transition to the realm of freedom is possible, and the slave does not anticipate the revolutionary proletariat. Additionally, the end of art, the moment at which figural representation is on the threshold of its sublation by concept formation, has been reached. But the moment for the realization of philosophy has been missed, and so art trembles on the lip of extinction, without visible means for progressing beyond a 'theatre of the absurd'. *Endgame* is the epilogue of subjectivity dramatized through the disintegration of art (Adorno 2019: 263).

According to Adorno the individual as a historical category, 'as the result of the capitalist process of alienation' and, as a defiant protest against it, has become openly transitory. Adorno maintains that 'the individualist position belonged . . . to the ontological tendency of every existentialism'. But 'the catastrophes that inspire *Endgame* have exploded the individual whose substantiality and absoluteness was the common element between Kierkegaard, Jaspers and Sartre'. Existentialism abstracts from historical existence to absolutize the individual and reduce historical concreteness to 'situations'. Beckett eliminates the purposeful and psychological context for personal unity and the meaningfulness of situations, reducing them to materials, thereby disclosing 'a specific and compelling expression—that of horror' (Adorno 2019: 246–7).

The elimination of the psychological unity of the individual and the unifying role of meaningfulness happens because rationalization disintegrates the subject, while positivism reduces metaphysical meaning to constellations of materials. Consequently, Adorno accepts the description of Beckett as a playwright of absurdism, but he locates the idea of 'an expression of meaning's absence' within an historical, rather than existential, context. It is important to notice that 'meaning', for Adorno, is therefore something transcendent, because he locates intentionality and semantics on the same plane as metaphysical teleology and ontological speculation. When he infers that 'affirmative metaphysical meaning is no longer possible' from Beckett's erosion of semantic meaning and psychological intentionality, Adorno strongly implies the identity of metaphysical meaningfulness with semantic significance (Adorno 2019: 238). For Adorno:

> The explosion of metaphysical meaning, which alone guarantees the unity of an aesthetic structure of meaning, makes the crumble away with a necessity and stringency which equals that of the transmitted canon of dramaturgical form. Harmonious aesthetic meaning, certainty at subjectification in finding tangible intention, substituted for that transcendent meaningfulness. (Adorno 2019: 238)

The fundamental reason for this is the complete instrumentalization of reason – the scheme of the play's progression is the endgame in chess – which leads Adorno to a restatement of the fundamental theses of *Dialectic of Enlightenment*. Instrumental rationality is triumphant in the extinction of nature and the mastery over the world leading to total domination. Morality is sundered from cosmology and formalized into a procedure guaranteeing coherence but lacking an ethical compass: 'the autonomous moral law reverts antinomically from pure domination over nature into the duty to exterminate' (Adorno 2019: 264). Rationality must seek the meaningfulness it has itself extinguished: 'the historical inevitability of this absurdity allows it to seem ontological; that is the veil of delusion produced by history' (Adorno 2019: 265).

Accordingly, for Adorno, *Endgame* is that schizophrenic disintegration of dramatic materials that happens when metaphysical meaning no longer anchors dramaturgical form, and authorial intentionality linked to aesthetic harmony can no longer substitute for the lost centre. The modernism of Strindberg had stripped away metaphysical meaningfulness from the totality of empirical human beings and the units of meaning, generating 'a tapestry in which everything and nothing is symbolic, because everything can signify anything'. Beckett removes the meaningfulness of semantic and syntactic units, so that 'not meaning anything becomes the only meaning': 'exposition, complication, plot, peripeteia, and catastrophe return as decomposed elements in a post-mortem examination of dramaturgy' (Adorno 2019: 254). As Adorno concludes: 'Drama falls silent and becomes gesture, frozen amid the dialogues. Only the result of history appears—as decline' (Adorno 2019: 243).

3

Habermasian social theory

Habermasian social theory is an extension and development of Adorno's social philosophy, albeit by communicative means. From the perspective of literature, therefore, the centrepiece of Habermas's social theory is the theory of communicative action, and the reflections on language and psychoanalysis, literature and culture, which surround his position on communication. Nonetheless, it is also important to understand Habermas's reformulation of the reification problematic, the prospects for the public sphere (and his revisions in light of criticism) and his understanding of the connections between ego maturity, moral dialogue and democratic deliberation. However, I do not intend to go into details about his theory of law and politics, translated as *Between Facts and Norms* (Habermas 1996b), or his reconstruction of pragmatic philosophy in relation to the natural sciences (Habermas 2005). I cannot discuss his interventions into contemporary politics, collected in *The Divided West* (Habermas 2006), *The Post-national Constellation* (Habermas 2001) and *The Intervention of the Other* (Habermas 1998a). Finally, I do not engage the technical debates with Rawls and Ratzinger, Gadamer and Luhmann, or recent controversies dealing with the role of religion in the public sphere, collated in *Between Naturalism and Religion* (Habermas 2008b). Instead, after discussing his reconstruction of historical materialism and the position of culture in his analysis of the crisis tendencies of contemporary capitalism, I turn to the two volumes of *The Theory of Communicative Action* [1980, 1981] (hereafter, *Communicative Action*, TCA1 and TCA2). Keeping in view the relation between ego maturity and the difference voices of communicative reason, especially the aesthetic-expressive dimension, I investigate the communicative reframing of the reification problematic and I notice some pertinent critiques of Habermas's formulations. Finally, I look at post-metaphysical thinking and Habermas's defence of the project of modernity, to frame the problems of literary rationality that concern the rest of the book.

Democratic politics and emancipatory critique

By positioning his reconstruction of the history of the public sphere as an 'inquiry into a category of bourgeois society', Habermas locates the work within the coordinate system of historical materialism. The main contention of *Structural Transformation* is that multinational corporations and bureaucratic administration undermine democratic government, citizen participation, social solidarity and discursive will-formation. Regressive developments, affecting the space of dialogue where modern public opinion forms, have rendered apathetic those engaged citizens who once formed a critical public, fundamental to democratic government. The apparently benevolent welfare state, with its administrative suppression of class contradictions through rational management of crisis tendencies, actually relies on systematic depoliticization, cultural anaesthetization and ideological manipulation.

Yet despite Habermas's basic agreement with Adorno's historical narrative of the rise of the culture industry and state capitalism, there is already a significant difference. Although the thesis of the 're-feudalization of the public sphere' is reminiscent of *Dialectic of Enlightenment*, its targets in instrumental rationality and technocratic ideology have a significant restriction. Adorno and Horkheimer suggest that Enlightenment science necessarily declined into a positivist cult of the facts. By contrast, Habermas, who regards advances in cognitive rationality as a crucial component of scientific experimentation, agrees with Karl Popper on the importance of the experimental falsifiability of scientific hypotheses. Habermas also thinks that calculations of efficiency and effectiveness in the labour process are entirely appropriate, and supports empirical controls on theory construction in the social sciences (Habermas 1988: 21–36). Habermas is also critical of Adorno's thesis that logical reasoning and propositional argumentation somehow necessarily culminate in the application of means-ends rationality to the entire social field (Habermas 1970c: 50–61). Nonetheless, Habermas critiques the lack of social contextualization and historical knowledge in Popper's positivism, arguing that this results in a technocratic ideology of social management (Habermas 1976: 198–225).

Likewise, Habermas disagrees with Adorno's thesis that there is no qualitative difference between parliamentary democracy, authoritarian socialism and fascist totalitarianism, as they are all forms of the integration of state and economy in the administered society (Wiggershaus 1994: 567–8, 84). The procedure of democratic will-formation through reasoned public debate, Habermas argues, is historically different from the ritualistic acclamation characteristic of medieval courtly display, as well as from staged acclamation in modern totalitarianism. Open discussion of matters concerning the general interest is an egalitarian ideal that depended on a historically vanishing critical public for its structural support. The problem with actually existing democracy is not democracy, but a process of the instrumentalization of communication that had contingent social roots (based in economic exploitation and class oppression), which might, in principle, be reversed.

Tracing the development of the public sphere in the eighteenth century, Habermas argues that a network of anticipatory forums, such as coffee houses, table societies and literary salons, were the training ground for the emergence of a free press, parliamentary parties, civic associations and social mobilizations, constitutive of the modern public sphere (STPS: 14–26 [70–85], 51–6 [117–22], 57–73 [122–42]). The ideals of liberty, equality and solidarity that emerged with the democratic revolutions around the notion of the social contract reflected the historical reality of a voluntary association between emancipated individuals who jointly direct society on the basis of open, rational deliberation (STPS: 79–102 [149–79]). According to Habermas, the public sphere provides a mechanism for making collectively binding decisions and thereby steering society towards goal attainment, particularly through the nation state, or 'public authority' (STPS: 30 [91]). It is crucial that the public sphere does not result in a totalitarian erasure of privacy or intimacy, as it mediates between the publicly engaged citizen, the private individual and their personal life. It is also important to notice that the notion of privacy, which in the bourgeois implementation of the modern project is coextensive with the economic sphere, is not automatically identical with its bourgeois definition. Privacy is simply that part of the social existence of the individual that is legitimately withdrawn from public scrutiny in the political community, while intimacy, coextensive in the bourgeois definition with humanity, but problematically reserved for women (Fraser 1995; Habermas 1992c), is the affective component of privacy that is reserved in a discretionary way for special figures (STPS: 43–51 [109–17]). The inclusiveness and rationality of the Enlightenment conception of the public sphere by no means implies the utopia of a completely transparent society that can be rationally managed right down to the intimate details. Instead, the democratic ideal, enunciated in declarations of universal rights and political independence, entails the principle that no individual may excluded from public deliberations in the political community (STPS: 89–140 [162–224]).

Habermas proposes that the corrosion of the egalitarian ideal of the public sphere from 1848 onwards reflects a tendency to return to forms of ritualistic acclamation, based on the display of political personalities. He identifies the corporatization of the media, the rise of manipulative versions of public relations, the advent of commodity aesthetics, the entrenchment of the special interests of powerful groups and the transformation of mass political formations into party apparatuses staffed by professional apparatchiks, as a potent set of regressive developments (STPS: 181–235 [276–342]). For Habermas, the ritualization of public debate is accompanied by the rise of 'technocratic ideology', the ideology of social efficiency through effective management, which rejects explicit political commitments and instead focuses on system maintenance and material prosperity (Habermas 1970c). In this context, Habermas warns about the 're-feudalization' of the public sphere, where the corporate media and parliamentary parties join with technocratic experts and powerful lobbies to transform politics into plebiscitary acclamation of elite figures (STPS: 231–2 [337–9]). The reduction of democracy to ritualized acclamation masks the conversion of politics into management of system problems. That is something that is facilitated by the transformation of citizens into consumers, oriented not to democratic citizenship but to 'civil privatism', the syndrome of an exclusive focus on career, family and leisure. Citizen participation becomes a steering problem for the bureaucratic administration, because democratic expectations reduce the capacity of the state to cope rapidly with complex economic crisis tendencies.

Legitimation crises

Habermas's reconstruction of historical materialism, which followed his work on the public sphere, results in a distinction between labour and interaction that maps, broadly speaking, onto a difference between political economy and the sociocultural subsystem (Habermas 1975a). In *Legitimation Crisis* (1975b), Habermas develops a deeper understanding of social complexity while insisting that contemporary capitalism remains subject to (post-classical) crisis tendencies. His analysis of the displacement of contradictions from the economic into the administrative and then the sociocultural subsystems makes possible a theory of the limits to the rational management of advanced capitalism. Meanwhile, the focus on linking crisis potentials of the capitalist system to the normative convictions of social agents implies a democratic-socialist practical intent. Furthermore, instead of the notion of a fusion of economy and state with the culture industries, Habermas proposes the relative autonomy of functional structures, based on a model involving three interrelated social subsystems. The economic, administrative and sociocultural subsystems are dynamized by different types of social action, steered by different media and subject to different antagonistic potentials.

The analysis presented in *Legitimation Crisis* represents a critique of the historical transition from the welfare state of the post-war settlement to the workfare state of the crisis decades from 1970 to 1990. Habermas indicates that he thinks that the generative matrix for capitalist crises is the tendency of the falling rate of profit, which aggravates the economic anarchy of the market with a long-term tendency to economic stagnation. Nonetheless, Habermas endorses the theory that state intervention 'has *transformed the contradiction of class interests into a contradiction of system imperatives*' (Habermas 1975b: 26). His analysis identifies a type of crisis tendency that is invisible in the framework of classical Marxism. In Habermasian terms, this is a 'rationality crisis', in which the irrationality of social production through anarchic competition is displaced onto the state, which then has to seek to intervene through rational planning and welfare measures. The constitutional framework of the vast majority of nation states mandates the preservation of private property in the means of production. That means that the irrationality of the market cannot be solved, because the rationality of the state is constrained by the need to merely ameliorate, rather than transform, the basic problem. In short, the burdens are unequally distributed, and citizens rightly see this as unfair, as a partisanship of the state that is unjust and unreasonable. Where Habermas innovates is by identifying two further crisis types that are the result of the administrative subsystem unloading its rationality crisis onto the sociocultural subsystem. In a 'legitimation crisis', society's consensus agreement on the just exercise of political authority is threatened by disagreement (i.e. social antagonism that can no longer be settled by dialogue, and which therefore gravitates towards resolution by force). In a 'motivation crisis', individuals' dispositions to engage in work performances, cooperate socially and support prevalent cultural values are eroded and phenomena of alienation, anomie and loss of meaning emerge (Habermas 1975b: 45, 49, 51).

Legitimation Crisis is particularly important to the topic of a communicative theory of literature because in that book, Habermas explicitly defends literature against Daniel Bell's neoconservative complaint about the 'adversary culture' of modernism. Bell deplores the contradiction between the corporate and bureaucratic structures, and the sociocultural subsystems. The economic and administrative subsystems need inputs of motivated workers and democratic citizens – respectively – that in liberal capitalism were supplied by classical structures in the sociocultural subsystem. Motivated workers were supplied by means of socialization into the post-Reformation work ethic, while democratic citizens were provided by the regulatory controls of a legal system framed by negative liberty. Bell supposes that the work ethic has become corroded by hedonistic orientations, while an excess of democratic expectations has led to a crisis of governance. Bell is particularly aggressive about the role of the modernist 'adversary culture' in the delegitimation of the work ethic and in promoting an anti-authoritarian counter-culture. For Bell, the solution is to depoliticize the administration in order to unload democratic expectations, while returning to religion in order to generate conformist personalities that have been re-oriented back to the work ethic. For Habermas, by contrast, emerging legitimation and motivation crises point to the need for a radical democratization of administration and economy, together with an expansion and deepening of modernist culture. The emancipatory potentials of modernity have been choked, because the economy and the administration, with their anonymous and amoral imperatives, have colonized the sociocultural system and the public sphere. Consumer hedonism is certainly a problem, but a modernist anti-authoritarian culture and a set of highly democratic expectations are part of the solution.

Communicative action

The theory of communicative action is an effort to rethink the foundations of Critical Theory developed through Habermas's reconstruction of historical materialism (after his dialogue with psychoanalysis, explored in Chapter 6). Habermas prolongs the distinction between system integration and social integration, which was central to the notion of legitimation and motivation crises, into an opposition between strategic and communicative action. This replaces the distinction between labour and interaction developed during the critique of Marxism. The fundamental social problem is not about a difference between two kinds of action that solitary individuals might engage in – labour or interaction. It is about how the various kinds of cooperative social action are coordinated: collective action can happen communicatively, or can be instrumentalized through what Habermas calls 'strategic action' and 'functional reason'. In functional systems, particularly the economic and administrative subsystems that are steered by anonymous media of money and power, cooperation is secured by exchange and command, which bypasses the process of reaching mutual understanding through dialogue. Additionally, in line with the notion of legitimation and motivation crises, Habermas divides the sociocultural subsystem into the legal subsystem and the cultural subsystem, where cooperation can also be instrumentalized through sanctions and status (respectively).

Speaking generally, strategic action involves the coordination of action through 'influence', defined as the resort to inducements for securing a consensus, bypassing reasoned argument. Influence may include money, commands, coercion, status, the idea of unquestioning obedience to traditional authority or recourse to persuasion by means of ideological misrepresentations. Social and cultural interactions normally involve communicative cooperation, but might also be directed by the instrumental distortion of communication, such as an appeal to prejudice, or the enforcement of a repressive law. By contrast, communicative action involves the coordination of action through consent, based on arriving at mutual understanding through dialogue. By consent, Habermas means assent to the possible justifications for a proposed action, which implies that participants in dialogue who are discussing their response to a situation assume that the potential exists to reach an unforced agreement between reasonable agents. Communicative action therefore implies the possibility for what

Habermas calls 'discourse', which is not just speech, or discussion, but the built-in potential for a suspension of action coordination while participants engage in debate. The process of dialogical justification through reasoned argument, which happens when communicative action is suspended while participants debate, entails the legitimacy of dissent and presupposes full reciprocity between participants.

The shift, from labour and interaction, to strategic action and communicative action, clarifies the descriptive intent of Habermasian social theory and sets the terms for his normative reframing of the problem of reification, as the colonization of dialogue-based cooperation by functional imperatives. Instead of classifying all actions into two groups – labour and interaction – Habermas builds up a descriptive typology of social action that corresponds to Weber's categories of social action and their correlative types of rationality. These action types are collaboratively enacted by collective agents who coordinate their individual efforts through the 'meta-actions' of communicative action and strategic cooperation. The implication is that instead of partitioning up the social system into two distinct domains, based on two different types of action, Habermas now has a flexible description of the whole social field as constituted by a multiplicity of action types, with communicative and strategic options at the disposal of participants who need to cooperate.

The key distinction is that between system integration, which involves the functional input–output relation between subsystems that depend on one another for resource exchange, and social integration, which involves the coordination of action between agents who depend on mutual understanding for achieving agreed ends. Generally speaking, when social action happens, both system and social integration also happens, because agents agree on the ends of a joint action whose (intended and unintended) consequences are the production of resources, resources which are the conditions of existence for other social actions. Furthermore, there is no automatic correlation between functional systems and strategic action, for the function performed by an action, and its integration with other functions, depends on the consequences of the action, not on the mode of cooperation. Accordingly, it is theoretically possible for the economic subsystem, for instance, to be functionally integrated by the consequences of the communicative coordination of collective labour (a situation which happens in lineage societies). Finally, Habermas refuses an automatic connection between strategic action, functional systems and technocratic rationality, for the coordination of action by money and commands is often necessary, for reasons of efficiency and complexity. When Habermas insists that society can be regarded from the perspective of an observer, as an ensemble of functional systems, and from the perspective of a participant, as a communicatively integrated 'lifeworld', he is refusing any ontological (as opposed to perspectival) bisection of society into 'good' versus 'bad' halves.

Nonetheless, there is a problem with the presentation of the analysis in *The Theory of Communicative Action*. As Axel Honneth documents, Habermas constantly slips between a two-dimensional social analysis and a two-tier social ontology (Honneth 1991: 251–80). Strategic action and communicative action, or functional and communicative reason, are sometimes represented as aspects of social practices and sometimes as distinct domains of the social. Habermas's description of the political system, supposed to consist of administrative rationality and legitimate interactions, is an excellent example of the two-dimensional analysis. Habermas's differentiation in kind between the economic and administrative systems, and the sociocultural system, however, is an illustration of the two-tier approach. Ultimately, the two-tier approach wins out, leading to the indefensible claim that the economic system is a norm-free zone of strategic action and that the sociocultural system cannot be rendered efficient by functional differentiation (TCA2: 256–8 [384–6]).

Habermas does not have sufficient reason to partition the social field into two distinct kinds of rationality and assign them to the warring empires of functional systems-rationality and communicative reason. Habermas's claim, that the sociocultural subsystem does not behave in the same way that the economy and administration do, really violates the logic of the application of the term 'system' to this domain. Despite this problem, Habermas's fundamental intuition – that 'disturbances of system integration endanger [the] continued existence [of a social formation] only to the extent that social integration is at stake, that is, when the consensual foundations of normative structures are impaired so that society becomes anomic' (Habermas 1975b: 3) – remains valid. Deficits of social integration cannot be compensated by system resources – it is difficult to buy motivations and orientations, just as it is impossible to coerce consent. The substitution of anonymous steering media, such as money and regulations, for discursive agreement, ultimately undermines the credibility of the entire social formation. I will return to the important question of whether communicative action is restricted to the sociocultural system, and strategic action to the functional logic of the economic and administrative systems, in a moment. But first I want to explore Habermas's signature contribution to the question of a normative standard for the critique of society, in the concept of discourse ethics.

Communicative reason and discourse ethics

To connect Weber's typology of social actions to the notion of communication, Habermas develops a correlation between different kinds of speech pragmatics and the distinct social actions that these speech acts coordinate. Agents orient to situations defined in terms of goal-directed (teleological) actions (value-rational action or purposive action), actions in conformity with norms (normatively regulated conduct) and actions that express the subjective stance of the actors (dramaturgical action). These action types are assessed according to different standards. Purposive actions (i.e. labour) involve means-ends calculations of success that are assessed according to criteria of efficiency and effectiveness. Value-rational actions are evaluated as 'fitting', or appropriate behaviour. Normatively regulated actions are considered in relation to notions of right conduct. Dramaturgical actions are regarded as valid when they truthfully represent the subjective state of the actor(s). The notion of standards of assessment for different types of action according to different kinds of validity brings us to the centre of Habermas's theory of communicative action. Every communicatively coordinated action proposal, because it presupposes the legitimacy of a participant saying 'no' and demanding an explanation, can be correlated with the relevant sort of 'validity claim', or reasoning procedure, that would be required to justify that proposal in the face of dissent. The process of argumentation about action proposals builds up referential 'worlds' that correspond to the situational domain of the action type – the objective world of the natural environment and social or psychological objectivity; the social world of norms and values; and the subjective world of needs and desires, feelings and beliefs. The process of the discursive redemption of validity claims constitutes a different register of rationality according to the referential world in question in the argument: cognitive claims about the truth of propositions concerning the objective world; claims to normative rightness and evaluative appropriateness, about the social world; and claims to the truthfulness of expressions about the subjective world. For the sake of intelligibility I intend to neglect evaluative claims to appropriateness for the moment. I also note that I have not discussed interpretive claims to the coherent meaning of symbols. I do this to highlight the fundamental architecture of Habermas's position: there is a neat 'triplicity' to Habermas's schema that flows from his somewhat Kantian approach.

Communicative reason is the totality of these different 'voices of reason'. Habermas argues that the process of the separation of cultural value spheres into expert specializations can be grasped from this perspective. Cognitive claims about the objective world are valid if they represent the truth about states of affairs, argumentatively redeemed through propositional logic and experimental falsification. Knowledge springing from these arguments forms the (natural and social) sciences and is deposited in the everyday lives of individuals as formal cognitive operations and verified hypotheses. Normative claims about the social world are valid if they represent guidelines for right conduct that can be agreed upon by all affected, argumentatively redeemed through universalistic moral reasoning. Knowledge springing from these arguments forms the moral basis for modern legislation and is deposited in the everyday lives of individuals as post-conventional moral discourses, such as utilitarian ethics and formal-universal (deontological) morality. Expressive claims about the subjective world of modern individuals are valid if they represent interpretations of human needs and cultural values that a community can accept as authentic, that is, as a truthful expression of desires and feelings that lead to healthy forms of individual self-realization. Knowledge springing from these arguments forms modern art and is deposited in the everyday lives of individuals as post-traditional motivations, that is, as a set of attitudes that enables modern persons to select a lifestyle for themselves in the context of pluralism.

To summarize, on Habermas's interpretation, each of the value spheres operates according to a distinctive logic, of cognitive (science), normative (law and morals) and expressive (aesthetic) reasoning, governed by the particular procedures by which their defining validity claims of truth (cognitive), rightness (normative) and truthfulness (aesthetic) are articulated symbolically and redeemed argumentatively. Because these domains are institutionalized as specialized forms of enquiry, liberated from religion, protected from the pragmatic pressures of everyday communicative action and purified from the intrusive predominance of one another's validity claims, they can develop expert knowledge about the objective, social and subjective worlds (respectively). Ideally, this flows back into the everyday existence of modern individuals through processes of translation, resulting in the release of rational potentials into cultural knowledge, social integration and socialized personalities. The intention here is to specify why it is that modernity is an advance on premodern community, because it leads to differentiated, secular knowledge and expanded possibilities for individual self-realization.

Habermas advances this schema of communicative reason in order to specify the normative grounds for the critique of capitalism and bureaucracy. Adorno advocates an existential judgement on capitalist society based in the prospect of reconciliation (or de-alienation), and proposes aesthetic mimesis as the alternative to instrumental rationality. By contrast, Habermas proposes communicative reason as the alternative to the technocratic management of functional imperatives, and advocates a critique of capitalism and bureaucracy grounded in the norm of free and open speech. Specifically, Habermas argues that the norm of consensus based on unconstrained dialogue provides a standard for the existential judgement on capitalism and bureaucracy that is not dependent on a Romantic utopia. Furthermore, Habermas wants to defend democratic participation and modern culture while reformulating the critique of reification as a critique of the colonization of everyday life by technocratic systems. In *Structural Transformation*, Habermas differentiated between the emancipatory potentials of the democratic public sphere and its bourgeois implementation. So too, in *Communicative Action*, Habermas distinguishes between the progressive 'cultural rationalisation' that happens through the process of 'value enhancement' in science, law and art, and the technocratic management of everyday life that instrumentalizes reason into bureaucratic formalism and economic calculation.

TABLE 3.1 *The Three Voices (Cognitive, Normative, Expressive) of Communicative Reason*

Referential world	Dimension of comm- unicative action	Validity claim as part of communicative reason	Cultural value sphere = institutionalized learning process	Structure-forming effect of expert knowledge
Objective	Cognitive	Truth	Science	Formalized cognition (formal-operational hypothetical attitudes to objective nature)
Social	Normative	Rightness	Morality	Normative universality (post-conventional moral discourses on the social world)
Subjective	Expressive	Truthfulness	Art	Post-traditional motivations (reflexively critical relation to cultural need-interpretations)

It is crucial to notice that in Habermas's work on discourse ethics, he rejects his initial formulation of rational consensus as an 'ideal speech situation', as highly misleading, implying a public sphere consisting of intellectuals or a kind of pure democracy impossible to achieve. The orientation towards unconstrained dialogue is a presupposition of speech rather than a particular social arena or historical condition. Every speech act is potentially rational to the extent that all participants presuppose that the speaker can provide rational grounds for their belief that the situation is just so, should the interlocutors object to an action proposal in this context. The dialogical justifications provided by speakers build up a network of rational arguments and consensus agreements that intersubjectively constitute the definitions of how the subjective, social and natural worlds are. In this process, agents manage to cooperate only insofar as they share common situation definitions – and therefore a common world – so that argumentative justification (rational action) generates at once individual autonomy and social solidarity. Accordingly, Habermas maintains that the programme of 'universal-formal pragmatics' involves rendering explicit 'the pre-theoretical grasp of rules on the part of competently speaking, acting and knowing subjects', rather than imposing on speakers a set of rules for reaching rational consensus (TCA2: 297–8 [443–4]).

Although the building-up of an intersubjective consensus does happen through the elaboration of traditions, modernity significantly rationalizes this process by means of expert specializations in the redemption of particular kinds of validity claims. The instrumental transformation of nature is grasped in relation to situation definitions in the objective world and redeemed through cognitive validity claims to truth that are institutionalized as learning processes in science. Debates about the regulation of conduct are redeemed through normative validity claims to rightness in the social world that are institutionalized as learning processes in moral philosophy and the law. Finally, expressive validity claims about the sincerity of feelings and beliefs, and the authenticity of needs and desires, are redeemed through expressive validity claims about the truthfulness of states of affairs in the subjective world and institutionalized as learning processes in art and therapy (TCA1: 75–101 [115–52]). Expert specialization in these independent validity spheres results in 'value enhancement' through the refinement of claims, leading to the decentring of the modern world view, which can no longer hold cognitive, normative and expressive claims together in a mythological unity. Communicative reason is procedural and argumentative, not substantive and mythic: 'communicative reason finds its criteria in the argumentative procedures for directly or indirectly redeeming claims to propositional truth, normative rightness, subjective authenticity and aesthetic harmony' (TCA2: 314 [466]).

The concept of communicative reason is intended critically as a universal normative standard, acceptable to every rational person, by which to judge the crisis tendencies of modern society and the implementation of the modern project. Unconstrained communication is a latent potential of communicative action that, although it is pervasively blocked by commodification and bureaucratization, provides a counterfactual ideal standard against which to measure an existential judgement on capitalism. The notion of a rational consensus is built into social cooperation through communicative action because participants implicitly commit to the resolution of disagreement through argument alone, rather than the resort to force. Furthermore, social domination and economic exploitation, by preventing the full participation of all speakers in a dialogue, are called into question by the ideal of unconstrained communication. The ideal of an egalitarian democratic community does not depend on the utopia of reconciliation or communist abundance, but instead on the norms that are presupposed by the possibility that any interlocutor might say 'no' to a proposal. Habermas rethinks the Frankfurt School's commitment to emancipation from domination and the achievement of a meaningful way of life through the idea of communicative reason. He articulates this as follows:

1. Every subject with the competence to speak and act is allowed to take part in a discourse.
2. (A) Everyone is allowed to question any assertion whatsoever; (B) Everyone is allowed to introduce any assertion whatsoever into the discourse; (C) Everyone is allowed to express their attitudes, desires and needs.
3. No speaker may be prevented, by internal or external coercion, from exercising their rights as laid down in (1) and (2) above. (Habermas 1999b: 89)

Habermas's definition of communicative freedom based on the fundamental right to say 'no!' has been extended and clarified by Rainer Forst in his theory of free speech as reflexive toleration (Forst 2013). Forst's presentation of non-violent disagreement based on respect for human dignity is a powerful alternative to Jacques Rancière's notion of disagreement as a clash between incommensurable language games (Rancière 1999). Rancière is concerned with the scenario in which a group, which is included in society but excluded from politics (e.g. women or workers, immigrants or plebeians), articulates its 'no!' as a radically singular claim, because it is not counted within the political universal. Voicing a widely shared concern about the 'ethics of the seminar room' versus the reality of disagreements in the public sphere, Rancière's criticism of Habermas is that Habermasian disagreement presupposes civility because it is a provocation to discourse among the already included. By contrast, the case of the political demonstration shows a moment where disclosure and critique unite in the presentation of an entirely new landscape of debate, something that is necessary for any emancipatory critical utterance to follow the 'no!' of the oppressed and excluded (Rancière 1999: 57–8). Rancière's case is certainly cogent on its own terms and it explains why he is interested in political aesthetics in exploring what happens when civil dialogue threatens to break down, because of paradigm-shifting ethical or political interventions (Russell and Montin 2015). But as Forst points out, from the Habermasian perspective, the interlocutor's 'no!' opens up the space of a reflexive shift that separates moral discourse from ethical conventions (and political universals) (Forst 2013: 459). Rancière, in other words, is pushing against an open door, but what he thinks is Habermas on the other side is his own foot jammed in it, in the form of a failure to recognize the distinction between ethico-political definitions of universality (i.e. conventions) and their rational critique. This is a really common misconception, and it leads to the assertion that the claims of the oppressed are radically arbitrary in relation to the reigning universal, something which is the logical consequence of adopting Rancière's perspective. The Habermasian perspective, especially as supplemented by Forst, is entirely different: the revolt of the excluded is both *rational* and *justified*.

This background is essential for grasping the stakes in Habermas's programme of 'discourse ethics', as a rational critique of power designed to spearhead the reconstruction of society within a democratic framework, through advancing post-conventional moral and legal representations. Discourse ethics goes beyond deontological morality because it allows speakers to consider generalizable interests as well as universal principles, consequences of action as well as norms of conduct. Among other things, Habermas intends this as a foundation for legislation that would set a normative ceiling on the forms of strategic action that can happen in the economy and administration. Having defined the conditions for rational discourse (above), he sets up 'D', the Discourse Principle, as:

> D   Only those actions norms are valid to which all possibly affected persons could agree as participants in rational discourse (Habermas 1996b: 107).

On this basis, he defines 'U', the Principle of Moral Universalizability, as:

> U   A norm is valid when the foreseeable consequences and side effects of its general observance for the interests and value-orientation of *each individual* could be *jointly* accepted by *all* concerned without coercion (Habermas 1998a: 42).

The reason why the demonstration of the excluded is legitimate is because the norms of power fail to meet this elementary standard of moral universality. Habermas's principle of moral universalizability is a response to Adorno's existential judgement on modern society. It is therefore not surprising that liberal and conservative interlocutors have objected that it is too demanding for present social institutions. Their objections entirely miss its critical implications as a principle of social transformation, but unlike Adorno's notion of reconciliation, the principle of moral universalizability is intended for application to the contemporary world. It is perfectly compatible with social complexity and democratic politics, but it does not reduce politics to ethics (Habermas 1996b: 110). Its intention, instead, is to provide the movements for the democratization of society with a reflexive moral standard that justifies their critique of the 'bourgeois implementation of the modern project' and guides their reconstructive efforts.

System versus lifeworld

Because of Habermas's own tendency to present this antagonism as an opposition between economy and administration, on the one hand, and the social and cultural systems, on the other hand, the critical potential of his analysis of crisis tendencies in the modern world has been almost entirely misunderstood. His illustration of the fault line by means of the protest politics of the new social movements – such as the environmental movement – rather than, say, mass democratic uprisings against authoritarian regimes, has contributed to the idea that this is a fair-weather social theory focused on the ameliorative politics of pressure groups in civil society. Interpreted in terms of Adorno's social theory, this would mean an idealist politics setting the cultural superstructure against the politico-economic foundation. That would be an essentially aesthetic revolt against functional imperatives, akin to the New Left's turn from political protest to counter-cultural rebellion. Indeed, Andrew Arato and Jean Cohen, interpreting the collapse of historical Communism in terms of a 'self-limiting democratic revolution' conducted by 'civil society within the political community', saw themselves as radicalizing Habermas's position, rather than implementing it (Arato and Cohen 1992: 221). Even cothinkers within the Frankfurt School tradition of Critical Theory have denounced Habermas's position as a conservative turn away from emancipatory struggle (Honneth 1991: 303).

The key to grasping Habermas's concept of the antagonism between system and lifeworld, however, is to return to his claim that he is the 'last Marxist', engaged in an analysis of the potential for emancipation in light of the crisis tendencies of the present. Habermas thinks that technocratic management has succeeded in dampening the crisis tendencies of the economy and administration, while 'colonizing' cultural institutions and civil society with a functional logic. Accordingly, crisis potentials have been displaced from functional systems into social integration, which relies on communicative action, creating a communicative disturbance in social cooperation expressed through crises of anomie (i.e. motivation crises), alienation (i.e. legitimation crises) and psychopathology (i.e. personality crises, e.g. epidemics of depression and narcissism). For the moment, needs-based struggles around material interests, such as labour mobilizations and union movements, have been integrated into the system. But egalitarian and democratic struggles around rights and recognition, human rights and political participation, ecology and meaningfulness, break forth from the 'seam between lifeworld and system' (TCA2: 392–6 [577–83]). I think that Habermas should have specified that what this means is the democratization of the economy and administration, as well as the revitalization of the public sphere.

Should Habermas have described the contradiction between lifeworld and system as setting democracy against capitalism? Perhaps, but the real problem concerns the democratic and communal steering of functional systems. Habermas corrects his dualist presentation of lifeworld versus system through the development of a discourse theory of law, according to which legal frameworks provide a normative ceiling to strategic action (Habermas 1991a). There are no 'norm free regions of strategic action'.

Equally, there are no power-free zones of communicative action. Instead, there is the problem of how to communicatively regulate steering media through democratic legislation. This has to happen without resorting to simplistic plans for the de-differentiation of functional systems, or utopian schemes for direct control through popular soviets. To this end, Habermas has advanced proposals for deliberative democracy, social rights and citizen participation.

The critical potential of Habermas's distinction between system and lifeworld, then, should not be restricted to the 'new social movements', or confused with an opposition between culture and society, versus capitalism and bureaucracy. Instead, it involves the difference between the democratic steering of society, based on a revitalized public sphere and egalitarian expectations, and the technocratic management of society, based on the needs of its functional systems. Should the economy and administration serve a democratic citizenry, or should de-unionized employees and depoliticized consumers service the requirements of the corporations and the state? In support of this challenge, Habermas builds up a set of distinctions based on the orientation to success of strategic action, versus the orientation to dialogue-based social cooperation, characteristic of communicative action. Where functional structures adapt to the system's environment, based on survival needs, the coherence of the lifeworld depends upon cultural reproduction, social integration and personal socialization.

The lifeworld is not a subsystem of society, but a perspective on social action, for all social action has intended goals that render it meaningful to the actors involved (TCA2: 122–35 [188–206]). At the same time, the consequences of these social actions are systematically integrated through functional relations happening 'behind the backs' of the actors. From the functional perspective, an author writing a book for a corporate publishing house is generating a consumer good for a market segment, something whose success can be described in monetary terms. Simultaneously, from the lifeworld perspective, that author is engaged in communication about a topic of mutual interest, with an audience whose evaluation of the book is discursive. That social action appears as meaningful against a background of assumptions, a 'culturally transmitted and linguistically organised stock of interpretive patterns', sustaining collective identity (TCA2: 136 [206–7]). The background assumptions constituting the lifeworld are a pre-theoretical and pre-reflexive horizon of pre-understandings that supply the context against which actions are intelligible (TCA2: 132 [202]). Assumptions are shaken from time to time and a new consensus forms on the basis of dialogue. This throws light on a region of the lifeworld, in a process that Habermas describes as 'cultural rationalisation'. But it is impossible to totalize the lifeworld and render it completely transparent.

According to Habermas, the lifeworld consists of three component strands – cultural knowledge, social norms and personality structures – while the reproduction of the lifeworld involves maintaining cultural continuity, reproducing the legitimacy of social institutions and socializing competent individuals. He distinguishes between the transmission and renewal of cultural knowledge – cultural reproduction – sustaining the solidarity of individuals through providing legitimate institutions – social integration – and the formation of personal identities motivated to participate in social life – personal socialization (TCA2: 137 [208–9]). Habermas tabulates the three components of the lifeworld – culture, structure, person – against the crisis potentials that a failure to reproduce a component of the lifeworld generates (TCA2: 142–3 [217–18]).

According to Habermas, social reproduction in the modern world involves the dialectically related processes of societal rationalization and cultural rationalization. In societal rationalization, the success-oriented strategic action happening in economic, administrative, social-legal and cultural subsystems becomes more effective and efficient by means of functional differentiation. In cultural rationalization, the discursive learning processes connected with communicative reason (cognitive – science; normative – law and morality; aesthetic-expressive – art and therapy) lead to increased autonomy of cultural value spheres and new discoveries about the objective, social and subjective worlds of

TABLE 3.2 *The Reproduction of the Lifeworld Provides for Consensual Knowledge, Legitimate Orders and Personal Autonomy (TCA2: 142 [217])*

Reproduction processes	Structural components		
	Culture	Society	Personality
Cultural reproduction	Interpretive schemes fit for consensus ('valid knowledge')	Legitimations	Socialization patterns Educational goals
Social integration	Obligations	Legitimately ordered interpersonal relations ('recognition frameworks')	Social memberships
Socialization	Interpretive accomplishments	Motivations for actions that conform to norms	Interactive capabilities ('personal identity')

TABLE 3.3 *Disturbances in Communicative Reproduction Lead to Anomie, Alienation and Pathologies, Affecting the Rationality of Knowledge (Culture), the Solidarity of Members (Society) and Personal Responsibility (Person) (TCA2: 143 [218])*

Kind of disturbance \ Structural components	Culture	Society	Personality
Cultural reproduction	Loss of meaning	Delegitimation	Crisis in orientation / Crisis in education
Social integration	Unsettling of collective identity	Anomie	Alienation
Socialization	Rupture of tradition	De-motivation	Psychopathologies

modern individuals. Ideally, these dynamics are maintained in a balanced equilibrium, by means of democratic will-formation and a vibrant public sphere, so that cultural discoveries become accessible to the mass of non-specialists, while functional improvements remain normatively regulated by social democratization. The problem created by what Habermas calls the 'bourgeois implementation of the modern project' involves the intrusion of functional logic into the communicative architecture of the lifeworld, through the monetization of social relations and the corporatization of the public sphere, as well as the bureaucratization of society and culture. What Adorno diagnosed as the plague of 'instrumental rationality' is alive and well, living in currently ascendant ideologies of technocratic management and neoliberal governance. Its results are widespread phenomena of anomie, de-motivation and pathologies such as epidemics of depression and narcissism (TCA2: 383 [564]).

Corporate colonization of the public sphere

The 'colonization of the lifeworld by the system' is Habermas's communicative reformulation of the reification problematic, which Adorno described in terms of instrumental reason (Sitton 2003: 84). Colonization generalizes the notion of 'legitimation crises', where system disequilibria in the economy and administration are displaced onto regions of the sociocultural lifeworld that depend on communicative, not strategic, action for social reproduction (TCA2: 384 [564]). On the new model, legitimation crises are supplemented by motivation crises and psychological pathologies, in a process that

Habermas describes as 'the juridification of social relations', that is, the regulation of social relations by formal processes to do with money and power (TCA2: 385–6 [565–8]). The idea is that regions of strategic action are steered by anonymous 'media', such as money and power, that coordinate the functional consequences of action without reference to communicative agreements. Individuals coordinating action by means of money and power can therefore act instrumentally to maximize utility, provided that they remain within the framework of the relevant 'juridified' regulations. System imperatives, represented by quantities of money and degrees of power, are transferred onto the lifeworld through its regulation in the corporate and bureaucratic interest. The fallout from economic stagnation or political crisis is thereby displaced onto the lifeworld, leading to well-known problems of loss of democratic legitimacy, breakdowns in social solidarity and the privatization of hope. As Habermas says elsewhere:

> I still explain these pathologies by referring to the mechanism driving capitalism forward, namely, economic growth, but I assess them in terms of the systemically induced predominance of economic and bureaucratic ... rationality, within a one-sided or 'alienated' communicative practice. (Habermas 1991a: 225)

But political representation and social status can also function as media anonymously transmitting influence through strategic calculations, alongside money and command. Accordingly, although the social and cultural systems might become dysfunctional as a result of the fallout from economic and administrative crises, the problem captured by the concept of colonization is a different one. When strategic calculations based on anonymous media systematically override communicative deliberation about the goals of social cooperation, then individuals are constrained to act instrumentally, bypassing dialogue and short-circuiting consensus. In the cultural field of the social system, for instance, the pervasiveness of calculations based on monetary success and cultural status (i.e. distinction) blocks literary experimentation. Instead of literary interventions into public debate and literary presentations of egalitarian ideals, the corporatization of global publishing means, more often than not, the routinization and trivialization of content (Schiller 1976, 1991).

The Habermasian reformulation of the critique of ideology in terms of distorted communication belongs to his effort to reframe the reification problematic in terms consistent with his formal pragmatics (Habermas 1970a, 1970b). According to Habermas, distorted communication happens when 'latent strategic action', that is, hidden resort to influence, operates undetected in action coordination (TCA1: 278 [333]). But it is also present when 'structural restrictions on communication' happen as consequences of domination, thereby preventing certain key debates or framing them in terms reflecting influence (TCA2: 194 [290]). Habermas's rejection of Gadamer's notion that interpretation is guided by an anticipation of closure – perhaps infelicitously expressed by the latter as a pre-judgement (*Vorurteil*) – is connected to the Habermasian critique of ideology. For Habermas, the paradigm of ideological misrepresentation is a distorted communication containing prejudiced representations that block the full participation of some agents in public dialogue (Mendelson 1979). It must not be imagined, however, that the critique of distorted communication involves a vision of interminable debate, based on the misconception that Habermas's critique of technocratic ideology implies that manifest, or explicit, strategic action is somehow wrong.

Indeed, Habermas insists that the reformulation or replacement of value-based agreements by legal frameworks, which represent system imperatives as rules regulating conduct, in 'juridification', is a two-sided process. On the one hand, legal relations carve out arenas for strategic action by formalizing relations between persons and making performances predictable. On the other hand, legal relations impose a normative ceiling on strategic conduct, setting limits to the instrumentalization of others. Accordingly, juridification is the shockfront in the imposition of instrumental regulations on efforts to reach consensus, and on the adjustment of one set of system performances – say, socialization and education – to the imperatives of another, such as happens in the monetarization of education or the bureaucratization of childcare (TCA2: 392–6 [577–84]). Habermas thinks that the transformation of citizens into clients of welfare bureaucracies and consumers of corporate products happens primarily through juridification. At the same time, however, juridification can function as the pacemaker for social change, when a new consensus is imposed as a formal performance on actors who otherwise might decide to perpetuate prejudice. Habermas illustrates this claim with reference to the regulation of normative conduct through rights-based protections and the notion, developed from T. H. Marshall's theory of democratic citizenship, of a progressive ascent through legal, civil, political and social rights (TCA2: 397–400 [584–90]).

Habermas proposes that legitimation crises remain the central concern of technocratic governments, because social solidarity, based on the legitimacy of institutional arrangements, is fundamental to the governability of a population. That solidarity is endangered by the corporatization of the public sphere and the bureaucratization of everyday life, which tends to transform democratic citizenship into the passive acclamation of political elites while choking public debate. The technocratic solution is to displace this onto problems of motivation and adjustment, as crises of anomie and psychopathology can be dealt with by thrusting responsibility for social suffering onto the individual. Habermas rejects neoconservative proposals to restore social solidarity through the re-imposition of religious ideologies as regressive utopias, pointing out that mythic world views are incompatible with role differentiation, scientific discoveries and moral autonomy, which refuses the prescriptive thickness of ethical systems. The real problems are that the modern lifeworld remains only partially rationalized, because of the sclerosis imposed by the re-feudalization of the public sphere, and that persistent social inequalities militate against meaningful democratic deliberation. As Habermas concludes, 'only in an egalitarian public of citizens that has emerged from the confines of class and thrown off the millennia-old shackles of social stratification and exploitation can the potential of an unleashed cultural pluralism fully develop' (Habermas 1996a: 219).

In line with this conception of democratic socialism, Habermas proposes a set of structural reforms. The public sphere needs to be reinvigorated by a reactivation of the democratic citizenry, in order to generate rational consensus on shared values and to transmit this, as democratic legislation, to the functional systems of a complex society. That will require the elimination of forms of social stratification that prevent participation, through redistributive measures designed to eradicate exploitation and oppression. The administrative system needs to be democratized, but through improved transparency rather than popular soviets, and a deliberative democracy set in place to ensure full representation of participants in dialogue. The key to all of this – and the connection between Habermasian politics and the cultural role of literature – is the rationalization of the lifeworld to generate egalitarian expectations among a critical public (Habermas 1996b: 364, 52, 440, 219).

Post-metaphysical thinking and utopian energies

My focus is on the 'young', Marxist Habermas, rather than the 'mature', liberal Habermas who emerges *after* the theory of communicative action, in recent works such as *Between Facts and Norms* (1996), *The Post-national Constellation* (2001), *The Divided West* (2006) and *Between Naturalism and Religion* (2008). I agree with some aspects of Michael Thompson's critique of the domestication of Critical Theory, which targets in particular the de-linking of Kant and Hegel from Marx and Freud (Thompson 2016: 15–38). Thompson also criticizes the idealism of supposing that the revitalization of social practices of democratic citizenship and open communication can alone lead to an egalitarian democracy, in the absence of structural transformation of functional systems (Thompson 2016: 39–62). However, Thompson misses his target with the claim that because language can become one-dimensional under conditions of technocratic ideology and functionalist reason, the communicative turn undertaken by Habermas is merely wishful thinking (Thompson 2016: 41). The intention of Habermas's speech-act theoretical reconstruction of the lifeworld is not to describe the intrinsically emancipated communicative practices of modern individuals, who merely need to be freed from the leaden weight of a reified public sphere. It is to work up a (quasi-transcendental) normative standard for the critique of capitalism and bureaucracy, while grounding proposals for structural reforms in the latent potentials of actually existing social practices. Contra Thompson, if modern individuals are completely 'corrupted' in their everyday social cooperation by a one-dimensional public sphere (Thompson 2016: 42), then they cannot possibly emancipate themselves or emerge from ideological mystification.

In proposing a reading of Habermas as a communicative reframing of Adorno's Critical Theory, I am certainly presenting a selective interpretation of Habermasian social theory and political philosophy. On the one hand, Habermas does indeed represent a turn away from Marx and Freud, towards Rawls and Kohlberg, as inspirations for Critical Theory. These thinkers are emblematic of the radical critique of modern society and its liberal amelioration, respectively, and they belong alongside a whole series of other theoretical sources and political intuitions pointing in the same direction. Where Adorno engages in negative dialectics, Habermas is involved with pragmatic reconstruction; where Adorno's 'reconciliation' resonates with Marxian revolution, Habermas expressly rejects social revolution as conceptualized by Marxism (Habermas 1996b: 372). On the other hand, Adorno's fundamental existential attitude towards modernity and enlightenment is relentlessly negative, whereas Habermas is a partisan of the enlightenment and a defender of modernity. The very processes that Adorno regarded as fragmentation and reification Habermas conditionally endorses as potentially liberating. These include cultural rationalization and functional differentiation, representative government and parliamentary democracy, moral autonomy and ego maturity and dialogue with non-radical positions. Furthermore, Habermas advocates 'post-metaphysical' formulations of critical theories that are based in empirical evidence and in-principle falsifiable, which excludes visions of the social totality as a singular utopia (Habermas 1992a: 18). In sum, Habermas has turned Critical Theory towards a moderate democratic socialism, while his dialogical temperament cannot possibly be described as 'intransigent'. Nonetheless, the communicative reformulation of Adorno's problematic is absolutely necessary, if Critical Theory is to engage with social complexity, democratic politics, post-metaphysical philosophy and contemporary social movements.

Habermas's refusal of a substantive utopian vision as a singular universal supposed to be applicable a priori to the whole of humanity has often been criticized as a waning of utopian energies in Critical Theory. Habermasian Critical Theory, it is sometimes claimed, risks degenerating through proceduralism and liberalism into a 'joyless reformism' that lacks any substantive convictions about the good life (Bernstein 1995: 35–57). Habermas does concede that 'the proceduralist concept of rationality that

I propose cannot sustain utopian projects for concrete forms of life as a whole' (Habermas 2002: 87). Post-metaphysical philosophy, which only has formal frameworks and plausible preferences, gives only conjectural responses to the question of a meaningful life. It can provide only 'the formal characterisation of the necessary conditions for the forms, not able to be anticipated, of a worthwhile life. There is no theory for these totalities themselves' (Habermas 2002: 82).

However, the idea that because Critical Theory cannot prescribe happiness to individuals, it has therefore renounced criticism of the structural conditions that cause social suffering, is entirely inaccurate. It misses the point of Habermas's defence of the rational potentials in modernity against a rising tide of irrationalism, authoritarianism and technocracy (Antonio 1989: 742). It also misses the importance of Habermas's reformulation of universality, not as a transcendental, *a priori* universalism that conceals its own particular situation, but as a restless movement of critical interrogation constantly seeking to expand and deepen the inclusiveness of dialogue (Habermas 1992a: 28–53). For Habermas, situated validity claims have a 'context transcending force' to the extent that they puncture, from within, the charmed circle of ideologically specified particular exemplifications of universality.

In conclusion, therefore, because I discuss the role of utopian wish-fulfilment in informing motivations and orientations further in the chapter on psychoanalysis, I want to close out by acknowledging an area where Habermasian theory has been critically reconstructed. This is particularly in the contributions to the public sphere and discourse ethics by Nancy Fraser, Rita Felski, Michael Warner and Seyla Benhabib, among others.

In a critique that departs from the problem of the opposition between a 'power-free lifeworld' and a 'norm-free system', Nancy Fraser questions the idea of an in-principle power-free lifeworld that includes the family (Fraser 1992: 109–42). If the public sphere characteristic of bourgeois society revolves upon a distinction between personal intimacy and private matters, in separation from the public role of the citizen, then that public sphere is gendered. As Fraser points out, Habermas's reconstruction of the emancipatory role of the public sphere neglects the whole dimension of the gendered division of domestic labour and the lack of political representation of women (Fraser 1997: 41–68). The implication is that the social roles of citizen and employee (intimate) person and (private) individual, which are structurally determined by the division of labour, sustain masculine domination and the subjugation of women. In response, Habermas concedes the justice of the criticisms (Habermas 1992c: 427–30), acknowledging the need for redrawing the intersections of gender and the public. He also accepts that counter-publics are central to the contestation of actually existing democracy (Habermas 1992c: 425–7). Nonetheless, although Habermas recognizes the problem of patriarchal familial structures and masculine domination, his perfunctory discussion of what Fraser calls 'recognition frameworks' prevents a deeper engagement (Fraser and Honneth 2003).

Fraser's challenge to the structuration of the public sphere, not just by gender and sexuality, but also by class and race, is also a contestation of the assumption of the homogeneity of the public sphere. In a critique of the social exclusions that hierarchically differentiate the public into strata with unequal access, she insists on the role of what she calls 'subaltern counter-publics', whose role is to 'formulate oppositional interpretations of [subaltern] identities, interests and needs' (Fraser 1992: 123). In light of the sometimes swingeing terms of Fraser's critique, it is important to recognize that its aim is to introduce strategic subtlety into emancipatory interventions into the public sphere, not to accuse Habermas of being an apologist for bourgeois or masculinist hegemony within that social space. I recall a point made at the start of this chapter: Habermas's analysis of the public sphere is a rejoinder to Adorno's crypto-Leninist dismissal of representative democracy as a manipulative façade concealing proto-totalitarian domination. Adorno's position, actually taken seriously rather than merely adopted as an intransigent posture, leaves only arrangements such as socialist technocracy or soviet power as alternative governmental forms. The problem with Habermas's defence of the emancipatory potential of the normative ideal of democracy, however, is that it lacks contact with textured political thinking.

The shift from stratified inequality towards inclusive egalitarianism involves thinking about dialectical conceptions of publics and counter-publics as engaged in struggles for cultural and political hegemony, on the terrain of the contestation of the inclusiveness of existing universals. As Rita Felski explains, 'unlike the bourgeois public sphere, the feminist public sphere does not claim a representative universality but rather offers a critique of cultural values from the standpoint of women as a marginalised group within society' (Felski 1989: 167). This aligns with Michael Warner's definition of subaltern counter-publics as defined dialogically against a 'cultural horizon . . . which is not just a general or wider public, but a dominant one' (Warner 2005: 119). Nonetheless, as Felski also notes, 'the feminist public sphere . . . serves a dual function: internally, it generates a gender specific identity grounded in consciousness of community and solidarity among women; externally, it seeks to convince society as a whole of the validity of feminist claims, challenging existing structures of authority through political activity and theoretical critique' (Felski 1989: 168). It constitutes a partial or counterpublic sphere based in an oppositional identification, yet insofar as it is a *public* sphere its arguments are directed outwards into the dissemination of feminist ideas throughout society.

Seyla Benhabib takes this further into a critique of Habermas's account of abstract selfhood in his developmental theory, which is based on Lawrence Kohlberg's theory of moral-cognitive developmental stages. For Benhabib, it is crucial to recognize that relations to the abstract, 'generalized other' (the sort of universal reciprocity that yields mutual respect and social esteem) are not the only dimension of moral existence. Relations to concrete 'particular others' are also crucial for caring and for responsibility to other individuals (Benhabib 1995). In her brilliant *Critique, Norm and Utopia*, Benhabib argues that although Habermas speaks about expressing feelings and interpreting needs, this is separate from normative debate. Flowing from this, she points out that 'all struggles against oppression in the modern world begin by redefining what had previously been considered "private" ... as issues of justice' (Benhabib 1992b: 100). Thus, Benhabib suggests, not only is the normative dimension of Critical Theory unnecessarily foreshortened into a procedural formalism, but the utopian dimension of needs interpretation and concrete sociality is also lost (Benhabib 1986). I intend to explore this response and critically develop the Habermasian position in the chapters on critique and psychoanalysis.

4

The literary discourse of modernity

Habermas's interpretation of modernity as a historically distinctive effort to generate a rational society, presented in his most controversial intervention, grounds the idea of a 'philosophical discourse of modernity' (PDM: 336–67 [390–5]).

Is there an equivalent, 'literary discourse of modernity', one that would stand as imaginative and expressive complement to post-Enlightenment philosophical conceptuality?

Habermas thinks that there is. Not only that. As explained in a moment, Habermas also thinks that the literary discourse of modernity displays the same dialectical dynamic of historical development that he detects in philosophy. He believes that an autonomous but popular literature, one which synthesizes aspects of realism with modernism, has the potential to contribute to a critical enlightenment. Where post-metaphysical social philosophy clarifies the prospects for the liberation of active citizens, modern literature potentially transforms the motivations and orientations of modern individuals.

In this chapter, I reconstruct Habermas's presentation of literary history, up to the moment of *Communicative Action* [1981], as the aesthetic complement to his mature social philosophy, which I presented in the last chapter. Although only four years later, in *Philosophical Discourse* [1985], Habermas changed his technical account of the status of literary communication, from 'critique' to 'disclosure', I think that the mature position on the history of modern literature presented in this chapter remains valid. When Habermas discusses literary movements from the perspective of communicative interventions in the public sphere and the reading community of modern individuals, he assumes that literature catalyses *both* critical debate *and* imaginative engagement. Likewise, Habermas's description of the structural transformation of the public sphere (including the 'republic of letters') implies that both the critical and imaginative potentials of literature are affected by commodification and bureaucratization.

Accordingly, I begin by situating the idea of a literary discourse of modernity in the context of Habermas's version of the dialectic of enlightenment. Then, I locate Habermas's approach to literary communication against the background of classical Frankfurt School aesthetics and explain how the communicative perspective transforms the basic questions. Next, I present the interlinked processes shaping modern literary history, processes of cultural rationalization and functional differentiation. From scattered remarks on art and literature in Habermas's early and mature work, I reconstruct that history with the assistance of Russell Berman's communicative interpretation of German literature. Finally, I pose two major questions for the Habermasian position that emerge from this discussion, to do with the prospects for an emancipatory literature and the role of the reader in literary communication.

Literary communication and philosophical discourse

According to Habermas, modernity is the historical era that generates its own normativity, through the unforced force of the better argument, without deference towards religion or tradition. That means that modernity is characterized by historically distinctive tendencies towards moral autonomy, political self-determination, rational consensus and ego maturity. Yet, for Habermas, modernity remains an 'incomplete project', a period with a potential for emancipation that has foundered on the limitations of the bourgeois implementation of the process of enlightenment:

> The project of modernity, formulated in the 18th century by the philosophers of the Enlightenment, consisted in their efforts to develop objective science, universal morality and law, and autonomous art, according to their inner logic. At the same time, this project intended to release the cognitive potentials of each of these domains from their esoteric forms. The Enlightenment philosophers wanted to utilize this accumulation of specialized culture for the enrichment of everyday life—that is to say, for the rational organization of social life. Enlightenment thinkers of the cast of mind of Condorcet still had the extravagant expectation that the arts and sciences would promote not only the control of natural forces, but also understanding of the world and of the self, moral progress, the justice of institutions and even the happiness of human beings. The 20th century has shattered this optimism. The differentiation of science,

morality and art has come to mean the autonomy of the segments treated by the specialist and their separation from ... everyday communication. This splitting off is the problem that has given rise to efforts to 'negate' the culture of expertise. But the problem won't go away: should we ... [therefore] declare the entire project of modernity a lost cause? (Habermas 1985: 10–11)

Evidently, Habermas's notion of a critical completion of the project of modernity indicates that the 'extravagant expectations' of the thinkers of enlightenment continue to animate his social theory and political philosophy. But because of the enlightenment spirit in Habermas's work, commentators have often ignored the fact that his position involves a dialectical *critique* of the historical Enlightenment. Although the notion of dialectics as involving 'thesis, antithesis and synthesis' can be somewhat schematizing, it usefully orients the present discussion. According to Habermas's criticism, the 'thesis', the philosophical discourse of the historical Enlightenment, is fatally inflected by the social reality of bourgeois life, which centres on the competitive individual of the market society. That reality is reflected in Enlightenment discourse through its 'philosophy of the subject', exemplified by Immanuel Kant's three critiques, a mode of philosophical enquiry that reifies the human being into a 'transcendental subject'. The necessity for a critique of the 'philosophy of the subject' becomes clear through the emergence of the 'antithesis', the Romantic rebellion against the Enlightenment. The Romantics rightly criticize the reification active in scientific positivism, the evacuation of ethical substance that corrodes moral formalism and the suppression of real questions of human happiness. But the Romantics mistake the social pathologies that result from the bourgeois implementation of the modern project for intrinsic problems of reason as such. Conflating reification with rationality, the historical Enlightenment with enlightenment processes, the market society with the modern project, the Romantic critique misfires, landing in celebrations of aesthetic revolt, archaic imagery drawn from unconscious processes, or political violence. Like Adorno, they are forced to look for an 'Other of Reason' to ground their position, leading to an aestheticization of rationality that Habermas politely describes as the conflation of philosophy with literature. Finally, the Romantic critique also misfires because it lack a valid social-theoretical framework for the contextualization of Enlightenment reason and its philosophy of the subject.

Accordingly, Habermas seeks a 'synthesis' of the Enlightenment's inauguration of the modern project with the Romantic critique of its bourgeois limitations. Developing critiques of late Romantics, such as Adorno, Nietzsche, Heidegger and Derrida, Habermas presents the case against the jettisoning of the modern project. The Romantics lapse into the 'performative contradiction' of a total critique of reason by means of reason itself, which is to say, they are forced to embrace irrationality. In the turn to intersubjectivity, by contrast, Habermas discovers a way beyond the philosophy of the subject. This is one that can be linked to his communicative reconstruction of Marxist theory and, therefore, to a practical critique of the market society. Habermas proposes to revitalize the project of modernity, rather than resort to the aestheticized reason of postmodernity. He advocates post-metaphysical thinking, grounded in communicative intersubjectivity, as a 'philosophical discourse of modernity' that is no longer ballasted by the assumptions of the bourgeois Enlightenment.

In his writing from the 1970s, Habermas interprets the history of modern literature in terms that are remarkably similar to his critique of the Enlightenment's philosophy of the subject (Habermas 1975b: 78–86; 1979a: 37–8, 53–4; 1981: 10–11). The rise of the modern novel, coextensive with the Enlightenment, indicates the emancipatory potentials of literary autonomy while siloing its liberating power within a peculiar form of literary communication. For three centuries, in the context of bourgeois forms of individuality, the realist novel has addressed members of a reading public as reciprocally isolated private readers who are ultimately concerned with intimate affairs. Just as Romanticism radically critiqued Enlightenment, the literary avant-garde mounted a critique of affirmative culture and the conformist individual. But the avant-garde antithesis to affirmative culture happened through the self-destructive framework of an effort to smash the autonomy of the aesthetic, in order to release its radical contents directly into everyday life. Instead of the aestheticization of the everyday, the avant-gardes risked the dissolution of the radical elements of the aesthetic.

Just like Adorno, Habermas also does not systematically differentiate between the avant-garde and modernism, because he regards them both as rejections of the culture industry – but in fact it makes sense to distinguish the radicalism of the avant-garde from the moderation of the modernists (Bürger 1984). The response of modernism was to barricade literature within a hermetic enclosure, defending the autonomy of art at the expense of emptying its communicative function. Modernism protected literary experience from the mass demand for 'entertaining reading' as generated by the culture industry, but only by retreating into esotericism. Thus, just as the Romantic critique of the philosophy of the subject drastically misfired, the avant-garde critique of affirmative culture also tragically miscarried.

Returning to these questions in the 1980s, however, Habermas detects an emergent synthesis of avant-garde insurgency and modernist intransigence, with realist accessibility, in literary interventions that defy formula fiction while retaining popular appeal (Habermas 1981: 12). What Habermas describes as 'post-avant-garde' literature situates fiction within literary communication by refusing atelic hermeticism, but it cannot be recruited to affirmative culture because of its critical negativity. For Habermas, such a literature of resistance is entirely different from literary postmodernism, which, unlike post-structuralism (a prolongation of the Romantic critique), represents the appropriation of modernist technique for cultural conformity (Habermas 1992a: 215–26). With only slight variations, then, Habermas's development of the idea of a literary discourse of modernity follows the path of the philosophical discourse of modernity.

Retrieving Adorno's insights

Against this historical background, the fundamental Habermasian argument is that the critical objectives of Adorno's defence of modernism can be fully successful only after the paradigm shift from transcendental subjectivity to linguistic intersubjectivity. Adorno's central strategy is not just to defend modernist dissonance, but also to locate in aesthetic mimesis the wellspring for a critical enlightenment. Habermas's response to the problem of critical enlightenment is communicative reason, which includes aesthetic rationality. Accordingly, Habermasian communicative aesthetics is not the negation of Adorno's aesthetic theory, but its intersubjective correction.

Adorno thinks that modernist art and literature, as the locus of an alternative to theoretical and practical rationality, is the last redoubt of spontaneous creative praxis. Through its autonomous forms and expressive contents, modernist art and literature refuses affirmative culture and the culture industry, and protests against the effects of reification and repression. For Adorno, aesthetic mimesis is the opposite of instrumental rationality, providing the basis for a non-coercive synthesis or non-identity thinking. Yet Adorno's insights remain locked up within a conceptualization of aesthetic mimesis that is fraught with theoretical difficulties and applied problems. Fundamentally, Habermas maintains, Adorno inverts the subject-object model of instrumental rationality, rather than breaking with it altogether (Habermas 1983: 99–110). Adorno intends to defend the protest of nature against the closing of the vice of rationalization. The problem is that 'the subjection of outer nature is only successful in the measure of the repression of inner nature, [which means that] technological mastery strikes back at conquering subjectivity' (Habermas 1983: 100). Because of the alignment between subject and rationality, Adorno's proposed object-subject relation results in a search for the 'exotic Other of Reason', one in concerning proximity to anti-Enlightenment Romanticism.

Nonetheless, it seems to Habermas that Adorno's quest for a critical enlightenment is a theoretical aim that deserves to remain at the very centre of Critical Theory, although it is necessary to 'moderate the idea of reconciliation to that of autonomy and responsibility' (Habermas 1983: 108). It is crucial to retain the aim of a non-coercive synthesis of particular and universal, one pointing towards an alternative to an instrumental rationality run wild and a culture industry choking the public sphere. This alone can provide the critical standard in reason by which Frankfurt School neo-Marxism brings an existential judgement against unbalanced forms of social life. Likewise, the notion of the 'political migration' of revolutionary potential into autonomous literature, while conceptually exaggerated, expresses a legitimate insight. Modernist dissonance testifies to a demand for happiness that bourgeois society has failed to satisfy, something modernism does by protesting the role of literature as consolation. Adorno's defence of the political implications of autonomous literature needs to be retained by Critical Theory.

Habermas's response is to reframe modernist dissonance within a theory of the emancipatory potential of the modern separation of cultural value spheres. The process of discovery based on the logic of value enhancement in autonomous domains brings with it the prospect of an increasingly rational society. A key component of that rationality is a post-traditional conception of human needs, which implies a set of motivations grounded in consensual agreement, rather than ones stencilled in by tradition, founded on aversions or reinforced by guilt. The aesthetic-expressive dimension of communicative reason provides for this possibility, in part through the indirect and reflexive communication performed by literary works. From the intersubjective perspective of communicative reason, aesthetic mimesis (existing symbiotically with art criticism) is one of the voices of rationality. Thinking intersubjectivity, in terms of the multiple voices of communicative reason, makes it possible to articulate an alternative to instrumental rationality – one that includes literary mimesis without resorting an exotic 'other of reason'. The aim of defending the radical potential of literary interventions can best be achieved through clarification of the autonomous logics of discovery in the cultural value spheres of science, law and art, and elucidating the contribution these make to emancipatory learning processes.

Resolving a key antinomy

The Habermasian shift to communicative intersubjectivity can also resolve the central antinomy of Frankfurt School literary theory, which is between literary autonomy and political commitment (Hunter 1985: 41–64). The antinomy arises because the competing notions of avant-garde mimesis and the author as producer, on which the antinomy is based, frame literature in subject-object terms, as authorial expression or writerly labour. By reframing expression within communicative intersubjectivity, and labour within functional integration of consequences, Habermas can reformulate literary autonomy and its social effects.

Debates in the 1930s and 1940s, between Adorno and Benjamin (among others), shuttled helplessly between the mutually exclusive poles of an aesthetically innovative but apolitical hermeticism, or an aesthetically conventional but political literature.

Defending political commitment under the slogan of 'the author as producer', Walter Benjamin attacked the conception of aesthetic autonomy. Aesthetic autonomy is an ideological illusion because artistic practice is part of capitalism's social division of labour, which implies that anything other than committed art is bourgeois apologetics (Benjamin 1970: 83–96). Furthermore, the industrialization of culture explodes the sublime illusion of the artwork as autonomous self-expression, making possible a democratization of aesthetic experience (Benjamin 1973: 219–54).

Adorno's response – the theory of political migration – involved the dialectical opposition between the culture industry and the avant-garde. Because aesthetic mimesis escapes instrumental labour, the work of art qua self-expression represents a form of creative praxis that 'resists by its form alone the course of the world' (Adorno 2007a: 180). Furthermore, the instrumental rationalization of cultural techniques does not democratize the work, but rather makes its expressive content the object of manipulation (Adorno 2007a: 194). Within the terms of this antinomy, a democratized modernism, one that refuses the instrumentalization of the communicative goal of literature, but exists within the functional frameworks of socialization and distribution, is impossible.

From the Habermasian perspective, the dichotomy happens because both conceptions of literature think the author as (instrumental or mimetic) subject and the work as (persuasive or expressive) object.

Both kinds of position, foregrounding the referential function of art in political commitment and the expressive function in mimetic autonomy, are based on the model of the labour process. Whether the work is theorized as a social representation produced for a calculated effect (Benjamin), or as free creative praxis expressing a mimetic relation to the object (Adorno), the social significance of the literary work is reduced to its relation to commodity production. The literary work is either a cultural commodity, or it refuses commodification completely. Accordingly, it either has a use-value (satisfying a demand for happiness) or it is useless (atelic autonomy). In that case: either its usefulness includes a consciousness-raising communication about the social world despite its pleasurable potential to offer false consolations; or, its forlorn uselessness constitutes an expression of the distress of the individual dominated by society. Within the model of labour processes, then, the referential aspect of literary utterances can be foregrounded only at the expense of literary autonomy. Concentrating on the autonomy of literary sentences has the effect of denying their capacity to represent the world.

Meanwhile, the exclusive modelling of literature on the labour process drastically foreshortens the role of the reader, tending to eliminate the imaginative response of the reading community.

The Habermasian turn to intersubjectivity reframes the liberating potentials of literary communication, without denying its functional role in processes of socialization. First of all, literature communicates. Literature is a reflexive communication between subjects engaged in an enlightenment process, something that happens through public dialogue and personal identification. From the Habermasian perspective, the cultural contribution of the literary text can be assessed in terms of its exploration of the subjective world of modern individuals. Literature communicates about the cultural interpretation of human needs and their means of expression, in relation to the social world (and natural environment), which satisfies – or frustrates – these needs. Literary texts that resist an affirmation of the status quo, by refusing stereotypical representations of social groups and traditional interpretations of human needs, provide material for public debate leading towards ego maturity. These texts, by refusing the conventional stencils of identity formation, potentially legitimate post-traditional interpretations of human needs, something consistent with autonomous and tolerant social identities. At the same time, from the functional perspective, the literary text is a material product generated within the literary institutions of the social division of labour. It is a cultural commodity whose use-value is a pleasurable form of sublimated gratification, but whose consequences are acts of identification that inform personality structures. Literature entertains and socializes. Here, alongside its role in cultural industries, literature functions by intervening into patterns of socialization through providing points of identification.

Of course, in literature, entertainment can be regressive, just as identifications can be conformist, and communication can be instrumentalized. I want to reinforce this point: it is no part of the Habermasian position that I am constructing to deny that the cultural region of the public sphere is being strangled by the entertainment corporations, whose interest is in making profits from regressive representations. In question is not just the trivialization and routinization of literature that happens because of the domination of the publishing industry by multinational entertainment corporations (Schiller 1976, 1991). There is also the effect on the process of socialization of identification with works permeated by commodity aesthetics (Haug 1986). Commodity aesthetics involves an admixture of erotic pleasure, accompanying sexualized representations, with aggressive satisfactions, connected to status competition and thrilling representations of violence. Popular fiction is an important area of study that is by no means to be dismissed as a 'reactionary swamp' of regressive representations. Nonetheless, the vast majority of literary texts are turned against enlightenment and towards reinforcing prevalent 'cultural fantasies' (Cawelti 1976). The Habermasian point is simply that this outcome is not a necessary entailment of the fact that literary texts have a use-value and a functional role in socialization processes.

In the next two sections, I want to explore the two perspectives on literature – the communicative lifeworld and the functional context of the cultural system – under the signs of literary autonomy in the cultural value sphere and the functional differentiation of literary institutions, respectively.

Value enhancement and literary autonomy

I have suggested that Habermasian communicative reason, including aesthetic rationality as one of its dimensions, is a prolongation of Adorno's effort to locate the basis for a critical enlightenment. Reframing the literary text as a reflexive communication between subjects engaged in an enlightenment process implies that emancipatory literature is a cultural intervention that aims at ego maturity. In modernity, what Habermas describes as 'aesthetic-expressive rationality' becomes an autonomous cultural value sphere, within which discoveries about the subjective world of modern individuals can happen.

Literature becomes autonomous to the extent that distinct cultural practices based on imaginative communication emerge, involving experiments with the redemption of claims to truthfulness about the subjective world. These experiments are discoveries to the extent that they become evaluated according to different values than those involved in truth claims about the objective world and normative claims about social conduct. Literature, in other words, becomes autonomous when it is no longer primarily dependent on forms of truth originating in (religious) cosmologies and (ideological) world views, or on (moral and legal) norms reflecting ethical life. The main sense in which modern literature is autonomous is that its practices are recognized as fictitious and amoral. In *The Theory of Communicative Action*, Habermas states that:

> To the degree that individual value spheres are separated out in their rational consistency, we become conscious of the universal validity claims against which cultural advances or enhancements of value are measured.... As soon as science, morality, and art have been differentiated into autonomous spheres of values, each under one universal validity claim – truth, normative rightness, authenticity or beauty – objective advances, improvements, enhancements become possible in a sense specific to each . . . . With regard finally to value enhancement in the aesthetic domain, the idea of progress fades into that of renewal and rediscovery, an innovative revivification of authentic experiences . . . . Advances in the domain of autonomous art move in the direction of an increasingly radical and pure – that is, purified of theoretical and moral admixtures – working out of basic aesthetic experiences. (TCA1: 177–8 [251–2])

Value enhancement in the aesthetic domain therefore involves the development of distinctive aesthetic-expressive procedures of evaluation that redeem (implicit or explicit) validity claims to truthfulness. As I will discuss in a moment, Habermas thinks that a sequence of such values – beauty, sublimity, authenticity, innovation – is generated historically, as aesthetic criteria progressively separate from admixtures of truth and rightness. From this perspective, the dialectical succession of literary movements is partly constituted by the discovery of aesthetic experiences that violate superseded artistic norms.

The central Habermasian claim, then, is that the purification of aesthetics results in an exploration of the subjective world of needs and desires, beliefs and feelings, one whose experimental logic of innovation involves discoveries about modern subjectivity. For instance, the modernist literary work of the interwar period raised implicit claims to truthfulness, to the degree that it explored new desires and feelings, together with developing new linguistic and aesthetic means of expression for them. The classic examples of this process were the frank presentation of sexuality as natural, and the depiction of anomic distortions of subjective experience, characteristic of D. H. Lawrence's and Franz Kafka's interwar modernism, respectively. These desires and feelings were judged to authentically belong to modern subjectivity, by readerships engaged in public debates, irrespective of prevailing ethical standards. According to David Seelow, the radicalism of modernism centres on the literary presentation of the Freudian discovery and its connection to the social arguments of the Freudian Left (Seelow 2005). In general, a whole series of 'scandalous fictions', from Flaubert's *Madame Bovary* all the way through to Kureishi's *The Buddha of Suburbia*, have attracted censorship attempts because they broke with traditional interpretations of human needs and proposed sexual tolerance (Dollimore 2001). At the same time, Flaubert's *Bovary* also led to a series of works, perhaps culminating in Nabokov's *Lolita*, that have, against the censor, asserted the autonomy of literature with respect to the conventional norms of ethical life.

The notion that artistic autonomy depends on the primacy of aesthetic value by no means precludes the literary work from commentary on the social world and the natural environment (for instance, the human social metabolism with the natural environment). The Habermasian position, as I reconstruct it, does not solely valorize experimental modernism or exclude forms of literary realism, science fiction and fantasy literature, or other popular fictions. Instead, literature is regarded as a fictive mapping of the subjective domain onto the social world and the natural environment, as an arena of potential (dis-)satisfaction. The point is not that autonomous literature must void the referential function of communication into a textualist poetics lacking contact with political commitments, but that the evaluation of literary innovation is independent of cognitive truth and normative rightness.

Although Habermas does not accept aesthetic mimesis as a replacement for social labour, the literary work does articulate a universal demand for happiness. Habermas lists: 'the desire for a mimetic relation with nature; the need for living together in solidarity outside the group egoism of the immediate family; the longing for the happiness of a communicative experience exempt from imperatives of purposive rationality; and, giving scope to imagination as well as spontaneity' (Habermas 1975b: 78). Literature does this by mapping the subjective world onto the external world, as if this latter were an arena for the satisfaction of human needs. It thereby clarifies the degree to which motivations and orientations, expressive resources and collective ideals serve the ends of socialized individuality, social justice, ecological balance and authentic fulfilment.

Literary institutions and socialization processes

Habermasian social theory corrects Adorno's nostalgic opposition to social fragmentation by introducing a positive appraisal of functional differentiation, which Habermas also calls 'societal rationalisation' (TCA2: 113–97 [174–293], esp. 179–83 [275–9]). The education and socialization of individuals that are performed by the cultural subsystem are necessary structural functions. These functions consist of the transmission of knowledge, the inculcation of norms and the formation of the personality. These processes proceed most effectively when differentiated institutions emerge that are dedicated to specific elements of this function. Only then can experimental discoveries in autonomous cultural spheres be institutionalized as learning processes that can be reliably transmitted to individuals during socialization. In relation to the cultural subsystem, functional differentiation in the modern world has resulted in the partial separation of education from socialization, in the splitting of school from family and church. The gains for moral autonomy and democratic citizenship are impossible to deny, relative to the premodern integration of church with school and family with economy. In relation to literature, Habermas speaks in a kind of Weberian shorthand of 'science, law and art' (e.g. TCA2: 146 [220–1]), to describe the emergence of institutions specialized in the redemption of differentiated validity claims to cognitive truth, normative rightness and aesthetic-expressive truthfulness. For Habermas, the exploration of specific forms of validity in differentiated cultural value spheres is incomplete, unless it is accompanied by the institutionalization of the relevant learning process in a corresponding apparatus. Expert specializations in science, law and art can be protected from the intrusion of other forms of validity only through institutional differentiation. But the laboratory, the courtroom and the museum also provide a set of formal arenas within which the relevant educational and socialization processes can be developed. These are then translated out of expert nomenclatures and transmitted to the mass of the population, through institutions such as the school and media.

Accordingly, Habermas has a powerful response to a critic such as Peter Bürger, for whom institutionalization and experimentation are antithetical. For Bürger, criticizing Adorno, the interwar avant-gardes (Surrealism, Futurism, Dadaism and Vorticism) aimed at the revolutionary abolition of the art institution. By contrast, modernism represented the institutionalization (and domestication) of avant-garde techniques within an aesthetic compartment of bourgeois society (Bürger 1984: 49). The postwar neo-avant-garde repeat, rather than resume, the avant-garde rupture, surrendering thereby to institutionalization as a late modernism, rather than constituting an autonomous movement (Bürger 2010: 705). Adorno is therefore criticized for his failure to distinguish the avant-garde from modernism and for the notion of 'autonomous art', which, for Bürger, reflects a lack of clarity on the difference between art institution and aesthetic autonomy (Bürger 1984: 84).

Although Habermas is invoked in support of the claim that autonomous aesthetics represents radical needs (Bürger 1984: 25), the Habermasian position would defend Adorno from Bürger's excess of Hegelian enthusiasm. Habermas has an historical response (explored in a moment) and a systematic response, which criticizes the dysfunctional character of the avant-garde's proposal. According to Bürger, the avant-garde programme is to transform all instrumentally rational social practices into aesthetic experiences, by smashing the separateness of the art institution from everyday life (Bürger 1984: 34). For Habermas (Habermas 1999a: 414–15), such an aestheticization of practice would not only be a regressive de-differentiation of society, but also a refusal of the learning processes connected with aesthetic rationality. Learning processes involve a regulated set of practices and resources (i.e. an institution), and for these to affect the three dimensions of the lifeworld – culture, society and person – they must be connected to reliable knowledge transmission, durable social norms and recognized personality structures. In the absence of these functional requisites, the protest of the avant-garde quickly expends itself in a fury of destruction whose abstract negativity never amounts to a dialectical sublation.

The central literary institutions of modernity are those connected with the 'republic of letters' in the public sphere, especially the publishing industry, literary journals, book reviews and prize committees. For Habermas, unlike Adorno, these institutions are autonomous despite their functional significance for the formation of democratic citizens, the education of new generations and the socialization of open-minded individuals (TCA2: 398 [587]). Alongside a defence of the utility of literature, Habermas also endorses the rationalization of literary technique. For Habermas, advances in technique do not threaten expression, but instead augment it, because instrumental rationality is legitimate as a subordinate aspect of self-reflexive literary communication. 'Avant-garde art', Habermas writes, 'achieved value enhancement in part by way of becoming reflective in its artistic techniques; the enhanced instrumental rationality of an art that makes its own production processes transparent is here in the service of enhancing aesthetic value' (TCA1: 177–8 [252–3]). Habermas's discussion of expression and technique resonates with Adorno's discussion of mimesis and calculation, but the dialectic is felicitous instead of tragic, because subjectivity can become 'experimentally unbound', rather than merely exhausted (TCA2: 399 [587–8]).

The problem is not that the literary text is a commodity, that is, a product with a monetary exchange value as well as a social utility. A socialist economy would also need to distribute products via some token representing socially necessary labour time and its ecological impacts – that is, in effect, red money – in order to functionally integrate the social division of labour. By commodification is meant not just the commodity character of the social product, but the real subsumption of the labour process into a production process that aims at profit. In plain terms, commodification refers to the submission of literary values to the demands of saleability, through the routinization of the writing process, the trivialization of contents and the formulaic nature of plots.

According to Habermas, then, the root of the problem confronted by modern literature is the 'bourgeois implementation of the modern project', that is, the capitalist structure of the literary marketplace and the political demands of the nation state. From the functional perspective, literary texts circulate in a cultural marketplace and have uses in the process of socialization, which implies that they have a functional role to play that springs from their character as literary communication. But this process, with its implicit requirement that the readership communities of literary movements develop a post-traditional relation to human needs and a post-conventional relation to cultural values, is extremely demanding in relation to citizen-critics. In the context of a division of labour determined by capitalist relations and the national state, societal rationalization, driving functional differentiation in the interests of efficiency and effectiveness *as defined through profit or nationalism*, has the potential to widen the gap between literary expert and lay reader. Literary specialization quickly leads to experimental forms of cultural expression that are isolated from everyday practices. Furthermore, market relations intrude into the literary process itself, in the interests of profitability, rather than provisionality.

The structural transformation of the republic of letters

Generally speaking, Habermas follows the trajectory set forth in the culture industry thesis, albeit without the bleak pessimism that flows from Adorno's monolithic social totality. In *Structural Transformation*, Habermas restricts his discussion of literature to the role played by a specific form of narrative fiction, the realist novel, in the formation of a critical public during the rise of liberal democracy. In *Legitimation Crisis*, however, Habermas brings his account of the fate of literature into line with his discussion of the decline of the public sphere (Habermas 1975b: 85–6). There, he discusses the modernist rupture with affirmative culture, including the misdirected rebellion of the historical avant-gardes, in the context of growing consumerism and bureaucracy. Habermas also endorses the efforts to break through the increasing reification of the public sphere by the post-war neo-avant-garde (Habermas 1975b: 121).

To these communicative theses, Habermas adds systems-functional reflections on the role of literature in the formation of the bourgeois individual. He attributes a formative role to literature in the differentiation of intimacy out from privacy and publicness, noticing that in bourgeois society this is coextensive with the distinctions between domesticity, economics and politics. The rebellion of the avant-gardes and modernists is therefore seen as a revolt against bourgeois subjectivity, within which literature and art protest against the alienation of certain human needs within bourgeois individuality. Considering the thesis of the 'end of the [bourgeois] individual' in *Legitimation Crisis*, Habermas criticizes the accommodation of late modernism to a situation in which 'phenomena of alienation are increasingly being replaced by manifestations of inauthenticity' (Habermas 1975b: 129).

I now want to explore this dialectic of cultural rationalization and functional differentiation in some detail, before returning to theoretical questions raised by Habermas in *Philosophical Discourse*, together with some problems with the Habermasian position on literature. Habermas's initial formulation of the social role of literature, from both the communicative perspective and the functional perspective, is set forth in his discussion of the rise and fall of the public sphere (STPS: 14–56 [70–121]).

In his discussion of the Enlightenment period's 'republic of letters', Habermas proposes that literature acted as a propaedeutic for critical debate about the general interest (STPS: 14–25, 51–6 [70–85, 117–21]). The salons, coffee houses and table societies of the eighteenth century encouraged the formation of a critical public skilled in debating representations of life in general. Habermas then proposes that the communicative aspect of the republic of letters became secondary to its social function during the nineteenth century. Drawing upon Ian Watt's *The Rise of the Novel*, Habermas suggests that the crucial dimension to this process is the partition of the premodern 'household economy' into the domestic sphere of intimate relations and the private sphere of economic interests (Habermas 1991b: 46–8; Watt 1963). The bourgeois novel, which had mercilessly satirized the seigneurial alliance of landed gentry and mercantile capitalists, now settles into its role as 'affirmative culture'. It presents a form of social subjectivity consistent with middle-class existence, by celebrating the privileged interiority of the domestic sphere as uniquely human, by contrast with political struggles and economic competition. Accordingly, the bourgeois novel is a lynchpin of the societal differentiation into the domestic realm (the intimate 'person') and the civil sphere of economic interests (the private 'individual'), whose difference from the public 'citizen' supports the syndromes of familial and civil privatism. Furthermore, the peculiarly personal reception of the bourgeois novel, as a form that is read in solitary contemplation, not collective audition, promotes the ideological illusion that the projection outwards of intimacy onto private and public spheres defines meaningful social participation. Thus, the gains in cultural rationalization of a form that catalyses the formation of loving reciprocity and legitimate feminine participation in romance, are offset by the functional effects of a form that reinforces depoliticization (STPS: 55–6 [120–1]).

In the second part of *Structural Transformation*, Habermas turns to the corporatization and bureaucratization of the public sphere, with implications for the republic of letters. For Habermas, not unlike Raymond Williams, the paradigmatic cultural form of twentieth-century mass culture is not the novel, but television (Habermas 1992c; Williams 1974). The cultural public sphere is transformed by the combination of commodity aesthetics and corporate entertainment, mediated by the spectacle, where 'televisual flow' becomes the visual equivalent to Adorno's 'regressive listening'. 'Serious involvement with culture', Habermas writes, 'produces facility, whereas the consumption of mass culture leaves no lasting trace; it affords a kind of experience which is not cumulative, but regressive' (STPS: 166 [256]). In combination with the syndromes of civic and familial privatism, 'the sphere generated by the mass media has taken on the traits of a secondary realm of intimacy'. Social relations appear as interpersonal connections, promoting 'sentimentality towards persons and corresponding cynicism towards institutions' (STPS: 172 [263]). Although Habermas does not specifically discuss twentieth-century literary formations, he does note the disintegration of the reading public (STPS: 174 [266]). As 'affirmative culture', even the prizewinning novels of world literature no longer unequivocally contribute to a critical republic of letters. Meanwhile, the bestseller and the blockbuster all too often appropriate advanced techniques for manipulative ends. The Habermasian position is that literary enlightenment as cultural intervention can happen only as part of a revitalization of the public sphere. His subsequent amendments to the concept of the public sphere indicate a theoretical space for literary counter-publics in opposition to the culture industry.

From affirmative culture to the modernist revolt

Habermas's endorsement of the notion of cultural counter-publics that support the political mobilization of social movements should be seen in connection with functions of socialization and education. Literary enlightenment needs to produce a new individuality that is beyond the current distribution of subjectivity into intimacy, privacy and publicity. That implies both a cultural strategy and an historical narrative, but the details need to be reconstructed from scattered remarks. Furthermore, when Habermas focuses on the communicative aspect of literature, he neglects discussion of the role of the readership. Yet the reception of literary communication by a community of (potential) interlocutors is crucial to the socialization and education functions of literature. However, Russell Berman's Habermas-influenced discussion of the shift from realism to modernism, which does focus on effects on readerships, can correct this defect.

Following Bürger historically, rather than systematically (TCA2: 436n57 [610]), Habermas thinks that the historical avant-garde marks the turning point at which the progressive potential of classical bourgeois art and literature is exhausted. In line with David Ingram's lead (Ingram 1987), I synthesize remarks from Habermas's work on the public sphere, legitimation crisis, communicative action and 'Modernity versus Postmodernity' (1981), to reconstruct the following narrative. Literary realism, initially a progressive force during the eighteenth century, becomes affirmative culture during the nineteenth century. It then becomes transformed by the culture industry into entertainment literature, especially during the twentieth century. Late Romanticism completes the cultural rationalization of the aesthetic value sphere by rebelling against morality and utility, while rejecting bourgeois subjectivity and refusing affirmative culture (Habermas 1981: 5–6). Right at the moment of liberation, however, things turn into their opposites: the emergence of the avant-garde marks the protest that breaks out once a reified public sphere effectively isolates the aesthetic discoveries happening in autonomous literature. The failure of the Surrealist revolt represents the moment in which literary and artistic avant-gardes discover that the aestheticization of the lifeworld cannot solve the social pathologies of capitalist modernity. Noticing that Habermas does not differentiate strongly between the avant-garde and modernism, progressive literature then divides into three streams. First, there are kinds of politically committed social realism that are prepared to sacrifice literary autonomy for political utility. Second, there is the neo-avant-garde, which prolongs the modernist rebellion into a protracted insurgency on the terrain of the literary institution (at the risk of becoming an empty repetition) (Habermas 1981: 6–8). Third, Habermas (perhaps hopefully) mentions forms of post-avant-garde literature which synthesize modernist forms with socially critical contents in an activist intervention (Habermas 1981: 12). Since the late 1970s, however, the formula fiction of popular culture has been joined by the affirmative appropriation of modernist technique in the interests of 'postmodern' literature (Habermas 1992a: 210–18).

Now, Habermas does mention that 'the exclusive concentration on one aspect of validity alone, to the exclusion of aspects of truth and justice, breaks down as soon as aesthetic experience is drawn into an individual life history and enters everyday life' (Habermas 1981: 12). But he is short on details, and does not relate the socialization of the personality to the enhancement of literary value in a systematic way. Russell Berman, however, in *The Rise of the Modern German Novel: Crisis and Charisma* (1986), does discuss these three counter-cultural strands of modern literature, in relation to the writer's effort to form a particular readership through aesthetic innovation. Berman begins by framing 'the rhetorical structures of texts as aspects of a communicative strategy designed to produce a relationship with the recipient, a relationship that is always social and therefore responsive to the social crisis' (Berman 1986: vii). The idea that literary communication is the constitution of a community of readers in the transmission of a reflexive message clearly resonates with, and is influenced by, Habermas.

Employing the Weberian matrix of the rationalization of authority as an interpretive framework, Berman grasps modernism in the context of the rational delegitimation of nineteenth-century affirmative culture. In the literary sphere, traditional cultural authority is linked to the persistence of inherited standards of value. By contrast, rational cultural authority is connected to the demand that the literary world be founded on rational principles and not on arbitrary conventions (Berman 1986: 53).

Literary realism reflects this rational demand in its totalizing vision of social existence, as represented by typical characters, operating plausibly in accordance with the historical forms of social relations, in the represented world. That totality is rational to the extent that the whole and its parts can be integrated according to the principle that the universal is reconciled to the particular through the notion of individuals' rationally universal self-legislation. Literary realism's affirmation of the social formation characteristic of the bourgeois implementation of the modern project, around private property and negative liberty, reflects its investment in the hegemonic cultural forms of the existing political community. But, 'as culture is transformed into a commodity, it becomes an object of mere display, robbed of its traditional substance'. Its rationality, based on the assumption of 'reasonable rules, the exchange of meaning between equals, and the transparency of language', enters a crisis of confidence, based on a scission between literary ideal and social reality (Berman 1986: 53–5). In response, in interwar and post-war modernism, the writer seeks to *create* the community that he or she addresses in a novel way, thus linking aesthetic innovation to social change in a characteristic combination. The author's self-invention as charismatic authority involves the envisionment of a radically new readership capable of grasping a refreshment of meaning so radical that it requires the inauguration of a new dialect, if not a private language.

In the emblematic series of Gustav Freytag (1816–95), Adalbert Stifter (1805–68), Theodor Fontane (1819–98) and Georg Hermann (1871–1943),

Berman traces out the disintegration of the bourgeois investment in literary realism and the transformation of its meaning-structures into the entertaining monologue of the culture industry. Initially, literary realism is insurgent against baroque literature, for 'the rules of baroque literature are based on the opaque enunciations of religion and inherited authority'. By contrast, 'while the rules of liberal bourgeois literature purport to be objects of rational scrutiny and therefore to take on the character of laws generated by a self-determining public' (Berman 1986: 57). The loss of cultural vitality within the bourgeois project is reflected in the degeneration of realism. This shifts from a rational communicative exchange to the monological presentation of a spectacle that the reader is forced to contemplatively accept. Trivialization, commodification and conventionality are imposed on the entertainment novel during the rise of the culture industry (Berman 1986: 161–78).

Late modernism and counter-hegemony

According to Berman, literary writing after affirmative culture is characterized by an effort to separate the reader from the existing reading community, forming them into a new individual in the process. By structuring new social relationships in the act of literary communication, literary modernism also implies a transformation of the social formation and the inauguration of a new political community. Charismatic figures such as Robert Musil (1880–1942), Hermann Hesse (1887–1962) and Elias Canetti (1905–94) sound the clarion of revolt against the culture industry.

> Modernism rebels against the culture industry, not with better or higher prose, but with multitudinous strategies for destroying the iron cage.... Modern writing presents itself radically as an alternative writing and therefore concerns itself expressly with reading and writing.... Whereas high realism... addressed social problems, modernism addresses literature itself as the social problem: the legerdemain of the culture industry, on which the overall system of domination vitally depends. (Berman 1986: 181)

The charismatic foundation of a new reading community around visions of post-bourgeois individuality grounds a counter-cultural revitalization of literature. In the figures of Ernst Jünger (1895–1998), Alfred Döblin (1878–1957) and Thomas Mann (1875–1955), Berman detects three alternative programmes of cultural renewal in German literature.

Both Jünger and Döblin envisage forms of collectivization. For Jünger, it is the fascist return to a racist conception of the nation, whereas for Döblin, it is the communist participation in proletarian class consciousness. These depend on the negation of the bourgeois individual's development towards maturity and the denunciation of participation in rational communication as social atomization. In fascist modernism, subjective interiority is replaced by stark power and moral autonomy by submission to necessity, exemplified by the battlefield, on which there is 'no time for novelistic development' (Berman 1986: 216 Jünger cited). The governing principle of the unfolding of action is mythical diachronic sequence rather than historical temporality, while cultural life becomes the site of classificatory description rather than developmental maturation.

In the work of Döblin, by contrast, post-bourgeois collectivized subjectivity happens through communist participation in the sovereign people. Instead of the fascist celebration of destiny, leftist modernism deplores the betrayal of the promise of happiness and denounces this as a denial of freedom. Seeking a social, rather than mythic, collective, it invites the reader to participate in the authorship of a collective documentation of oppressive social conditions. 'The work is no longer merely fictional, because it is ethnographic; it is not simply a realistic description of the real life of the people, but a text written by the people itself', framed in the characteristic diction of the plebeian classes (Berman 1986: 260).

Finally, in the work of Thomas Mann, Berman detects a non-collectivist form of post-liberal individuality, in which intimacy and privacy are not erased (Jünger), and literature is not dissolved into ethnography (Döblin). Rather, a modernist focus on language makes a new sort of social engagement possible, because the 'ambivalence of narrative speech establishes an interlocutory encounter with the recipient'. The reader is thereby 'wrested out of passive contemplation and drawn into the contradictions of the textual debate' (Berman 1986: 283). In light of the social character of the represented world, readerly participation in communal reception of the literary work facilitates Mann's socialist repoliticization of the public sphere.

Against the background of Berman's Habermas-influenced reconstruction of the literary history of the bourgeois epoch, I now want to discuss the fundamental political stakes in Habermas's communicative aesthetics. In *Legitimation Crisis*, Habermas provocatively sides with the rebels against the neoconservative functionalists, to propose an insurgent reading of post-war avant-garde literature. Modernism 'expresses, not the promise, but the irretrievable sacrifice, of bourgeois rationalisation' (Habermas 1975b: 86).

> Genuinely bourgeois ideologies, which live only from their own substance, offer no support in the face of the basic risks of existence ... do not make possible human relations with ... nature ... Permit no intuitive access to relations of solidarity ... Allow no real political ethic .... Only bourgeois art, which has become autonomous in the face of demands for employment extrinsic to art, has taken up positions on behalf of

the victims of bourgeois rationalisation. Bourgeois art has become the refuge for a satisfaction even if only virtual, of those needs that have become, as it were, illegal in the material life process of bourgeois society .... Bourgeois art, unlike privatised religion, scientistic philosophy, and strategic utilitarian morality, did not take on tasks in the economic and political system. Instead, it collected residual needs that could find no satisfaction within the system of needs. (Habermas 1975b: 78)

The explosive potential of modern art emerges when discontent surfaces about the antagonism between individual and society. The hopes for a reconciliation of universal and particular, built into the holistic totality of the aesthetic illusion, are then either false or betrayed. On the one hand, in modernism, formal developments, such as juxtaposition, reveal the conventional character of the realism effect. On the other hand, in popular culture, techniques of mechanical reproduction demystify the literary aura surrounding the 'great author'. The technological and conceptual demystification of art destroys the affirmative role of the aesthetic illusion:

[Modernism] radicalised the autonomy of art vis-à-vis contexts of employment external to art. This development produces for the first time a counter-culture, arising from the centre of bourgeois society itself and hostile to the possessive individualistic, achievement and advantage oriented lifestyle of the bourgeoisie .... The alter ego of the commodity owner – the human being, which the bourgeois could at one time encounter in the solitary contemplation of a work of art – thereupon split off from him and confronted him in the artistic avant-garde, as a hostile power, at best a seducer. In the artistically beautiful, the bourgeoisie that once experienced primarily its own ideals and the redemption, however fictive, of a promise of happiness that was merely suspended in everyday life but in radicalised art, soon had to recognise the negation rather than the compliment of its social practice. (Habermas 1975b: 85)

Accepting neoconservative functionalism's central thesis but inverting its negative evaluation into a valorization of the counter-culture, then, for Habermas, the main question is whether an oppositional art and literature can avoid the polarization between aesthetic specialization and mass consumption. His perspective reverses that of Adorno: the problem is not the potential intrusion of instrumental rationality into literary form, but the encapsulation of literary interventions within an anodyne culture of the entertainment industries. The problem is how to burst out, not what might break in; it is a problem of the routinization and trivialization of meanings, before it is one of the programming of forms and the instrumentalization of technique.

Communicative reason and the postmodernism debate

Habermas supports the idea of literary enlightenment as a 'secular illumination' of the subjective world of modern individuals, one that happens through a popular synthesis of literary innovation with realist literature. This position, however, which communicatively reframes Adorno with a synthesis of insights from Benjamin and Marcuse, suffers from a significant lack of clarity around some key points. The most important problem concerns the questionable nature of aesthetic rationality, something that I will broach in a moment by looking at the absence of the reader from Habermas's model of literary communication. But the other problem concerns the desirability of the effort to bridge the 'great divide' between literary modernism and mass culture, especially in light of the post-1970s debates about 'postmodern literature'. Although I do not intend to reprise the entire postmodernism debate (Frow 1997: 1–57), I do need to indicate a difference between the German and English engagement with the question. Explication of that difference will help explain why the Habermasian position, despite hostility to the idea of philosophical postmodernity, might be receptive to dissident elements of literary postmodernism.

The debate about postmodernism in the English-speaking world has been dominated by Fredric Jameson's description of it as the 'cultural logic of late capitalism' (Jameson 1991). That description valuably points to the appropriation of modernist technique for cultural affirmation in ludic postmodernism. But Jameson's topographic framing of postmodern culture as a superstructural reflection of late capitalism – in contradiction with his theoretical recognition of social complexity (Jameson 1981: 17–102, esp., 34–40) – restricts the terms of debate to the functional fit between the cultural and economic subsystems. Further, in a way that is deliberately reminiscent of Adorno (Jameson 1990), the relation between literature and commodification is defined through an evolutionary sequence of cultural stages (Jameson 1992: 156–7). These involve increasing reification (as reification invades the literary sign) and reflexivity (naïve realist representation, reflexive modernist allegory). Like Habermas, albeit in an entirely different theoretical lexicon, Jameson too looks forward to a popular synthesis of realism and modernism that evades the postmodern lapse into affirmative culture, claiming to detect it in science fiction (Jameson 2005: 164–5, 96–7, 213).

By contrast, the postmodernism debate in the German-speaking world has been mainly inflected through intellectual history rather than cultural movements, partly because of the influence of Habermas and cothinker, Albrecht Wellmer (Wellmer 1991, 1998). In relation to literary history, however, Peter Bürger's interventions, characterized by a defence of the historical avant-garde (Bürger 1984) and critique of the neo-avant-garde (Bürger 2010), have defined the terms of debate. Where do modernism and postmodernism fit in the schema of the radical avant-gardes versus the reactionary culture industry? Bürger's basic schema involves the moderation of an avant-garde guerrilla insurgency into post-/modernism's democratic participation in the republic of letters. He castigates Adorno for failure to recognize modernism's lack of revolutionary intentions, a condemnation which necessarily also includes Habermas (Bürger 1984: 104n83). Postmodernism, from this perspective, leads a 'pseudo-autonomous pseudo-life' consistent with the commodification of moderate modernism into neoconservative affirmation (Wellmer 1991: 86–7). The problem is that this schema prevents the identification of dialectical processes *within* these movements, or of tensions *between* their internal poles. The notion of a 'dissident postmodernism' opposed to 'ludic postmodernism' (Maltby 1991), for instance, is thereby excluded.

The work of Albrecht Wellmer is sometimes critical of Habermas, but revolves around the question of the communicative dimension of postmodernism, as opposed to its historical status. Wellmer criticizes Bürger's application of cognitive truth claims to literary works and points out that only a focus on aesthetics makes it possible to frame expressive claims (Wellmer 1991: 30–1). A focus on the communicative aspect of the aesthetic dimension reframes literary autonomy not as a question of institutional specialization, but as a distinctly artistic arena for the exploration of (social) relations between universal and particular. Specifically, Wellmer detects, in the shift from juxtaposition and allegory to pastiche and irony, 'the opening up of the work of art, the dissolution of its boundaries . . . [something] closely related to an enhanced capacity for the aesthetic integration of the diffuse and the disparate' (Wellmer 1991: 89). To be certain, problems of routinization and trivialization do not disappear, along with the need to critique celebratory transformations of destructive negativity into affirmative playfulness (Wellmer 1998: 283). Nonetheless, like Huyssen, Wellmer also sees postmodernism as a prolongation of the neo-avant-garde, aimed at setting modernist conventions in institutional context. Postmodernism is a critique of modernism's false universalization, conducted through a release of non-totalizable particularity (Wellmer 1991: 30–2; 1998: 169–70).

The work of Andreas Huyssen, although also sometimes critical of Habermas, supports this line of argument. Huyssen suggests that postmodernism is misread as affirmative culture, when it is in reality a prolongation of the radical intentions of the neo-avant-garde. Just as modernism continued the revolt of the avant-garde after the failure of their effort to destroy what Bürger calls the 'art institution', postmodernism prolongs the neo-avant-garde resurgence of the 1950s and 1960s (Huyssen 1986: 3–15). The neo-avant-garde, Huyssen argues, is a resumption of the avant-garde strategy, but in the context of a critique of the separation of modernism from mass culture.

It too fails, because museum culture and coffee-table modernism cannot be destroyed without also inadvertently corroding aesthetic experience, as the degenerative logic of the post-war ready made demonstrates. Huyssen proposes that postmodernism is a road out of this apparent impasse, for it aims to deconstruct the opposition between high modernism and mass culture while refusing conformity with museum values. Modernism's dialogical negation of mass culture made hidden reference to its (eroticized yet denigrated) other (Huyssen 1986: 44–62). What postmodernism does is to apply the avant-garde strategy, with reference not to the opposition between literature and everyday praxis, but between literary modernism and mass culture (Huyssen 1986: 160–78). Postmodernism is an effort to bridge the great divide in a progressive way, by dialectically preserving the autonomy of literature while engaging with popular culture. The only thing that needs to be added is that it remains important to notice that the ludic wing of postmodern literature, defined by its exclusive focus on the metafictional paradoxes of 'narcissistic narrative', entirely lacks connection with any agenda of progressive cultural intervention (Hutcheon 2013).

Reception aesthetics as a missing dimension

It is striking that although the Habermasian focus on literature as communication implies a critique of any exclusive concentration on the author as producer, his work does not explore the role of the reader. Accordingly, Pieter Duvenage has called for the integration of reception aesthetics into Critical Theory (Duvenage 2003: 133–7). As explained in the introduction to this book, the role of the reader is central to my overall argument. That is because reframing 'critique' and 'disclosure', which in Habermas represent mutually exclusive accounts of literature, as different receptive attitudes of the reader, clarifies why I think that the 'reciprocity of critique and disclosure' is possible.

I therefore want to close out this chapter by surveying some aspects of reader-response theory that are relevant to this project. Broadly speaking, Wolfgang Iser's hermeneutics of imaginative concretization bears most strongly on 'disclosure', and therefore on the capacity of literature to directly affect the personality structure of the reader. Meanwhile, Hans Robert Jauss's concept of surprised expectations connects with 'critique', with its focus on literary innovation and its connection to debates about what counts as authentic individuality. However, Iser's hermeneutics of reading logically precedes Jauss's historicization of literary experience and so comes first in my account, despite being discussed second in this book. I discuss Jauss in the next chapter.

According to Wolfgang Iser, literary language is characterized by a distinctive structure of negativity – a structuration consisting of blanks and negations – that not only distances the literary message from the real world, but also fills the text itself with a peculiar structure of gaps. In *The Act of Reading* (1978), Iser develops the phenomenology of reading of Roman Ingarden, who maintains that there is a fundamental indeterminacy about the stratum of presented objects that the literary text purports to depict. We know, for instance, that in the Jorge Luis Borges story, 'Tlön, Uqbar, Orbis Tertius', volume T-U of the *Anglo-American Cyclopedia* is on the bookshelf in the hallway, but not what other volumes are on the bookshelf, how the hallway is lit and so forth. Literary texts guide the reader by providing a sequence of descriptions of the represented action that gradually, but always incompletely, concretize the imaginary world (Iser 1980: 170–9). But at the same time, the text maintains a structure of gaps that solicit the reader's participation in the imaginative completion of the possible world that the text suggests, so that, although the reader is guided by certain schemas, their active response crucially defines what reading means (Iser 1980: 135–51). In the terminology that Iser develops, the active imagination that constitutes the reader's response involves the constitution (or concretization) of the text as a work, in a temporalized process involving anticipation and correction, being guided by the text and freely completing its inviting gaps (Iser 1980: 195–202).

Although Iser refuses the terminology of content and form, his notions of repertoire of conventions and narrative strategy are, in effect, coextensive with the traditional vocabulary. The repertoire of the text consists of an ensemble of conventions that regulate social and literary norms, which lends to the text its ability to plausibly represent social worlds and psychological realities (Iser 1980: 68–85 and 96–8). The strategy of the text selects and combines the materials of the repertoire in line with a determinate process of structuration, something which may range from formulaic narrative trajectories, through to paratactic techniques of montage. According to Iser, a dynamic equilibrium exists between the horizon of the work – the imagined world represented by the text as completed by the reader – and the theme of the work – the materials that are conceptually foregrounded by the narrative progression. The reader is therefore solicited to select from the multiple perspectives available in the text in a process of concretization that involves the evolution of meaning-structures, as well as the imaginative rendering of represented objects, actions and persons (Iser 1980: 139–51). Furthermore, the reader is also involved in the reconstruction of a story – the cause-and-effect sequence of actions and their consequences, in their correct temporal order, that constitutes the basis for the narrative – from the plot – the sequence of events that is represented in the text by the narrating agent. Iser describes this process as the way in which the text provides segments, each of which constitutes a field of vision, that the reader is invited to reassemble into the sequence of the story. For Iser, this activity involves more than simply decoding the plot in order to logically reconstruct the story, because as readers select different segments as interpretive keys they must necessarily force the other segments into the background. The text therefore consists of a structure of segments and blanks, as well as indeterminate objects and the gaps around them, that constitutes the syntagmatic axis of the reader's interaction with the text. As the reader passes along the syntagmatic chain of the narrative, the range of possible concretizations of the text as a work either shrinks, in the case of a realistic narrative, or expands, in the case of a narrative that sets deliberate puzzles before the reader. Iser theorizes the expansion and contraction of possibilities in terms of selections from the paradigmatic axis provided by the text and he proposes that the activity of concretization is therefore strongly connected to negation and negativity (Iser 1980: 212–30).

What Iser calls reading is the moving locus of determinacy and indeterminacy that unfolds along the succession of sentences in the text, depositing the imagined work in the wake of the interplay of perspectives that happens at along this locus. This is different from the 'ideal reader', a reading-position supposed to know everything, to saturate the text by exhausting its meaning-potential. Instead, the implied reader is a transcendental construct, an inference from the repertoire and strategies of the text to its context of relevance and horizon of expectations. The implied reader is 'a textual structure anticipating the presence of a recipient without necessarily defining' the reader, a 'network of response-inviting structures which impel the reader to gasp the text' (Iser 1980: 34).

In summary, theories of active readership explain how reception in a critical mode leads to 'critique', the dialogical testing of the accuracy and legitimacy of interpretive constructions, as well as social criticism that draws on literary representations in arguments about changing the world. But theories of active readership also explain how reception in an imaginative mode leads to 'disclosure', the envisionment of new forms of individuality in new social worlds, as well as the refreshment of language and imagery. Here, theories of imaginative transportation in reading experience clarify how the reader's active construction of a literary work enables the literary text to act as an agent of socialization. Both aspects of reading – critique and disclosure – have to do with the links between innovation, imagination and individuality. This connects up with the Habermasian reconstruction of literary history as an exploration of the subjective world that has the formation of a new individuality as its most significant potential.

5

The nature of literary critique

Habermas frames the enlightenment vocation of progressive literature in terms of its contribution to cultural rationalization, by virtue of literature belonging to communicative reason – specifically, to the dimension of communicative reason that he calls 'aesthetic-expressive rationality'. In the architecture of the theory of communicative action, that means that literature is called upon to play a demanding, structurally essential role. The three voices of communicative reason – cognitive, normative and expressive – explore and develop the objective, social and subjective worlds of modern individuals, respectively. To the extent that expert specializations in these dimensions of communicative reason are located in differentiated institutions – such as scientific and legal institutions – the learning processes connected with their experimental discoveries can (in principle) be transmitted to the general population.

The system of connections here – dimension of reason, referential world, specialized procedure, expert knowledge, institutional locus – is crucial, because without it, there is no ground for supposing that modernity might be a potentially fulfilling way of life. For instance, a dimension of reason and its referential world – say, the subjective – might, for structural reasons, be underdeveloped in modernity; modernity might be an historical epoch characterized by technological progress, the juridification of society and subjective impoverishment. Alternatively, modernity might be characterized by a fertile exploration and discovery of the subjective world, but one which, for lack of an influential institution, remains forever locked up in an expert specialization. Critics of modernity have argued both cases – that modernity is soulless and that its art is hermetic – and Habermas's defence of modernity as a potentially rational form of society must confront the force of these objections.

As the bearer of 'aesthetic-expressive rationality', literature is charged by Habermas with the exploration and development of the subjective world of modern individuals. It does this by making experimental discoveries about the cultural interpretation of human needs and the means of their social expression. Furthermore, the literary institution is responsible for the transmission of these radical innovations back into the everyday lives of the general population. Unfortunately, however, although Habermas often refers to the triplicity of 'science, law and art' as a shorthand for the architecture of modernity, the notion that literature is functionally or communicatively equivalent to science and law does not survive inspection. The problem is not that literature lacks social impact, for it is obvious that popular fiction has a tremendous influence. The real question is whether this impact extends beyond entertainment and/or indoctrination, to embrace anything remotely resembling the experimental discoveries of the sciences, or the rigorous argumentation of the law. It therefore needs to be shown that literature has a credible emancipatory vocation that can, in principle, be transmitted to the general population.

But it is not at all obvious why an imaginative practice such as literature should be regarded as a dimension of rationality in the first place. Why should literature be assimilated to procedures involving rational dialogue, when fictional narratives are manifestly not forms of propositional argumentation? Furthermore, even supposing that a plausible explanation for recruiting literature to argument can be found (for instance, as I shall argue, that literature sparks critical debate, so forming a symbiotic literary-critical practice), there remains the question of whether the results are rationally binding. Scientific discoveries are universally binding on rational beings by virtue of the procedures of experimental replication and falsification of hypotheses, whereas critical readings notoriously remain trapped in the 'conflict of interpretations'. Is the subjective universality of an aesthetic judgement a strong enough basis for the transmission of literary discoveries to rational individuals? Should reasonable persons *really* let arguments about imaginary universes and invented characters affect their motivations and orientations in the actual world?

This chapter explains the nature of 'aesthetic-expressive rationality' and clarifies the role of literature and criticism in the rationalization of the subjective worlds of modern individuals. Through a series of approximations and corrections – based on positions of Habermas – it builds up a plausible Habermasian model of literary communication as belonging to communicative reason.

Part I: The literal model

I begin by claiming that there is a 'literal model' of literature at work in some moments of the theory of communicative action, according to which the literary text is the form of argumentation that corresponds to a fundamental type of social action, what Habermas calls 'dramaturgical action'. On this model, literature is therapeutic, because, like therapy, it is about the truthfulness of expressions of subjectivity. The dialogue that it involves, in which the author and reader can alternate between roles of analyst and analysand, has the effect of clarifying individuals' sociocultural relation to human needs. Progressive literature, on the literal model, brings readers to the developmental stage where it is finally understood that impulses are cultural interpretations of desires and feelings. These are valid or invalid in relation to the rational agreements behind communal standards, rather than being inherently 'normal' or 'abnormal', intrinsically 'natural' or 'unnatural'. The role of the critic is to propositionally formulate the implicit arguments that the text presents in a narrative form, just as the role of the therapist is to present interpretive constructions to the analysand for their consideration. However, the proximity of literature to therapy naturally raises the question of whether the clinic might not be a better institutional candidate for the structural role that Habermas assigns to literature.

Expressive rationality

In Chapter 3, I explored the basic architecture of the theory of communicative action, with its schematic triplicity of cognitive, normative and expressive validity claims to truth, rightness and truthfulness (respectively). Action coordination using speech acts is halted when participants say 'no!' to an action proposal, which triggers a suspension of speech pragmatics and a shift to reflexive communication. Then, participants examine the warranted assertions about situation definitions that speakers provide for their proposals. The assertive warrants of speakers are redeemed through argumentative debates about the validity of their claims regarding the objective, social and subjective referents of their discourse. Each type of claim is redeemed through a specific argumentative procedure, something whose ultimate foundation lies in the differences between the action types that are the source of the disagreement. Questions about dramaturgical actions (explored in a moment) refer to the subjective world of beliefs and intentions, desires and feelings. These are contested through validity claims to expressive truthfulness – this constitutes the *expressive* dimension of communicative reason. Expert specialization in each of the resulting cultural value spheres leads to learning processes, summarized by developmental psychology, in terms of the achievement of hypothetical attitudes (Jean Piaget), post-conventional morality (Lawrence Kohlberg) and post-traditional need-interpretations (Jane Loevinger) (Habermas 1979b: 75–8).

According to Habermas, these learning processes constitute autonomous domains of inquiry, where pragmatic concerns are suspended and the rival claim types of the other cultural value spheres are excluded (or subordinated). It is crucial that these autonomous cultural value spheres, with their associated learning processes, are institutionalized in a form that makes possible knowledge transmission into the education system and the public sphere. The 'structure forming effect of expert knowledge' that results from successful institutionalization is how communicative reason is supposed to influence society. In Chapter 3, I presented a table as a *provisional* schematization, which reflected Habermas's often-used shorthand for cultural modernity: 'science, morality and art' (e.g. TCA1: 141 [213]). But there are four really obvious reasons why, despite using the shorthand 'science, morality and art', Habermas does not always directly claim that literature plays the same role in relation to the subjective world that science performs in relation to the objective world. Although Habermas's central contention is that literature is experimental, it is clearly not experimental in the same sense that science is experimental. Additionally:

1. Psychotherapy is a significantly better candidate institution than literature.
2. Literature is an imaginative discourse, not a form of propositional argumentation.
3. Debates sparked by literature are restricted to particular readerships and remain controversial.
4. Literary criticism evaluates according to literary standards, not the truthfulness of expressions.

The force of these leads to the following amendment: Habermas should speak of 'science, law, and, the expressive institution, including therapy & literature'. I will clarify the relation between 'therapy and literature' in a moment. Meanwhile, the fact that literature is an imaginative discourse is not fatal to the thesis that literature constitutes the expressive institution, because the relevant definition of 'literature' here embraces both fiction and criticism. Criticism turns fiction into argumentation, in a way to be explained, just as Habermas thinks that therapy embraces both clinical analysis and the dream report. The other two objections structure the movement of this chapter, and I will attend to them in a moment. But I have stated these objections right from the beginning, because I do not want my reader to go insane with frustration. I nonetheless intend to persist with building up a literal model that these problems negate, because I believe that a dialectical presentation is warranted by the subject matter.

There is a powerful reason why Habermas resorts to the shorthand 'science, morality and art', in relation to the communicative architecture of modernity. In every speech act, Habermas maintains, the actor raises three potentially challengeable validity claims with each utterance:

(1) that the statement is true;
(2) that the statement involves right conduct; and

(3) 'that the manifest intention of the speaker is meant as it is expressed' (TCA1: 99 [150]).

The truthfulness of expressions therefore seems to be a fundamental dimension of the rationality of communication in everyday praxis. Literature seems to have an expressive relation to the subjective world. But does literature – meaning, 'literature and criticism' – *directly* express this?

To attack this question requires some preliminary definitions. The human being has natural instincts, but lacks a stereotypical repertoire of instinctual satisfactions amounting to a behavioural programme, depending rather on interpretations of needs that are culturally formulated (KHI: 312). In what follows, a 'drive impulse' is the psychic representation of a natural instinct. Drive impulses are articulated onto potential objects as 'desires', *Wünsche*, or wishes, which are (unconscious) archaic images of impulse satisfaction, or as 'demands', intersubjectively accessible linguistic symbolizations of a request to the other for impulse satisfaction. Both desires and demands are 'need-interpretations'. Human needs are generalizable forms of need-interpretation, ones that can in principle be affirmed by every rational person. The development of post-traditional need-interpretations involves finding new forms for the symbolization of human needs, not the discovery of new needs or the structural modification of a biological endowment.

Post-traditional need-interpretations are a symbolic representation of the impulses arising from the instinctual spectrum, in terms that make explicit the fact that these need-interpretations are consensus agreements, not natural facts (Loevinger and Blassi 1976: 14–28). For Habermas's source (Habermas 1979b: 76), Jane Loevinger, post-traditional need-interpretations, or 'self-evaluated standards of impulse control', are correlated with post-conventional stages of moral development. This includes respect for the uniqueness of others' personalities and tolerance of their particular need-interpretations (Loevinger and Blassi 1976: 25). Conversely, semantic renewal in relation to self-expression is necessarily a reinvention of the cultural description of the spectrum of needs, which includes desires and feelings (TCA1: 92–3 [137–8]). From this perspective, the semantic renewal conducted by literature seems to be a likely candidate for expressive learning processes, with a key role to play in modernity. As Habermas says, 'we need those rescued semantic potentials if we are to interpret the world in terms of our own needs, and only if the source of these potentials does not run dry can the claim to happiness be fulfilled' (Habermas 1979a: 57).

Expressive truthfulness and authentic literature

Against this definitional background, I want to return to the question of whether literature and criticism *directly* expresses subjectivity. Sometimes,

Habermas seems to think so. He proposes that validity claims to expressive truthfulness arise from 'dramaturgical action', an action-type involving 'an encounter in which the participants form a visible public for each other and perform for one another' (TCA1: 91 [137]). According to Habermas, 'in bringing something of [their] subjectivity to appearance, [they] would like to be seen in a particular way', which means that they 'have to behave towards [their] own subjective world' (TCA1: 91 [137]). Such an agent must presuppose a relation between subjective realm and social world in which argumentative warrants can in principle be advanced in support of the intersubjective validation of their subjective experience. They are neither deceiving themselves about what they truthfully want, nor demanding communal satisfaction of completely idiosyncratic interpretations of human needs (TCA1: 20 [41–2]). When challenged by the audience to provide warrants for the performance, the actor must reflexively shift into the argumentative redemption of validity claims to expressive truthfulness.

Such claims have two varieties, connected to two completely distinct aspects of the subjective world, which in turn correspond to two entirely different procedures for the redemption of their argumentative warrants. Claims about beliefs and intentions are *sincerity* claims that are redeemed through the consistency of subsequent conduct, which is compared with the implied intention of the utterance (TCA1: 91–2 [137–8]). These are not relevant to literature. By contrast, validity claims about desires and feelings are redeemed through debate about the *authenticity* of the expressed need-interpretation, which involves the conformity of a human need to the standards and traditions of the speaker's community (TCA1: 93–4 [139–40]). In claims to authenticity, speakers maintain that a form of self-realization is legitimate because it fits with a consensus that a community might reach about the link between human needs (i.e. generalized motivations) and communal value standards (i.e. particular orientations). Habermas summarizes this entire chain of argumentation as follows:

> Dramaturgical actions embody a knowledge of the agent's own subjectivity. These expressions can be criticised as untruthful, that is, rejected as deceptions or self-deceptions. Self-deceptions can be dissolved in therapeutic dialogue by argumentative means. Expressive knowledge can be explicated in terms of those values that underlie need interpretations, the interpretation of desires and emotional attitudes. Value standards are dependent in turn on innovations in the domain of expressive evaluations. These are reflected in an exemplary manner in works of art. (TCA1: 334 [497])

On the Literal Model, then, literary texts, including fictional narratives, are imaginative suggestions about the subjective basis for authenticity (truthfulness) claims, which might be raised in the context of a challenge to coordinating dramaturgical action. Literary texts present imaginative speculations that critical debate then transforms into propositional form, in authenticity claims to expressive truthfulness connected to conjectured, exemplary new forms of self-realization. A critically interpreted literary work is a proposal for an authentic form of life. How would this work?

Following Alessandro Ferrara, modern authenticity claims have to be grasped as involving morally autonomous individuals asserting that a novel particular form of self-realization is exemplary and therefore creates new standards for all members of that community (Ferrara 1998). These exemplary new forms of self-realization can involve a transformed interpretation of human needs, a fresh form of the sublimation or expression of desire or a revaluation of values gained by a work that sets new expressive standards. According to the literal model, then, the role of literature is therapeutic. Its conjectural status makes it possible for individuals to experiment imaginatively with new forms of self-realization before committing themselves to the relevant forms of praxis. In *Communication and the Evolution of Society*, Habermas expressly allocates just such a role to literature as the literal model supposes:

> Inner nature is rendered communicatively fluid and transparent to the extent that needs can, through aesthetic forms of expression, be kept articulable or be released from their paleo-symbolic pre-linguisticality. But that means that internal nature is not subjected, in the cultural preformation met with at any given time, to the demands of ego autonomy; rather, it is only through an independent ego that the individual finally obtains free access to the interpretive possibilities of the cultural tradition. In the medium of value-forming and norm-forming communications in which aesthetic experiences enter, traditional cultural contents are then no longer simply the stencils according to which needs are shaped; on the contrary, in this medium, needs can seek and find adequate interpretations. (Habermas 1979b: 93)

David Colclasure's exposition of *Habermas and Literary Rationality*, especially his extended reading of Wolfgang Hilbig's experimental novel, *Ich*, demonstrates that the literal model can generate a fascinating commentary on literary works (Colclasure 2010: 102–10) – provided that they are considered as imaginative presentations of authenticity claims. Progressive literature, on the literal model, brings readers to the developmental stage where it is finally understood that impulses are cultural interpretations of desires and feelings, rather than 'normal' or 'abnormal', 'natural' or 'unnatural', and it expands the coping mechanisms that a culture has for dealing with human needs. The role of the critic is to formulate propositionally the implicit arguments that the text presents in a narrative form, just as the role of the therapist is to present interpretive constructions to the analysand for their consideration.

However, the proximity of literature to therapy naturally raises the question of whether the clinic might not be a better institutional candidate for the structural role that Habermas assigns to literature.

Literature and therapy: Limits to the literal model

The literal model not only implies a directly therapeutic role for emancipatory literature and literary criticism, but also assigns to the literary institution the key task of supporting subjective learning processes in modernity. But why load up *literature* with this responsibility when therapy exists? On the one hand, there are good reasons to worry that literature can only be *indirectly* therapeutic. On the other hand, an irresolvable 'conflict of interpretations' seems a highly fragmented foundation for an expressive institution. By contrast, therapy works (more or less) and exists in a social form with the plausible capacity to support the role allocated to the expressive institution by the theory of communicative action. The therapeutic institutions are regulated and centralized in a way that public discussion of literary texts is not. This is because, while literary debate remains within the conflict of interpretations, therapy is guided by practical success.

Intuitively speaking, forms of therapy – especially psychotherapy, which is what Habermas mainly means – are a strong contender for the role of expressive institution. Habermas holds a functional and social-contractual theory of social institutions, inherited from Talcott Parsons (TCA2: 166–72 [249–54] and 199–300 [297–444]). According to this perspective, an 'institution' is a cluster of organizations that is dedicated to a particular kind of joint action, performs one or several structural functions, is susceptible to change depending on its collective acceptance and which has a 'structure-forming effect' on society. For instance, 'science' consists of organizations such as laboratories, universities and agencies, dedicated to making experimental discoveries about the natural environment, sociological structures and the material substrate of human mentation. The discoveries of science function to advance technological potentials, particularly in relation to the economic subsystem, something which significantly protects the scientific method from potential delegitimation because of its corrosive impact on traditional world views. Finally, the formalizations and falsifiability of scientific hypotheses mean that scientific knowledge can be reliably transmitted via education into society, where it contributes to the formation of hypothetic cognitive attitudes and informs deliberations in the public sphere.

In all of these respects, the credentials of the therapeutic organizations are strong, especially when access to mental healthcare provision is subsidized by the state. Therapy consists of organizations such as the laboratories and clinics of the psychology profession, psychoanalytic schools, psychiatric hospitals and a network of counsellors throughout social institutions. Although Habermas denies the possibility of a scientifically reductive account of psychology that would entirely eliminate interpretation, the discoveries of therapeutic research direct, in a disciplined way, clinical practice, which in turn contributes to the falsification of hypotheses about therapeutic effectiveness. Psychoanalysis, for instance, which for Habermas is paradigmatic of 'therapy', although it deserves a sceptical reception as a science of mind (Grünbaum 1984), does in fact include falsifiable hypotheses (Kline 2014), has been tested empirically (with mixed results) (Masling and Bornstein 1994–2005), has somewhat successfully guided psychiatry (Ellenberger 1981) and currently, in a modified form, informs scientific research in neuropsychoanalysis (Kandel 2005). Habermas (as we shall see in the next chapter) regards it as a hermeneutic rather than a science, but this does not detract from its social influence via the therapeutic organizations. The psychoanalytic clinic is effective in treating some disorders (Fonagy 2015), despite a proliferation of schools that is the consequence of the unresolvable status of the conflict of interpretations. Psychoanalysis as a whole has without doubt entered the broader popular imagination while alleviating the suffering of many. Meanwhile, cognitive behavioural therapy and developmental psychology, for instance, are unquestionably on a firmer empirical footing, as practical treatments and theoretical methodologies, respectively. Additionally, despite its weak credentials in relation to communicative reason, there is a supplementary sector of organizations best described as consisting of wisdom literature and meditation therapies, ranging from self-help books through to Zen Buddhism. Literature would have to meet most of these standards to act as the expressive institution, and it simply cannot do so.

Of course, in this argument, 'literature' is a placemarker for the creative media in general, including the visual and plastic arts, music and dance, theatre and architecture, cinema and television, computer gaming and virtual reality. From the communicative perspective, however, literature has an exemplary status by virtue of its special connection to language. But even supposing that literature can act as a placemarker for the creative media in general, it is surely plausible to suppose that the role of the media actually only supplements that of the organizations of therapy. A central reason for this is that therapy is dialogically organized as a learning process, in a context within which the dream report, which bears some resemblance to the literary text, is a pretext for dialogue, rather than the entire substance of the communication. Freud's interpretive procedure, which insists on the analytical dissection of the elements of the dream through free association to key experiences, implies that the dream report is treated as consisting of disguised propositions that can be translated by interpretation into the form of statements. With the restoration of the continuity of the narrative of their life history, now unbroken by repression and its distortions of selfhood, the analysand practically corroborates the therapeutic theory through the resumption of everyday praxis.

By contrast, readers actively participate in the concretization of an imaginative work from the literary text, and then – turned critics – they discuss their interpretations of the relevance of these imaginary worlds for actually existing society. Because the literary text becomes an imaginative work by virtue of readerly participation, the propositional statements that emerge from literary debate concern the readers' experience rather than authorial subjectivity. Furthermore, this discussion is strictly interminable, in the sense that the conflict of interpretations can neither be ended by recourse to some final theory or definitive interpretation, nor be referred to a criterion of practical success that *directly* tests interpretations as therapies.

In short, the analysand *learns*; the readers only *discuss*.

Part II: The rhetorical model

In summary, communicative reason needs an expressive institution based in expressive truthfulness and having therapeutic effects. Habermas thinks that literature is a good candidate, springing from dramaturgical action and leading to progressive literature. But therapy is a better candidate, and it provides for learning processes based in direct expressions of subjectivity. The 'rhetorical model', which results from consideration of these limitations, is probably the main implicit model of literature in the theory of communicative action. It corrects the assumptions of the literal model by foregrounding the difference between literary rhetoric and individual self-expression, rhetorical criticism and therapeutic dialogue. From the perspective of the rhetorical model, literary texts employ rhetorical techniques on expressive materials to present potential structures of feeling. Where therapy works with individuals, literature relies on a readership community, which implies that literary texts seek to persuade in intersubjective (i.e. generalizable), rather than interpersonal, terms. Literature's rhetorical strategies present generalized structures of feeling, which implies a commentary on the relation between the individual and society, and an intervention into ethical life. Nonetheless, these generalized structures of feeling are the referent for literary presentations, and, to this extent, the literal model is vindicated.

Literary critique

For Habermas, both criticism and therapy are forms of 'Critique', rather than of the formal or logical demonstrations constitutive of 'Discourse', such as science and law. By contrast with 'Discourse', which results in universally binding rational agreement, forms of 'Critique' involve an art of judgement. Of course, in the field of literary studies, the philosophical terminology of 'Discourse' and 'Critique' is potentially confusing. Narrative discourse refers to the rhetorical formation of the fictional narrative – the manner of the storytelling – as opposed to plot and story (Genette 1983). Literary critique describes a particular critical practice situated within the hermeneutics of suspicion, which unmasks ideological misrepresentations or reveals symptomatic silences, generally in the name of Marx, Freud or Nietzsche (Felski 2015). To avoid misunderstanding, therefore, I intend to modify Habermas's terminology in the following way. I shall capitalize formal demonstration as 'Discourse', but describe literary rhetoric as narrative discourse. I shall describe interpretive argumentation as 'critique', but refer to the hermeneutics of suspicion by name when I mean a particular practice of literary critique. By critique, I mean the Kantian practice of 'exhibiting the universal and necessary conditions of possibility for a phenomenon'. Marxian ideology-critique, for instance, consists in a discussion of the social and cultural conditions of possibility for the distorted presentation of economic conditions. Habermas develops the concept of critique from a reflection on expressive truthfulness that it is worth citing at length:

> We call a person rational who interprets the nature of [their] desires and feelings in light of culturally established standards of value, but, especially, if [they] can adopt a reflective attitude to the very value standards through which desires and feelings are interpreted. Cultural values do not appear with a claim to universality, as do norms of action. At most, values are candidates for interpretations under which a circle of those affect can describe and normatively regulate a common interest. The circle of intersubjective recognition that forms around cultural values does not yet in any way imply a claim that they would meet with general assent within a culture, not to mention universal assent. . . . Arguments that serve to justify standards of value do not satisfy the conditions of Discourse. In the prototypical case, they have the form of aesthetic Critique. (TCA1: 20 [41–2])

From the Habermasian perspective, then, literary critique emphatically does not reduce to the various schools of the hermeneutics of suspicion. Habermas is most interested in the rational status of literary and therapeutic critique, rather than being specially invested in particular critical methodologies, or psychoanalytic theories. Literary critique means, foremost, the conflict of interpretations around the republic of letters. To that extent, literary critique is a meta-critical descriptive term that designates the entire spectrum of interpretive practices. In relation to communicative reason:

> [Critique] is a form of argumentation in which the adequacy of value standards, the vocabulary of our evaluative language generally, is made

thematic. . . . In this context, reasons have the peculiar function of bringing us to see a performance in such a way that it can be perceived as an authentic expression of an exemplary experience, in general, as the embodiment of a claim to authenticity. . . . In aesthetic Critique, grounds or reasons serve to guide perception and to make the authenticity of a work so evident that this aesthetic experience can itself become a rational motive for accepting the corresponding standards of value. This provides a plausible explanation for why we regard aesthetic arguments as less conclusive than the arguments we employ in practical, or, even more so, theoretical Discourse. Something similar holds for the argument of a psychotherapist [whose role is to let the patient] . . . see through the irrational limitations to which [their praxis] is subject. . . . Freud examined the relevant type of argumentation in his model of the therapeutic dialogue, [the process of] clarifying systematic self-deception in therapeutic Critique. (TCA1: 20-1 [44])

Forms of critique are rational and argumentative, as plausible judgements relative to a single individual or a value community, but not susceptible to demonstration, and therefore subject to the conflict of interpretations. All forms of critique rely on a logic of exemplification, which requires a reflexive determination (the invention of a universal rule to fit a particular case). That is why both criticism and therapy are presented through the form of the case study, rather than exclusively through methodological considerations or metapsychological speculations. Nonetheless, both forms of critique engage judgements of the legitimacy of proposals about the relation between human needs and value standards. What is at stake is the connection between motivations and orientations, that is, between the subjective and the social.

What is meant by authentic self-realization is the intersubjective judgement that a style of individual fulfilment or an ideal of human flourishing represents a satisfying relation between accepted motivations (i.e. need-interpretations) and legitimate orientations (i.e. communal standards) (Ferrara 1998). From the perspective of the rhetorical model, literary affirmations persuade readership communities that a style of living is a form of authentic self-realization, while literary negations persuade that a way of life is a mutilation of human flourishing. The expressive institution, then, seems to involve a division of labour between therapeutic and literary critique (TCA1: 23 [46]). This division of labour concerns the difference between expressive truthfulness and authentic self-realization. Therapy clarifies the personal history of a specific individual's developmental progress, while literature illuminates of the social context of individuals' authentic self-realization.

On this construction, literature is a persuasive communication that uses rhetoric and figuration to get the reader to imaginatively entertain a new 'structure of feeling'. Literature (affirmatively or negatively) maps the subjective world onto the social domain (and the natural environment), as if the social domain were an arena for the satisfaction of human needs. Criticism then translates this into post-traditional need-interpretations, together with suggestions about the corresponding reformation of the social world. The implication is that literary criticism deals with the social possibilities for human happiness. Dialogical assent belongs to the collective readership as a critical community. Dialogical assent does not imply a saccharine literature of affirmative culture, or license a depoliticized criticism. By translating the literary work into a propositional argument, literary critique is inevitably social advocacy.

On the rhetorical model, then, literature is about 'affective mapping', the projection of generalizable feelings from the subjective domain onto the social world and the natural environment, as if these were domains for the satisfaction of human needs. Expressive impulses are combined with literary materials, which include the most advanced rhetorical strategies and figurative potentials available to the author, and creatively synthesized into a symbolic repertoire. The literary material is then provided with textual form through the imposition of literary technique, consisting of representational conventions and composition procedures, which guides selection and combination from the repertoire. These literary techniques are rhetorical strategies for the representation of the relation between the individual and society, a persuasive presentation of a structure of feeling to the readership. The rhetorical model therefore constructs the text as a persuasive message that sparks a critical debate, in which the contending parties argue about the degree to which a way of life is fulfilling or mutilating. The main means of evaluation of the message's appropriateness is consideration of how it intervenes into existing mappings of the subjective domain onto the social world. The rationality of this procedure is restricted, however, by the communal character of the values in question. Forms of literary critique remain within the conflict of interpretations to the degree that ethical life is characterized by value pluralism.

Part III: The communicative model

The problem with the rhetorical model is that literary communication cannot be reduced to a persuasive message about a determinate referent, in the subjective world or anywhere else. More simply, there is no aesthetics in the rhetorical model, only persuasive strategies that could, in principle, be extra-literary. There is no consideration of what Lukács called the 'specificity of the aesthetic', which would introduce the irreducible link between form and content in literary texts.

In *Philosophical Discourse*, discussing the 'poetic language hypothesis' in the aftermath of the theory of communicative action, Habermas (correctly, I think) denies that textual messages can be assimilated to ordinary language. There are significant differences between aesthetic presentations of possible experience and extra-literary forms of rhetorical persuasion. The point of literature is not just to allude to the relation between the individual and society in a way that persuades the reader to imagine a different structure of feeling. It is also to invent a new language for the expression of the transformed relation between the subjective domain and the social world that this implies.

Literature, in short, shakes up the relation between language and reality, as well as experimenting with new realizations of human needs that are no longer stencilled by cultural traditions, or stereotyped by ideological distortions. But instead of revising the rhetorical model, Habermas abandons the link between literature and critique entirely. I now want to propose an alternative, a communicative model that sublates the rhetorical model.

Fictive utterances and the ambiguity of reference

On the communicative model, literature is an *indirect* presentation of a mapping of the subjective domain onto the social world, rather than a *direct* and persuasive one, as implied by the rhetorical model. This is an alternative to abandoning the link between literature and critique. The extent to which this is Habermasian depends on whether the communicative model can accommodate the points that Habermas makes in his argument against the rhetorical model.

Habermas makes his arguments against the rhetorical model in *The Philosophy Discourse of Modernity* in the context of revising the 'science, law and art' paradigm of communicative reason. Despite Habermas's endorsement of speech act theory in relation to the pragmatics of social coordination, he is critical of the application of speech act theory to literature, because this fails to consider how literary communication has an aesthetic dimension (PDM: 201–4 [237–40]). In the work of Mary Louise Pratt, Habermas encounters a sustained effort to refute the structuralist 'poetic language hypothesis', the hypothesis that formal characteristics of literary language set it apart from ordinary speech (Pratt 1977). The basic idea is that although literature suspends the normal illocutionary force component of the speech act (and so is non-pragmatic), it does not thereby depart from the realm of ordinary communication. Narrative reports about sequences of speech and action happen constantly in ordinary communication. They have the status of perlocutionary sequences (i.e. rhetorical strategies), intended to persuade interlocutors that something exemplary took place. Actors then return from this non-pragmatic and reflexive break in action coordination, with a better understanding of their current situation. Unlike rational argumentation – which is also a non-pragmatic and reflexive break in action coordination – telling stories does not involve propositional formulations. These arise only if the interlocutors disagree about the relevance of the narrated report.

Now, Pratt's *Towards a Speech Act Theory of Literary Discourse* is effectively the same as what I have called the rhetorical model. Habermas's rejoinder to Pratt, conducted in an excursus within *The Philosophical Discourse of Modernity*, is also a dialectical negation of the rhetorical model implicitly proposed in *The Theory of Communicative Action*. He elegantly demonstrates that she introduces, but does not explain, an aesthetic criterion of 'tellability'. This is a placemarker not only for a judgement of the exemplary status of the reported event, but also of the manner in which it is told, the story's 'worthwhileness' (PDM: 203 [239]). Habermas adds:

> What grounds the primacy and structuring force of the poetic function is not the deviation of a fictional representation from the documentary report of an incident, but the exemplary elaboration that takes the case out of its context and makes it the occasion for an innovative, world-disclosing and eye-opening representation, where the rhetorical means of representation depart from communicative routines and take on a life of their own. (PDM: 203 [239])

I will return to world-disclosure in the second part of this book. Meanwhile, the defamiliarization of practical communication that happens in literary language (i.e. 'poetic language') leads to the autonomy of literature. This explains the nature of fictional reference, while at the same time separating literary communication from rhetorical persuasion within everyday contexts. In particular, the Habermasian position on fictional utterances cannot involve a special literary illocution ('make believe that once upon a time . . .') that suspends pragmatics without altering everyday speech (Currie 1986, 2008), or the notion that fictive utterances are pretended speech acts ('let's pretend that . . .') (Searle 1975; Sutrop 2000).

To develop this point, Habermas turns to the poetics of Roman Jakobson (PDM: 200–2 [235–8]). According to Jakobson's well-known model of the six functions of communication, every utterance constitutes a relation between six factors – addresser, addressee, code, message, contact and context – which are the loci for the 'emotive' (addresser), 'conative' (addressee), 'phatic' (contact), 'referential' (context), 'metalinguistic' (code) and 'poetic' (message) functions (Jakobson 1987: 62–94). Jakobson proposes two key theses about literature. The first is that literature is constituted by the dominance of the poetic function of a 'set towards the message', a focus on the message for its own sake. In particular, poetry is characterized by a 'projection of the principle of equivalence [i.e., similarity – GB] from the axis of selection into the axis of combination' (Jakobson 1987: 69, 71). The Jakobsonian 'set towards the message' is equivalent to the formalist concept of estrangement, according to which the distinctive characteristic of literary language is its defamiliarization of everyday speech. The second is that, for Jakobson, in the utterance, the paradigmatic axis of selection, based on similarity, is the locus of metaphor, while the syntagmatic axis of combination, based on contiguity, is the locus of metonymy. Furthermore, poetry releases metaphorical potentials of language, while realism releases metonymic potentials (Jakobson 1987: 19–27 and 368–78). The implication is that mimetic narrative is a projection of the principle of contiguity from the axis of combination into the axis of selection. It involves 'the condensation of the narrative by means of images based on contiguity that is, avoidance of the normal designative term, in favour of metonymy or synecdoche' (Jakobson 1987: 25).

In narrative fiction – for instance, Pasternak's fiction – factual reporting on a causal sequence of enchained events is systematically replaced by succession of metonymic moments, one whose logic is that of synecdoche, not causation. Jakobson cites Pasternak, for instance:

> Somewhere nearby . . . a herd . . . was making music . . . The music was sucked in by blue-bottles. Its skin was rippling to-and-fro, spasmodically and surely.
>
> Those were aerial ways, on which, like trains, the rectilinear thoughts of Liebknecht, Lenin and the few minds of their flight departed daily.
> (Jakobson 1987: 309 Pasternak cited)

In the first quote, the sound made by something assumes the thing's function; in the second quote, an abstraction becomes objectified. Both are forms of metonymy or synecdoche. Jakobson's note that this often happens to the detriment of the plot indicates its significance as a distinctive characteristic of narrative fiction. This marks out the difference between (the temporally arranged causal sequence of) a report on a social action and a fictional narration of such actions.

The precise details of Jakobson's alignment of metonymy with the syntagmatic axis of combination and metaphor with the paradigmatic axis of selection have been questioned, but they have also been strongly defended (Waugh 1980). In general, Jakobson's approach has turned out to be reasonably robust (Bradford 1994), and it certainly explains the peculiar 'double reference' that happens in literary works. Jakobson proposes that the resulting subordination of the referential function by the poetic function foregrounds the capacity of language to generate new references, at the expense of a 'splitting of reference'. The speaker and the interlocutor are doubled into the narrating agency and the narrated addressee, while reference is split into worldly context and imagined world. Contemporary theories of fictional utterance also highlight that literature involves a bracketing of normal reference, best grasped in terms of the idea that the literary text designates what is relevant through resemblance, without referring through predication. The result is a thorough-going ambiguity regarding who is representing what for whom. In Jakobson's analysis of Shakespeare's Sonnet 129, for instance, the result is significant difficulty in sorting out addresser and addressee in the poem. Additionally, the formal characteristics of the sonnet structure make the referent of the discourse shift between a metaphorical invocation of mortality and a metonymical naming of immorality (Jakobson 1987: 198–215, esp. 2–3).

Literary semblances

The rhetorical model involved literary texts as direct communication about the generalizable feelings towards the world that authors seek to persuade readers to adopt. The communicative model that I propose depends on the thesis that literary communication involves an indirectly presented rhetorical message. The indirectness of literature is evidently connected with the features of poetic language – the dominance of metaphor and metonymy over causal enchainment; and, the double reference of fictional narration – which 'wrap' rhetorical persuasion in a playful form. So, let's quickly round up the usual suspects – the ambivalent feelings that literature expresses, the notorious ambiguity of literary meaning, the equivocal character of literary reference – and make the standard allegation. Here is a field of imaginative play, rich in interpretive consequences, but poor in propositional or referential specificity. Literature is, of course, guilty as charged. But in bringing down the verdict, I think we need to proceed slowly.

Following Albrecht Wellmer, I intend to describe the aesthetic dimension of the literary text – the dimension that transcends rhetorical persuasion – as 'semblance' (Wellmer 1991). On the communicative model, literature involves semblances, coherent presentations of speculative experiences.[1] These semblances resemble real situations while referring to an imaginary world; that is, they designate their relevance to reality only through salience. Nonetheless, literary communication is always 'about' feelings towards the world, even when that 'aboutness' is elusive, because the semblance is a peculiar kind of interjection into lifeworld situations. It is precisely this

---

[1] Wellmer describes these as coherent presentations of *possible* experiences. But this would exclude the literature of the impossible – science fiction, fantasy literature and metafictional paradoxes. Hence: 'speculative'.

indirectness which opens up a space for readers to play with possible experiences and for critics to debate interpretations of the relevance of the work.

Now, the idea that semblances are speculative experiences invites the misconception that they consist of fused complexes of cognitive, normative and expressive validity claims, in an aesthetic form such that 'the whole exceeds the parts'. Literary texts present – or envision – worlds through poetic language: they are an imaginative envisionment of new perspectives on reality; just as philosophy is a reflexive and conceptual totalization of reality. The argument is seductive:

> The aesthetic 'validity' or 'unity' that we attribute to a work of art refers to its singularly illuminating power to open our eyes to what is seemingly familiar, to disclose anew an apparently familiar reality. This validity claim admittedly stands for a potential for 'truth' that can be released only in the whole complexity of life-experience; therefore, this 'truth-potential' may not be connected to (or even identified with) one of the three validity-claims constitutive for communicative action, as I have previously been inclined to maintain. The one-to-one relationship which exists between the prescriptive validity of a norm and the normative validity claims raised in speech acts is not a proper model for the relation between the potential for truth of works of art and the transformed relations between self and world stimulated by aesthetic experience. (Habermas 1998b: 415)

In that Wellmer-influenced position of Habermas, literary semblances catalyse a 'truth potential' that is released in the life praxis of readers through their transformation of speculative experience into actual experience. This is consistent with the concept of literary disclosure, something that I discuss in later chapters, but its present effect is to sunder literature from critique.

The difference between Habermas's disclosing model and the communicative model that I am proposing is the following. The disclosing model constructs literary semblances as potential experiences – fused validity claims – alloyed by poetic language, which are swallowed whole by readers. The communicative model proposes that rhetorical persuasion is detoured into indirectness by aesthetic construction, which has several consequences, none of which rules out critical analysis. First, semantic renewal is included in affective mapping, so that the literary text is not just a structure of feeling, but also a new means of articulation. This is the great insight of Georgy Lukács in his late aesthetics: 'literature is a projection from the intensive totality onto the extensive totality.' Second, because of their manifestly fictive status, literary semblances are characterized by equivocal reference, which means that it is uncertain whether the affective mapping is onto the imaginary world or social reality. That creates a space of vicarious experimentation, in which the reader can entertain imaginative possibilities while considering their potential implementation. I want to call this 'equivocal reference'. Third, the play of form and content, in the space of symbolic coherence, transforms the reader's horizon of expectations by alternating moments of surprise with spreading illumination. The reader is defamiliarized, relative to routinized forms and stereotypical contents, but they are simultaneously re-socialized in to a new symbolic coherence, thus transforming their receptivity to the imaginative possibilities suggested by the work. I want to call this 'symbolic coherence'. Literature is a playful provocation, an invitation to a thought experiment conducted in the subjunctive mood, rather than simply an aesthetic disguise for rhetorical persuasion. Nonetheless, its 'rational kernel' is rhetorical persuasion about generalizable feelings towards social reality, or what I have called affective mapping.

These considerations further clarify how the Habermasian perspective communicatively reframes Adorno's aesthetics of negation as an aesthetics of transformation. According to Adorno, expressive spontaneity, externalized through aesthetic mimesis, results in creative praxis as an anticipation of utopia, which is a negation of social reality. From the Habermasian perspective, literature involves the transformation of the relationship between the subjective domain and the social world, an intervention into the motivations and orientations of modern individuals. According to Adorno, the rationalization of aesthetic materials through advanced technique results in the artistic negation of existing art, generating an irreversible history of aesthetic progress as a sequence of radical and annihilating breakthroughs. From the Habermasian perspective, literature transforms the receptivity of individuals to semantic renewal and novel affective mappings, by inviting them to dialectically transcend their horizon of expectations. I now want to consider these two communicative reformulations, concerning equivocal reference and symbolic coherence, respectively, in more detail.

Literary interventions and equivocal reference

Literary semblances communicate about the (dis-)satisfaction of human needs in the social world, suggesting realignments of the motivations, orientation and meanings of modern individuals. Literary semblances supplement rhetorical persuasion about generalizable feelings towards the social world with an invitation to a vicarious experience in which the reader can experiment with fundamentally new attitudes. Equivocal reference is crucial to this capacity of literature to experiment with alternative forms of existence, because the play, or slippage, between resemblance to reality and reference to an imaginary world invokes the possibility of different ways of coping with that reality. But this shift, from currently existing motivations and orientations to a new set, arrived at by dialogue but prompted by literature, is not simply a 'translation' – in both the linguistic and the mathematical senses – that brings the reader from one position or semantics to another. Instead, it is a transformation. For the interpretive position that the reader ultimately arrives at is the result of a playful provocation in the subjunctive mood, and the critical or reflexive reader remains aware that it might have been read otherwise. Precisely because of equivocal reference, ambiguous meanings and ambivalent feelings, interpretations, ultimately about the relation to human needs, are rendered provisional and perspectival; in short, they are ironized, becoming post-traditional need-interpretations rather than dogmatic convictions about motivations and orientations, or a fixed semantics rigidified by stereotypes. Literary semblances communicate *ironically*, and this is central to their role in the exploration and development of the subjective world, for it explains how literature contributes to the formation of ego maturity, as well as to cultural tolerance, imaginative sympathy and reflexive authenticity.

The distance between a report on a chain of events and a fictional narrative has been specified through the poetic language hypothesis, which states that the predominance of metaphor and metonymy in literature suppresses (but does not eliminate) causal enchainment. A different way to state this insight would be to say that the resemblance to reality of literary semblances depends on their coordination of representations of reality with elements of invention. A point made by Kathryn Hume, though, is that describing *mimesis* and *phantasia* as 'impulses', rather than 'elements', makes it clear that it is impossible to analytically differentiate the two in any semblance, that is, in anything fictional that resembles reality (Hume 1984: 21). It is not as if the literary text can be neatly sorted into a heap of fictional bits and a pile of descriptions of real things. The literary semblance references an imaginary world at the same time that it resembles reality – but this relation of resemblance must be *global*, between the imaginary world and actual reality, not *piecemeal*, between a constellation of representations and items in reality.

The global relation between representation and reality creates a plausible possibility or potential vision of the world – a way of coping with reality – that is *relevant* to the readership. In Alfred Schutz's discussion of relevance as a lifeworld phenomenon, Schutz proposes that relevance involves arriving at the perception that an assumption needs to be questioned (Schutz 1970: 28). The notion of relevance, then, registers the surprising possibility that something significant might escape our attention, rather than the complacent assurance that all of the important factors have been taken into consideration. Social action transpires mainly through 'typified' schemes of interpretation that have become routinized and habitual. Perceptions become 'topically relevant' when they require an interpretation that goes beyond the current typification, while they become 'interpretively relevant' once the anomalous percept is systematically compared with the actor's 'stock of knowledge' (Schutz 1970: 54–66). At the same time, percepts are 'motivationally relevant' to the degree that the salient stock of knowledge concerns the values of the agent, especially survival (Schutz 1970: 35–44). Literature's capacity to represent, then, involves presenting a potential vision of the world that is a plausible possibility, relative to some definition of its relevance that makes the literary percept interpretively and motivationally significant.

Global equivocal reference through resemblance to reality happens in a space of playful provocation that, because it is both fictional and non-propositional, must be grasped as taking place in the subjunctive mood. This mood, which expresses an attitude towards something which is unreal (because futural, wishful, judgemental, opinionated or conjectural), opens an ironic potential that has immense developmental – or maturational – significance. Claire Colebrook, in her work on irony, points out that it is based on a gap between speaker's intention and the meaning of the statement (i.e. performative insincerity), or on a gap (i.e. performative inauthenticity), both of which point to its intrinsic relation to subjectivity (Colebrook 2004). Both types may be represented within literature. Specifically literary irony typically involves the gap between utterance and context, and depends on techniques of citation, pastiche, juxtaposition or satirical exaggeration. But the purpose of this is only sometimes to expose the emptiness (e.g. the lack of feeling, or the blind stereotyping) of something cited ironically. Sometimes it is to disturb any absoluteness of judgement about the structures of feeling towards the world presented in the work. This kind of irony, typical of contemporary fiction, which tends to be global, rather than local, relativizes judgements about human needs and the social world, making the recipient aware that their position is entirely provisional (Hutcheon 1988: 45). In the work of the German Romantics, such as Friedrich Schlegel, consciousness of provisionality was inflated into thinking in contradictions, so that 'irony is the form of paradox' (Colebrook 2004: Schelegel cited). By introducing a pragmatic theory of truth within the framework of intersubjectivity, in a context where it is certainly possible to revise statements in light of discoveries about the things they designate, Habermas removes irony from the Romantic locus of subjective relativism (Habermas 1998b: 343–82).

The significance of literature's mapping of the subjective world onto the social world *as provisional* can be seen in Habermas's long article on 'Moral Development and Ego Identity' (Habermas 1979b: 69–94). There, Habermas advances the notion of the maturity of the ego (or 'ego identity') as the criterion by which to measure the rationality gains made in science, morality and literature in the modern world. The concept of ego identity – a psychoanalytically derived and post-metaphysical replacement for idealist notions of the autonomy of the transcendental subject – is the enlightenment ideal that unconstrained communication presupposes (Habermas 1979b:

93). Ego identity means the ability to narrate a unique life history as a developmental sequence 'under the guidance of general principles and modes of procedure', within which impulse satisfactions are integrated with cognitive and moral accomplishments (Habermas 1979b: 91). Accordingly, ego identity integrates the three aspects of personality development which relate to the three referential worlds of external nature, internal nature and the social world: cognitive development, moral development and motivational development. In a characteristic schematizing move, Habermas proposes that the general stages of development in each aspect of personality are all reciprocal preconditions of one another, so that the structures of the ego can be clearly related to degrees of reflexivity (Habermas 1979b: 91). The following table summarizes this discussion (Habermas 1979b: 84).

The exact details of Piaget and Kohlberg's developmental models need not detain us here. In relation to motivational structures, Habermas's reconstruction of the ego-psychological, object-relations, interactional-psychological and empirical-developmental literature is exhaustive (and inconclusive), but its main thrust is a prolongation of his discussion of psychoanalysis in *Knowledge and Human Interests*. I discuss this in detail in the next chapter – a brief summary suffices for now. The quasi-biological notion of instinctual impulses must be replaced by the notion of the psychic representation of drives acquired via the process of socialization, without this losing its conceptual connection to its somatic basis in the natural body.

TABLE 5.1 *Habermas's Theory of Referential Domains and Psychological Development*

External nature (Cognitive development via Piaget)	**Social world (morality)** (Moral development via Kohlberg)	**Internal nature (motivation)** (Motivational development via reconstructive argument)
Stage I Pre-operational	*Stage I* Pre-conventional	*Stage I* Egocentric pleasure/pain continuum
Stage II Concrete-operational	*Stage II* Conventional	*Stage II* Quasi-natural 'culturally interpreted needs [whose] satisfaction depends on following socially recognized expectations'
Stage III Formal-operational	*Stage III* Post-conventional	*Stage III* Post-traditional 'critique and justification of need interpretations' as action orientating motivations

Habermas describes these as 'cultural need-interpretations' and rejects the idea that the dynamics of these drives can be described through the notion of libido. Instead, focusing on clinical practice, Habermas argues that these are best described linguistically, in terms of culturally symbolized motivations arising from socialized need-interpretations, and repressed material with the character of 'linguistically excommunicated' need-interpretations. Motivational development consists of integrating repressed components into the individual's narration of their life history, which is equivalent to a dismantling of ego defences and a reduction of superego pressure, together with the global restricting of the ego to reflect a new relation to interpreted needs (Habermas 1979b: 70). In short, the mature ego is capable of reintegrating formerly repressed inclinations into socially legitimate motivational dispositions by means of a critique of the limitations of their cultural tradition (Habermas 1979b: 93). This conception of ego flexibility in terms of a reflexive relation to motivational dispositions then connects with flexibility towards cognitive and normative questions. These strictly defined stages of development all express a reflexive de-centring of experience where persons become capable of adopting hypothetical attitudes towards the natural world, taking up the moral positions of others, and considering the need-interpretations of other cultures (or counter-cultures) as potentially valid.

Literary innovation and symbolic coherence

Critical debates sparked by literary interventions potentially transform individuals' relation to human needs, from traditional to post-traditional frames, while bringing into question the institutional arrangements and social values that belong to now-superseded need-interpretations. At the same time, because literary interventions present conjectures about transformations of subjectivity, they must break with the routinized means of expression that merely sediment stereotypical or prejudicial relations between motivations and orientations. Accordingly, critical debates about literary semblances necessarily include dialogue about aesthetic innovation, but from a communicative perspective, these arguments involve a relation between literary text and public context. Considerations of the dialectics of materials and technique, and form and content, relate to the horizon of expectations relevant to this context. Literary innovation is a question of a novel opening in meaning and experience, in a relevant situation and for a concrete readership, before it is a matter of the coherence of aesthetic form and social content.

The poetic language hypothesis explains how literary materials and writing techniques are combined into a repertoire of aesthetic contents, which are provided with form through the activity of the 'projection' of 'principles' in the distinctive formations of poetry and prose. A fictional narrative consists of a succession of events activated or experienced by characters, in which a chain of contiguous images provides the illusion of a linked sequence of actions (the plot), one that seems to unfold in diegetic time by virtue of implied or explicit causal connections (the story). In other words, the novel is about 'the experience of what happens', the enigma of an exemplary event, something which supplementary formal operations of parallelism, marking and sequencing help the readership to feel and see. Formal operations in the text (such as parallelism, marking and sequencing) lead to a cognitive process in decoding the symbolic coherence of the literary text, at the same time as the network of similarities and differences that they support in the imagined world leads to conjectures about the work's relevance to the individual and society. These considerations make it possible to communicatively reframe Adorno's position. Habermasian literary aesthetics accepts, from Adorno, the dialectical relation between form and content, and its relevance for the question of the individual's relation to society. But the communicative perspective insists that the temporal unfolding of fictional narration structures the reception of the literary message in a specific way, as a process of the violation and revision of expectations, within which the imaginary world exists in flux. Accordingly, 'the dynamic of reading is not only a process of the formation, development, modification and replacement of hypotheses ... but also, simultaneously, as the construction of frames, their transformation and dismantling' (Rimmon-Kenan 1983: 123–4). It is this process, within which readers transiently entertain constructs and undergo vicarious experiences, together with an associated ambivalence, ambiguity, uncertainty and provisionality, which sparks the interpretive debate between readers.

These considerations bring the communicative perspective into dialogue with the reception aesthetics of Hans Robert Jauss, who reframes literary experience within the concept of the horizon of expectations, a concept that he develops from the same hermeneutic sources as Habermas used to develop the concept of the lifeworld. Jauss proposes to reconceptualize literary history, not as a history of authorial production, but as a history of transformations of the readers' horizon of expectations, by radical literary innovations (Jauss 1982a: 46–75). The implied reader approaches the text from a cultural background that informs in advance the literary expectations and imaginative repertoire that can be brought to bear on the task of the concretization of the work. The text that minimizes the gap between poetic language and everyday communication maximizes the likelihood that it will be regarded by the reader as plausible, at the cost of the failure to disturb the ideological assumptions layered within the horizon of expectations. The text that disturbs the horizon of expectations in a way that is transformative rather than simply idiosyncratic effectively restructures this horizon, widening or shrinking it, and thereby deposits itself is a crucial element of the cultural heritage. The sequence of texts that is regarded at any moment in historical time as canonical is therefore in actuality a sequence series of horizons of expectation that: (1) is permanently susceptible to revision and (2) constitutes the genealogy of the present. Literary history is not an evolutionary sequence regulated by a developmental law. Accordingly, the aesthetic of reception developed by Jauss is an aesthetics of negativity that differs from Adorno's notion that the radical works consign the rest to the dustbin of history only in its inclusion of the reader in the process of sorting the garbage.

Following the publication of Adorno's aesthetic theory, Jauss turned from the aesthetics of negativity to the question of whether literature could be both progressive and positive, corresponding to communication with an enlightened readership (Johnson 1987). For Jauss, the valorization of modernist dissonance in the aesthetic of negativity has the potential to result in a form of cultural elitism that denies the communicative potential of literature and equates illegibility with innovation (Jauss 1982b: 13–21). The validity of Jauss's position depends on the continued existence of critical public sphere, which is questionable. But what Jauss and Adorno both neglect is the possibility that an emancipatory literature might communicate positively with an enlightened *counter*-public sphere, while at the same time (implicitly or explicitly) negating the bourgeois public sphere of 'actually existing democracy'. Meanwhile, strangely, for Jauss, although the needs and desires communicated by the text do not have to be separated from the question of the entertainment value of the text, the pleasure of reading that he proposes is a disinterested pleasure distinct from play. Like Adorno, he thinks aesthetic pleasure involves an unmediated surrender of the ego to the (imaginary) object. From the Habermasian perspective, the distinction between instinctual gratification in commodity aesthetics and sublimated pleasure gained from literary experience is best grasped in terms of how the playful text solicits the critical engagement of the ego and proposes ego ideals as points of identification. A literary intervention involves literary innovation to the degree that its transformation of the horizon of expectations of a determinate, concrete readership leads to critical engagement and sparks emulation, resulting in an emancipatory shift in attitudes. From the Habermasian perspective, the key to this is the way that novel forms of symbolic coherence make new social contents – a transformed subjective world – relevant to readerships, so that even though literary history can be constituted through localized sequences of innovative rupture, a completely formalist approach is excluded.

6

Silenced needs, hidden desires

In the present chapter, I deepen the idea of the therapeutic social role of literature by exploring the connection between literary critique and psychoanalysis. At the same time, I expand the notion of the socially critical role of literature, through the idea that literature criticizes socially silenced human needs and expresses culturally hidden desires. In the last chapter, I proposed that literary critique involves the articulation of post-traditional need-interpretations. It is now necessary to acknowledge that traditional need-interpretations often involve the repression – the silencing and hiding – of 'unnatural' needs and 'abominable' desires. Post-traditional need-interpretations are therefore generally the result of the retrieval of silenced needs and hidden desires. The Habermasian idea of psychoanalysis as both a depth hermeneutic and a cultural dialogue provides the key to the process of recovery of repressed material. Habermas's concepts of repression as the 'ex-communication of forbidden need interpretations', and therapy as the reverse operation, a 'linguistification of the unconscious', point towards the specific role of literature in the process. Poetic language and the dream report have many common features, making literature another 'royal road to the unconscious'. The difference is that whereas the therapeutic setting involves the resolution of symptoms, literary dialogue involves new forms of sublimation. However, it is crucial not to confuse sublimation with affirmative culture, for new forms of sublimation may be culturally insurgent and socially critical.

Unfortunately, because of Habermas's problematic encounter with psychoanalytic theory, specifying how this works is something that demands a critical reconstruction of Habermas's position. Accordingly, I begin this chapter by returning to Habermas's reading of Freud in *Knowledge and Human Interests* (1968), in order to reclaim his insights into psychoanalytic theory. I show how Habermas twists his reading of Freud in order to fit it into an alien problem – the derivation of a human interest in emancipatory knowledge, which Habermas himself subsequently abandoned – and in the process, de-natures his psychoanalytic source, Alfred Lorenzer. Once Habermas's position on psychoanalysis is amended, it becomes both defensible and plausible, providing Critical Theory with a post-metaphysical philosophical anthropology that yields a human interest in the integration of the subjective world. That interest supports the demand for human happiness that Habermas's discourse-ethical position otherwise struggles to explicate. Framed in narrative terms as the coherent reconstruction of a life history, this connects with both Eriksonian theories about successful ego maturation and Alessandro Ferrara's ideas about self-fulfilment as reflexive authenticity. Furthermore, it clarifies the stakes in literature's critical revelations about silenced needs and experimental testing of hidden desires, linking the therapeutic role of literature to the critique of irrational forms of social authority.

Knowledge and human interests

The keys to a Habermasian transformation of Freud are implied by his reading of psychoanalysis, not as a scientific psychology, but as a depth hermeneutic. 'The object domain of depth hermeneutics', Habermas explains, 'comprises all of the places where, owing to internal disturbances, the text of everyday language games is interrupted by incomprehensible symbols' (KHI: 226 [278–9]). The task of depth hermeneutics is to translate these 'privatized hieroglyphs' into intersubjective symbolizations, rather than to provide explanatory causes modelled on the physical sciences. The model here is Hegel's notion of the 'causality of fate': unmastered intersubjective influences manifest in the lives of individuals as an external objectivity – 'fate' – causally determining their activities as if they were subjected to a 'second nature'. The aim of critical analysis is to dissolve quasi-natural determinations back into the historico-social intersubjectivity from whence they came, releasing the ego from ideological mystification or unconscious self-deception.

Against this background, in *Knowledge and Human Interests*, Habermas seeks to do three things simultaneously. First, he proposes a post-metaphysical philosophical anthropology – a theory of human nature from a pragmatic perspective – as the foundation for social critique, thereby linking science, morality and therapy to human interests in the objective, social and subjective worlds. Second, Habermas advances towards the theory of communicative action by reconstructing science, morality and therapy after the linguistic turn, as fields of intersubjective agreement rather than as domains of positive knowledge of facts. Third, he suggests that social critique, as grounded through this intersubjective and post-metaphysical approach, issues in a new conception of emancipatory praxis, one that is oriented to critical dialogue rather than directed by the vanguard party. Throughout, the aim is to replace the philosophy of the subject with a materialist theory of ego formation, grounded in the insight that 'the achievements of the transcendental subject have their basis in the natural history of the human species' (KHI: 312 [383]). At the same time, linguistic intersubjectivity indicates how human interests 'derive both from nature and from the cultural break with nature' (KHI: 312 [383]).

According to Habermas, humanity has three 'knowledge constitutive human interests' (technical, social, emancipatory), which result in scientific, normative and critical knowledge. To clarify this insight, he proposes a post-metaphysical philosophical anthropology consistent with pragmatist philosophy. Instead of speculation about human nature, Habermas focuses on working backwards from knowledge formations to a reconstruction of the knowledge-constitutive human interests that can be inferred from the varieties of propositional discourse. In this construction, natural instincts are inferential presuppositions of human interests, rather than speculative constructions that ground analysis in a metaphysical foundation. The natural instinct for self-preservation may be assumed to be the driver for a persistent struggle for technical control over the natural environment, which clarifies why there exists a knowledge-constitutive human interest in scientific knowledge. A social instinct for communicative interaction may be assumed to be the driver for a human interest in political order and social justice, presumably animating the knowledge-constitutive human interest in practical knowledge. Finally, there is an emancipatory human interest in liberation from power, which means that there is a knowledge-constitutive human interest in critical reflection – paradigmatically, psychoanalysis (KHI: 313 [384]).

Although Habermas is right to seek an alternative to the Leninist militarization of politics, there are definitely questions about the proposal to replace political intervention with psychoanalytic dialogue (McCarthy 1996: 75–90). But I do not think that is the main problem. The main problem is that Habermas believes that he has to ground the praxis of liberation in a specifically emancipatory human interest in critical self-reflection. After reconstructing the natural sciences and practical hermeneutics, Habermas turns to psychoanalysis to provide a model. Here, Habermas proposes that psychoanalysis discovers a human interest in freedom from quasi-natural constraints imposed by power. This intention, subsequently abandoned, interferes with Habermas's reading of Freud as a depth hermeneutic aimed at reconnecting normative orientations with their underlying motivations.

At this precise point, Habermas turns Freud into Fichte. Nowhere is this more evident than in Habermas's wholesale revision of the concept of the id. According to Habermas, id equals alienated ego: 'the ego [takes] flight from itself . . . the self's identity with the defended-against part of the psyche [i.e., the repressed] is denied; the latter is reified, for the ego, into a neuter, an id (it)' (KHI: 242–3 [296]). Here, the Freudian model of repression is drastically revised to exclude the possibility that basic repression includes the ego turning aside potentially anti-social libidinal and aggressive drives, which classically lead to incestuous and murderous wishes. Instead, the action of repression is entirely attributed to the superego, 'which anchors in the personality structure itself the repressive demands of society against "surplus" instinctual aims', directing the ego to 'ex-communicate' socially prohibited need-interpretations (KHI: 243 [297]). 'The psychically most effective way [for the ego] to render undesired need dispositions harmless is to *exclude from public communication the interpretations* to which they are attached' (KHI: 223–34 [275]). Accordingly, '*what is unconscious is removed from public communication*', ex-communicated, forming a static reservoir of privatized motivations, or semantic contents, which can be expressed only through the 'foreign language' of symptoms (KHI: 238 [290]). The implication is that, contra Freud, it *is* theoretically possible to empty the unconscious. There is no quasi-natural kernel to human subjectivity, no *limit* to what Habermas otherwise rightly calls the 'linguistification of the unconscious'.

Now, following Thomas McCarthy's penetrating critique, Habermas abandoned the emancipatory interest in critical self-reflection and rethought its intersubjective and post-metaphysical aspects as the theory of communicative action. In the process of retreating from the extravagant claim to have detected a naturally related human interest in emancipatory critique, Habermas also jettisoned – rather than corrected – important aspects of the concept of the unconscious, emptying out the notion of linguistification. Although Habermas did not entirely renounce psychoanalysis, what did happen was that the role of psychoanalysis changed valence in the architecture of Habermas's thought. Crucially, Habermas claimed that he had shifted from a symbolically mediated version of psychoanalysis to the psychoanalytic ego psychology of Heinz Hartmann and cothinkers, and then to the developmental psychology of Piaget, Kohlberg and Loevinger (Habermas 1979b). But it would be wrong to imagine that developmental psychology replaces psychoanalytic theory entirely. Habermas continues to look to psychoanalysis to relate the theory of defence mechanisms to intrapsychic and interpersonal disturbances. Loevinger, meanwhile, is merely 'filling in a gap in psychoanalytic facts and theories' (Loevinger 1983: 347).

Habermas: The linguistification of the unconscious

Against the background of these qualifications, Habermas's interpretation of psychoanalysis as the 'linguistification of the unconscious' reframes psychoanalysis after the linguistic turn. The cornerstone of Habermas's reading of Freud is the claim that psychoanalytic 'depth hermeneutics' became reified because Freud lacked a theory of language that might have articulated a symbolic conception of the unconscious (KHI: 238 [293]). For Habermas, the unconscious consists of socially prohibited need-interpretations that have been split off from public discourse, 'excommunicated' into a 'privatized' quasi-language, so that unconscious desires can now only be expressed in a distorted, disguised form, as symptoms (KHI: 240–2 [295–7]). Psychoanalytic therapy consists in the 'linguistification of the unconscious', the cooperative invention of a manual of translation, a 'Rosetta Stone' for the 'foreign language' of the analysand's symptoms, which releases the forbidden need-interpretations back into communicative circulation (KHI: 227–30 [282–6]). The linguistification of the unconscious makes it possible for a Habermasian position to reframe the classical Frankfurt School's idea of the utopian vocation of literature as the therapeutic role of literary critique. Instead of an anticipation of the eroticization of the personality, the therapeutic role of literature involves the restoration of the narrative continuity of individuals' life histories, as a communicative working through of repression. Furthermore, critique oriented by psychoanalysis recasts the diagnosis of surplus repression and regressive desublimation as deformations to personality structures, caused by increasingly primitive defence mechanisms.

Habermas argues that psychoanalytic therapy can succeed only in the medium of dialogue because repression involves the splitting-off of need-interpretations from linguistic symbols – 'what is unconscious is removed from public communication' (KHI: 227 [282]). He reinterprets Freud's claim that repression involves the sundering of 'word presentations' from 'object presentations' (linked to affective intensities) as the 'splitting off of individual symbols from public communication [which] means at the same time the privatisation of their semantic content' (KHI: 242 [295]). The symptoms characteristic of neurosis (hysteria, obsession, phobia), perversion (fetishism) and psychosis (delusional projections and ego fragmentation) are therefore attempts by the self to restore communication with itself about its own identity. This process is grasped clinically in terms of the restoration to continuity of the narrative of an individual life history, in which the gaps and rents inflicted by repression are filled in by a conscious self-formative process of the maturation of the ego (KHI: 227–30 [282–6]).

The restoration of the lost portion of a life history is a process of emancipation, not just of enlightenment, because the superego, which governs the censoring of the instincts, is a representation of socially sanctioned expectations. The superego 'anchors in the personality structure itself the repressive demands of society against "excessive" instinctual aims', so that the elimination of repression is simultaneously a revolution against the superego (KHI: 243 [296]). The 'libidinally bound basic propositions' of the superego, hitherto 'immunized against critical objections', are thrown into question by a mature ego now capable of self-regulating and self-governing (KHI: 244 [297–8]). Psychoanalytic therapy simultaneously 'changes a life' by finding culturally acceptable need-interpretations, and sparks a critique of power leading to the resolution of personal suffering (KHI: 212, 284 [254, 341]).

According to Habermas's reconstruction of Freud's developmental typology, the infantile ego is confronted by cultural prohibitions of some of its interpretations of needs, in the form of parental representations of social authority and its potential sanctions. The result is that the ego takes flight from its own desires, hiding these in and as the id, so that 'the "id" is then the name for the part of the self that is alienated through defense mechanisms, while "ego" is the agency that fulfils the task of reality-testing and censorship of instinctual impulses' (KHI: 242 [295]). In sum:

> The learning mechanisms described by Freud... make understandable the dynamics of the genesis of [these] ego structures at the level of symbolic interaction. The defense mechanisms intervene in this process when and where social norms, incorporated in the expectations of primary reference persons, confront the infantile ego with unbearable force.... The child's development is [thereafter] defined by problems whose solution determines whether and to what extent further socialisation is burdened with the weight of unresolved conflicts and restricted ego functions – or whether the socialisation process makes possible a relative development of ego identity.... [T]his history is represented schematically as a self-formative process... that has as its telos the self-consciousness of a reflectively appropriated life history. (KHI: 257–9 [318–21])

Habermas's recasting of ego, superego and id as loci, within a subjectivity constituted through linguistically mediated intersubjectivity, facilitates the replacement of 'hypotheses about instinctual vicissitudes with assumptions about identity formation' (TCA2: 389 [544]). In particular, the linguistification of the unconscious makes it possible to 'take up the theory of defense mechanisms in such a way that that interconnections between intra-psychic communication barriers and communication disturbances at the interpersonal level become comprehensible' (TCA2: 389 [544]). The Habermasian interpretation of drive energies as need-interpretations is intended to shift psychoanalysis, via the linguistic turn, into a form of post-metaphysical philosophy:

> It is only from the point of view of a reifying theory of the drives that the extra-linguistic referent of both the structure and autonomy of 'inner nature' gets lost, along with the vocabulary of instinct and drive energy, cathexis, displacement and so forth. The essential difference consists

only in replacing 'drive energies' with 'interpreted needs', and describing 'instinctual vicissitudes' from the perspective of identity formation. On this reading, inspired by the theory of communication, inner nature is not in any way vaporised into a culturalist haze. (Habermas 1998b: 426–7)

But as Joel Whitebook has shown in a major critique of the Habermasian reading of Freud, there is a significant problem with Habermas's conception of the unconscious as a 'secondary process' resulting from social pressures, rather than a 'primary process' based on impulses (Whitebook 1995). In concert with several other critics (Alford 1987; Flynn 1985; MacKendrick 2008: 58–85), Whitebook argues that the central Habermasian claim, that unconscious wishes are best described as need-interpretations (KHI: 241–2 [296]), represents an erasure of nature (Whitebook 1995: 184).

Habermas: Post-metaphysical psychoanalysis

Habermas is not prepared to ground the critique of surplus repression in the vicissitudes of the instincts. This is because it seems to him to mortgage Critical Theory to a philosophical anthropology based in speculative metaphysics. For Habermas, the critique of surplus repression must be grounded in an analysis of ego deformation and communicative distortion. But in explicating this through an entirely linguistic conception of the unconscious, Habermas misses the opportunity to specify the action of symbolization on the imagistic content of repressed material, and its relation to naturally derived impulse potentials.

According to Whitebook, Habermas's excessively social conception of the human being presupposes a notion of the absolute plasticity of natural instincts that is hopelessly idealist (Whitebook 1979). In (rightly) going beyond the Marcusean conflation of 'perversion and utopia', Habermas neglects the 'thicket of non-linguisticality at the centre of the subject' (Whitebook 1995: 167). He therefore loses sight of the unruly naturalness, the asocial sociability, at the heart of the human being, as well as the human animal's belonging to the natural environment. Habermas does so at exactly the same moment that he turns aside from his own insight: the 'store of semantic energies', based in biology, which criticism must redeem from aesthetic traditions, holds the key to humanity's motivation for struggling for a better world. For Habermas, 'we need those rescued semantic potentials if we are to interpret the world in terms of our own needs, and only if the source of these potentials does not run dry can the claim to happiness be fulfilled' (Habermas 1979a: 57).

Specifically, Whitebook argues that an exclusively symbolic conception of the unconscious is unsustainable from any psychoanalytic perspective that claims inspiration from Freud. This is because 'something that is wished is represented ... as a scene' (Whitebook 1995: 186 Freud cited). Now, Habermas's position on the characteristics of unconscious symbols and their relation to natural instincts is often expressed in terms that seem exclusively linguistic – 'privatized semantics', 'need-interpretations' – especially when Habermas rejects the concept of drive energy.

Habermas's focus on a symbolic conception of the unconscious, together with the idea of ego, superego and id as intersubjectively constituted loci, has led to the observation that 'Habermas is remarkably close to Lacan' (Dews 1995; Whitebook 1995: 181). Actually, that is not so surprising, since Habermas's source is the psychoanalysis of Alfred Lorenzer, a figure whose work is convergent with Jacques Lacan (Heim 1980). In a highly condensed discussion, Habermas claims that instinctual impulses are accessible only as motivational structures that are symbolically mediated, which is what he means by need-interpretations (KHI: 252–3 [313]). But it is also important to notice that Habermas gets Lorenzer wrong. He conflates the intersubjective constitution of the psyche with an *exclusively* social and symbolic conception of the unconscious. Habermas summarizes:

> [As] linguistically interpreted needs ... motivations are not [quasi-natural] impulses ... but subjectively guiding, symbolically mediated and reciprocally interrelated, intentions .... Impulse potential, whether incorporated in social systems of self-preservation or suppressed instead of absorbed, clearly reveals libidinal and aggressive tendencies. That is why an instinct theory is necessary [but] ... the concept of instinct ... is derived privatively ... from a motivational structure that depends simultaneously on publicly communicated, and repressed and privatised, need interpretations. The original defensive process ... removes from public communication the linguistic interpretation of the motive of action that is being defended against. In this way, the grammatical structure of public language remains intact, but portions of its semantic content are privatised: symptom formation is a substitute for a symbol whose function has been altered. The split-off symbol has not simply lost all connection to public language, but its connection has, as it were, gone underground .... The essentially grammatical connection between linguistic symbols [now] appears as a causal connection between empirical events and rigidified personality. (KHI, 255–9 [312–16])

The problem is that this incompletely surveys a crucial part of the work of Lorenzer, on whom Habermas relies for his conception of psychoanalysis as a depth hermeneutic concerned with unconscious symbolism (KHI: 256n19 [313n64]). It is certainly the case that Lorenzer proposes that a symbol or symptom in the dream or practice represents a personal semantics rather than a public communication (Lorenzer 1970a: 70–1; 1970b: 66–7). But for Lorenzer, the id precedes the ego, just as the primary process of the unconscious precedes the secondary process of consciousness. The unconscious is not the alienation of the ego, but a dynamic reservoir of 'symbolic figures' for 'scenic representations', which are connected to 'impulse potentials' (Lorenzer 1986: 40–4). 'The unconscious is a non-verbal, non-conventional system of meaning, which is contrary to the symbolic order that an individual is inserted into'; furthermore, the unconscious is 'autonomous', 'systematic' and 'meaningful', because its symbols are representations of memories (Lorenzer 1986: 46–7).

Following Lorenzer, it becomes possible to modify Habermas's position that motivations are symbolically mediated need-interpretations, by acknowledging that they *do* have a quasi-natural origin and they *are* based on scenic representations. I think that the most economical way to do this is to refer to the familiar Peircean distinctions between (caused) indices, (motivated) icons and (conventional) symbols. An 'index' is a sign causally related to its referent (e.g. signature, fingerprint). An 'icon' is a sign that refers by means of resemblance (e.g. onomatopoeia, pictures). Such signs are 'motivated' by their (historically and socially variable) verisimilitude as images of the referent. A 'symbol' is unmotivated, or entirely conventional, in its relation to the referent. The implication of the symbol's lack of motivation is that every referent can be described in a transfinite number of ways by the total repertoire of a culture's signifying resources. It is just a question of inventing new articulations.

Notice that on this definition, a symptom is a pseudo-symbol, because it is a motivated sign. It is close to an icon. This is part of the sense of symptoms as 'hieroglyphs' and dreams as a 'rebus'. On Freud's definition, which Lorenzer retains, the symptom is a compromise formation, between the pressure of the id and the censorship of the ego. The obsessive ritual or somatic conversion is motivated, via a chain of associations, by the forbidden need-interpretation that it distantly resembles. But the semantic content of this resemblance is repressed, privatized.

For Lorenzer, in the unconscious, natural instincts are represented in the psyche as impulse potentials linked to elemental scenic representations, or, archaic images. Lorenzer's theory of the unconscious as a dynamic reservoir of 'scenic representations' implies that subsequent satisfaction events resemble the original event. Paradigmatically, for psychoanalysis, such iconic images are erogenous zones located on the bodily image of the ego and cathected to part objects located on the image of the body of the other. The unity of an impulse potential with an iconic image, or scenic representation, is a need, which Habermas (confusingly) describes as a 'paleo-symbol'. Following Lorenzer once again, Habermas describes this as the semantic content of a symbolized desire. What the term 'desire' adds to the semantic content of the need is a request for satisfaction (equivalent to a demand for recognition), that is, speech addressed to the other. Conversely, linguistification of the unconscious is a process, not of draining impulse potentials, but of converting privatized icons into public symbols.

DIAGRAM 6.1 *A motivation is a need-interpretation, where a symbolization of desire is the interpreter of a semantic content that is imagistic and impulsive*

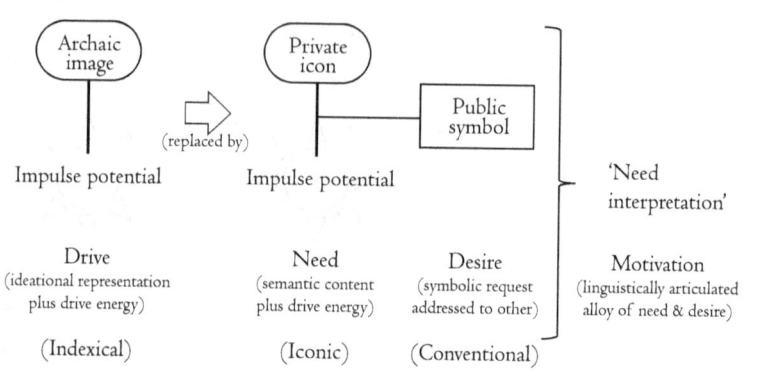

A motivation is therefore, as Habermas says, a need-interpretation, that is, a semantics of desire linked to a symbolization of desire. This is ego-syntonic when it can be articulated through public communication. It is ego-dystonic when can be articulated only through inhibitions, symptoms and anxieties. Lorenzer's version of the linguistification of the unconscious, in other words, also leads to a social psychoanalysis, but it does so without dispensing with the peculiarly imagistic and libidinally dynamic character of unconscious thinking.

The distinction between motivated icons and conventional symbols clarifies the concept of 'fixation', linked to repression, for motivated signs are by definition 'fixed' by resemblance, whereas conventional signs are 'unfixed', capable of transinfinite articulation. It also clarifies Habermas's insight that neurosis is a private mythology, for this is formed from iconic signs which, through relations of condensation and displacement, and in the context of ambivalence, have an articulation that strongly resembles mythological and magical thinking.

The task of psychoanalysis is to transform fixated, iconic (i.e. mythical) imagery into conventional symbols, which can then be flexibly re-articulated onto new need-interpretations. Such a modification accepts the force of Whitebook's critique but maintains the *Bilderverbot*, the ban on images, in the transition to linguistically mediated intersubjectivity. The figurative potentials of language, evident in literary uses of poetic language, are therefore a crucial resource in the transformation of need-interpretations into generalizable motivations. Habermas thinks about the resulting mature ego identity in terms of it becoming 'unconstrained' and 'flexible'. It is to a non-metaphorical interpretation of those terms that I now turn.

Ego maturity and life history

According to Habermas, reframing psychoanalysis through linguistically mediated intersubjectivity makes it possible to reformulate 'hypotheses about instinctual vicissitudes, as assumptions about identity formation' (TCA2: 389 [544]). In particular, the linguistification of the unconscious makes it possible to 'take up the theory of defense mechanisms in such a way that that interconnections between intra-psychic communication barriers and communication disturbances at the interpersonal level become comprehensible' (TCA2: 389 [544]). It should therefore be possible to reformulate pathological defence mechanisms as communicative disturbances that result in ego deformations. That links the critique of ideology as distorted communication to the normative standard provided by the ideal of ego maturity. It is important to notice that this critical standard is extraordinarily demanding:

> The model of [mature] ego identity is richer and more ambitious than a model of autonomy developed exclusively from perspectives of morality .... The transition ... from a formalist ethic of duty to a universal ethics of speech can be found in the fact that need interpretations are no longer assumed as given, but are drawn into the discursive formation of will. Internal nature is thereby moved into a utopian perspective; that is, at this stage, internal nature may no longer be merely examined within an interpretive framework fixed by the cultural tradition in a naturelike way .... Inner nature is rendered communicatively fluid and transparent to the extent that needs can, through aesthetic forms of expression, be kept articulable or be released from their paleosymbolic pre-linguisticality. But that means that internal nature is not subject, in the cultural preformation met with at any given time, to the demands of ego autonomy; rather, through a dependent ego it obtains free access to the interpretive possibilities of the cultural tradition. In the medium of value-forming and norm-forming communications into which aesthetic experiences enter, traditional cultural contents are no longer simply the stencils according to which needs are shaped; on the contrary, in this medium, needs can seek and find adequate expression. (Habermas 1979b: 93)

The transformation of need-interpretations from cultural icons stencilled by tradition to post-traditional symbolizations evidently connects with the programme, influenced by Lorenzer, of socio-symbolic psychoanalysis. But Habermas's reliance on Lorenzer is tempered by his interest in both ego psychology and developmental psychology (Habermas 1998b: 389). Although this reflects encyclopaedic reading in psychology and psychoanalysis (Habermas 1979b: 73n7), it also risks a confusing proliferation of terms. I therefore want to specify the hierarchy and relation of categories involved, as follows.

DIAGRAM 6.2 *Partitioning of the subject – ego, superego and id – into functional domains*

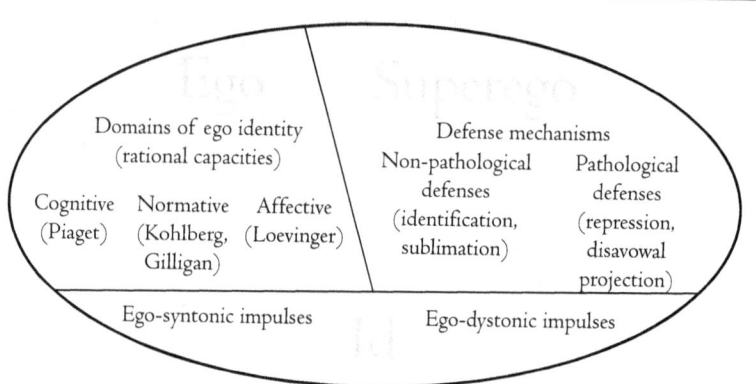

The category of ego identity embraces both the three subdomains of ego capacities dealt with by developmental psychology, *and* the coordination of defence mechanisms with the superego, dealt with by ego psychology. Methodologically, the construction is legitimate because developmental psychology originates from ego psychology and represents a specialization within it. Its genesis is Heinz Hartmann's explorations of the synthetic (i.e. rational) capacities of the ego when it is motivated by ego-syntonic impulses and oriented by guilt-free ideals. Accordingly, the distinction between the two regions – ego capacities and ego defences – has to do with the mobile border between ego-syntonic and ego-dystonic impulses, with their corresponding need-interpretations. In effect, there is a division of labour between ego psychology and developmental psychology. In general, developmental psychology investigates how, in ego maturation, ego-*syntonic* impulses are placed under the ego's rational control through an ascending series of developmental stages in thinking capacity. Meanwhile, ego psychology investigates how ego-*dystonic* impulses are repelled or transformed by the defence mechanisms of the ego, often resulting in pathological symptoms.

What, then, is a *mature* ego identity? When Habermas uses the term 'maturity' [*Mündigkeit*], he generally does so in a context defined by the normative concept of moral autonomy (Habermas 1999b: 116–94). It might therefore seem tempting to think that ego maturity involves ticking off the highest stages in all three developmental boxes, in the context of passing the hurdle requirement of an ego identity that does not significantly rely on pathological defence mechanisms. But two considerations militate against this neat schema.

The first has to do with the fact that the expressive subdomain of affect regulation, involving rational controls over impulse potentials, achieved through symbolizations of need-interpretations, does not actually exhibit 'stages of development' (Kohlberg et al. 1983). Developmental psychology describes the subdomains of ego-syntonic synthetic activity in terms of structural stages that are universal, hierarchical and irreversible (except through regression), with good success in relation to cognitive (Jean Piaget) and normative (Lawrence Kohlberg and Carol Gilligan) capacities. The subdomain of impulse control and affect regulation, by contrast, has proven stubbornly resistant to formalizations that pass tests of cultural neutrality. That is probably because investigation in this region is troubled by the same limitation (i.e. the problem of evaluative judgement) that restricts the universality of critique relative to discourse. There is no universally applicable list of 'higher' and 'lower' need-interpretations, so that traditional and post-traditional need-interpretations are not susceptible to sorting into two classes. Indeed, beyond adopting the idea of post-/traditional need-interpretations, Habermas is highly critical of Jane Loevinger's efforts to formulate 'stages' of ego identity based on affective development (Habermas 1979b: 75). What this suggests is that the concept of post-traditional and traditional needs is a quality of synthesis (reflective and unreflective), rather than a description of two stages in impulse control, traditional and post-traditional.

The second is that ego identity passes through several phases of maturation. The life history that defines an ego identity does not reduce to a binary distinction between immature and mature stages. Habermas and cothinkers Gertud Nunner-Winckler and Rainer Döbert are certainly alert to this reality (Habermas 1979b: 74 n13), but Habermas does not elaborate. Following Habermas's own hint (Habermas 1979b: 74 n9), I suggest that the Eriksonian framework of ego identity, which is a version of ego psychology, is consistent with both the developmental and psychoanalytic components of Habermas's position. Methodologically speaking, phases of a life history are defined by the coordination of culturally defined ages with socially derived expectations about developmental stage acquisition. These phases therefore cannot sustain the requirement of universality that applies to structural stages. This is because cultural age combines biological maturation with social learning of cultural roles and the 'socially appropriate' expression of impulses. In this connection, it is crucial to notice that Erik Erikson's phases of identity formation, despite their cultural-age-based nomenclature, are functionally defined. The phases identified by Erikson aim at the ego as a whole, rather than at its cognitive, normative or affective-expressive subdomains, and they relate affective-expressive development, grasped through cultural age, to structural stages in cognitive and normative development (Kohlberg et al. 1983: 326). From this perspective, on the basis of age-appropriate stage acquisition, maturity describes the capacity of the ego to surmount the crisis potentials typical of transitions between specified phases of life, without resort to pathological defences.

Now, Erikson is best known for his elaborate conception of eight (eventually, nine) stages of identity formation in the maturational process, each characterized by specific crisis potentials and a characteristic identity tension, broadly speaking, between social role and authentic self (Erikson 1974, 1994). Indicating the culturally relative nature of his construction, despite claims to universality, he describes these in terms of a maturational task and its corresponding virtue. The first three stages (infancy – 'hope'; toddler – 'will'; and childhood – 'purpose') recapitulate, in modified form, Freud's psychosexual stages and strongly relate drive impulses to ego development. The next three (pre-teen – 'competence'; adolescence – 'fidelity'; youth – 'love') invoke the characteristic crises of the transitions from home to work, via school. The final two (adulthood – 'care'; late maturity – 'wisdom') involve parenthood and senescence, invoking the generational cycle and the reality of death. For Erikson, these stages of development represent capacities of the ego to cope with social reality (and the natural environment of the human body) in the context of drive impulses that may have retained their disruptive potency. Each stage poses specific questions of desire and therefore concerns the capacity of the ego to articulate and satisfy needs.

Erikson's eight phases extends and corrects Freud, while combining a libidinal perspective with the notion of ego-syntonic adaptive tasks, and he focuses on the notion of a dialectical development of the ego through maturational crises. The definition of Erikson's phases of childhood, adolescence, adulthood and late maturity combines cultural age with stage of thinking via the notion of distinctive conceptual-existential problems to be solved in the different phases, but the correspondence between phase and virtue indicates its cultural relativity. Indeed, Erikson's own claims in this regard are undermined by the historical specificity of his fusion of moral and ethical horizons, guided by the need to integrate the superego with the ego, which it would be the task of a Habermasian process of moral reflection to separate. Nonetheless, Erikson achieves a high level of generality, as acknowledged by Kohlberg and cothinkers: Erikson's 'functional phases of development appear to be facilitated by the optimal interaction or matching of structural stage abilities and cultural age responsibilities' (Kohlberg et al. 1983: 324). What this means is that the notion of identity *formation* is relatively successful because it is subtended by the universal structural stages of cognitive and normative development, even though cultural traditions of need-interpretation cannot attain the same scope of application.

Ego deformations and defence mechanisms

Post-metaphysical psychoanalysis 'conceptualises clinical intuitions about deviant and successful processes of ego development by making defence mechanisms comprehensible as inner-psychic communication disturbances' (Habermas 1998b: 426).Unfortunately, despite provocative hints, Habermas does not follow through with the integration of a typology of pathological defence mechanisms correlated with communicative disturbances. The Habermasian reconstruction that follows also aims to throw light on his observation that the main problem confronting the critique of ideology today is not ideological false consciousness, but the fragmentation of subjectivity (TCA2: 355 [497]).

Although Anna Freud lists nine mechanisms, including sublimation and identification (A. Freud 1967: 41–53), the pathological defence mechanisms can be reduced to a threefold typology of increasing severity. The first is repression. For Anna Freud, conversion hysteria, obsessional compulsions and phobic anxieties were all 'neurotic' products of the mechanism of repression. From the communicative perspective, the defence mechanism of repression involves the motivated forgetting of a prohibited symbolization of a need-interpretation, which typically returns as a 'hieroglyphic' symptom. The communicative disturbance in question is an interruption of discursive flow by an unintelligible interjection – a misfired speech act, private ritual, corporeal disturbance or phobic avoidance – which introduces gaps into both argument and narrative. The second is disavowal. For Anna Freud, the defence mechanism of disavowal was connected to perversion and involved a fixation on a partial object, a fetish, which simultaneously affirms and denies the forbidden object of desire (A. Freud 1967). From the communicative perspective, the defence mechanism of disavowal involves self-contradiction, as the ego simultaneously affirms and denies its attachment to a prohibited symbolization of a need-interpretation. Octave Mannoni perfectly sums this up as the discourse of performative contradiction: 'I know very well, but all the same . . .' (Mannoni 2003). Finally, the third and most severe is projection. For Anna Freud, this defence mechanism involves projecting warded off impulses and their symbolization onto the other, who typically becomes integrated into a delusional construction as a persecutory figure (A. Freud 1967). Projection is related to the splitting of the ego (into all-good and all-bad components), in a disintegration of the subject that results in a Manichaean world view or in the phenomena of the *doppelgänger* (Rank 1971). For Kernberg, 'borderline conditions', such as 'narcissistic personality disorder', also depend on the mechanism of projection as their basic defence (Kernberg 1975). Communicatively speaking, it is the psychotic certainty that accompanies the delusional construction, which entails an orthogonal relation to intersubjective testing, that is the main disturbance. These considerations result in the following table.

Now I want to relate this provisional tabulation to problems of ego deformation, via consideration of the implications of communicative disturbances for intersubjective dialogue. The absolute certainty that accompanies projection implies potential resort to violence, because dialogue is excluded from the beginning. The interlocutor is positioned as either the

TABLE 6.1 *Mapping Defence Mechanisms and Typical Symptoms as Communicative Disturbances*

Defence mechanism	Typical symptom	Communicative disturbance
Repression	Conversion hysteria Obsessive ritual Phobic avoidance	Ineradicable gaps or blanks, filled in by hieroglyphs
Disavowal	Fetishization	Persistent self-contradiction
Projection	Delusion	Absolute certainty

recipient of a revelation or an ally of persecutory forces. At the same time, as the literature of the double imaginatively explores and the testimony of mental illness corroborates, powerful disintegrative tendencies are activated by projective mechanisms, alongside a tremendous shrinking of the ego to narcissistic concerns. The ego exists inside its own idiosyncratic mythology, involving the terror and excess of completely unmastered impulses, and it recruits all contact with reality – such as others – into this delusional universe. Adorno and Fenichel were probably correct to point to projection as the fundamental mechanism operative in fascist propaganda and to link the splitting of the ego to political violence.

By contrast with projection, disavowal prevents full participation in dialogue rather than blocking discourse entirely. Because Habermas has explored the problem of performative contradiction in a philosophical context, it is probably the best illustration of the implications of disavowal for intersubjective dialogue. A performative contradiction involves conflict in an utterance between what is affirmed by the enunciation and what is affirmed by the statement, and is a subspecies of self-contradiction generally. *Persistent* self-contradiction as an argumentative strategy or subjective style, however, is a communicative disturbance that denies the interlocutor the capacity to meaningfully say 'no' to the speaker. Everything happens as if the speaker has two stories about themselves and two sets of arguments about the world, one public and the other private. The private set is incorrigible, immunized against critical objections by the strategy of simultaneous affirmation and denial: 'I'm not a racist, but . . .'. The contradictory maintenance of conflicting attitudes and stories means that the history of the ego's formation is necessarily incoherent, inconsistent. A private mythology is permanently juxtaposed to public narrative such that, at best, the fragments of exoteric history allegorize an esoteric fixation whose form can only be presented through forbidden images of transgression and punishment.

Finally, repression prevents the speaker from fully accessing their own motivations in an intersubjectively accessible way. Argumentatively, this means that the speaker must resort to mythic narratives and iconic suffering in those places where propositional justification should be. This is different in degree to a literary intervention in intersubjective dialogue to the extent that the key to the personal mythology of the neurotic, necessary for understanding the significance of the narrative, remains entirely private, hidden away even from the speaker themselves. There are ineradicable blank chapters in the narrative presentation of the life history of the speaker, where someone or something has inscribed enigmatic symbols, diagrams for a conjuration that the speaker categorically resists performing.

The following table summarizes this reconstruction, intended in the spirit of an overture to discussion.

It is now possible to specify how ego deformations relate to social structures, thereby specifying a communicative interpretation of surplus repression. The 'ego exercises the function of censoring impulses under the supervision of the superego', which is the 'intrapsychic extension of social authority' (KHI: 243 [297]). By social authority is meant the ethical values and social ideals that regulate the lifeworld of a social formation and its political community, i.e. its framework of mutual recognition and the cultural traditions that subtend ethical life. For Habermas, superego

TABLE 6.2 *Communicative Disturbances as Manifestations of Regressive Defence Mechanisms Leading to Blockages in Dialogue and Ego Deformation*

Defence mechanism	Typical symptom	Communicative disturbance	Ego deformation
Repression	Conversion hysteria Obsessive ritual Phobic avoidance	Continued resort to inarticulate justifications	Narrative has ineradicable gaps or blanks, filled in by hieroglyphs, which point to a private mythology that cannot be integrated with public history
Disavowal	Fetishization	Persistent self-contradiction	Narrative juxtaposes public history with a private mythology resulting in contradiction
Projection	Delusion	Absolute certainty	Narrative eclipse of public history which disappears inside the private mythology resulting in archaic terrors

commands are elementary prescriptions and fundamental prohibitions whose libidinal investment prevents, by means of guilt, the questioning of authority in respect of basic ideals (KHI: 244 [298]). It is crucial to notice that this entails that superego injunctions, which represent forms of the good, are not the same as the categorical imperative, which demands, as a voice of reason, the universalistic critique of ethical life. Indeed, as Slavoj Žižek proposes from a Lacanian perspective, universality is 'beyond good and evil' (but not beyond right and wrong), precisely because it constitutes a confrontation with the values represented by the superego (Žižek 1996: 213–41). Conversely, the 'malevolent neutrality of the superego' describes its enforcement of pseudo-universalistic particular specifications of potentially universalizable frameworks (e.g. the universal rights of men, but not women and slaves). It follows from this that the superego exercises influence in relation to communicative reason and so is a fundamental defensive line in the protection of existing social arrangements, including social asymmetries and political exclusions. This also includes those traditional need-interpretations which anchor inequalities in the motivations of individuals whose orientations are supplied by obedience to the relevant forms of social authority.

Challenges to social arrangements that involve existing motivations and orientations inherently involve a confrontation with the influence of the superego, for those individuals whose need-interpretations and value orientations are placed in question. Under these circumstances, the superego, which is psychically indispensable yet represents a permanent potential blockage to communication, may trigger repression, disavowal or projection. It is certainly possible that this will result in the development of ego deformations, as the resulting communicative disturbances become integrated into the personality through the constant necessity for defensive struggle. But the moderation of superego commands and their reconstruction along different lines is also possible, through the symbolic re-articulation of images of social authority. The superego is the result of identification, not directly with beloved figures, but with the idealized image of social authority that they represent (KHI: 244 [298]). As Shakespeare's *Measure for Measure* dramatizes, the ideal of 'that demi-god, Authority' is supported by the imagery of terror, as well as the affect of disgust and the mechanisms of guilt and shame (1.3.5 and 2.1.4). Cultural traditions generalize the imagery of delight and terror as iconic presentations of idyllic and abhorrent possibilities – angels and demons – providing a mythological repertoire of need-interpretations whose stereotypical figuration supports superego influence. But symbolic articulations of alternative possibilities shake up these stencils and set them once again in communicative motion. Together with critiques of the immoderate nature of superego commands, these supplement the linguistification of the unconscious with a deflation of the potency of authoritarian imaginaries.

The human interest in subjective integration

Against this conceptual background, I now want to return to the post-metaphysical philosophical anthropology essayed in *Human Interests*, to propose a human interest in subjective integration. According to Habermas:

> The human species secures its existence in systems of social labour and self-assertion through violence, through tradition-bound social life in ordinary-language communication, and with the aid of ego identities that at every level of individuation reconsolidate the consciousness of the individual in relation to the norms of the group. Accordingly, the interests constitutive of knowledge are linked to the functioning of an ego that adapts itself to its external conditions through learning processes, is initiated into the communication system of a social lifeworld by means of self-formative processes, and constructs an identity in the conflict between instinctual aims and social constraints. (KHI: 313 [384])

The implication of this intention, in light of the discussion of developmental psychology, is that the idea for Habermas's three 'knowledge-constitutive human interests' actually originates in the subdomains of ego functioning, within a dialectically evolving ego identity that unifies these components. This ego identity is based on the interdependence of the universal structural stages of cognitive and normative reasoning on the one side, and the cultural connections between motivations and orientations, embedded in ethical life and cultural traditions, on the other. Two remarks are now necessary.

The first concerns the human interest in social cooperation that results in practical knowledge and normative development, in relation to Habermas's speculative 'human interest in liberation from power'. It is discourse ethics which is heir to the 'emancipatory knowledge through reflexive critique' that is rightly modified after *Human Interests*. This is because discourse ethics, which introduces motivations and consequences into deontological formalism, is a hinge in the entire construction. It articulates the universality of cognitive and normative discourse to the restricted generalizability of evaluative and expressive critique, while at the same time bringing together the rational capacities of the ego with its synthetic abilities to reconcile superego demands to need-interpretations. Theory is linked to practice, and virtue to hope, before they are coupled together in discourse ethics, and then used to support deliberative democracy, renovated publics, reflexive tolerance and cosmopolitan peace. The critical standard of unconstrained communication that belongs to the human interest in social cooperation is a post-metaphysical reformulation of the initial idea of an emancipatory interest.

The second concerns the way that therapeutic knowledge implies a human interest in subjective integration, located not at the level of impulse control in the affective subdomain, but at the global level of the maturation of ego identity. Subjective integration from this perspective means successful (i.e. non-pathological) surmounting of the typical crises that are characteristic of the various phases of ego maturation. A final glance at Eriksonian psychology clarifies these claims, because his discussion indicates that what is at stake is the identity of a *human subject* whose functionally defined psychological agencies are integrated within a unique personal style. A mature ego is part of this, but so too is a moderate, rather than ferocious, superego and a set of need-interpretations that tolerably regulate impulse potentials. In his extended analysis of the 'dream specimen of psychoanalysis', Freud's 'dream of Irma's injection', instead of deploying a hermeneutics of suspicion that discards the manifest content as a semblance concealing the latent materials, Erikson points to the relation between latent and manifest, as well what is revealed in analytic dialogue (Erikson 1954). 'In addition to a dream's striving for representability, then', Erikson writes, '[I] would postulate a style of representation which is by no means a mere shell to the kernel, the latent dream; in fact, it is a reflection of the individual ego's peculiar time-space, the frame of reference for all its defenses, compromises, and achievements' (Erikson 1954: 21). This is the nucleus of Erikson's subsequent development of a phase theory of ego maturation, designed to exfoliate a personality's mode of individuation, or style, from the narrative of a succession of surmounted identity crises that engulf their entire subjective world.

Subjective integration is therefore a question of dynamic psychological equilibrium, under conditions short of extraordinary stress and outside of extreme situations (Menninger 1954a, 1954b). The implication of this reconstruction of Habermas's third human interest is that it modulates the normative content of the universal demand for human happiness. Subjective integration cannot be mistaken for a formula for personal or social happiness, which is why it can only have the negative normative significance of a demand for peaceful circumstances. That is a precondition for any emancipatory dialogue, because that presupposes full participation by agents who are sufficiently integrated to be able to narrate continuous life histories and thereby explain their motivations and orientations truthfully. There is a human interest in the lifting of surplus repression and the elimination of pathogenic circumstances, but there is no formula for the social arrangements that might lead to human happiness. These must be discovered in political debate, not deduced from a philosophical anthropology.

Ferrara's concept of reflexive authenticity repositions this insight on the terrain of an ethical theory that takes its bearings from psychoanalytic research as well as normative and aesthetic considerations (Ferrara 1998: 80–105). Authenticity indicates a unique personal style of self-realization that attunes truthfully expressed needs to socially appropriate values, something which becomes reflexive, rather than merely adversarial, when it acknowledges the intersubjectivity involved in socialization and the individual's reflective relation to traditions. Only morally autonomous individuals can become reflexively authentic, because this depends on social recognition of the exemplary character of a particular style, in a context of respect and tolerance, but only subjectively integrated persons can hope to have a truthful relation to their needs and desires (Ferrara 1998: 70–80). The 'exemplary' character of a reflexively authentic existence is potentially generalizable, under the guidance of reflective judgement, based on intersubjective evaluations of its four dimensions, each of which is modelled in literature as well as exhibited in life (Ferrara 1998: 127–47). These dimensions are as follows. Coherence is 'the possibility of summing up the modifications undergone by an identity during the lifetime of its bearer in the form of a narrative'. Vitality 'designates the experience of joyful empowerment which results from the fulfilment of one's central needs', in congruence with who one has been and is becoming. Depth is 'a person's capacity to have access to his or her own psychic dynamisms and to reflect such awareness in the construction of his or her identity'. Finally, maturity describes 'the ability to come to terms with the facticity of the natural and social world, as well as the internal world, without compromising one's coherence and vitality' (Ferrara 1998: 80, 87, 96, 100).

Literature and human interests

Turning to literature, I think that Ferrara develops this insight in a problematic direction. For Ferrara, textual criteria of cohesion, vividness, depth and continuity are the doubles of evaluative judgements on an individual's coherence, vitality, depth and maturity (Ferrara 1998: 138). A work of literature can 'succeed' when it exhibits these features, just as an individual can be 'authentic'. But this entails a continuity between text and life that is based in the identity of the medium of 'experience', which excludes consideration of the specificity of literary experience (Ferrara 1998: 143). By contrast, Habermas's communicative reformulation of Adorno makes it possible to see that literary semblances catalyse the kind of debate that Ferrara describes, without belonging to it.

The Adorno-influenced literary theory of Fredric Jameson provides a dialectical starting point for this concluding reflection. Jameson proposes to relate literary history to narrative disturbances through a schematization that maps cultural periods onto defence mechanisms. According to Jameson, the reification of the sign involves the fragmentation of its components (signifier, signified, referent), such that modernism registers a sundering of sign from referent, while postmodernism reflects the splitting of signifier and signified (Jameson 1992). Modernist juxtaposition, reflecting self-reflexive knowledge of the conventionality of the sign, then promotes the repression of nature and a hysterical subjectivity. By contrast, postmodernist pastiche registers the self-reflexive knowledge of the arbitrary bond between signifier and signified, which promotes the schizophrenic splitting of the ego. Manifestly, literary realism provides a critical standard of aesthetic and subjective wholeness. This schematization evidently resonates with Adorno's cultural typology of Beethoven, Schönberg and Stravinsky, and it has proven a highly influential intervention into debates about postmodern literature. I think that the problem with this schematic construction is that it schematically aligns literary techniques with communicative disturbances, as if juxtaposition and pastiche were automatically symptomatic of regressive defence mechanisms. Its problem, in other words, is that it suffers from the main defect of all formalisms, namely, it neglects the substantive question of whether a narrative form articulates a generalizable content or a privatized mythology. Communicative disturbances and ego deformations are privations because of semantic privatization, not because they fail to meet a formal standard of harmonious wholeness, organic totality or literary realism.

It was Lacan, and not Lorenzer, who proposed that 'the unconscious is structured like a language' and that condensation and displacement are best grasped as the rhetorical tropes of metaphor and metonymy (respectively) (Lacan 2006). Although a debate on the theoretical status of Lacan's insight is beyond the scope of the present discussion, his insight suggests how poetic language evokes dreamlike processes in a way that bears upon the question of the therapeutic role of literature. Metaphor and metonymy, constitutive of poetic language, symbolically represent – without necessarily being identical with – dream mechanisms, providing an environment for the articulation of hidden desires and silenced needs. Additionally, the equivocation of reference characteristic of literature opens a space of affective ambivalence, semantic ambiguity, potential irony and the play of form and content. In combination, these aspects of poetic language mean that the literary work tests out forbidden wishes in a space where every possible affirmation is simultaneously also a potential retraction. At the same time, its figural potentials evoke unconscious thinking without necessarily resorting to the incommunicable iconography of an entirely private mythology. Certainly, with Jameson, literature can be a social symptom of prevalent ego deformations and communicative disturbances. But it can also be a form of cultural sublimation that makes a special intervention into the process of dismantling surplus repression and restoring communicative openness. It is to a work that does just this that I now want to turn.

7

Habermas and the Devil

A communicative reading of *Doctor Faustus*

Theodor Adorno's brief appearance as Mephistopheles in Thomas Mann's *Doctor Faustus* (1947) fatefully connects Mann's masterpiece with the core philosophical problems of the Frankfurt School (DF: 253–4 [301–2]). Subtitled *The Life of the Composer Adrian Leverkühn, As Told by a Friend*, the novel presents the narrative, by humanist professor, Serenus Zeitblom, of the descent into madness of the musical genius, Adrian Leverkühn. In the story, Leverkühn achieves an avant-garde breakthrough into atonal dissonance modelled on the twelve-tone row of Arnold Schönberg. Like Schönberg, Leverkühn's compositional problem involves the historical obsolescence of the organic totality of the harmonic symphony, which necessitates dissonant experimentation in order to achieve the only authentic expressivity that remains possible, namely, anguish (256 [304]). Yet because Leverkühn's compositional brilliance is made possible by a diabolical contract (facilitated by deliberate contraction of syphilis), the ultimate result of his breakthrough is personal disaster. Zeitblom, whose narration tracks the interwar decades and Germany's wartime experience, insistently relates this aesthetic impasse to the problem field of modernity itself. This especially concerns the combination of irrational motivations with the application of an aesthetic logic to politics, as released during the rise of fascism. Not surprisingly, then, Mann's novel acts as a touchstone in discourse on the political implications of both modernism (the aesthetic movement) and modernity (the cultural-historical period). Because of the influential role of Adorno in Mann's reworking of the Faust legend (Schmidt 2004), that connection has generally been regarded from the perspective of *Dialectic of*

Enlightenment (1947) and *Philosophy of Modern Music* (1949). The tragedy of *Doctor Faustus* is often thought to be one whose ultimate stakes are best expressed in Adorno's lapidary negation of modernity: 'Enlightenment is totalitarian' (Adorno and Horkheimer 2002: 4).

According to the standard reading, then, the degeneration into insanity of the avant-garde composer is an allegory of Germany's downfall into Hitler's orgy of destruction. What I shall call the 'allegorical interpretation' reigned in the 1950s (Fetzer 1996) and has since been reformulated by liberal (Jendreiek 1977) and leftist critics – most notably in Evelyn Cobley's recent Adorno-inspired analysis of 'fascist atonality' (Cobley 2002b). According to this reading, the autonomy of modernist art and literature leads to the release of ethical controls over aesthetic experimentation. This is something that Leverkühn, in a desperate effort to win an artistic breakthrough irrespective of the human cost, radicalizes into a deliberate re-barbarization of musical culture. That allegorizes the Nazi attempt at civilizational renewal, which begins from a Nietzschean 'revaluation of values' that is guided by a thorough-going ethical relativism. Because of the fascist indifference to the suffering of the victims, the alleged civilizational breakthrough attained by this aestheticization of politics leads only to a return to barbarism. The idea that Mann's book is an allegory of the fascist 'aestheticization of politics' is completed by adding a critique of modernity to this indictment of modernism. Supposedly, modernity, as the cultural epoch inaugurated by the Enlightenment, secretes totalitarian potentials in its pervasive rationalism, something that the novel dramatizes through Leverkühn's quasi-mathematical compositional techniques. As the leading contemporary proponent of the standard reading sums up: 'when Mann associates Leverkühn's serial experiments with Hitler's totalitarian regime, his novel must then be suggesting . . . that Auschwitz is a possibility always-already implicit in the project of modernity' (Cobley 2002a: 69).

The allegorical interpretation of *Doctor Faustus* presents a frontal challenge to the philosophy of the leading representative of Critical Theory today, Jürgen Habermas. For a German philosophical defender of cultural modernity and an advocate of the modernist movement in contemporary art and literature, the stakes could not be higher. The entire work of Habermas, from his defence of the emancipatory potential of democracy in *The Structural Transformation of the Public Sphere* (1962) onwards, has been aimed at bringing German philosophy into the democratic light. His thinking vigorously repudiates the anti-Enlightenment Romanticism of figures such as Nietzsche (mobilized by the Nazis as a source of intellectual authorization) and Heidegger (whose Nietzschean philosophy actively and explicitly supported the Nazis). For Habermas, totalitarianism is not the result of modernity, but of the incompleteness of the modern project, the fact that the democratic and rational potentials of modernity have become blocked. What Habermas calls the 'bourgeois implementation of the modern project' has stifled democracy and called forth irrational reactions. But he insists that the way forward is the humanist completion of the modern project, in social democratization and a post-metaphysical enlightenment, not its retraction.

By contrast, from the Adornian perspective represented by Cobley, the humanist response to the problems of modernity that Habermas represents is deeply complicit with the disaster of fascism (Cobley 2002b: 29). Fundamentally, that is because humanism is powerless to prevent the reification characteristic of capitalist modernity. What Cobley describes as 'fascist atonality' is represented through Adrian Leverkühn, whose compositions emerge from a social and historical context dominated by reification. In other words, Cobley's accusation is that the Habermasian diagnosis of the origins of totalitarianism fails to point the finger at capitalism: in effect, she enlists *Doctor Faustus* in a rejoinder to Habermas's critique of Adorno. Cobley thereby brings the severe judgement of Habermas's mentor, Theodor Adorno, to bear on Habermas's 'irresponsible' defence of modernity (Cobley 2002b: 29–30).

In this chapter, I explore a Habermasian reading of *Doctor Faustus*, seeking to elaborate an alternative to the allegorical interpretation while demonstrating the potential insightfulness of a communicative approach to literary modernism. Part of my interpretive strategy is to contrast Adorno with Habermas, in order to exhibit why his communicative reformulation of Adorno's aesthetics is valid. The communicative approach thinks literary semblances as indirect communication about an historical situation, using poetic language that is irreducibly characterized by the equivocation of reference and aesthetic consistency. The equivocation of reference means that what is at stake in a reading of Mann's novel is not an illegitimate detour through the historical referent that lands in a debate about the nature of German fascism. Instead, interpretation must work out how an exploration of that imaginary Germany, which Mann populates with culturally representative figures, makes the novel relevant to the post-war context of its reception. The novel's tragic trajectory and ambivalent structure of feeling, centred on the problem of 'the role of the daemonic in human affairs' (4 [5]), has to be linked to the difficult task of reconnecting two sundered systems of symbols, musical and spoken. That points readers in the direction of what Habermas calls the 'linguistification of the unconscious' through cultural sublimation, and explains why Mann is engaged in a project of humanist myth-making as his response to the catastrophe of fascism.

At the same time, the meaning of *Doctor Faustus* is inextricably connected to Mann's literary technique of perspectival construction, in the preparation of his cultural and historical materials. Those materials themselves explain nothing about the novel without consideration of how the resulting perspectives are consistently connected through the relation between content and form. This is especially evident in Mann's inflection of the Faust legend through Nietzsche and Shakespeare, which has the effect of focusing novel onto the 'discontents of civilization' and condensing these onto the figure of Adrian Leverkühn. The novel suggests its relevance to the post-war context in terms of thinking through a civilizational failure to provide alternatives to 'sympathy for the abyss', Romantic fascination with, and captivation by, the instinctual excess that Freud interprets as 'death drive'. Mann's novel plays off Nietzschean Romanticism, captivated by deathwishfulness, against Freudian Enlightenment, determined to supplant the id with the ego. It therefore sets fascist fascination with instinctual regression against democratic cultivation of ego maturity, and proposes a new humanism as a form of sublimation capable of achieving civilizational renewal. For Mann, Enlightenment is the bulwark against totalitarianism, not its entrance.

Part I

From the communicative perspective, novels are cultural interventions into historical situations. They aim to spark debates and transform readerships, through the mediation of critical debate and reader identification. From this perspective, Mann's novel has been a paradoxical success. Its initial reception (1947–55) triggered debate around the social and cultural coordinates of fascism, but in the registers of hostility and bewilderment (Fetzer 1996: 1–16). That, presumably, was the debate Mann wanted, but not in the key he hoped for. Lukács's reading in terms of the 'tragedy of modernism' and the contribution of Adorno scholars set up the allegorical interpretation as counterpoint to post-war conservative rejection. The archival discoveries (1955–75) springing from Mann's *The Story of a Novel* (1961) represented a tremendous enrichment and complication, through source criticism, of the allegorical interpretation (Fetzer 1996: 17–54). Formalist methods provided a new possibility, reading Leverkühn's life as a musical chord and the structure of the novel as replicating Leverkühn's imaginary music (Bergsten 1969). But it was not until the post-1960s working through of German history that these formal possibilities were supplemented by recognition that Leverkühn is not exactly the same as Schönberg (Dahlhaus 1982). Although that might have opened a fresh political reading of the novel, instead, biographical and autobiographical readings, released by Mann's posthumous diaries, dominated reception (Fetzer 1996: 55–114). Meanwhile (1975–95), critical formalism highlighted structural ambivalence and equivocation, paradox and doubt (Fetzer 1996: 70), something that the new formalism of deconstruction (and allied schools) have perpetuated in the period post-1995. In a context where political readings are strangely uncommon, Berman's Habermas-influenced interpretation of Mann's efforts to forge a post-bourgeois individuality is refreshing (Berman 1986). Yet it is rare to find a political reading that makes sustained contact with the formal structures of the novel, without suspending the analysis on the note of ambiguity. The recent entry of cultural-materialist Shakespeare criticism into this field, via Mann's use of Shakespeare in the novel, has therefore been especially welcome (Döring and Fernie 2015). Nonetheless, it is reasonable to say that the novel remains enigmatic, which sets the tone for what follows.

After describing the novel's representation of artistic modernism and the character of Leverkühn, I intend to explore the unreliability of Zeitblom's narrative and the novel's critique of the complicity of liberal humanism. The limitations of both Leverkühn and Zeitblom, combined with the dangerous political implications of the allegorical interpretation, imply that the novel is actually perspectival rather than allegorical. I then investigate a modified Adornian reading of the novel. For Adorno, the tragedy of modernism illuminates the sociocultural matrix that generates fascism, because the impasse of modernism is caused by reification. Yet in the world of the novel, Leverkühn does what is impossible in the historical world as described by Adorno, namely, he combines regression and repression, reactionary and progressive modernisms, into a single figure. That contradiction centres on love, not reification, and it strongly suggests that the book is about the communication of hitherto hidden desires, rather than a representation of the economic structures that facilitate fascist politics.

Leverkühn and modernism

The novel is the fictional biography of the avant-garde composer Adrian Leverkühn (1885–1940), retrospectively narrated in the period 1943–6 by his lifelong friend, the humanist professor of classics, Serenus Zeitblom. Accordingly, Zeitblom's narrative happens in the historical moment of Mann's actual composition, during the darkest days of the twentieth century, between the Nazi offensive at Kursk and the terrible discovery of the extermination camps. But the main action of the novel concentrates on the fictive sequence of musical inventions, achieved by Leverkühn in his twenty-four years of diabolically inspired genius, between 1912 and 1936. Consequently, Zeitblom's reconstruction of the descent into madness of the musical genius mainly engages the cultural coordinates of fascist emergence in the interwar decades.

Leverkühn's background is a complex representation of the cultural situation that generated fascist politics, in the peculiar combination of forced technological modernization and romanticized traditional backwardness – reactionary modernism (Herf 1984) – specific to Germany. On Mann's analysis, presented in speeches during the war, fascism was neither solely the result of anti-modern Romanticism, nor exclusively the consequence of instrumentally rational, means-ends calculations, but a peculiar synthesis of both. He described it as a 'the combination of robust timeliness, efficient modernness, on the one hand, and dreams of the past [i.e., memories of medieval glory], on the other hand—in a word, highly technological Romanticism' (Mann 1973: 16). Consistent with this position, despite becoming an avant-garde composer, Leverkühn prefers provincial Germany to the cosmopolitan cities of Europe, just as his work is described by one character as *Boche dans un degré fascinant* (422 [510]).

Mann locates his representation of Leverkühn in a force field of cultural influences that includes the German transformation of the Faust legend from a tragic figure into a triumphant criminal. This decision was historically determined by the prevalence in Nazi ideology of the Spenglerian idea of 'Faustian self-assertion'. For Mann, the voluntaristic self-assertion that was originally celebrated in Goethe's *Faust* is closely related to the German Romantic notion that defiance of divine law and moral principle is the key to greatness (Mann 1961: 30). According to Mann, in his essay 'Germany and the Germans', because of the backwardness springing from the failure of democratic and then socialist revolutions, the Europeanization of Germany was fatally conflated with Germanization of Europe (Mann 1973: 10–12). In *The Story of a Novel*, Mann therefore interprets the book's representation of the Faust motif in terms of the conflation of the break out of isolation into the great world, with the breakthrough conducted through *Blitzkrieg* (Mann 1961: 72). Swinging between introspection and grandiosity, and between inferiority and arrogance, German intellectuals integrated the motif of self-assertion with romantic nationalism and a certain 'sympathy for the abyss' that belongs to confusing authenticity with primitivism (326 [394], 387 [464]). Yet this was combined with 'historical consciousness', the awareness that historical variability, moral conventionality and cultural contingency imply the groundlessness of all grounds.

Accordingly, Leverkühn's character note is cold distance and intellectual arrogance, instant disdain for conventionality and sentimentality, as expressed through his constant mocking laughter. Leverkühn's incipient creative paralysis, generated by hypertrophy of historical consciousness, is resolved by desperate means when, in the central incident of the work, Mephistopheles manifests, to propose a 'Faustian Bargain' to Leverkühn (238–65 [283–318]). According to the Devil, Leverkühn is granted twenty-four years of creative genius, in return for renunciation of human warmth and erotic love. The agent of the diabolical pact is the prostitute 'Esmeralda', from whom Leverkühn deliberately contracts syphilis, amidst a series of eerie coincidences. Leverkühn's inability to love is therefore caused both by diabolical coldness and by the onset of neurosyphilitic symptoms, and his masterworks are produced by a combination of diabolical inspiration and syphilitic insanity. In the twenty-four years of explosive creativity that result from the destruction of inhibitions, caused by neurosyphilitic general paresis, Leverkühn develops compositional breakthroughs that result in expressive release. Underlying Leverkühn's eventual breakdown is a psychoanalytically consistent representation of the character's pathological narcissism (one that Mann's diaries reveal was grounded in personal experience) (Böhm 1990). In the meantime, however, Leverkühn's erotic (Rudi Schwerdtfeger) and familial (Nepomuk Schneidewein) loves meet strange and terrible deaths.

As a radical experimental composer, whose dissonant compositions combine experimental atonality with regression to medieval polyphony (Mann 1961: 36, 46), Leverkühn is an enigma to the narrator, Serenus Zeitblom. It is a critical commonplace about the book to note that Leverkühn's invention of the compositional method of the twelve-tone row is closely modelled on Schönberg's serial procedure, as set forth in Schönberg's 'Twelve Tone Composition' (1923) and interpreted in Adorno's *Philosophy of Modern Music* (1949) (Adorno 2007b; Mann 1961; Schönberg 1975: 207–8). Too seldom noticed, however, is the fact that Leverkühn makes not one, but two, musical discoveries in his twenty-four years of feverish genius. For the dodecaphonic method, arrived at in 1928 – chapter XLVI (504–15 [608–22]) – is preceded by his 1912 invention of a primitivistic form of atonal polyphony entirely different from serial regularity – chapter XXVII (277–90 [333–50]). These inventions make possible a disturbing music whose expressive intensity is – paradoxically – strictly related to the imposition of order. This happens either through musical adaptation to rhythms of speech external to the refrain, or through the clinical precision of a mathematical compositional technique that infiltrates the work.

Many critics – notably Helmut Jendreieck – have interpreted Mann as presenting, through the figure of Leverkühn, an indictment of the complicity of modernism with the disaster of fascism (Jendreiek 1977: 432). Modernism, on this interpretation, involves the sundering of aesthetics from ethics, something that makes possible an artistic breakthrough won at a terrible human cost. According to the standard reading, then, the novel allegorizes the fascist effort at a convulsive breakthrough into a new civilization, through a 'revaluation of values' that lost contact with humanity and descended into orgiastic release. The main authority for that reading is Mann himself, who states that the figure of Leverkühn represents 'the craving of a proud mind, threatened by sterility, for an unblocking of inhibitions at any cost, and the parallel between a pernicious euphoria ending in collapse and the nationalistic frenzy of fascism' (Mann 1961: 64). On the allegorical interpretation that Mann provocatively flashes in his authorial commentary, Leverkühn represents in fictional form the analysis presented in 'Germany and the Germans'. From this perspective, Leverkühn is quintessentially German: provincial yet arrogant; symptomatically Lutheran, insofar as inhabited by an undigested medieval irrationalism; and, a cynical Nietzschean, sickened unto death by historical consciousness.

Zeitblom and humanism

But there are two main reasons why readers should be extremely wary about accepting the allegorical interpretation. The first is, as Michael Beddow has pointed out, that it is incoherent – even dangerous (Beddow 1994: 81). The second is that the 'intentional fallacy' it involves requires a naïve conflation of Zeitblom with Mann – something expressly contradicted by the author (Mann 1961: 90). Consideration of Zeitblom as a character suggests that the novel is not an allegory, but a multi-perspectival representation, in line with the strategy of perspectival relativism that Mann employed in his other works (Vaget 2002). That leads to the idea that the novel presents the two broken halves of modern German culture: modernism and tradition, Romantic radicalism and liberal humanism. Mann's novel represents a civilizational crisis whose solution remains impossible, because of a failure to develop the right cultural resources. German history involves a cultural failure to cope with a disturbing element of the human condition, in terms other than the complete liquidation of normative values.

I turn first to the allegorical interpretation. Beyond their generation within the same set of cultural coordinates, the connection between aesthetic breakthrough and political totalitarianism is remote. What is the relation between the composer's 'Faustian Bargain' (aesthetic innovation in return for inhuman coldness) and the 'Faustian Bargain' struck between Hitler and Germany (politico-military breakthrough in return for radical evil)? Does the one allegorize the other? That would be extremely disturbing, for while Leverkühn's breakthrough results in genuine greatness (at tragic cost), Hitler's breakthrough results in... what? It is inconceivable that Mann, who fled from Hitler's Germany into American exile and broadcast regularly on behalf of the Allies, thinks that the Nazi *Grossdeutschland* was somehow historically authentic. Conversely, is the reader to suppose – along the lines of Cobley's idea of 'fascist atonality' – that avant-garde experimentalism, banned and burned by the Nazis, whose artistic preferences were for neoclassicism, is somehow 'Nazi'? That the music of the Jewish Schönberg, whose last statement on the Holocaust was the atonal lament, 'A Jew in Warsaw' (1947), is a fit candidate to allegorize the politics of Adolph Hitler? The idea is incoherent – or monstrous. Yet these are the highly problematic implications of the allegorical interpretation.

I turn next to the problems raised by the narrator-as-character. Although the notion of Zeitblom as an unproblematic authorial proxy is suggested by his many narrative intrusions, this functions to occlude a quite different unity – the 'secret identity' of Zeitblom and Leverkühn (Mann 1961: 90). That secret identity is complex, however, and it problematizes, rather than eliminates, the appearance that Zeitblom ventriloquizes Mann's position. Zeitblom, who, like Mann, distrusts music, effectively proposes that Melos is the subterranean connection, that secret corridor, in which Eros transforms into Thanatos (10–11 [12–13]). He links sympathy for the abyss to Romantic fascination with the fusion of death and desire, a fusion that is particularly evident in Wagnerian music and opera (Fetzer 1991). This perspective is explicated by Mann's comment, in 'Germany and the Germans', that: (1) the Germans are Faustians (i.e. partisans of heroic-tragic self-assertion), and (2) the Germans are musical (i.e. emotionally disposed to instinctual release devoid of rational controls); so that (3) a new German Faust figure would have to be a composer (Mann 1973: 5). In short, Zeitblom raises the question of the cultural coordinates of German fascism and, like Mann (Mann 1973: 11–12), he locates them in a Romantic fascination with the abyss of introspection that leads to what he describes as the 'daemonic' [*Dämonische*] (6 [6]). Should the reader, then, not simply accept Zeitblom's judgements as transparent representations of Mann's position?

Several considerations suggest that this apparent identity is merely a lure. Zeitblom, diegetically the author of (most of) *Doctor Faustus*, is a character, not the extra-diegetic author. Zeitblom is in some ways the *opposite* of Mann, for Zeitblom is a member of that 'inner emigration' that Mann castigated as politically complicit. Although the allegorical interpretation relies on the assumption that Zeitblom's narrative transparently represents Leverkühn's destiny, in actuality Zeitblom's discourse insists on its own unreliability in three major respects. The first is that Zeitblom concedes from the outset that he has always avoided thinking about the 'daemonic in human affairs' and has no sympathy for the Dionysiac implications of music (10–11 [12–13]). The key point here is that Zeitblom's perspective is represented by the novel as intrinsically limited – it overlooks something crucial, namely, insight into the daemonic. The second is that Zeitblom unhesitatingly interpolates scenes and ideas into the narrative that he has not witnessed at all, but instead has (feverishly?) reconstructed in imagination (455 [550]). There are two crucial types of scenario involved – the scenes of Leverkühn's romantic imbroglios and Zeitblom's interpretation of Leverkühn's masterpieces, *Apocalypsis cum figuris* (1919) and *The Lamentation of Doctor Faustus* (1928). In relation to musical interpretation, Zeitblom superimposes a theological resonance onto the musical stave, speaking of a 'diabolical glissando' in *Apocalypse* and the 'high G of redemption' in *Lamentation* (394 [472], 515 [635]). The third kind of unreliability must be inferred, but it explains the enthusiasm that Zeitblom has for scenes of fiasco and rejection: Zeitblom is unrequitedly in love with Leverkühn. The homoerotic dimension of Leverkühn's and Schwerdtfeger's interlude in Palestrina is represented allusively yet unmistakeably. That this encounter is based in Mann's own conflicted homosexuality is something delicately attested to in *The Story of a Novel* and corroborated in considerable detail in his diaries (Böhm 1990). No doubt, Mann put a lot of himself into Zeitblom. But he put even more of himself into Leverkühn. In the final analysis, he is neither: writing is a means of gaining distance on his own life history, a form of working through a personal past that condenses key episodes in German intellectual history into its expansive compass.

Novelistic anamorphosis

It is worth noting that Mann's 'story of a novel', his authorial commentary on *Doctor Faustus*, is just that – a narrative fabrication, rather than an authoritative interpretation. Mann's decision to supplement the original novel with an authorial commentary arose in a post-war context of critical rejection and accusations of plagiarism (Beddow 1994). In this respect, *The Story of a Novel* is a labyrinth of evasions, an elaborate fiction about the exhaustive research conducted by Mann in preparation of the novel. This is designed to minimize the degree to which *Doctor Faustus* relies on the compositional techniques of Arnold Schönberg and the musical philosophy of Theodor Adorno. Inter alia, Mann exonerates himself from the charge of having generated an ambiguous representation of a historical situation involving radical evil. The interpretation of the novel by György Lukács (i.e. the allegorical interpretation) is pressed into the service of a counter-attack against the right-wing critics (Lukács 1964; Mann 1961: 142–3). Lukács is at the origin of a long line of critics who collapse the narrator into the author and fail to consider the possibility that Zeitblom is as limited as Leverkühn. The Adornian perspective, too, fails to interpret the novel *as a novel*, rather than as testimony about an imaginary artist, or the imaginative figuration of a theoretical truth expressed elsewhere in propositional form.

To motivate the plausibility of that claim, as well as to advance the communicative reading, I now want to consider a modified version of the allegorical interpretation. A modified Adornian reading of *Doctor Faustus* focuses the allegorical interpretation on Schönberg-as-Leverkühn, as a figure whose fate exemplifies the 'whole cultural crisis' of the modern epoch, rather than on Leverkühn-as-Hitler. The problematic conception of 'fascist atonality' is not really consistent with Adorno's thinking, which is rather that the tragedy of the modernist artist illuminates the fatal dialectic of modern culture. Both Susan von Rohr Scaff (Von Rohr Scaff 2002: 178) and Hannelore Mündt (Mundt 2004: 186) present Adornian interpretations of the novel keyed by this assumption. For Adorno, fascism and modernism are dialectical opposites, but also historical complements. Atonal dissonance, as discussed in *Philosophy of Modern Music*, is an aesthetic protest against capitalist reification. Fascist regression, meanwhile, critiqued in *Dialectic of Enlightenment*, is the result of reification, evidence that enlightenment regresses to mythology under the fatal spell of instrumental reason. From Adorno's perspective, however, although modernism and fascism are opposites, they are both generated within the same set of social and cultural coordinates. Artistic tragedy and social atrocity are consequences of reification. Adorno, it seems, was prepared to consider *Doctor Faustus* as a representation of the aesthetic theory presented in *Philosophy of Modernism* (Vila-Matas 2012).

Yet although this is an improvement on the notion of 'fascist atonality', it cannot establish that Mann's representation of the 'whole cultural crisis' centres on instrumental rationality. For it misses the most salient fact about the novel, which is that it is not about Leverkühn (and still less, about Schönberg-as-Leverkühn, as I will show in a moment). It is about Leverkühn and Zeitblom, as two perspectives dislocated by their reciprocal failure to grasp the object of their focus, namely, the daemonic. Indeed, it is instructive to contrast Mann's use of representative figures in *Doktor Faustus* with those of *Der Zauberberg*. In *Magic Mountain*, traditional humanism (Settembrini) contests a series of philosophical set pieces with modernist radicalism (Naptha) [i.e. Lukács], with the Dionysian, Mynheer Peeperkorn, disturbing the neutrality and innocence of the protagonist, Hans Castorp, while problematizing the intellectualism of Naptha and Settembrini. In *Doctor Faustus*, the proxy for the reader and the vehicle for authorial interpretations, in the figure of Castorp, is gone. This is because the novel – in typical modernist fashion – transposes the problem of interpretation from the characters onto the reader. Providing that we identify the role performed by Peeperkorn with music itself (and with Mephistopheles), however, the rest of the diagram remains the same. The difference is that the encounter with fascism has inverted Mann's politics, from sympathy for the conservative revolution, to sympathy for socialist humanism (Lee 2007: 1–21).

The strong implication of this construction of the novel, as consisting of two flawed perspectives whose dislocation prevents them from adding up to a whole, is that *Doctor Faustus* involves novelistic anamorphosis. Originally a painterly technique, this describes the way that an object hidden in the representational field (for instance, a death's head) can be abruptly revealed by a shift in perspective. In Mann's novel, it is music that is the seemingly meaningless, non-symbolic stain in the foreground of the narrative, which suddenly flashes into visibility because of the failure of the two perspectives to achieve closure. Music is the bearer of a deathwishful sensuality that combines the demonic and the Dionysiac into the 'daemonic'; Melos is where Eros and Thanatos secretly intertwine.

Beyond its role in preventing the closure of the two main perspectives in the novel, the most important narrative consequence of the intrusion of the daemonic is that it dislocates Adrian Leverkühn himself. I now want to demonstrate that Mann's novel cannot be successfully interpreted through the lens of Adorno's notion of the tragedy of modernism. For Mann's Leverkühn does what Adorno rules out, namely, he simultaneously combines reactionary and progressive variations on modernism. The reason for this is that Leverkühn's deepest problem is not, in fact, the dialectics of reification. Leverkühn's deepest problem is with love – specifically, the expressive problem of an erotic sublimation of forbidden desire.

The Stravinskyian *Apocalypse*

The Adornian reading of *Doctor Faustus* depends on not noticing that 'Schönberg' and 'Stravinsky', opposites in Adorno's aesthetic theory, are combined in the figure of Adrian Leverkühn. Adorno's interpretation of Stravinsky's 'reactionary' anti-modernism involves the effort to evade the modernist dialectic, through instinctual regression that is achieved by means of techniques of entertainment, that is, the penetration of the culture industries into artworks. By contrast, Adorno's Schönberg refuses release through disciplined expression (implying repression), something consistent with symptom formation but not with orgiastic regression – further, Adorno's Schönberg is a dissonant protest.

Mann's Leverkühn does what Adorno's Schönberg cannot, namely, develop a musical atavism that is expressed through the diabolical glissando and parodic citation. On Adorno's interpretation, musical primitivism involves the effort to evade the modernist dialectic, something achieved by three basic means. These are: the decomposition of musical form; the heteronomous surrender to entertainment music; and, the re-naturalization of music through acoustic icons. The result is instinctual regression to primary narcissism, equivalent to schizophrenic depersonalization. Leverkühn's *Apocalypse* is a 'Stravinskyian' work that responds to all three of these regressive themes.

The decomposition of musical form indicates, for Adorno, a failure of coherence grounded in the work's lack of autonomy, that is, its failure to legislate its own forms. Zeitblom describes Leverkühn's *Apocalypsis cum figuris* work as having 'a fugal feeling, although the theme is never fatefully repeated, but rather is itself developed along with the development of the whole, so that a style, to which the artist apparently wished to subject himself, is dismantled and carried, so to speak, to absurdity' (379 [456]). The decomposition of musical form makes possible the introduction of heteronomous determinations into the musical material. In *Apocalypse*, the dissonant elements of the work are expressions of culture, while the harmonic and tonal elements are expressions of a world of banality that is hell on earth (394 [473]). The work contains parodies of diverse musical styles of popular cultural taste, ranging from Tchaikovsky to the Music Hall and Jazz (395 [474]).

What makes the work most 'oppressive, dangerous, malevolent' (394 [472]), however, is the adaptation of the totality of music to the voice. That is, the decomposition of musical form also introduces the desperate search for an acoustic iconography capable of the re-naturalization of music. The work as a whole is a fictional example of musical ekphrasis, for '*Apocalypsis cum figuris* pays homage to Dürer', although 'Adrian's monstrous fresco [does not] programmatically follow those 15 illustrations by the man from Nuremberg' (377 [454]). Nonetheless, the work as a whole is punctuated by a contamination of instrumental pitches by vocal sounds, and vice versa, the chorus is instrumentalized and the orchestra vocalized (393 [471]), so that the whole resembles diabolical laughter. Decisively, just as with Stravinsky, 'the rhythm, lacking all consideration of symmetry and surely adapted to the accents of speech, changes in fact from bar to bar' (395 [472]). This happens especially in the climax to the first part:

> This sardonic *gaudium* of Ghenna sweeps across 50 bars, beginning with the giggle of a single voice, only to spread rapidly and sees choir and orchestra, then, amid rhythmic upheavals and counter blows and jettison is, to swell to a horrible fortissimo tutti, to a dreadful mayhem of yowls, yelps, screeches, bleats, bellows, howls, and whinnies, to the mocking, triumphant laughter of hell. (397 [479])

The mocking laughter of hell is then echoed in the beginning of the second part in the 'totally strange and wonderful children's chorus' that uncannily reprises the diabolical laughter (397 [479]) of the first part. The infection of music by voice therefore contains a 'recollection of the pandemonium of laughter, of infernal laughter, that forms the brief, but ghastly conclusion of the first part' (397 [479]). Finally, Zeitblom speaks of 'that gruesome call assigned to the mocking, bleating bassoon' (393 [472]), adding that there are glissandos of the trombone, timpani and voice:

> There are ensembles that begin as speaking choruses and only by stages, by way of the oddest transitions, arrive at the richest vocal music; choruses, that is, that move through all the shades of graduated whispering, antiphonal speech, and quasi-chant, on up to the most polyphonic song. . . . Frozen within it, as a naturalistic atavism, so to speak, a barbaric rudiment of pre-musical days, is the sliding tone, the glissando—a musical device that, for profoundly cultural reasons, is to be employed with utmost caution, and in which I have always tended to hear something anti-cultural, indeed anti-human, even daemonic. (393 [472])

Now, for Adorno, Stravinsky's heteronomous music leads to psychological regression, because its atavistic re-naturalization of music implies the re-awakening of archaic instincts. Likewise, Mann's Leverkühn engages in an aesthetic breakthrough that is won at the cost of a 'deliberate rebarbarization' (389 [469]). That begins with instinctual chaos, but ends in primitivist celebration of de-humanization:

[An] onrushing welter of brass in an inordinate host of voices at the extremes of their range, giving the impression of an abyss that will engulf everything in its hopeless maw. . . . [A]ccompanied by sounds that begin a simple noise, as magical, fanatical African drums and booming gongs, only to attain the highest music. How often has this for bidding work—with its urgent need to let music revealed the most hidden things, from the beast in man to his most sublime emotions—incurred reproaches both of bloody barbarism and bloodless intellectuality. (380 [456], 393 [472])

Adorno's claim was that Stravinsky's work expresses a schizophrenic depersonalization that is related to the triumph of the collective and a return to the archaic. In Leverkühn's *Apocalypse*, that is literalized in a primitivist regression that leads to a demonic laughter, which cynically strips the human voice of warmth and makes it echo with cold despair. Finally, *Apocalypse* is the surrender of aesthetic autonomy to functional utility, for Leverkühn's expression of his 'longing for a soul' (397 [479]) is subordinated to a neo-ecclesiastical music that aims at collective cohesion. 'Its ambition', Zeitblom comments, 'is to create community out of atomisation, which seizes upon means that belong not only to an ecclesiastical stage of civilisation, but to one that is primitive as well' (392 [471]).

The Schönbergian *Lamentation*

By contrast with Adorno's Stravinsky, Adorno's Schönberg attains release only through disciplined expression (implying repression), something consistent with symptom formation, but not with schizophrenic regression. Accordingly, Adorno's Schönberg expresses a dissonant protest against the banalization of culture and the de-humanization of persons, in a work of mathematical formalization that paradoxically makes possible expressive release. Mann's Leverkühn of *The Lamentation of Doctor Faustus* resembles Adorno's Schönberg point-for-point, up to and including the 'magical square' for calculating variations from a tone row. Leverkühn's *Lamentation* is a 'retraction' of Beethoven's 'Ode to Joy', which closes the *Ninth Symphony* (501 [604]), but it is also a kind of 'retraction' of the regressive atavism of Leverkühn's breakthrough work, *Apocalypse*. That is because the work represents the 'reversal, that is, of calculated coldness into an expressive cry of the soul', which, for Zeitblom, represents not only a fresh breakthrough, but also the recovery or perhaps the reconstruction of expression (509 [614]). It is a reversal of demonic coldness and mocking laughter, of the longing for a soul, into 'the sound of the human voice returned as a sound of nature, revealed as the sound of nature, in essence a lament, nature's melancholy' (510 [615]). Most importantly, it is also a retraction of formal disintegration, especially rhythmic decomposition and the depersonalization of the voice, something that is made possible by the 'strict style' of formal composition. Leverkühn's late process of composition, of course, resembles that of Schönberg so closely that Mann was eventually obliged to acknowledge the composer's originality.

What catalyses Leverkühn's transition from 'Stravinsky' to 'Schönberg'? Certainly not reification! In *Lamentation*, noting that in German, 'B' is written 'H' and 'E-flat' is written 'Es', the fundamental tone row is the *Hetaera Esmeralda* theme. The melody of the cantata is:

> determined by permutation of its basic motif of five notes, the symbolic letters H-E-A-E-Es. [It is based on a] magic square . . . technique that develops the utmost variety out of materials that are always identical, a style in which there is nothing that is not thematic . . . variation of something forever the same. (510 [617])

That is: H-E(ter)-A-E-Es(meralda). Leverkühn's masterpiece insists on the centrality of love, but under the sign of the intertwining of desire and death, sexuality and syphilis, the passionate and the daemonic.

For Leverkühn, music goes from being symptom to sublimation. As a symptom, it is a classical compromise formation, combining the repressed wish for forbidden desire with diabolical censorship of expressions of love. As sublimation, especially in the forms of musical notation, librettos and cantatas, it is a system of conventional symbols that supplements speech and expresses ambivalent feelings. The 'magic square' of the tone row is central to both, and the mysterious location of this discovery in the novel is the final clue that *Doctor Faustus* is about repression, before it is about reification.

In the diegetic chronology created within Mann's novel, the transformation of the 'Stravinskyian' Leverkühn into the 'Schönbergian' Leverkühn is musically underdetermined, even if it is psychologically overdetermined. Leverkühn's inspiration for the 'magic square' is related in chapter XXII, during events which place it against the narrative background of the composition of music for a symphonic version of *Love's Labor Lost*, music which is completed in 1913. The magical square, Zeitblom informs the reader, first makes its presence felt in the thirteen *Brentano Lieder* resulting from this process. These songs are begun in Palestrina, in 1912, while on holiday with Adrian's Platonic love, Rüdiger Schildknapp (205 [245]). Palestrina is also the setting for the dialogue with the Devil that is related in the fateful chapter XXV of the novel. The chapter narrating the *Apocalypse* – chapter XXXIV – happens *after* the Shakespeare symphony, and marks the inception of Leverkühn's opening to breakthrough by describing a work completed in 1919. Supposedly, the magical square is important to this 'Stravinskyian' work. Finally, the description of the *Lamentation* happens towards the end of the novel, in chapter XLVI, imagining a work completed in the period 1928–30. The magical square is also central to that final, 'Schönbergian' cantata (511–12 [618–19]). Although Zeitblom describes *Lamentation* as another breakthrough, the narrative motivates this only biographically (the murder of Schwerdtfeger and the death of Leverkühn's nephew) but not musically. By contrast with *Apocalypse*, which displays a heterogeneity of elements and the decomposition of form, however, *Lamentation* generates its elements endogenously through a principle of composition which guarantees formal consistency. It is, in other words, composed using the magic square. Zeitblom registers the break emphatically: 'in general, Leverkühn's late work has little in common with that written in his thirties [i.e., with the works that culminate with *Apocalipsis cum figuris*]' (513 [620]). Yet the narrative fails to attribute two different compositional procedures to *Apocalypse* and *Lamentation*, for instance, by bringing forward the magical square to a position later in the narrative, where it would make musical sense as the difference between the two works.

The reason is simple. Mann attributes an entirely different significance to the magical square compared with Adorno. For Adorno, the magical square reduces music to reason. For Mann, the magical square is a cipher for love. I will discuss what magic it is that the square holds, via connecting Palestrina, Shakespeare and Leverkühn, in a moment. For now, I want to notice that the difference between *Apocalypse* and *Lamentation* concerns more than just the opposition between heterogeneous and endogenous form. Leverkühn's fundamental musical problem, the problem of conventionality, has two registers: musical breakthroughs quickly ossify into new conventions; but, also, musical conventions are *conventional*, not indexical. While the first register determines Adorno's response, it is the second register that is crucial for Mann. The problem of conventionality confronted by Leverkühn involves arbitrariness, the lack of true necessity in musical conventions. The transition from the 'Stravinskyian' *Apocalypse* to the 'Schönbergian' *Lamentation* is from natural to logical necessity. In *Apocalypse*, musical notes are motivated, because they are icons of mocking laughter. In *Lamentation*, musical notes unmotivated, symbolizing forbidden desire in a culturally regulated way.

The development of a musical language for the expression of anguish is centred on its ability to encode the repression of forbidden love, emblematized by the Hetaera Esmeralda matrix in *Lamentation*. Certainly, the semantics of a mythological coincidence of opposites remains the underlying theme of Leverkühn's entire work, for 'the same identity that reigns between the crystal chorus of angels and the howls of hell in the *Apocalypse* has now [in *Lamentation*] become all-embracing' (512 [619]). That is the significance of the 'wicked and good Christian' refrain that structures the final work. In *Apocalypse*, ambivalent feelings towards romantic love and sexual passion find expression through acoustic icons that have an archaic – theologically medieval – quality. By contrast, in *Lamentation*, this ambivalence is expressed not through iconic resemblances, but, instead, 'as a result of the absoluteness of the form, music is liberated as language' (512 [619]).

Part II

Leverkühn's discovery of the magic square pivots on the coincidence of two events: his sojourn in Palestrina with Schildknapp and the visitation from Mephistopheles. This highlights something crucial about the novel that the Adornian perspective misses: it is about a Faustian Bargain, about the conjuration of the Devil. The novel is written in the mode of the literary fantastic, which involves a structurally determined hesitation between natural and supernatural explanations of events (Todorov 1975). That mode generates a systematic uncertainty, partitioned between Zeitblom and Leverkühn, as to whether we are dealing with the Dionysian – that is, the pressure of repressed instinctual forces, resulting in transgressive pleasure – or the demonic – that is, the diabolical evil that results from willing the opposite of the moral law. Deciding prematurely that what is at stake is the instinctual, that is, uncritical acceptance of Zeitblom's perspective, not only leads to overlooking *the fact that we hesitate* – it also leads to a second blindness. This is to the fact that the opposition between the Dionysian and the demonic does not exhaust the field of possible registers of the uncanny. From the Freudian perspective that Mann adopts, Romanticism creates a subterranean link between life and death within music. Melos is the medium for that Wagnerian fusion of death and desire that Mann calls 'the abyss', and that Freud, thinking about repetition compulsions that go beyond the pleasure principle, described as 'the daemonic'. The nature of this fusion of death and desire so perplexed Freud that he deferred any decision to the celestial and chthonic gods, Eros and Thanatos. Mann, by contrast, stages the problem through the cultural divinities, Shakespeare and Nietzsche, a 'coincidence of opposites' that he frames into a new, Freudian myth for the twentieth century.

Shakespeare: Gravity's revolt to wantonness

The limitations of the two perspectives in German modernity – the Goethean humanism of Zeitblom (an angelic repression of desire that prepares the Romantic symptom) and the Romantic modernism of Leverkühn (a symptomatic revolt to diabolical enactment that delights in transgression) – are initially focalized around Shakespeare. An exceptional figure, because one of the only non-German cultural intellectuals in the novel, Shakespeare provides both a model for aspects of Leverkühn's narrative and a set of cultural coordinates for thinking beyond repression and symptom. On the one hand, Mann was highly influenced by Frank Harris's psychobiography, *The Man Shakespeare and His Tragic Life Story* (1909) (Mann 1961: 166–7), which serves as pattern both for deliberately induced syphilitic genius and for a series of disastrous love triangles (Cerf 1981: 476–80). I shall deal with this first. On the other hand, on the reading implied by Mann, Shakespeare's plea for a moderation of superego ferocity is the key to his grasp of the secret connection between death and desire in guilt. I shall deal with this second.

The novel insists on a parallel between Leverkühn and Shakespeare. In line with Mann's endorsement of the Harris thesis, Shakespeare's name is foremost on the list of syphilitic geniuses that Mann itemizes (alongside Dürer, Nietzsche and Schumann) (Mann 1961). In the novel, the parallel is mediated by Shakespeare's romantic comedies, *Love's Labour Lost* in particular, and the relation between them and the sonnets that Harris proposes. 'Adrian', notes Zeitblom, 'always carried with him a pocketbook edition of the sonnets' and particularly admired the ambivalent passion and cynicism of Berowne's monologues in *Love's Labour Lost* (230 [260]). Mann accepted the interpretation according to which these monologues ventriloquize Shakespeare's disillusionment after a catastrophic romantic triangle. For Harris, Shakespeare attempts to woo the 'dark lady', Mary Fitton, by proxy through the 'fair youth', William Herbert, while being sexually in love with the former and idealistically in love with the latter. By contrast with Harris, Mann's homosexuality sensitized his reading of Shakespeare's 'fair youth' sonnets. Accordingly, although the first love triangle, between Leverkühn, Schildknapp and (the absent, merely represented) Esmeralda involves romantic idealization, there is a strong homoerotic component. While it is possibly the case that the 'shared chastity' of Leverkühn and Schildknapp is 'the foundation of their friendship', it is no wonder that the songs they collaborate on are 'an unrelenting, tense game played by art at the very edge of impossibility' (233 [277], 235 [280]). The object of their collaboration introduces the third elements into the triangle, for the music is none other than the song 'Oh Sweet Maiden'. That song is an invocation of Esmeralda: 'it all comes from one basic figure, from a row of intervals capable of multiple variation, taken from the five notes: B-E-A-E-E-flat [H-E-A-E-Es]' (205 [245]). Leverkühn's second impossible/forbidden love then follows the same triangular pattern, but now involving reversal into homosexual consummation rather than romantic idealization. The relationship between Adrian Leverkühn, Rudi Schwerdtfeger and Madame Godeau has the classical structure, based on wooing by proxy (442 [526], 459 [551], 467 [564]), but Madame Godeau is at best idealized by Leverkühn, while it is strongly implied that Schwerdtfeger is his lover (369–70 [443–4]).

Shakespeare's importance to *Doctor Faustus*, however, goes beyond a narrative template for romantic fiasco with a homoerotic subtext. The theme of the apparently trivial comedy *Love's Labour Lost* is central to the problem of the daemonic. As Alexander Honold has shown, there is a hidden relationship between the text of *Love's Labour*, the magic square of serial composition and the combinatory of elements at work in *Doctor Faustus* (Honold 2017: 70–94). The encounter with Hetaera Esmeralda functions for Leverkühn in the same way that the love cure works for the characters in *Love's Labour*, where 'the vehement rejection of love soon turns into desperate lovesickness and personal obsession' (Honold 2017: 79). In *Love's Labour*, this theme is provided with formal expression through linguistic games that turn out to logically exhaust of the space of romantic communication. The same basic compositional principle is at work in Leverkühn's music, once he discovers the serial method in the development of *Love's Labour Lost*. The apparently arbitrary designation of a tone row and its mapping out in the magical square of compositional possibilities provide for a conclusive exploration of the space of the refrain. This is guided by the permutations known as the sequence, inverse, retrograde and inverse retrograde, as explained in Adorno's manuscript on Schönberg. The point of the logical character of twelve-tone composition is that it renders music entirely conventional – that is, symbolic, rather than iconic – and therefore completes its transformation into a language.

In the process, the selection of the Hetaera Esmeralda sequence as the basis for the *Lamentation* indicates that Leverkühn finds a constructive way to evade diabolical censorship. By inventing a musical language capable of the symbolic expression of forbidden desire, Leverkühn is engaged in a curious combination of potential sublimation and actual repression. It is repression to the extent that the sexual content of the magical square, evident to Zeitblom, remains closed to Leverkühn. It is sublimation, to the degree that Leverkühn's articulation of an impossible/forbidden love through controlled forms of musical expression that are socially accepted, that potentially provides a satisfying alternative to enactment. What should by now be evident is that Leverkühn's efforts towards sublimation fail, for his music is rejected and his illness renders him catatonic after *Lamentation*. Meanwhile the intensification of repression associated with the failure of sublimation generates a further symptom – focalized through the character Nepomuk – explored in a moment. But it is worth considering forbidden love briefly, for biographical scholarship on Mann has now conclusively established that he, like Leverkühn, experienced a lifetime of furtive and/or frustrated homosexual passion (Böhm 1990). The 'Shakespearean' love triangles of *Doctor Faustus* indicate the delicacy with which this theme is raised in the novel and point towards the culturally progressive expansion and deepening of love that is involved. The magic square – a combinatory exploration of the entire field of exogamous love – is a fitting emblem for the plea that the novel enters on behalf of romantic freedom.

For Mann, however, Shakespeare provides a model for literature as diagnosis as well as therapy. The diagnostic theme is grasped in a motif repeated several times in the novel:

> The blood of youth burns not with such excess
> As gravity's revolt to wantonness? (231 [270])

Moral righteousness calls forth, in other words, transgressive rebellion. According to Jonathan Dollimore, there is an underlying continuity between *Love's Labour Lost* and *Measure for Measure*, probably the play that is closest in spirit to Mann's diagnosis of the cultural roots of fascism (Dollimore 2017: 30).

> The . . . idea of the most savage kind of wantonness emerging from, and being intensified by, gravity is also dramatized in *Measure for Measure*. Angelo, the Puritan upholder of religion and law, suddenly becomes wrecked by illicit sexual desire for the chaste Isabella, who aspires to a nunnery. . . . We could call it the vicious dialectical intensification of evil by good: evil irrupting from within the good, and taking from it a certain intensity which in turn invests evil with a virulence that it does not intrinsically have. (Dollimore 2017: 31)

Where repression engenders symptoms, surplus repression brings forth an intertwinement of forbidden desire with superego guilt. This is an alloy of sexuality and aggression that twists love into hate, infatuation into destruction. This clarifies the paradoxically deathwishful eroticism at stake in the novel, the puzzling entwinement of Eros and Thanatos. It is not that opposites meet. Rather, forbidden desire, twisted by superego-induced guilt, irrupts symptomatically as unspeakable transgression. In Leverkühn himself, the anxiety that the 'revolt to wantonness' might take the form of promiscuity laced with degradation is defended against, by means of its inversion into an icy distance freighted with murderous aggression. When this defence collapses, the abyss of an abominable crime opens, a personal guilt (501 [604]) that is the echo of historical guilt (325 [386–7]).

The figure of Nietzsche

The figures who focalize this theme of abhorrent transgression and terrible guilt, in Mann's novelistic inscription of a new myth for Germany, are Nietzsche and Luther (respectively). To say that Mann utterly detested Luther would be an understatement, for in 'Germany and the Germans', Mann proposes that the cultural predominance of Luther's 'medieval' religiosity is the correlate to German historical belatedness (Mann 1973: 4). The Reformation in Germany, freighted with arcane demonology and righteous intolerance, strangled the Renaissance in the sixteenth century, and then choked off Goethean humanism in the nineteenth century. Luther is therefore the origin of that (for Mann) peculiarly German hypertrophy of the superego that leads to oscillation between judgemental arrogance and self-lacerating guilt. Luther's moral absolutism dialectically summoned forth the spirit of Romantic transgression around the conjurer's diagram of

German 'depth of spirit' (i.e. introspective grandiosity laced with provincial inwardness) and 'fascination with the abyss' (i.e. captivation by the atavistic and irrational, coupled to corrosive relativism) (Mann 1973: 15–18). In short, Nietzsche is the symptom of Luther.

The figure of Nietzsche is invisible yet pervasive in the text (Mann 1961: 32), inflecting Mann's imaginary composer with a political significance impossible for 'Stravinsky' or 'Schönberg', or even 'Shakespeare'. Mann invests Leverkühn with the biographical details of Nietzsche's life according to his source texts (particularly TW Brann), especially the episode of the Cologne brothel and Nietzsche's wooing of Lou Andreas-Salomé by proxy (Bergsten 1969: 55–61). Indeed, Mann's response to the supposed equivalence of Leverkühn with Schönberg is worth citing:

> The idea that Adrian Leverkühn is Schönberg, that the figure is a portrait of him, is so utterly absurd that I scarcely know what to say about it. . . . *Doctor Faustus* has been called a Nietzsche-novel, and indeed, the book, which for good reasons avoids Nietzsche's name, contains many references to his intellectual tragedy, even direct quotations from the history of his illness. It has also been said that I had bisected myself in the novel, and that the narrator and the composer each embraced a part of me. That, also, contains an element of truth. (Bergsten 1969: 56, 58 Mann cited)

Nietzsche is significant for the German descent into fascist irrationalism for two basic reasons. The first reason is the ideological role of Nietzscheanism in legitimization of Nazism. Mann's essay on Nietzsche – an 'essayistic postlude to *Faustus*' (Mann 1961: 221) – interprets the philosopher as a symptom of proto-fascist cultural conditions, rather than a direct cause of fascist politics (Mann 1959: 152). Nonetheless, in relation to the second reason, the cultural role of Nietzsche in Romantic fascination with the abyss, Mann is categorical. The kernel of irrationality in Nietzsche's philosophy springs from the distinctly Romantic combination of relativism with vitalism (Mann 1959: 157). Fascism is a form of political Romanticism, one that responds to Germany's historical belatedness and cultural backwardness by seeking civilizational renewal, gained through the desperate route of a convulsive transformation achieved by irrational means. The implication is that the novel is not about the rationalization of aesthetics, but about the aestheticization of reason, and the political consequences of the cultural and libidinal forces that Nietzsche's philosophy represents.

Mann's focus on Nietzsche centres on the philosopher's reading of the problem of historical consciousness, where self-reflexive cognition of the conventionality of values leads to instinctual inhibitions, because the will is paralysed by knowledge of the arbitrariness of every civilization. The relativity of values, the idea that civilizations are bounded wholes whose values are merely relative to the civilizational totality, implies that civilizational transformation – the "revaluation of values" – is an arbitrary process. Faced with this knowledge, the modern individual cannot discover anything binding about their own civilizational values, so that, like Leverkühn confronted with the conventionality of music, everything seems to be a parody of seriousness and meaningfulness.

Conversely, though, Nietzsche argues the vitality of transgression when it is connected to instinctual release, proposing that although the revaluation of values involves doing what is forbidden, the result is a revitalization of historical culture. The entailment is that a supreme crime, involving radical evil, is necessary to every social inauguration, in what amounts to the arguments of Chaim Breisacher in the novel: a deliberate re-barbarization as the key to civilizational renewal. A further implication, explored in Mann's *Mario and the Magician* (about Italian fascism) (Mann 1988), is that the Romantic radical thinks of civilizational formations as imaginative conjectures. They therefore accept the notion that the foundation of new forms involves a combination of magus and artist – someone like Zarathustra, prepared to trick the masses into a new ideology. It is worth noting that Mann's critique of Nietzsche is also a self-critique of Nietzsche's influence on Mann's aesthetics and politics before the 1920s. *Doctor Faustus* is Mann's 'retraction', not only of Nietzsche, but also of Nietzschean strain of cultural Romanticism (Schopenhauer, Wagner) that was formative for Mann (Lesser 1950, 1951). The essay on the German catastrophe that identifies the ideological origin of fascism in fascination with the abyss is thereby clarified as a persistent Romantic strain in German culture.

Beyond the personal characteristics of Nietzsche that are reflected in Leverkühn – arrogance, narcissism – the novel opposes the captivation by images of destruction, represented in the 'Stravinskyian' phase of Leverkühn's work, to the development of a musical language capable of articulating desire, represented in the 'Schönbergian' stage of Leverkühn's work. In a series of ways, Mann links the captivation by images to atavistic regression, an insight that directs his engagement with cultural struggle during the Nazi period. This is the explanation for why as soon as Hitler took power, Mann began work on his Joseph novels, which oppose the Jewish Law, especially its *Bilderverbot*, to polytheistic paganism. A series of Romantic themes – the coincidence of opposites, mythological imaginary, apocalyptic imagery and the iconography of the godhead, through to the disintegration of the bodily image and the fragmentation of the self – are thereby rejected. The 'paleo-symbolic pre-lingusiticality' of these libidinal images brings Nietzsche into contact with German mythology in ways reminiscent of polytheistic paganism. That points not just to a residue of the premodern in Germany's belated modernity, but also to mythologies of the tribe as ideologies of transgression, that is, as pre-Axial and anti-universal.

In *Doctor Faustus*, the atavism of the Romantic transgression that guides Nazi ideology is traced to the ultimate regression, from exogamy to endogamy. The incest theme is a condensation of themes of isolation and inwardness, but also an exploration of the anti-universal roots of German culture in its archaic mythology. Mann's novella on the Siegfried myth, about the incestuous union of Siegfried's parents, Siegmund and Sieglinde, clarifies his implicit claim about German mythology (Mann 2001: 289–317). Indeed, the captivation by images of German Romanticism implies not a release of inhibitions through instinctual regression, as evident in the incest theme in Mann's novel (Hoelzel 1988).

Mann provides systematic hints towards incestuous desire in Leverkühn, centred on the coincidence of his mother's striking eyes with the eyes of the prostitute, Hetaera Esmeralda (Pelikan-Strauss 1987). But he also accepted the account of TW Brann, who believed that Nietzsche had an incestuous relation with his sister and was infatuated with Salomé as an image of his sister (Bergsten 1969). Leverkühn's bizarre confession at the inaugural performance of *Lamentation*, about the 'little mermaid' as his 'sister and bride' (524 [632]), confirms that his case is the same. Leverkühn's completion of his cantata is an act of both mourning for, and contribution about, his nephew, Nepomuk, whom he calls 'Echo', treats as an infatuated father would, and names as his son (525 [633]). Is Nepomuk, in fact, the child of Adrian and his sister Ursula? Textual details, including his speech on marriage at his sister Ursula's wedding and the details of his sister's children, strongly imply sibling incest within the novel. Leverkühn hints at her wedding that the real barrier to desire is the difference of the other (implying that desire desires the identical) (201 [239]). This might simply imply narcissism, were it not for Zeitblom's pointed noting of Nepomuk's eyes (484 [576]). This clinches it. Nepomuk has blue eyes, as does Adrian and his father, Johann, while Ursula has her mother's brown eyes; Ursula's husband has brown eyes too. Ursula's first children, in 1911, 1912 and 1913, are then followed by a long interval until Nepomuk is born in 1923. This happens after Adrian's Faustian Bargain, which includes the Devil assigning him the 'little mermaid' as his wife (246 [292]).

Freud in the twentieth century

Mann's retelling of the Faust legend is part of the gigantic project of crafting a new myth for Germany. Freud is central to that myth: in *Doctor Faustus*, Shakespeare and Freud are opposed to Luther and Nietzsche. As presence of the incest theme indicates, Mann's engagement with Freud is total – lock, stock and barrel – for Freud replaces Nietzsche as Mann's guiding star. The implication is that Mann is engaged in a specifically Freudian diagnosis of Nietzsche, as well as a cultural repudiation of political Romanticism.

In this connection, it is worth briefly contrasting Freud's concept of repression with Nietzsche's notion of inhibition. In *The Genealogy of*

Morals (1887), Nietzsche proposes that civilization depends on imposing moral restraints on natural instincts, which leads to a whole swathe of inhibitions (*Hemmungen*). There follows a multiplication of prohibitions, eventually resulting a society that is hostile to Life (i.e. instinctual release) (Chapelle 1999: 37–50). In *Civilization and Its Discontents* (1930), in an apparently similar way, Freud argues that increasing renunciation of instinctual satisfactions, concomitant with industrial discipline, leads to growing repression of drive components (S. Freud 1930). The frustration connected with increasing repression implies, he maintains, the need for a surplus pressure on the repressed material. In his article on melancholia, Freud has already argued that this is achieved by turning aggression against the ego via the superego, with the risk that the superego becomes 'a pure culture of the death instinct' (S. Freud 1923: 53). But for Freud, repression differs from both inhibition and sublimation: an inhibition is an alteration (de-sexualization) of the aim that retains its object (the other) – 'inhibition'; a sublimation is an alteration (de-sexualization) of the aim now directed to a substitute object (an idea) – 'deflection'; repression is the substitution of an object (an idea), accompanied by the turning backwards of the (sexual) aim – 'arrest' (S. Freud 1926: 87–90, 110). The arrested sexual aim – the 'satisfaction held in abeyance' (S. Freud 1926: 113) – provides the dynamic pressure behind the chain of associations that develops in the unconscious, between the original object and subsequent ideas, and that sometimes returns in symptom formation. The ramifying network of forbidden ideas that results generates the typical pattern of phobic, obsessional and hysterical patients, namely, a spreading web of irrational taboos. These are designed to avoid trigger circumstances where the return of the repressed might overrun the defensive trench system around the ego. On Freud's account, it is precisely this embattled condition that leads to the ego drawing on the aggressivity of the superego to maintain its increasingly precarious salients. But the superego then acts pre-emptively, accusing the ego of surrender to instinctual forces before battle is even joined (S. Freud 1926: 116–17).

Against this background, the link to Romanticism is best established through consideration of Freud's reversal, in *Inhibitions, Symptoms and Anxieties*, of the relation between anxiety and repression. For the mature Freud, anxiety is experienced in the ego, when objects associated with repressed ideas enter the ego's proximity – the result is repression, a defence mechanism that protects the ego from excessive anxiety (S. Freud 1926: 108–9). Anxiety, Freud argues, is aroused in the ego – itself a 'bodily ego' (S. Freud 1923: 23), that is, an imago that maps permitted instinctual aims onto erogenous zones and thence to the partial objects located in the other person – as the spectre of shattering punishment by the superego, should prohibited instinctual impulses be released (S. Freud 1926: 118). From the perspective of the neurotic, then, death is the flipside to desire, something imagined as a destruction of the ego, a disintegration of the bodily image in dismemberment and mutilation. This is paradigmatically evidenced in castration phantasies (S. Freud 1926: 128–9). The problem is that the pre-emptive cycle of anxiety and repression results in arrested development, a suspension of sexuality at the Oedipal moment, for fundamentally, the re-structuration of the ego is a necessary element in maturation. That is not just a question of Freud's developmental theories about the unification of the component instincts in genital sexuality, the intensification of identification with one parent and the substitution of an acceptable sexual object for the other parent, and the destruction of the repressed material of the Oedipal conflict (S. Freud 1924). It is fundamentally a question of the renunciation of that image of potency that Freud calls the phallus and links to infantile sexuality, something that Freud affirms happens through the symbolization of the objects of the sexual instinct within the framework of exogamy. These linguistically mediated frameworks are generally articulated through religious taboos, divine laws and cultural codes, and are sometimes supplemented by iconographies of the demonic and the divine. But, not surprisingly, Freud thinks that the shift to a monotheistic formulation supported by a ban on images is a major cultural advance (S. Freud 1939: 83–6).

From the Freudian perspective, then, Romanticism is a neurotic registration of the crisis of repression. This results from a civilizational moment in which maturation is necessary, but impossible – because of the lack of any symbolization of desire. Under these conditions, death and desire appear as a fusional unity: a captivating image of disintegration; the fascinating spectacle of the abyss.

Mann's substitution of Freud for Nietzsche, then, is not simply a politically inspired transfer of allegiance from the German Romantic disciple of Schopenhauer to his Jewish Enlightenment counterpart – although that motivation is certainly present (Lee 2007: 1–21). Instead, in the novel, 'psychology' is positioned between Romantic 'theology' and conservative 'humanism' (p. 201), because of their attitudes towards 'daemonic' repressed instinctual impulses. Humanism phobically avoids confronting the daemonic; Romanticism is neurotically fascinated by the release of the daemonic; only psychoanalysis grasps the need for mature ways of coping with instinctual demands. Freud, Mann affirms, is the humanism of the future, because psychoanalysis confronts the daemonic without surrender to the *Liebestod*, Wagnerian images of the fusional unity of death and desire (Mann 1947a: 360), or Schopenhauer's speculation about the transformative and transgressive power of the irrational instincts (Mann 1947b: 408). In *Doctor Faustus*, Mann powerfully and cogently 'retracts' his own German Romanticism, in the name of Freud's evocation of the 'voice of reason' (Mann 1947c: 428). In Mann's *Joseph Tetralogy*, Mann worked in dialogue with Freud on a representation of the theses eventually contained in *Moses and Monotheism*, effecting a new humanist reading of religious mythology. Mann intervenes in the dissemination of the distinctively modern myth, the

Faust myth, to represent psychoanalytic theories as a cultural cure for the German disease of metaphysically inflated Romanticism.

Coda: Communicative reading

Thomas Mann's *Doctor Faustus* is an indirect communication about the failure of German culture to provide a civilizational defence mechanism capable of withstanding the surge of irrationalism that resulted in fascism. That is the significance of his claim that 'the central idea is the flight from the difficulties of the cultural crisis into the pact with the devil' (Mann 1961: 30). That brings me to the question of Mann's diagnosis of the cultural coordinates of fascist politics. What the communicative perspective clarifies is that, for Mann, these coordinates are in surplus repression. Specifically, it is about the problem of 'gravity's revolt to wantonness', the problem that surplus repression is not the same as instinctual inhibition. Repression pre-emptively summons the forces of superegoic aggressivity against the immature ego, resulting in symptomatic returns where desire and death are intertwined. The startling truth is that Mann's explanation of fascism is superstructural, not infrastructural; it is metapsychological, not metapolitical.

It is worth contrasting Mann with his double, DH Lawrence, to grasp what is at stake here. For Lawrence, the crisis of civilization is the result of sexual inhibition, caused by a life-denying moral conscience that is buttressed by obsolescent religious doctrines. A frank naturalism about sexuality (and rather more sexual enjoyment all round) is the cornerstone to releasing a whole series of inhibitions, including those on masculine aggressivity. Lawrence thought that these generated those masochistic and introverted personalities who were the compliant drones of industrial alienation. What Mann realizes, which Lawrence does not, is that moral gravity does not revolt to frank naturalism when conscience is troubled by a ferocious superego. The repressed is infused with transgression and punishment, carrying a tremendous energy of anxiety along with its libidinal charge, investing it in the captivating imaginary of the disintegrating body. For the weak ego, 'desire is death', but acting out the spectacle of destruction remains a possibility, when the superego is delegated to the leader. Rectitude's rebellion is to transgression; Weimar conservatism revolts to fascist atrocity. While Lawrence, who does not understand this, becomes a proto-fascist, Mann, who understands this, becomes an anti-fascist exile.

Mann's entire work is dedicated to the problem of the historical transformation of the liberal individual into an empty shell, and the correlative rise of a Romantic counter-culture that cultivates an asocial individuality through the embrace of aestheticized irrationality. The early story 'Tristan' (1902), for instance, explores the antinomy of the philistine bourgeois Klöterjahn and the decadent aesthete Spinell, in the context of a critique of Wagner's opera. The characters' fascination with the Wagnerian fusion of death and desire – the *Liebestöd* – represents the yearning for a necessary transformation of subjectivity, but only in the morbid form of the destructive imaginary (Mann 2008: 113–68). In *Death in Venice* (1912), the antinomies are intro-reflected into the individuality of Aschenbach, in the conflict between his social role as a successful author of neoclassical forms and his deepest personal longings for ecstatic release, of a transgressive, yet aestheticized, erotic variety. The contradiction between the 'ethics' of the ego (i.e. bourgeois morality) and the repressed 'aesthetics' of the depths (i.e. Romantic radicalism) irrupts when solitude and encounter make possible a lifting of moral censorship – what emerges is not healthy homoerotic desire, but deathwish, and self-destruction (Mann 2008: 249–343). The advent of the twentieth century means that the autonomous individual of the liberal epoch of Goethean humanism is finished, but against the depersonalization advocated by the spokespersons of fascism, and the collectivist de-individualization of the communists, Mann advocates a post-individualist psychology and a socialized individual (Berman 1986: 261–86). However, it is not until Mann's renunciation of Nietzsche and his turn to Freud, emblematically marked out in *Doctor Faustus*, that Mann can specify how the re-structuration of the individual is to be achieved, without embracing the abyssal fusion of death and desire.

8

Imaginative disclosure and literary identification

In his work on the philosophical discourse of modernity, Habermas spectacularly reverses the position on literature implied by his theory of communicative action. In the theory of communicative action, Habermas proposed to discover the 'unity of reason in the diversity of its many voices' (Habermas 1992a: 115–48). As discussed in the chapters on critique, Habermas detected in aesthetic and expressive rationality two intertwined voices of communicative reason that explore the subjective world. The paradigm for the aesthetic-expressive dimension of communicative reason is literature (and criticism), because of its links to language. Indeed, as we have seen, he often spoke of 'science, morality and art' as the institutional loci of the discoveries made within cognitive-instrumental, normative-evaluative and aesthetic-expressive rationalities, respectively. In sum, the theory of communicative action implicitly grasped literature as a moment of reflection, akin to argumentative debate, and literary criticism as a dimension of reason.

In his intervention on the philosophical discourse of modernity, by contrast, Habermas develops an opposition between philosophy and literary criticism, directed at an about-face on literature and reason. Philosophy is interpreted as a discourse on the universally binding propositional dimensions of communicative reason (i.e. the cognitive-scientific and normative-legal). These are framed as the problem-solving capacities of society. Literary criticism, however, is grasped as a discourse on the literary imagination and its cultural opening up of forms of significance. The term chosen to express the difference between propositional argumentation and the literary imagination is 'world-disclosure'. The ultimate aim of Habermas's revision is to oppose literary criticism to philosophical discourse, in the context of a polemic against deconstruction's conflation of the two discursive modes.

In an oft-quoted statement, Habermas declares that literary criticism 'administers potentials for world-disclosure', while philosophy 'administers capacities for problem-solving' (PDM: 207 [243]).

Now, a significant component of Habermas's presentation of the claim depends on his argumentative strategy against deconstruction – qua conflation of literary criticism with philosophical reasoning – which drives the stark distinction between critique and disclosure proposed in *The Philosophical Discourse of Modernity*. Nonetheless, Habermas's reversal of the communicative position also happens following debate with fellow critical theorist Albrecht Wellmer, and so it is by no means entirely an artefact of the polemic against deconstruction. In an important retraction of the position articulated in the theory of communicative action, Habermas maintains that in the literary work, the whole is greater than the parts. He states that it is impossible to tease apart the literary work's presentation of possible experience into validity claims that might be adjudicated for their truth value. Instead, the imaginative vision presented in the literary work is integrated into the life history of readers. Accordingly, Habermas maintains that literary works express a 'truth potential', rather than stake validity claims, and the subsequent notion of 'world-disclosure' is an effort to explain what 'truth potential' might mean.

The effect of the stark distinction between critique and disclosure is twofold. First, it exiles literary criticism from critique. Literary criticism becomes restricted to the explication of imaginative visions of possible experience. Second, it prevents the literary work from sparking critical debate. Literary works now may only provide points of identification. I think that this is a disastrous position, on two major counts. First, it undermines the fundamental architecture of the theory of communicative action and its defence of the modern project. Once Habermas revises his position on literature, the role of literature in the learning processes connected with the subjective world is placed in serious question. Literature expands subjectivity by enhancing the imagination. It no longer contributes to the exploration of the subjective world by reason. That negates a significant component of 'aesthetic-expressive rationality'. It is equivalent to saying that in modernity, subjectivity grows like topsy, but we don't really know anything about what it is that is growing, unless it one day presents in a clinical context for inspection by therapeutic discourses. Second, Habermas's revised position conceptualizes literature through a false dichotomy – critique *or* disclosure – that is stated by means of highly problematic formulations. In Habermas's efforts to clarify how the category of disclosure is supposed to work, he relies on questionable constructions. Habermas thinks that literary wholes cannot be analytically decomposed into conjectural validity claims. But Habermas's work on religion indicates that this is a false position. Religious mythologies are presented as holistic narratives, yet he affirms that an ethical core can be analytically extracted from religions. Habermas also presents a 'stimulus-response' model of disclosure. He proposes that holistic presentations of possible experience 'cause' the effect of disclosure. By contrast, I am going to propose that this effect depends on an active stance of reception.

At the same time, the idea of disclosure conveys an authentic insight. Literary works *do* holistically present imaginative visions of possible experience. Sometimes, readers *do* identify with the work's presentation as a legitimate way of seeing the world. Then, the work is taken to disclose, reveal, an authentic potential form of existence. Identification with this aspect of literary works can affect a person's life history. It does so through a transformation of their personality structure – their character – that modifies their ego identity. Individuals release the potential for truth of an imaginary form of existence by living the experience that it presents as possible. The literature of religious proselytization is an excellent example of how this works. But so too is the secular literature of modern love, for romance as passion is mainly a literary invention. A second important insight follows from the notion of literary disclosure. The role of literature as bearer for imaginative visions necessitates a literary-critical standpoint capable of retrieving the holistic meaning-potential of the text. Known as the 'hermeneutics of recovery', critical explication of the ways in which the literary work presents an imaginative vision has been neglected in Literary Studies. The discussion of disclosure reframes the hermeneutics of recovery as a legitimate partner to the better-known hermeneutics of suspicion. It also points forward to empirical studies of reception that might move Literary Studies beyond theoretical speculations that lack robust engagement with actual readers.

The category of disclosure

The term 'disclosure' can seem perplexing. In the context of continental philosophy, disclosure does not have its everyday meaning of divulging a specific secret, but rather means, more generally, bringing things to light. The category of disclosure in the English-language representations of the debate originates as a translation of Martin Heidegger's German terms: *Unverborgenheit*, unconcealedness; and *Erschlossenheit*, disclosedness. These are themselves Heidegger's idiosyncratic translations of the Greek term *Aletheia*, manifest truth, normally translated into German as *Wahr* and *Wahrheit*, truth and truthfulness. Another translation of *Aletheia* is, of course, 'revelation'. Habermas, meanwhile, studiously avoids *Unverborgenheit* and *Erschlossenheit*, instead employing *Welterschliessung*, literally, the generation of worlds, or world-building (PDM: 201, 207 [236, 243]). However, Habermasian *Welterschliessung* is translated into the English-language debate with the same term as Heideggerian *Unverborgenheit*, disclosure.

Accordingly, in the Habermasian context, disclosure might be glossed as 'opening-up', or, even, 'bringing to light', provided that the constructive activity (and therefore the fictional provisionality) of 'world-building' is retained. In disclosure, something is provisionally brought to light. A topic is opened up in a new way. For Habermas, a disclosure is a special representation that reveals, or opens up, an 'eye-popping' new perception, or a 'striking' new meaning (Habermas 1998b: 383–402). It has the potential to change our attitude towards the world in some important respect. In that regard, the concept of disclosure acts like the categories of 'vision' and 'envisionment'. It makes something able to be 'seen' – perceived, experienced, intuited, conceptualized – that before was 'unseen'. These days, ocular metaphors are, so to speak, on the nose, because of the supposed objectification they perform (Jay 1994). But because I think that this specular taboo is fashionable nonsense, I intend to use 'vision' and 'disclosure' interchangeably.

The philosophical origins of disclosure are concerning, because it arrives from the history of philosophy, as it were, dripping with blood. The provenance of the underlying concept from within the work of Heidegger – philosophical Romantic and Nazi sympathizer – marks it out as potentially problematic. In translations of Heideggerian philosophy, disclosure often gets the grandiose prefix – '*world*-disclosure' – because it is assigned to something truly mysterious, an 'Event' in the 'Sending of Being' (Heidegger 2008: 425). In his essay on the 'origin of poetry', Heidegger proposes that this sort of numinous rupture happens when a great poet sets forth a new vision of how the world is, populating the canvas of Being with a fresh conception of earth and sky, mortals and gods (Heidegger 2008: 139–212). Poetry discloses complete worlds in an entirely new way. The philosophical implication of this position is that we inhabit our fictions in the strongest possible sense, namely, that poetic world-disclosure acts transcendentally to inaugurate the categories of rationality, to define what entities exist, and therefore to constitute possible experience. There is no outside. Societies exist as a multitude of holistic totalities whose ontology and normativity are entirely different and whose languages are therefore ultimately untranslatable. The parallels between this idea of world-disclosure and the notion that civilizations are founded by prophetic revelations that not only define what reality is for an historical epoch, but also delimit what counts as reason, are unmistakeable.

It is a short step from this Romantic position to claims about how civilizations are closed totalities that are completely immiscible and entirely incommensurable, and whose clash is therefore regulated solely by force. Or, in Heidegger's case, to the anti-Semitic idea that modernity is a Jewish intrusion into Western civilization (Di Cesare 2018). On Habermas's interpretation, Heidegger shifted from 'the conscientious project of an individual concerned about his existence', and therefore motivated to disclose the hidden assumptions that precede propositional argumentation, to something else altogether. This is the 'anonymous dispensation of Being that demands subjection', and whose concrete social form was, with Heidegger's active support, ominously realized. Habermas argues that for Heidegger, disclosure ultimately happened through the 'historical existence of a nation yoked together by the *Führer* into a collective will', a nation capable of projecting a world as if it were a world-constituting transcendental subject (PDM: 155-7 [184-7]).

Not surprisingly, then, Habermas wants to signal his critical relation to the history of philosophy when discussing disclosure. He explicitly develops the category through critique of Heidegger's *Unverborgenheit*, so that the result is something provisional and constructive, Habermasian *Welterschliessung*. He seeks to deflate its scope, from the disclosure of an entire world, to acts of world-building within the existing world. He restricts its authority, from an emphatic Truth about the world to an imaginative vision with a truth-potential, something that can ultimately be redeemed only through dialogue. And he localizes its effects and brings it down to earth, from a prophetic revelation of how the world is in the dispensations of the gods, to a poetic disclosure of a new way of looking at certain things. In hermeneutic terms, the basic Habermasian idea of disclosure depends on acknowledgement that events and entities become intelligible and relevant by virtue of their embeddedness in the lifeworld. This background network of unquestioned assumptions and pre-given interpretations provides the shared horizon of expectations for actors seeking to communicate and cooperate. A disclosure points out something in this background in a new way, makes it freshly salient, so that it can become thematized in dialogue or incorporated into an individual's life history.

Language and disclosure

Heidegger's Romantic conception of poetic language assumes that the grey and plastic medium of the universe is susceptible to an infinity of arbitrary, world-projecting disclosures. In a sense, this is the supposed Truth about truth that his philosophy triumphantly announces. In her article contrasting Habermas and Heidegger on world-disclosure, Christina Lafont probes the linguistic theory that is the foundation for the Romantic position (Lafont 2000: 179-247). The supposed capacity of disclosures to generate entire worlds rests upon the so-called triple-H (Humboldt, Herder, Hamann) theory of language, which influences thinkers as politically distinct as Martin Heidegger, Jacques Derrida and Charles Taylor. It is worth dwelling on this briefly in the context of Habermas and literature, because the Heideggerian claims will strike the reader from a literary-critical domain as eerily familiar, despite being deprived of their standard Saussurean intonation. In technical terms, the 'triple-H' theory involves three postulates about language that are effectively identical with the Saussurean vulgate popularized by the literary-critical reception of post-structuralism:

1. Intensional truth semantics: meaning determines reference and designation.
2. Language holism: languages are internally related totalities.
3. Descriptivism: names are definite descriptions not rigid designators.

The first claim maintains that the meaning of an expression constructs the properties of the referent through predication. It follows that the truth of a statement is really a question of the correct application of semantic relationships. (The opposite of intensional semantics is extensional semantics, the claim that to understand the meaning of a statement involves grasping the conditions under which it is a true proposition about a designated aspect of reality.) The second claim ultimately entails the proposition that language as a whole constructs reality. There is no term-by-term reference to the world. Languages are internally related semantic totalities, so that the meaning of one expression depends on the meaning-potential of all of the other possible expressions. Conversely, the introduction of a new meaning implies a redistribution of the totality of meanings possible in the rest of the language that also repartitions reality by introducing a new referent. (The opposite of linguistic holism is linguistic atomism, the view that the units of language, generally statements rather than signs, are discretely defined, either intensionally or extensionally.) The final claim holds that all names are definite descriptions, so that 'the author of the First Folio' can be substituted for 'William Shakespeare' without loss of referential accuracy. The most extreme version of this hypothesis holds that even proper names consist of definite descriptions consisting of general concepts, so that, for instance, 'The Moon' can be replaced by 'celestial orb', or, perhaps, 'the onwards up-shining'. (An opposite to the theory of definite descriptions is the theory of rigid designation, the idea that proper names are semantically empty placemarkers for the historical event of naming a designation.) Within literary studies, the work of Christopher Norris is instructive, in terms of both the relation between these three claims and Saussurean linguistics (Norris 1987), and also in terms of his subsequent rejection of intensional holism and definite descriptions (Norris 2001).

It is the combination of the three claims that leads to pernicious relativism, because the triple-H theory denies the capacity of language to designate, so that there is no linguistic equivalent to ostension. Sentences cannot pick out things in the world in a way that is independent of the predication applied to them, which entails the position that there is no rational ground for the revocability of statements. In the particular intensional theory of Heidegger (as with Ludwig Wittgenstein and Charles Taylor), the basic problem of the conflation of designation with denotation is present, together with the resulting problem of the impossibility of revisions concerning predication of the referent (Lafont 2000). According to Humboldt, the origin of this position, all words denote general concepts – even proper names denote general concepts – and because this is assimilated to the relation of designation, individuals are simply particular aggregations of general concepts. Because meaning determines reference and all meanings are general, language transcendentally constitutes possible experience, which entails the claim that there are no phenomena that are not completely described by the resulting world view. The holistic theory of meaning compounds this because it implies global reference; that is, language only picks out particular things via the detour of the totality of language qua system of internal relations. The consequence is that the individuation of objects is conventional, because no relation between meaning and predication can possibly be conceptually motivated, from which it follows that language is arbitrary in relation to the designatum. If every statement I make about the world happens within a set of presuppositions about the world that are built-in to the very language that I use, how can I possibly be wrong about the world when my syntax is correct? What possible reason might I have for the revision of statements concerning fundamentals? As Lafont summarizes her argument against the triple-H theory, 'an explication of the relation of designation . . . not assimilated to the relation of predication, is central to any attempt to view the revisability of our knowledge as a possibility which is built into language' (Lafont 1994: 55). Lafont contrasts Heidegger with the theory of rigid designation to show that a theory of language is possible within which designation can succeed even when the characterization of the referent is incorrect.

The key to acknowledging the disclosing power of language while refusing pernicious relativism is to introduce distinctions between designation, denotation and predication. It is crucial not to conflate the ability of speech to pick out things in the world (i.e. designation) with the ability of language to assign these things a meaning (i.e. denotation), and critical to maintain the difference between these and the ability of language to refer to things by describing their attributes of things (i.e. predication). The textbook case is Venus: 'the Morning Star' and 'the Evening Star' are two denotations of the celestial phenomenon designated by these terms, the second-brightest object in the night sky, whose referent may be . . . a god, a planet, or two gods, Phosphoros and Hesperos, corresponding to the Western and Eastern manifestations of the phenomenon. How did the Greeks go from two gods to one? Pythagoras is credited with the discovery, based on a reconstruction of probable orbital motion that would explain the phenomenon as manifestations of a single celestial wanderer. In other words, because the two denotations, linked to the two referents through predication as sons of Astraios and Cephalus (respectively), had a single designatum – the brightest object in the night sky except the moon – it became possible to revise the denotation to a single deity and grasp the referent through its predication as an essentially variable goddess.

In terms of the example developed a moment ago, for the Romantic wing of the triple-H school of linguistics, there is no difference between 'the second-brightest object in the night sky', 'the evening star', and 'the morning star': all are denotations. The predication of two different bodies follows from the determinative role of the opposed denotations, with no possibility for a revision of any statement about the world based on appeal to the designated phenomenon. The generality of intension and global, or holistic, reference, leads to the theory that languages are monadic world views, arranged in a contingent sequence of arbitrary disclosures. Accordingly, instead of theories of the revisability of statements based on practical engagement with the designatum, the Romantics developed theories of sudden radical shifts in fundamental ontology. These are the purported result of new languages, speculative conjectures, religious transformations, revolutions in the game and so forth.

Literary disclosure and truth-potential

It is Habermas's polemic against Derrida's Heidegger-inspired deconstruction that frames his presentation of the difference between the 'extraordinary domain of fictive discourse and everyday discourse'. Habermas's acknowledgement of the world-disclosing capacity of natural languages is tempered by his insistence on the pragmatic connection between meaning and validity, which is itself dependent on the potential of speech to designate an extra-discursive reality. He proposes that the problem with Heidegger's presentation of disclosure is therefore not that it is false, but that he has transposed literary experience onto pragmatic contexts, neglecting the problem-solving capacities of language, for a one-sided exploration of its world-disclosing potentials. On the Habermasian interpretation, Derrida's Heideggerian inflation of the world-disclosing potential of language and his corresponding neglect of the problems-solving aspect of language lead to a systematic dissolution of the distinction between philosophy and literature. Everything becomes rhetoric, which makes possible Derrida's next move, which is to deny the distinction between literature and literary criticism, along with rejection of the belonging of literary criticism to the field of propositional reasoning (PDM: 190 [224]). Accordingly, Derrida can apply forms of literary criticism to philosophical rhetoric while claiming that there is no difference in kind between deconstructive critique of philosophy and literary rhetoric itself, which leads to the field of the 'general text' (PDM: 190–1 [224–5]).

For Habermas, literary criticism and philosophy belong to propositional reasoning, differing in their object domains, which are, respectively, the disclosing potentials of language as exhibited by literature and the problem-solving capacities of language as demonstrated by science and law. The difference between literature and reason, meanwhile, is framed as a distinction between truth-potential and validity claims. In Habermas's presentation, that particular construction of the difference between literature and philosophy results in the accent falling on three distinctive characteristics of literature:

1. Although it is a reflexive suspension of action coordination whose meanings may be innovative and whose referents are fictive, it designates something salient to a situation in a way that is 'worthwhile' or 'tellable'. That is because the narrative presents an exemplary construction of possible experience with the capacity to modify intersubjective expectations about a relevant, newly thematized element of the lifeworld.

2. It consists of poetic language as defined by Roman Jakobson; shorthand – releases the rhetorical and figurative potentials of language for innovative expressions and arresting perceptions.

3. It is a holistic presentation of possible experience that imitates reality because its representation of existence depends on a fusion of validity dimensions that cannot be analytically separated into differentiated validity claims without neglecting the potential impact of the whole.

For Habermas, this revision of the communicative position is intended to do justice to some salient facts about literature, while at the same time opening up a critical position on deconstruction. Setting the inter-school philosophical debate to one side for the moment, Habermas was responding to probing intra-school evaluations of communicative action. These came from within the Frankfurt School, by Albrecht Wellmer and Martin Seel. In explaining and clarifying his shift in position, Habermas maintained that the inclusion of aesthetic processes within communicative reason was incorrect for the following reason:

> The aesthetic 'validity' or 'unity' that we attribute to a work of art refers to its singularly illuminating power to open our eyes to what is seemingly familiar, to disclose anew an apparently familiar reality. This validity claim admittedly stands for a potential for 'truth' that can be released only in the whole complexity of life-experience; therefore, this 'truth-potential' may not be connected to (or even identified with) one of the three validity-claims constitutive for communicative action, as I have previously been inclined to maintain. The one-to-one relationship which

exists between the prescriptive validity of a norm and the normative validity claims raised in speech acts is not a proper model for the relation between the potential for truth of works of art and the transformed relations between self and world stimulated by aesthetic experience. (Habermas 1998b: 415)

What this means is that communicative reason must be restricted to cognitive truth and normative rightness. What Habermas is seeking to do justice to is not only the problematic status of literary critique, but also the fact that when literary experience is integrated into the narrative of a life history, it goes beyond 'renewing the interpretation of needs that colour perceptions'. Rather, 'it reaches into our cognitive interpretations and normative expectation and transforms the totality in which these moments are related to each other' (Habermas 1998b: 414–15). That means, Habermas argues, that the illuminating power of art relates to representations of the social totality, rather than to reflexivity about the subjective world. Instead of expressing post-traditional need-interpretations, literary works 'harbour a utopia' because they present the desire for 'a balanced and undistorted intersubjectivity in everyday life' (Habermas 1998b: 415). Acknowledgement of this situation, Habermas thinks, means conceding that Albrecht Wellmer is right:

> Neither truth nor truthfulness may be attributed unmetaphorically to works of art, if one understands 'truth' and 'truthfulness' in the sense of a pragmatically differentiated everyday concept of truth. We can explain the way in which truth and truthfulness—and even normative correctness—are metaphorically interlaced in works of art only by appealing to the fact that the work of art, as a symbolic formation with an *aesthetic* validity claim, is at the same time an object of an experience, in which the three validity domains are unmetaphorically intermeshed. (Habermas 1998b: 415 Wellmer cited)

In other words, Habermas believes that he must decide between literature as mimesis of life in its totality and literature as an exploration of need-interpretations alone.

The debate on disclosure

The aftermath of *The Philosophical Discourse of Modernity* was marked by a vigorous debate among Critical Theorists on disclosure. Proposals and counter-proposals went back and forth, for disclosure as an alternative voice of reason or disclosure as a supplement to argumentation. The linguistic and conceptual background that I have just explicated is essential to understanding the stakes in this debate. In the context of the communicative position that I have been reconstructing in this book, the linguistic background indicates that disclosure happens pre-eminently within literature. The equivocation of reference characteristic of literary semblances explains why. Literature refers to an imaginary world but resembles the real world. The inference is that literature is the only domain in which the triple-H theory could possibly be true. That is because the peculiarity of literary reference is that predication determines designation by constituting the schema for an imaginary object. Accordingly, debate centres on the problem of how disclosure can extend beyond literature. The conceptual background is crucial too. As introduced by Habermas in a literary context, disclosure is foremost a literary phenomenon. But the implication of his framing of the problem is that it is generated by poetic language (Duvenage 2003: 120–41). Habermas wants to separate the 'extraordinary domain of fictive discourse [from] everyday discourse' (PDM: 194 [224]), but if poetic language becomes available through the rhetorical potentials of language, then this separation is hard to maintain.

In the chapter on critique, I proposed that literary semblances aesthetically wrap rhetorical persuasion in two ways that make a difference, namely, the equivocation of reference and aesthetic coherence. However, although that means that there *is* a clear distinction between fictive discourse and everyday persuasion, this by no means settles the question of whether disclosure can also happen in everyday speech. The idea that imaginative disclosure is an aspect of everyday language, rather than a special function, is perhaps the most intriguing, yet most difficult, element of the debate on disclosure. Of course, the Critical Theorists involved in the argument have no intention of erasing the distinction between pragmatic speech acts and fictional utterances, or between literature and philosophy. Their claim is that a focus on a particular aspect of everyday speech highlights the disclosing dimension that is present in ordinary language. Intuitively speaking, it does happen, but a full discussion of that possibility would take me too far afield. Instead, I want to explore the question of the scale of disclosures – whether literary or extra-literary – and discuss whether they are best grasped as events of world-disclosure or more localized effects.

For several participants, the distinction between non-propositional truth-potential (disclosure) and propositional truth (discourse) is equivalent to the difference between utopia and resignation, respectively. Particularly within the so-called 'inflationary' camp, the motivation behind participation in the debate seems to be the idea that without the capacity to imagine a social alternative, Critical Theory is likely to remain stuck within the critique of 'actually existing democracy'. For Nikolas Kompridis and Lambert Zuidervaart especially, Habermas's insistence that disclosures only have a potential for truth, one that must be discursively redeemed through propositional argumentation, limits critical standpoints to the horizon of existing social expectations (Kompridis 2006: 249–50; Zuidervaart 2004: 119–20). The core idea is that a Critical Theory with emancipatory intent needs a vision of de-alienation in order to direct its critique of the totality of existing social arrangements beyond the horizon of what seems conventionally possible. The so-called 'deflationary' camp, however, is by no means arguing for resignation. For James Bohman, for instance, a successful disclosure completely alters readers' perceptions of certain social questions. It alerts them to salient aspects of a situation that have hitherto been unquestioned, or to descriptions of what is possible that have so far been considered implausible or imprudent. Strikingly, Bohman interprets Michel Foucault's *Discipline and Punish* as an instance of disclosure that aims to alert readers to the dystopian perception that modern institutions have the potential to transform modernity into a 'carceral archipelago' (Bohman 1997: 197–221). The leading concern of the deflationary camp is that the inflation of disclosure into something equivalent to truth fails to prevent the validation of problematic visions, alongside the celebration of utopian energies.

I think that the perspective of the reciprocity of critique and disclosure makes it possible to acknowledge the cogency and integrity of both sides, through a synthesis focused on what is specific about literary disclosure. For Bohman, disclosures are momentary interruptions in argumentation within which the speaker foregrounds the rhetorical potentials of language, in order to present a perception of hitherto unthematized aspects of the world, with the potential to alter the direction of dialogue (Bohman 1994). It is not a question, he proposes, of innovative disclosure versus everyday speech, but of the ability to entertain possibilities within a mature and flexible ego capable of coping with provisionality, versus ego rigidity and dogmatic fixation on conventional situation definitions (Bohman 1994: 87). Disclosure makes something newly relevant to participants in dialogue, resulting in a multiplication of possibilities that can be discursively tested (as opposed to a reduction of the space of possibility consequent upon confirmation of biases). 'If this is the proper analysis of the dialogical construction of certain aspects of the social world', Bohman comments, 'disclosure is not any sort of mysterious event. It is best understood as a certain effect of expressive speech . . . on a specific type of audience . . . best grasped through the concept of relevance' (Bohman 1994: 89). As Bohman notes, 'relevance' involves foregrounding the relation between assumptions by thematizing their interconnection within a holistic background. Disclosures pick something out and make it at once perceptible and expressible, but they do so poetically, that is, equivocally yet accessibly.

By contrast, for Zuidervaart, 'artistic truth', equivalent to imaginative disclosure, is another kind of (non-propositional) truth (Zuidervaart 2004: 121). Zuidervaart's Adorno-inspired concept of artistic truth seems to me to involve the emphatic judgement of a work's global significance (Zuidervaart 2004: 136–9). Invoking criteria of integrity and authenticity as markers for significance, Zuidervaart says that he intends to 'close the gap' between the artwork's aesthetic validity and its truth-potential (Zuidervaart 2004: 130). I think that this postulates a relation between 'imaginative cogency' (the consistency of an imaginary world that is the result of a coherent representational strategy, that is, criteria of aesthetic validity qua 'integrity') and the new validity claims that result from putting insights from the work into practice (i.e. its truth-potential). But that means that – on this construction – both aesthetic validity and truth-potential are *discursively redeemable* as propositionally articulated validity claims. In light of this fact, I believe that 'artistic truth' could be reframed, without loss of content, as an argumentatively grounded anticipatory speculation about the work's future significance. That significance depends on its 'truth potential', which is a way of speaking about how art gets integrated into individuals' lives.

For Kompridis, disclosure is 'another voice of reason' that makes possible 'disclosing arguments' that are 'successful disclosures' (Kompridis 2006: 116, 18, 44). He is adamant that disclosure cannot be restricted to aesthetics, and that it also includes transcendental speculation, dialectical arguments and narrative reconstructions (Kompridis 2006: 119–20). Kompridis presents disclosing truth as different to validity claims, but what he specifically means is that 'successful disclosure' is how we retrospectively describe a disclosure that has passed pragmatic testing (Kompridis 2006: 144). This rules out the validation of toxic visions, because of their intersubjective consequences. Successful disclosures are (1) 'capable of enlarging the cultural conditions of meaning', (2) facilitate 'the resolution of epistemological crises' and (3) thereby 'revitalise the future', re-opening modern history (Kompridis 2006: 144). I think that describing an anticipatory speculation to the effect that a particular disclosure is going to have a certain outcome, as a different voice of reason, as opposed to a claim about truth-potential, is unnecessarily confusing. Instead, I want to suggest that Kompridis's notion of the truth-potential of a successful disclosure, as something revealed through its pragmatic consequences, can best be grasped as the following argument. Disclosure is not a kind of speech or a voice of reason: it is what individuals *do* with poetic language, when they do not mobilize it as a prompt for critique, but instead imaginatively integrate its implications into their life histories.

The reciprocity of critique and disclosure

Having summarized the debate on disclosure within Critical Theory, I now want to show that it can be resolved through the claim that literature is *neither* critique *nor* disclosure; these are responses to literature. In advancing a proposal for the reciprocity of critique and disclosure, I am specifically following Pieter Duvenage's work on Habermasian aesthetics (Duvenage 2003). The difference is that while Duvenage's concentrates on disclosing language as the aesthetic dimension of communication, my focus is restricted to a discussion of literary disclosure. Furthermore, I approach the problem from a different perspective: the role of the reader as critic and convert. It is important to notice that this is not in contradiction with the three characteristics claimed for literature by Habermas – fiction, holism and salience; the only problem is that he associates these exclusively with disclosure. The reason that Habermas does this is that he neglects the questions of reception and response, conflating the literary text with the reader's active concretization of the imaginative work, and the work with the reader's response to its relevance as providing a vision of new possibilities. That lacuna is symmetrical with the conflation of the literary text with rational critique in the theory of communicative action, where Habermas also short-circuits the questions of reception and response. It is probably simplest to begin by presenting my argument diagrammatically, before explaining it conceptually (Figure 8.1).

In *Communicative Action*, as explained in the chapter on critique, in what I have called the 'literal model', Habermas locates literature and criticism as symbiotically related contributions to expressive critique, happening within the space of rational argumentation. Other moments in *Communicative*

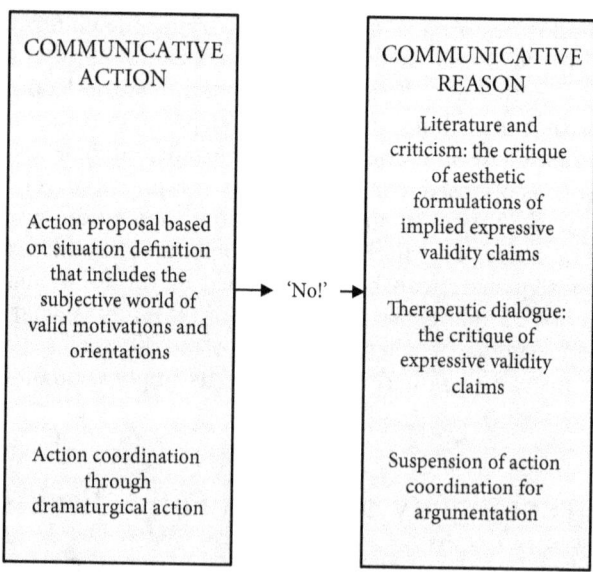

FIGURE 8.1 *Habermas's 'literal model' of literature and criticism.*

IMAGINATIVE DISCLOSURE AND LITERARY IDENTIFICATION 201

Action complicate this with a 'rhetorical model', which separates therapy and aesthetics, but this model continues to locate both literature and critique in the space of reason. By contrast, in *Philosophical Discourse*, Habermas splits literature from criticism and opposes imaginative disclosure to rational argumentation (Figure 8.2).

Now both literature and criticism are exiled from the field of communicative reason. Therapy may or may not remain within rational argumentation, alongside cognitive and normative validity claims; here, I have presented the most generous interpretation, which is that it does. The two positions, that of *Communicative Action* and that of *Philosophical Discourse*, are symmetrical, parallax errors, missing the relation between literature and reason by overlooking the reader's response to literary experience.

By contrast, I propose that literature is a form of the suspension of action coordination that happens when a participant in dialogue, instead of presenting an argument that contests a situation definition, presents a narrative that potentially reframes perceptions of the situation, or the means of its expression. Strictly speaking, narratives may take factual or fictional forms, and both are relevant to reframing situations (think of the

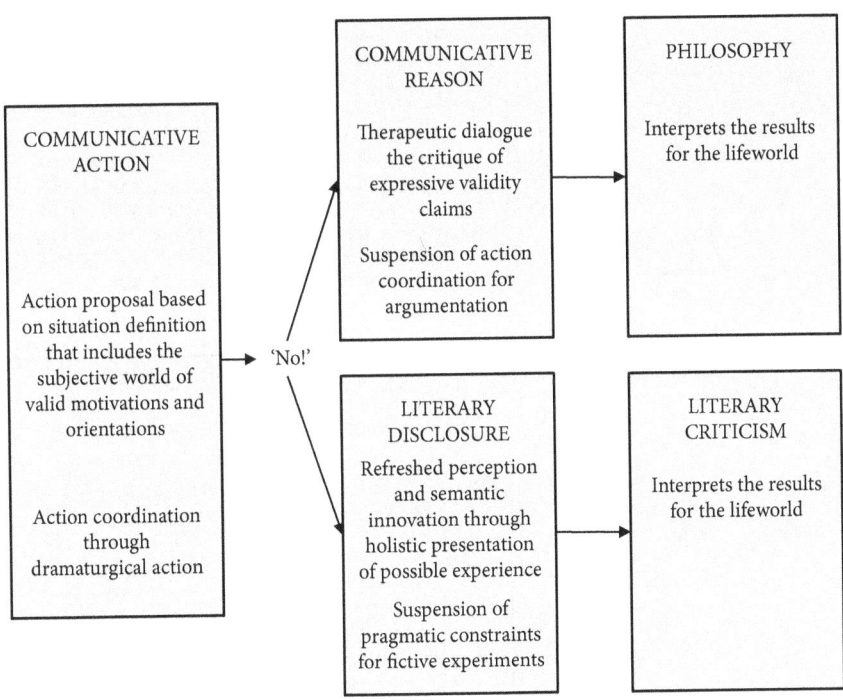

FIGURE 8.2 *Habermas's opposition between critique and disclosure (PDM: 207 [243]).*

effects on debate of historical narration or life histories), but for reasons of scope I intend to consider only fictional narration. On this account, fictional narratives can be received publicly, through debate about meaning and significance, or personally, through acts of identification that modify personality structures (Figure 8.3).

The claim here is that 'disclosure' names the effect of readers' identification with a fictional narrative as a vision of possible experience; disclosure is what readers call it, when they are profoundly affected by it. The implication is that in taking a narrative as a disclosure (through identification), readers 'jump the gun' on dialogue around the validity of the interpretation of the world presented in the fiction; they just go right ahead and incorporate its vision (which is partly their vision, by virtue of active reception of the text as work) into their life histories, without waiting for the critical debate.

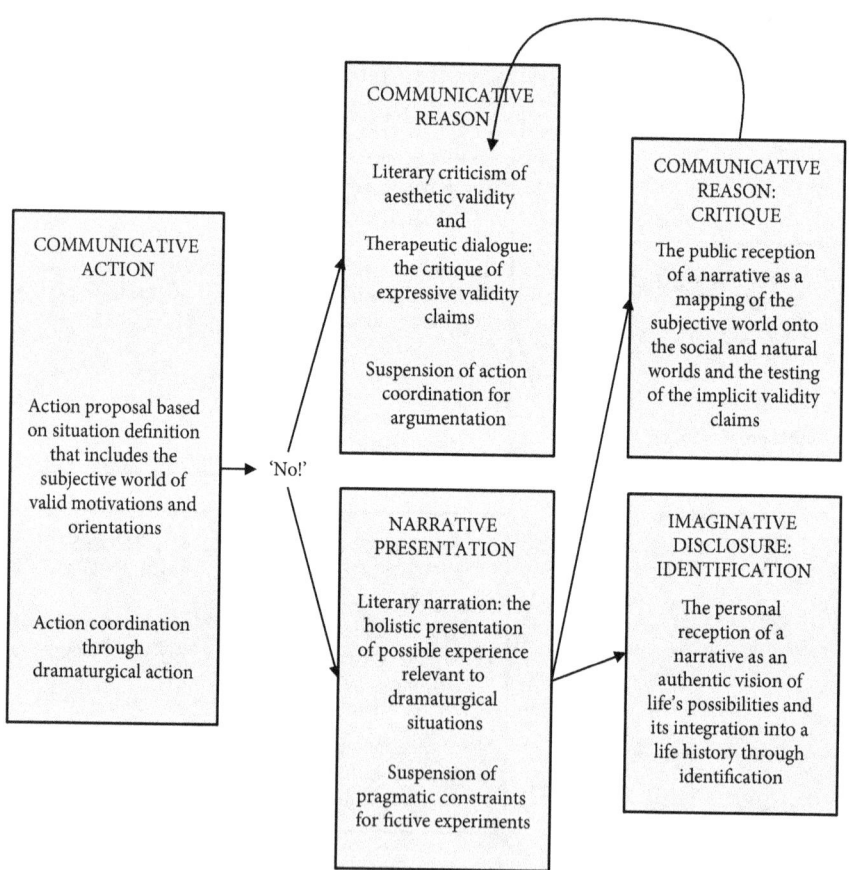

FIGURE 8.3 *Critique and disclosure as two modes of reception of literary narrative.*

Hermeneutics of retrieval

The interpretation that I have just proposed of disclosure, as an effect of identification with elements of a literary vision, implies a programme of reading the work as a holistic presentation of possible experience. Following Paul Ricoeur's celebrated distinction, the retrieval of coherent meaning from a fictional narrative might be described as a 'hermeneutics of restoration', as opposed to the 'hermeneutics of suspicion' (Ricoeur 1970: 32). 'According to one pole' of the hermeneutic field, Ricoeur states, 'hermeneutics is understood as the manifestation and restoration of a meaning addressed to me in the manner of a message, a proclamation, or, as is sometimes said, a kerygma'. By contrast, 'according to the other pole, [hermeneutics] is understood as a demystification, as a reduction of illusion' (Ricoeur 1970: 27). Speaking of biblical hermeneutics, Ricoeur describes the 'recollection' of the semantic content of the message as involving the restoration of its meaningfulness, the retrieval of 'the *something* intended in ritual actions, in mythical speech', the 'reality of the religious object', the 'sacred' (Ricoeur 1970: 29). What is restored in Ricoeur's hermeneutics of recovery, then, is not just meaning, but existential *meaningfulness*, the relevance of an ensemble of meanings for the ultimate concerns of human beings. This emerges because of the relation of religious discourse to the designatum of the sacred, which Ricoeur specifies as the object of belief (Ricoeur 1970: 29). Ricoeur's procedure, developed from his work on religious symbolism, while suggestive, is ultimately problematic. I now want to sketch a Habermasian 'hermeneutics of retrieval' that is significantly different on some key points from Ricoeur's 'hermeneutics of recovery'. Furthermore, reading Ricoeur 'after Adorno', what I shall call the hermeneutics of retrieval by no means commits the interpreter to the assumption that the imaginative work is an organic whole (AT: 141–3 [251–2]).

From the Habermasian perspective, the biggest problem with Ricoeur's hermeneutics of recovery for an interpretation of literature is its presupposition that fictional narratives all have a single, secular relevance, just as religious narratives also have a single, sacred relevance. In this respect, it is worth noticing the difficulties that happen in the three volumes of *Time and Narrative*. Ricoeur is convinced that the resemblance of modernism is to the temporal flow of lived experience – the moments of protention, present and retention – and that in fact experimental narrative involves playing with the various temporalizations that can happen through different constructions of their inter-relation. Accordingly, the 'structural identity of historiography . . . and fictional narrative' leads up to the 'deep kinship of their truth claims', namely, that 'the truth claim of *every* narrative work is the temporal character of human experience' (Ricoeur 1984: 3). Such a hermeneutics of recovery in literary studies would have the effect of a radical simplification of the literary field, at the cost, let us say, of a certain richness of imaginative experience.

Through Ricoeur's lens, works as varied as *Remembrance of Things Past*, *Mrs Dalloway* and *The Magic Mountain* all turn out to be about the same thing, the disjunction between lived time and chronological time, and between the intersubjectivity of chronology and the monumental time of authoritative history and human mortality (Ricoeur 1985: 112, 30, 52). Ricoeur's thematic interpretation of temporality is insightful, but the presentation of this theme as exhaustive is, I think, entirely false.

I suggest that fictional texts are the only place where descriptivism is true, which has the consequence that the objects of a literary work are entirely internal to its imaginary world. When the reader traces out the way that meaning determines reference within the text, they populate the imagined world with objects, which their active reception then supplements. When the reader does this, they are presented with a vision that resembles some aspect of the world, some situation. That vision is not entirely idiosyncratic, for the schemata of the text and their relation to the implied reader are the framework for the reader's participation its concretization. And when the reader identifies with some part of that vision, it is because they find this guided concretization relevant to some of their concerns. The relation of relevance is not arbitrary, just as the activity of concretization is not capricious. Relevance is motivated by the way that the visionary framework of the text relates to the implied reader, modelling the relation between the work and the reader, who is in the real world.

The response to semblances

Against this conceptual background, the hermeneutics of retrieval involves reading for the vision that the literary work presents, relative to relevant social and historical situations and to the horizon of expectations of the implied reader. I now want to explore a potential point of departure for a Habermasian version, which would converge at many points on the reader-response criticism of Iser, whose work I introduced at the end of Chapter 4, and of Northrop Frye, whose work I introduce now. I have argued that literary semblances are characterized by equivocal reference and aesthetic coherence. Equivocal reference involves the imaginary world's resemblance to a situation, but this situation has both practical and cultural coordinates, for its context of relevance includes a socio-historical conjuncture and to a set of cultural expectations. It involves, in other words, what Iser calls the 'repertoire', the cultural conventions and historical thinking invoked by the text as the material for defining its situation (Iser 1980: 69). A consequence of this is that all literature references other literature, forming a literary symbolization of non-literary reality that Frye describes as a 'circular labyrinth' and as a 'secular scripture'.

According to Frye, the imposition of formal patterning on arrangements of words constitutes verbal art, whose effect is to deprive the 'sign' of its designative capacity, rendering it a 'symbol' (Frye 2000: 73). The totality of meanings in a text, generated through the interplay of semantics with patterning, determines the imaginary reference of the work (Frye 2000: 74–5). Consequently, Frye describes literary experience as entry into a circular labyrinth that is separated from reality, and which leads not outwards, to the external world, but inwards, to its formal principle of structuration (Frye 2000: 73). At the same time, to remain a kind of communication, textual symbols must be sufficiently plausibly arranged to resemble assertions and to be reminiscent of experience (Frye 2000: 272). Literary content achieves this through mimesis, which involves emptying descriptions of particularity (Frye 2000: 265). 'The poet's job', he argues elsewhere, 'is not to tell you what happened, but what happens: not what did take place, but the kind of thing that always takes place' (Frye 1964: 63). Frye describes this tension as the 'quizzical antithesis' between 'delight and instruction, ironic withdrawal from reality and explicit connection with it' (Frye 2000: 82). It is synthesized through what might be described as acknowledgement of the 'as if' character of literature. In Frye's terminology, literature is 'analogous' to reality as a whole, rather than designating an object in reality, and so literary criticism must proceed 'hypothetically'. That happens through the discussion of the internal consistency of the work, rather than 'descriptively', through explanation of the work's extra-textual reference to a context (Frye 2000: 93).

Frye's attention to how in literary semblances there is an interplay between negation of reality and resemblance to reality leads him to considerations of relevance. The literary work is a totality that is analogous to reality as a whole and that, through its imposition of a formal principle onto extrinsic content, generates a satisfying representation of the world. As such, the literary work is analogous to social labour in its metabolism with nature and its transformation of society – in its creation, in other words, of a habitable world. But literary messages are the communicative complement to social labour: not the instrumental transformation of raw materials, but the specification of what is story-worthy about this, why anybody would want to do this in the first place. Defining desire as 'the energy that leads human society to develop its own form', Frye proposes that 'desire is liberated and made apparent by civilization': 'the efficient cause of civilization is work, and poetry has the social function of expressing, as a verbal hypothesis, a vision of the goals of work and the forms of desire' (Frye 2000: 106). Literary works present 'out of the society we have to live in, a vision of the society we want to live in', representing the theoretical and practical accomplishments of a civilization as strivings towards 'home', a world that is worth making (Frye 1964: 140). Frye synthesizes the generality of mimesis, the principle of imaginative form and the social function of literature, in the claims that literature is concerned with symbolic action, that literary characters are typical and that the world of literary imagery is 'totally symbolic' (Frye 1964: 75).

Frye's 'total symbolic order' of the text is another description of Iser's repertoire. But the repertoire is complemented by narrative strategies, which select and combine the repertoire into distinct perspectives – the narrator, the protagonist, the characters, the world – through which the reader 'wanders' in the act of reading (Iser 1980: 108–9). The network of strategies generates aesthetic coherence, grasped through material and technique, content and form, and explains the way that the reader is solicited to active concretization. According to Iser, blanks and voids appear through the relation of strategy to repertoire: the sequence of selections from and the combination of elements of the repertoire, in the unfolding strategy, represents an invitation to the reader (also known as suspense, intrigue, engrossment, etc.). Part of this is simply the activity of working out the plot/story relation. But another part of it involves guessing why it has been so presented, and evolving imaginative conjectures about what can be expected next. Iser discusses this in terms of theme and horizon: the reader is constantly moving back and forth between foregrounded themes and the background horizon, puzzled about the relation and surprised in their expectations, permanently engaged in a process of revision. For the real reader, as opposed to the ideal reader – which is merely a structure of possibilities – the process of imaginative conjecture can lead to total involvement in the imaginary world.

Contemporary psychological research into the effects of engrossment in narrative discusses the imaginative experience in terms of 'immersion' in the diegetic (or narrated) world and 'transportation' to a situation where the reader vicariously experiences the events of the narrative (Gerrig 1993). The (material) state of immersion involves being physiologically unresponsive to some real-world stimuli and being psychologically absorbed in cognitive and emotional processing of events in the narrated world (Gerrig 1993: 12). That makes possible the (psychological) state of transportation, in which the reader imaginatively undergoes a series of vicarious experiences which imply a modification to the reality principle for the duration of immersion (Gerrig 1993: 16). Having 'lost track of reality' and 'lost themselves in the narrative', the reader empathetically identifies with the protagonist and imaginatively moves in a world constructed from the book's imagery, guided along a series of emotionally charged episodes by the narrative's mediation of experience (Green and Brock 2013). According to Richard Gerrig, the traditional notion of the 'willing suspension of disbelief' in the imaginary world that the theory of transportation reformulates is best grasped through the psychological finding of the expenditure of will that is required to fully 'return to reality'. Naturally, the reader knows that they have stopped reading, but studies indicate that there is a deliberate effort involved in the subsequent construction of disbelief about whether the ideas of the narrative can be projected onto the real world. Readers struggle with the suggestion that the relation between character and outcome in the real world does not, in fact, follow the pattern of the narrated world (R. Gerrig and Rapp 2004).

Immersion and transportation

The reader who becomes immersed in a fictional narrative can become transported into a condition where their emotional responses and perceptions of reality are significantly influenced by the literary work. This is especially, but not exclusively, in relation to their understanding of the link between character and consequences, or, personality structures and ways of coping with reality. Changes to the beliefs and attitudes of readers that happen during transportation are surprisingly resistant to real-world correction after reading and turn out to be extraordinarily durable, since psychological research shows that lasting alterations to personality structure can happen as a result of the repetition of strongly impactful reading. Beginning from pre-theoretical conjectures about the influence of literature right through to contemporary psychological studies, the kernel of the ability of readers to change themselves through reading has been believed to lie in the process of the reader's identification with the characters, and recent research that combines narrative poetics with empirical psychology has confirmed this hypothesis. Furthermore, new research in cognitive psychology delineates the scope of the phenomenon of identification with characters and indicates that it involves both recognition (the reader sees themselves in the character) and mimicry (the reader imitates key aspects of the character's psychology or engagements). Although identification with characters is not the only mode of transported reading (two others exist: a focus on emptions and awareness of poetic language and aesthetic imagery), it is the most socially significant because its implications for identity formation are that literature can intervene in both socialization, and re-, or counter-, socialization.

According to the classic construction of transportation by Victor Nell, the reader who reads for pleasure and becomes transported gets 'lost' in the story (Nell 1988). Becoming lost involves both physiological arousal and entry into a psychological trance, one that is unlike dreaming only to the extent that the reader's ego does not abdicate. This is a condition that is perpetuated by a virtuous pleasure/reinforcement cycle, when readers read stories that they expect to like (Nell 1988: 262–5). That raises the question of whether readers can engage in transportation when their expectations are *disappointed*, that is, when confronted by literary innovation or social critique, and the answer is that they can, but only when they feel that emplotment and characterization plausibly address the reader's concerns. Although the dispiriting implication is that it is easy for authors to lose readers because of angular characterization or tenuous plotting, it is reassuring to know that changes in belief caused by plausible narration can be significant and durable. Jeffrey Strange, for instance, gives the example of the role of Harriet Beacher-Stowe's *Uncle Tom's Cabin* in building support for manumission as a goal of the American Civil war, in a context where this was strongly contested (Strange 2013). However, the concerns of the reader are foremost existential concerns, to do with security and hope, before they are social concerns, to do with social stratification and authority structures (Nell 2013). Nonetheless, it seems that when both existential and social concerns are persuasively addressed, narrative form itself tends to push readers towards an orientation to just outcomes, and this effect is so strong that readers find it difficult to suspend belief in their normative judgements, even when they are given good reason to doubt the story (Green and Donahue 2011). The narrative representation of imaginary experience implies the fore-interpretation of that experience because every event is located within the cause-and-effect sequence of emplotment, something which dramatically influences readers' constructions of the potential consequences and normative value of certain motivations and orientations, actions and attitudes (Gerrig and Rapp 2004). The results of transportation are identification with characters and transformations of the self, with impacts including the alteration of cognitive beliefs and social attitudes, as well as affective dispositions (especially sympathy) and perceptions of the real world (Green et al. 2004).

Keith Oatley's cognitive model of identification (Oatley 1995), now supported by neuroscientific research (Cheetham et al. 2014), involves readers using fiction as a simulation of experience. This requires adopting a character's goals, forming mental images of their world, receiving speech acts addressed to both character and reader, and integrating disparate elements into a unified vicarious experience. The resulting changes affect cognitive attitudes, normative orientations and emotional dispositions, including impulse control and affect regulation, which prompts Keith Oatley to describe the alteration to the personality structure that happens through identification in terms of modifications to both the superego and the ego The superego shifts, sometimes dramatically, in the direction of different cultural ideals and social norms, while the ego gains new capacities to control impulses, to disagree with society and to construct personal identity.

Subsequent research shows that although identification is central, it works in concert with other aspects of transportation. In a review of the scientific and psychological literature on what she calls 'transformative reading', Olivia Fialho discusses how a substantial body of experimental research connects readers' 'strategies of defamiliarisation' to 'changes in personal meanings' (Fialho 2019). That terminology, which is empirical-psychological rather than literary-critical, is potentially confusing: de-familiarization describes the reader's distance from their self-construct, not poetic language's estrangement from ordinary speech. These strategies – identification with characters, focus on emotions and awareness of aesthetics – turn out to be the modes of transported reading identified by Green and cothinkers. In particular, Fialho documents supporting evidence for the hypothesis that emotional attunement, leading to empathy towards characters in the narrative ('insights into others'), complements identification, which is often with the protagonist ('insights into the self') (Fialho 2019: 8). A focus on aesthetic expression can lead to transformations in personal meanings that have to do with perceptions of reality and expressive resources, rather than personality structures, with some subjects reporting a move towards saturation, richness and depth of experience (Fialho 2019: 7). The core of the connection between the two sorts of insight has to do with the relation between dispositional attribution (what persons are like – e.g. their integrity, or their irascibility) and situational judgement (what the right or the wrong thing to do in a situation is) (Gerrig and Rapp 2004: 272). Just such a character does the right (or the wrong) thing under those circumstances because of the kind of person that they are, and that kind of person is the sort of character that the reader would like to be like (or not), or can sympathize with (or condemn). It is important to notice that these transformations involve 'personal meanings'; that is, they depend on the active response of the reader and they are individualized through participation, or 'expressive enactment', in the context of an individual's life history – for instance, striking transformations often happen after personal crises (Fialho 2019: 9).

These experimental findings on transportation and transformation, focusing on identification, might be summarized most simply by saying that there is a way in which Wayne Booth was right all along. Fictional characters are 'the company we keep' (Booth 1988), and we rely more than we think on the advice of these imaginary friends (and a gallery of rogues). Booth proposes that readers assemble a repertoire of situated judgements about ethical decisions, in the form of an ensemble of familiar characters that are connected to the moral judgements about their virtues (and vices) as suggested by their narratives (Booth 1988). Every reader's fictional library then provides a plug-and-play inventory of thought experiments linking character to outcome, under various ethical circumstances, which can be drawn upon as analogues for moral experience, when forming judgements. They help connect dispositional attributes – what Habermas describes as the relation between motivation and orientation – with social situations and ethical judgements – what Habermas calls the lifeworld, or, ethical life (*Sittlichkeit*). The reason for this is probably that emplotment, which often presents the relation between character and consequences in an idealized way, inherently suggests the idea of 'just deserts'. Getting lost in a narrative and hoping for poetic justice turn out to be strongly related.

Martha Nussbaum is, of course, the contemporary philosophical figure who has championed the idea that the vocation of literature is its presentation of poetic justice, and I want to briefly indicate the distance between the Habermasian position and Nussbaum's Aristotelian stance. For her, the central feature of literature is the link between narrative emplotment and poetic justice, something that she argues with reference to Wayne Booth's Aristotelian understanding of emplotment (Nussbaum 1997: 124 n9). It should be noted that for Nussbaum, literature stimulates a reflective attitude rather than catalyses the experience of transportation, so literature contributes to ethical knowledge rather than provides moral instruction. The difference between the Aristotelian and the Habermasian position should therefore be clear. Nussbaum and Booth are proposing an Aristotelian understanding of *critique*, one that restricts literature's socially critical role to variations within the existing arrangements of ethical life. By contrast, Habermas thinks that the therapeutic role of literary critique includes ruptures with conventional morality and traditional needs, while the Habermasian understanding of *disclosure* encompasses, but is not restricted to, the morally instructive potential of literary works. Transportation results in alterations to attitudes about existential and social questions, alterations that are 'sticky', durable, if not permanent, as a consequence of a readerly orientation to immersion in the vision presented by the literary work. Poetic justice is certainly part of that picture, but it is important not to forget that a transformed relation between motivations and orientations fundamentally belongs to readerly transportation.

9

Literary visions and the social imaginary

How do literary disclosures influence the social formation? How should critics who engage in a hermeneutics of retrieval 'read for the vision'? In this chapter I propose that literary visions refine and re-define the collective space where motivations and orientations are collectively developed. Literary visions contribute to that arena within the social imaginary that has been called the 'imaginative topocosm'. This is an intersubjectively accessible, imaginary map of dread and desire, which literature particularly generates and explores. The imaginative topocosm is where the 'motivational anchoring... of post-traditional moral and legal representations' (TCA1:199 [279]), critical to modernity, happens. It is also where human potentials are mapped out as desirable or undesirable, providing the basis for the cultural socialization of motivations and orientations. The implication is that reading for the vision is about retrieval of the meaning structures that lead readers to locate themselves somewhere on this map. Accordingly, the claim in this chapter is that every literary communication is an intervention that both indicates, and further elaborates, the (region of the) social imaginary that would be needed for its vision of human flourishing. At the same time, it is also an invitation that projects an ideal readership community, one capable of engaging with its structures of feeling and its semantic horizon.

In what Charles Taylor has described as the 'secular age' of the modern world, that vision of human flourishing is fundamentally articulated as humanism. Humanism combines an affirmative and this-worldly (or materialist) relation to reality, with an affirmative stance towards pleasure (i.e. psychological hedonism), including the consolations of illusion. Humanism advocates human desires as basic motivations and human values as valid orientations. In modernity, the basic vision of literary humanism projects a bourgeois form of social individuality. The main characteristics of bourgeois individuality are its partition into personal, private and public components, each with a distinct dimension of self-realization (romance, career, nation), combined with its insistence that the pursuit of human happiness should be left to private discretion. Literary visions have immensely influenced the formation of this humanist social imaginary and its hedonistic imaginative topocosm, something that is especially visible in the roles played by romance fiction, in relation to personal life, and adventure stories, in relation to private careers. Yet in the twentieth and twenty-first centuries, the imaginative topocosm has begun to fragment. Today, reading for the vision is no longer simply a matter of locating literary identifications within the spaces mapped out by bourgeois forms of literary humanism. Humanism now has powerful and credible interlocutors, while bourgeois forms of individuality are increasingly besieged.

To argue these claims I need to first clarify their relation to the cognate claim that literature involves 'ideological interpellation'. After critically discussing the Althusserian position and a few of its sequels, I propose that the category of the social imaginary is a better frame for a communicative hermeneutics of retrieval. Accordingly, I turn to Charles Taylor's concept of the modern social imaginary and explicate its connections with the Habermasian category of the lifeworld. Taylor's history of the Western European and North American social imaginary within modernity as a 'secular age' provides narrative depth and categorial structure to the lifeworld concept. Against this background, I introduce the specifically literary component of the social imaginary through Northrop Frye's idea of the 'imaginative topocosm'. Setting aside Frye's schematic template for literary history, I suggest that his concept of a 'secular scripture' is nonetheless immensely fertile and suggestive for communicative investigations within literary studies. In conclusion, I illustrate these claims with a discussion of two influential forms of popular fiction – romance and adventure.

Literary identification and ideological interpellation

The conception of the social impact of literary disclosures that I am suggesting is an alternative to functionalist theories. Literary identification is often discussed in literary studies through the lens of the theory of 'ideological interpellation' developed by Structural Marxism around Louis Althusser and cothinkers, but it is important to notice that Althusser's theory is not a psychology of literature. Instead, the theory developed by Althusser is a functional account of the role of culture in the fitting of biological individuals into social roles, which is why it speaks of interpellation, that is, a (vocational) calling or (militant) recruitment, in terms of the function of institutional apparatuses (Althusser 1971: 127–86). Althusser's use of psychoanalysis in this context (Althusser 1971: 187–219) 'trails Lacanian resonances without meaningful correspondence' (M. Barrett 1993: 175), lending the theory the appearance of a social psychology without the substance. Indeed, Pierre Macherey's adaptation of the concept of ideological recruitment to his theory of literary production explicitly rejects psychological interpretations of the operation of literature (Macherey 1978: 85–7). The latent unconscious disclosed by the text is neither a form of meaning, nor truly inside the book (Macherey 1978: 150), but rather, it is the absent presence of social structures, which generates a dialectics of 'measured silences', especially through the 'tacit positiveness [of language], which makes it into a truly active insistence' (Macherey 1978: 89). The unconscious in the text is the set of social assumptions, sedimented through language, that history deposits, in the form of what cannot be spoken or thought under a particular mode of production.

Of course, that did not long detain post-Althusserian theory from presenting a construction, as influential as it is elaborate, in both cinema (Metz 1982) and literary studies (Jameson 1981), which attempted to treat the text as *simultaneously* the archaeological site where the plans for the mode of production are buried *and* an authoritative social document housing definitive psychological identifications. From a Marxist perspective, the construction is intuitively appealing because it articulates credible insights into the social role of literature. Fictional narratives *surely do* record something of their historical context of enunciation as well as make indirect statements about aspects of society. The social ideals presented in literary texts *surely are* influential in supporting individuals' psychological identification with authority and so definitely do perform an important role in the process of socialization. The first problem with the Althusserian position (and its post-Althusserian sequelae) is that any hermeneutics of retrieval is constantly menaced by the threat of a functional reduction of meaning, through the treatment of literary structures as 'cultural programming' (Jameson 1992: 166). The second problem is that structures of feeling suffer a scientistic reduction to forms of 'cognitive mapping' (Jameson 1991: 1–40), as an after-effect of the problematic of thinking literature as an architectural sketch of an absent totality. These are the consequences of Althusser's (always inexplicit) one-dimensional functionalism (Clarke 1980) and its transposition into the connection between literature and ideology, which generates Durkheimian assumptions about collective representations and their reflection (and perpetuation) in literary texts (O'Neill 1988).

Nonetheless, there are two important aspects of the Althusserian programme that are not commonly noted, but that I want to keep in sight in what follows. The first is Althusser's insight into the link between ideological misrecognition and mutual recognition (Althusser 1971: 181 n22). Ideology is practical, not theoretical: it is the handshake, not the handbook;

normative, not cognitive. Insofar as 'ideology' for Althusser, as 'lived experience', is co-extensive with what Habermas describes as the lifeworld, the central Althusserian insight is that the lifeworld is centred on ethical life. Now, ideology is a cognitive misrecognition of the functional totality of the regional structures of the mode of production, but this is not how it is socially effective. Instead, ideology functions through subject formation in practical contexts, fitting human individuals into functional roles through their enculturation into social subjectivity. Göran Therborn, who strongly takes up this theory of occupational socialization while correcting some of Althusser's most reductive gestures (such as the fusion of civil society with the state institutions in 'ideological *state* apparatuses') (Therborn 1980), provides the second aspect. The framework of mutual recognition as the basis for ethical life can be described as encompassing a set of 'positional or inclusive ideologies', which have to do with the social authorization of groups or the collective to issue legitimate instructions, especially in the context of material asymmetries. Mutual recognition is tilted towards powerful groups. When mutual recognition challenges through inclusivity that is inconsistent with positional authority, it clashes with functional social roles, and the result is dysfunction, that is, a potentially transformative crisis.

However, Therborn's most striking insight is that positional ideologies have to be supplemented by 'existential or historical ideologies'. The existential component in ideologies has to do with mortality, finitude, sexuality and belonging to communities, whether this belonging is inclusive or positional (self-other relations) (Therborn 1980: 15–30). This is explicitly an effort to come to grips with what 'provides meanings related to being a member of the world' (Therborn 1980: 23), but I suspect that it also secretes an insight along the lines of 'every ideology is a theodicy'. What I mean by that is not a theoretical explanation for human suffering, but a practical way of coping with the realities imposed on human beings by virtue of our finitude and mortality, as well as a rationalization for social suffering.

The concept of the social imaginary

Nonetheless, because of its hermeneutic impoverishment, I want to suggest an alternative to the Althusserian starting point, in the concept of the social imaginary. The concept of the modern social imaginary, as articulated by Charles Taylor, supplements Habermas's stratospherically abstract description of the lifeworld with a concrete narrative of its historical genesis and a detailed account of its structural tensions. This narrative clearly indicates the place of humanism in the modern social imaginary, while the account of its tensions amplifies Habermas's concerns about the totalitarian potentials of functional rationality. Furthermore, as Taylor's nomenclature indicates, the visionary dimension of knowledge formations, mutual recognition and the interpretation of human needs is foregrounded by the social imaginary concept.

Of course, we enter here upon a complex terrain, and there are two theoretical debates that I need to flag while indicating that I cannot discuss their detail within the scope of this book. The first is that the positions of both Taylor and Habermas on the social imaginary/lifeworld, cultural transformation, the provinciality of Europe and the role of religion are contested, and the debates span social theory, political philosophy, historical scholarship and the philosophy of religion. The key issue is the extent to which either thinker generalizes from Western European historical experience in their formalization of the discursive conditions of social existence and rational argument (respectively). Taylor states that his theories of the modern social imaginary as a 'secular age', and the modern moral order based on negative liberty, are specifically restricted to Western Europe and its settler colonies, while Habermas has shifted from 'universal' to 'formal' pragmatics in response to awareness of the provinciality of 'occidental rationality' (Habermas 1998b: 92). However, Habermas mainly considers modernity from the perspective of time-consciousness, rather than spatial-consciousness, which makes it difficult to acknowledge multiple modernities, or to fully provincialize Europe. At the same time, Habermas (I think rightly) insists that scientific discoveries and human rights are fully universalizable and applicable globally (Habermas 2001: 149). Nonetheless, there is scope for Habermas's universalism to acknowledge local variation, because Habermas's post-conventional morality, post-traditional need-interpretations and decentred ego-maturity each involves a succession of reflexive and universalizable transformations of conventional, traditional and centred conceptions.

The second debate concerns what is probably the most important and influential alternative to the Taylor/Habermas position on the social imaginary or the modern lifeworld. This alternative focuses on the democratic revolutions as a radical rupture in the historical continuum, by a novel form of social institution. Here, the positions of Habermas and Taylor contend with those of Claude Lefort and Cornelius Castoriadis. At first glance, Lefort and Castoriadis would seem to be the natural allies of the Habermasian position, rather than Taylor. Lefort and Castoriadis highlight the idea of a political constitution of society, by means of the idea that the democratic revolution inaugurates modernity through its dissolution of the placemarkers of certainty. According to Lefort, democracy empties the locus of sovereignty, the place of power, with the consequence that unlike the premodern prince, the governing party cannot claim to be the incarnation of the collective will (only its delegate) (Lefort 1986, 1988). In democracy, society is constantly unmade and remade, which implies acceptance of provisionality and awareness of the transience of conventions. Castoriadis has a theory of the distinction between institution and imagination grounded in psychoanalysis that makes it possible for him to foreground the utopian aspect of political constitution (Castoriadis 1997). The problem with this notion of the political constitution of society is its voluntarism. Habermas's critique focuses on the implied conception of society as a subject, but it also notices that the notion of social inauguration through political revolution represents a return to the utopian de-differentiation of complex societies (PDM: 327–35 [380–9]). By concentrating on revolutionary spontaneity, Lefort and Castoriadis fail to note the long duration, the historically extended preparatory role of cultural changes and social practices in any major transformation.

By contrast, in a way consistent with Habermas's insistence that the lifeworld is a 'conservative ballast', Taylor emphasizes the crepuscular and variegated movement of cultural change in the emergence of the modern social imaginary. According to Taylor, the social imaginary is the result of the sedimentation of those meanings that interpret social practices and render them meaningful from the perspective of the participants in social action, so that it is 'not a set of ideas; rather, it is what enables, through making sense of, the practices of society' (Taylor 2003: 2). Social imaginaries, he states, are 'the ways people imagine their social existence, how they fit together with others, how things go on between them and their fellows, the expectations that are normally met, and the deeper normative notions and images that underlie these expectations' (Taylor 2003: 23). The institution of the ways that individuals imagine society is not a question of a singular event of radical rupture:

> To transform society according to a new principle of legitimacy, we have to have a repertory that includes ways of meeting this principle. This requirement can be broken down into two facets: (1) the actors have to know what to do, have to have practices in their repertory that put the new order into effect; and (2) the ensemble of actors have to agree on what these practices are. (Taylor 2003: 115)

Accordingly, Taylor's concept of the modern moral order focuses on the 'society' dimension of the lifeworld/imaginary, something described by Hegel's concept of ethical life (*Sittlichkeit*). For Taylor, the modern moral order is based on a set of highly abstract but simple principles governing conduct, which are clearly delineated from premodern moral orders, and which are susceptible to multiple concrete articulations (as liberalism, as socialism, as nationalism, etc.) (Taylor 2003: 3–21). These principles were once (in the seventeenth century) the arcane theories of an insurgent class, but they have become sedimented into the modern way of life to the degree that they now represent principles guiding practical conduct that are independent of their origins in classical liberalism (Taylor 2003: 28–9). The modern moral order is based on the principle of mutual benefit from individual actions (as opposed to the premodern moral order, based on hierarchical complementarity between collective actions), which might be summed up as the social theory of negative liberty (Taylor 2003: 3–4). Its basis, summed up in natural law, is the natural right of individuals to survival and the natural order that arises when these rational agents voluntarily cooperate. Nonetheless, in broad agreement with Habermas's idea that the lifeworld consists not just of normative frames regulating society, but also of the cultural transmission of evolving traditions and an accepted range of personality structures, Taylor acknowledges the importance of imaginative articulations and socialization practices.

Moral orders and recognition frameworks

Taylor's claims resonate with the classical Marxist analysis of the 'political theory of possessive individualism', which traced classical liberal doctrines of social contract, negative liberty and political rights back to their origins in market society (MacPherson 1962), but Taylor clarifies how this need not remain a 'dominant ideology' to be socially effective. At the same time that the modern moral order (MMO) is based in negative liberty, it also depends on equality for its specifically modern character, and there is no doubt in Taylor's mind that a tension exists between these two aspects. Modern equality – as distributive justice, rather than spiritual collectivity – springs from the symmetrical mutual respect that naturally alike agents must demonstrate in order to peacefully cooperate. Finally, the individual pursuit of happiness under conditions of negative liberty requires a basic frame in moral autonomy. This particular conception of moral autonomy supports the notion of authentic individuality as a necessary consequence. The Romantic notion of authenticity as personal self-realization involves an individual definition of flourishing that is consistent with both liberty and equality, having significant cultural and political consequences (Taylor 1991).

Taylor's notion of the MMO is compatible with the theory of struggles for recognition worked out by Habermas's fellow Frankfurt School thinker, Axel Honneth. The concept of a recognition framework, co-extensive with ethical life, describes the customary norms that govern reciprocal expectations of social conduct in terms of three dimensions of ethical identity – self-love (the integrity of the body), self-respect (based in mutual respect) and self-esteem (based in social esteem) (Honneth 1995). These result in frameworks of love, rights and solidarity that guide practical action in everyday life, and which become the basis for normative grievances in social mobilizations, when they are violated (in the respective forms of abuse, disrespect and denigration) (Honneth 1995). Indeed, it is a crucial feature of recognition frameworks that *only privations* trigger struggles for recognition. These are struggles for restitution that *only sometimes* transcend existing norms. Further, norms of mutual respect are *often* asymmetrical, with different rights for different status groups, and norms of social esteem are *usually* asymmetrical, with different contributions valued in rank order (e.g. the Nobel Prize is not awarded for solid efforts). This aspect of Honneth's theory is intended to account for the fact that recognition frameworks reflect the reciprocal expectations between members of historical societies and is consistent with the observation that mutual recognition is ideological misrecognition.

Honneth's discussion of modern struggles for recognition further clarifies how this concept should emphatically not be restricted to questions of cultural recognition or special rights – as it is in Taylor's conception (Taylor 1994) – but must be considered a general description of the normative grievances that inform social movement activation. According to Honneth, modernity breaks up the hierarchical premodern 'alloy' of rights and esteem and replaces these with equal rights and the performance principle (the 'meritocratic' distribution of esteem according to measurable achievements). The result is a chain of struggles for the expansion and deepening of rights, which proceeds along the sequence of legal, civil and then social rights, something that accords with Habermas's notion of rights claims as the pacemaker for modern emancipatory struggles. Nancy Fraser in debate with Honneth introduces notions of (economic) re-/distribution and (political) representation, alongside (legal) rights and (sociocultural) esteem (Fraser and Honneth 2003), and it is worth considering how this modification throws light on what recognition frameworks are and how they relate to functional systems. The economic interests that agents are structurally allocated from a functional perspective are exactly the same as the distributive and redistributive claims that they normatively articulate from the participant perspective. Whether the agents mobilize around 'interests' or 'ideals' is actually a question of whether strategic or communicative action coordinates their activation, not a question of an ontological distinction between two different types of embeddedness.

The intervention of Seyla Benhabib into these debates around the centrality of moral identity to ethical life brings into focus the role of culture generally and narrative specifically, from a perspective that is feminist and multiculturalist, as well as an advocacy of deliberative democracy (Benhabib 1996). Benhabib's articulation of discourse ethics insists on the significance of personal history to moral identity and thus the importance of narrative in linking moral grievances and recognition struggles to the capacity of agents to participate in public debate or political mobilization (Benhabib 1992b: 190–4). Contesting the sufficiency of Habermas's universalizability principle, based on the idea of taking the perspective of the generalized other, she proposes that this becomes adequate only when coordinated with the reality of dialogue with a concrete other. 'The standpoint of the concrete other', she writes, 'requires us to view each and every rational being as an individual with a concrete history, identity and affective-emotional constitution. In assuming this standpoint, we abstract from what constitutes our commonality and focus on individuality . . . [where] our relation to the other is governed by the norms of equity and complementary reciprocity' (Benhabib 1992b: 159). Universalizability must be supplemented by recognition, and narrative has a central role to play in making that possible, because its construction of personal history and group identity locates ethico-moral problems in a social situation that facilitates a 'historically self-conscious universalism' (Benhabib 1992a: 330–69; 2002: 24–48). I now want to focus more generally on the role of narratives in the social imaginary.

The secular age of exclusive humanism

According to Taylor, the MMO would not be possible without its embedding in what he describes as the 'immanent frame' of a set of cultural knowledge formations, which affirm the necessity and sufficiency of the natural against the supernatural, immanence as exclusive of transcendence (Taylor 2007: 542). The key to the integration of the modern naturalistic world view into everyday life is its transformation of subjectivity, connected to what Taylor calls 'instrumental individualism', from a porous to a bounded form of selfhood. Modern individualism coordinates Romantic expressive authenticity within the frame of Enlightenment moral autonomy and liberal forms of negative liberty, and it is deposited into the lifeworld of individuals through the familiar partitioning of spheres into personal, private and public. By describing this as a 'secular age' characterized by 'exclusive humanism', Taylor points not to an absolute eclipse of belief, but to 'how something other than God could become the necessary objective pole of moral or spiritual aspiration, of "fullness"' (Taylor 2007: 26). Literature is central to this process.

Although Taylor advocates the multiple modernities approach, in *A Secular Age* he focuses solely on the modernity of Western Europe and its settler colonies, with the consequence that his discussion of 'religion' is specific to the denominations of Christianity. Against this background and in the context of the resurgence of most of the world religions to socio-political visibility, Taylor discusses three possible interpretations of the 'secularization hypothesis'. Acknowledging the implications of functional differentiation for religious institutions and accepting the tendency to the increasing separation of church and state after the Westphalian Settlement, Taylor zeroes in on the other two. Declining church attendance is not directly indicative of a decline in faith because spiritual beliefs are persistent, but Taylor does think that in general it is now 'so hard to believe in God in (many milieux of) the modern West, while in 1500 it was virtually impossible not to' (Taylor 2007: 539). The focus of his enquiry is therefore turned towards the privatization of religious belief, as conviction faith rather than public orthodoxy (or orthopraxy), as the key to modern secularization. Taylor's historical reconstruction of the successive phases of the complex process of the privatization of faith is also an opportunity to explore the 'sources of the self' under the lens of how personal, private and public are linked in the social imaginary.

> [Secularization] describes a process which is undeniable: the regression of belief in God, and even more, the decline in the practice of religion, to the point where from being central to the whole life of Western societies, public and private, this has become sub-cultural, one of many private forms of involvement which some people indulge in. (Taylor 1989: 309)

Taylor's historical narrative of alienation is dialectical, involving gains and losses. It passes through transitional stages of the Enlightenment's providential deism and then the classical liberal vision of the impersonal order of the market society, before a confident post-Enlightenment secularism begins to 'dragoon' individuals into confessional privatism (Taylor 2007: 221–504, esp. 445). By the mid-nineteenth century, humanism has adopted its definitive modern form:

> I would like to claim that the coming of modern secularity in my sense has been coterminous with the rise of a society in which for the first time in history a purely self-sufficient humanism came to be a widely available option. I mean by this a humanism accepting no final goals beyond human flourishing, nor any allegiance to anything else beyond this flourishing. Of no previous society was this true. (Taylor 2007: 18)

Of course, Taylor accepts that humanist Christianity exists, from Erasmus and Montaigne through to Maritain, but this does not meet the threshold of exclusivity set by 'accepting no final goals beyond human flourishing'. By contrast, what he calls 'providential Deism', belief in an abstract deity whose beneficent providence governs the cosmos and prepares an afterlife by virtue of being a sort of prime mover or universal origin, shifted society historically, and perhaps now shifts individuals in their life histories, towards an exclusively naturalistic world view. Taylor has a long list of literary figures – from Matthew Arnold and Jane Austen, through Hopkins and Ibsen, to Oscar Wilde and Virginia Woolf – who he describes as decisive contributors to modern humanism, either because of their explicit humanist convictions, or because their humanist literary concerns rendered invisible, within their texts, faith convictions that were mainly private and sometimes exclusively personal. At the same time, thinking about figures such as Christopher

Dawson, TS Eliot, Hilaire Belloc and GK Chesterton, literature is also the site for the contestation of humanism, for it is 'one of the prime loci of expression for [converts'] newly discovered insights' into the possibility of something beyond human flourishing (Taylor 2007: 733).

Taylor therefore concludes his monumental survey by looking at diremption in contemporary ethical life. He plots out divisions between reflexive forms of humanist religion and exclusive humanism, on the one side, and the 'immanent counter-Enlightenment' and fundamentalist religion, on the other side (Taylor 2007: 636–7). The potentially anti-democratic and anti-enlightenment forces described by Taylor are exactly the same ones that Habermas identifies. On the one hand, the sceptical destruction of modern normativity, dissolved in the will-to-power, and often allied to a technological celebration of the dominating potentials of instrumental reason, is visible in Nazism. On the other hand, the desperate fundamentalist defence of the unquestionable authority of traditional doctrines is an effort to restore certainty and thereby stabilize reciprocal (usually hierarchical) expectations, by a renewed socialization into unquestioning obedience and orientations anchored in divine law (Habermas 1975b: 74–5; 1987: 384–96).

In summary, the concept of the social imaginary accommodates the insights of functional theories of ideological interpellation into the relation between ideological misrecognition and mutual recognition, while providing scope for hermeneutic depth that they lack. Taylor's nuanced history of the social imaginary lends important texture to Habermas's lifeworld concept and clarifies what is meant by the humanist imaginary of the modern period, while describing the emergence of diremption in the modern context. This locates the narrative contribution to the social imaginary in terms of the contestation and renegotiation of social mythologies, especially those cultural narratives which synthesize recognition frameworks with responses to existential questions. In exploring this aspect of the social imaginary, the approach of both Habermas and Taylor to religion is particularly suggestive, because it illuminates the role of mythological narratives.

Religion and the modern social imaginary

In relation to the role of narrative, literature and religion are cognate phenomena. Not surprisingly, then, Habermas's position on religion duplicates his insights into and problems with literature. In *Communicative Action*, Habermas proposed that communicative reason's 'linguistification of the sacred', in combination with the profanation of the lifeworld by instrumental rationality, results in 'disenchanted', or 'demystified', modern secular societies. As Eduardo Mendieta notes, the concept of the 'linguistification of the sacred' presupposes that religious representations are complexes of cognitive, normative and aesthetic-expressive validity claims, hopelessly fused into mythological narratives (Mendieta 2000: 132–3). The task of reason is to analytically separate these validity claims, in order to extract from the husk of myth a kernel of normative rightness that can be propositionally expressed through post-conventional moral reasoning:

> The disenchantment and disempowering of the domain of the sacred takes place by way of a linguistification of the ritually secured, basic normative agreement; going along with this is a release of the rationality potential in communicative action. The aura of rapture and terror that emanates from the sacred, the *spellbinding* power of the holy, is sublimated into the *binding/bonding* force of criticisable validity claims. (TCA2: 77 [108])

Habermas's claim about religion in relation to normativity is entirely cognate to his claim about literature in relation to expressivity. So too is his reversal, for when Habermas notices that literary semblances are holistic presentations of possible experience that are irreducible to one-dimensional validity claims, he also realizes that mythological narratives point to things that cannot be exhausted by procedural reasoning. In an explicit revision of his initial statements, Habermas now insists that the Abrahamic faiths have positively contributed to modernity. These contributions include: a permanent source of inspiration (rather than a persistent phenomenon); a wellspring of substantive thinking about the good life and an acknowledgement that affection and solidarity in remembrance are most possible against the background of belief in an afterlife and the soul. 'This legacy', he concludes, 'substantially unchanged, has been the object of a continual critical reappropriation and reinterpretation . . . and . . . we [Europeans] must draw sustenance now, as in the past, from this substance' (Habermas 2002: 150–1).

It is remarkable that when Habermas itemizes the cultural contributions of the Abrahamic faiths, however, his impressive list – egalitarianism, autonomy, solidarity, emancipation, conscience, human rights, democracy – is exclusively normative. The implication of my observation is that Habermas's *replacement* of the 'linguistification of the sacred' with acknowledgement of the validity of religion not only misrepresents his own intuitions about the matter, but also misses the opportunity to specify the *reciprocity* of critique and disclosure. Both Duvenage and Mendieta, however, do see the possibility, and it is worth describing their perspectives because of the potential illumination of literature that they provide.

Mendieta proposes that Habermas's revision sublates the opposition between reason and religion into their constant reciprocal interplay. Theological rationalization and evangelical re-envisionment shift back and forth within Christianity, for instance, suggesting that 'disenchantment' and 're-enchantment' ebb and flow within religious life. But following theologians such as Rudolf Bultmann, Karl Barth, Jürgen Moltmann and Helmut Peukert (Mendieta 2000: 125), it is crucial to grasp critical disenchantment – critique – as a process of de-mythologization (where a narrative is grasped as fictional but relevant to a spiritual context), rather than demystification (where a narrative is denounced as a false reference to an absent pseudo-reality). From this perspective, re-enchantment – disclosure – is not necessarily the destruction of reason, but can instead involve the renewal of mythology, in imaginative ways that make a kerygma relevant to new contexts. Re-mythologization and de-mythologization are the ways that the imaginative component of a narrative can be socially influential and critically activated (respectively), regardless of whether the truth-potential of the narrative is spiritual or secular. Duvenage focuses on the way that the distinction between substantive reason and procedural formalism overlaps with the difference between disclosure and critique, in the context of a discussion of how both religious doctrines and political aesthetics provide the definitions of the good life that are otherwise absent from modernity (Duvenage 2010: 349–50). A substantive conception of the good – a 'utopian image' that is also a teleological value – can only be active in the modern public sphere through the life histories of individuals and their collective organizations.

I think that it is unfortunate that instead of articulating the reciprocity of disclosure and critique, or re-mythologization and de-mythologization, Habermas instead developed the category of 'post-secular society' to underline the persistence of religion in modernity. The terminology is confusing and apparently in conflict with the notion of a 'secular age', but its definition actually suggests that it is not a description of the social imaginary, so much as an instruction to social scientists to give up on one-way secularization hypotheses and modernization theories. Habermas's concept of 'post-secular society' is defined as a multi-faith society, with secular political institutions of the democratic variety and religious doctrines that are consistent with human rights and non-violent disagreements in the public sphere (Habermas 2008a, 2008c). Specifically raised in the context of inter-cultural dialogue (as opposed to the implicit violence and communicative closure of a 'clash of civilizations'), Habermas's interventions are aimed at the future of democratic politics rather than the historical trajectories of the social imaginary. But in the present context, it is the dialectics of disenchantment and re-enchantment that is most suggestive for the specifically literary contribution to the social imaginary.

The literary inscription of the imaginative topocosm

Following Northrop Frye, I now want to suggest that literature contributes directly to one element of the modern social imaginary, the component that is responsible for linking motivations to orientations, the 'imaginative topocosm'. The imaginative topocosm is a mythological cartography of fortune and misfortune whose simultaneous generation and exploration happen particularly in the world-building of narrative fiction, and which represents a collective inscription-and-description of idyllic and abhorrent potentials. Although Frye positions this within a schematizing vision of civilizational cycles that is subtended by a speculative anthropology, I nonetheless think that several communicative concepts can be extracted from the labyrinthine passages of his 'anatomy of criticism'. Frye insists that literature communicates a vision that is irreducible to scientific or moral claims, for it concerns the relation between imagination and desire (conceptualized in Aristotelian, rather than Freudian, terms) (Frye 1964: 421). Frye maintains that the imaginative topocosm is constructed around two types of myth – myths of concern; and, speculative, or utopian, myths:

> There are two social conceptions which can be expressed only in terms of myth. One is the social contract, which presents an account of the origins of society. The other is utopia, which presents an imaginative vision of the *telos* or end at which social life aims. These two myths both begin in an analysis of the present, the society that confronts the mythmaker, and they project this analysis in time or space. The contract projects it into the past, the utopia into the future or [elsewhere]. (Frye 1970: 109)

By 'social contract' Frye means any imaginary social foundation, such as divine law, natural right or human dignity, and the utopian speculations that he speaks about are those which transform nature into garden and collectivity into civilization. Evidently, myths of concern are mainly the narrative kernels of divine law or political philosophy, while utopian myths are what certain kinds of speculative literature pre-eminently build. The entire edifice of Frye's literary criticism is contained within this notion. It is crucial not to miss its sweeping implications, as well as Frye's own sceptical and ironic temperament. Of course, there is a functional thesis implied in the distinction between concern and utopia that warrants Fredric Jameson's Althusserian appropriation of Frye in the development of his concept of the 'ideologeme' as a semantic 'dipole' of 'ideology and utopia' (Jameson 1981: 94–5). For Jameson, *every* literary text is constructed through an assemblage of dialogically arranged ideologemes, constituting a partisan diagram of desirable (and detestable) social possibilities. From the hermeneutic perspective, however, Frye's thesis is equally intriguing, because what he really thinks is that the difference between concern and utopia is partly just a difference in historical authorization:

> Every human society, we may assume, has some form of verbal culture in which fictions, or stories, have a prominent place. Some of these

stories may seem more important than others: they illustrate what primarily concerns their society. They help to explain certain features in that society's religion, laws, social structure, environment, history or cosmology. Other stories seem to be less important, and of some at least of these stories we say that they are told to amuse or entertain. This means that they are told to meet the imaginative needs of the community, so far as structures in words can meet those needs. The more important stories are also imaginative, but incidentally so: they are intended to convey something more like special knowledge, something of what in religion is called revelation. Hence they are not thought of as imaginative, or even of human origin, for a long time. (Frye 1976b: 6–7)

As is visible here, the Reverend Professor Frye has a complex relation to the de-mythologizing (but not de-mystifying) theology of Karl Barth and Rudolf Bultmann (Potter 2014). According to Frye, an author, such as John Milton, operating against the background of a religious cosmology and seeking to communicate a literary vision of the myth of concern, must constantly work within the dialectic of the presentation of religious revelation, and the representation of that presentation as demonic parody of prophetic insight (Frye 1976a: 201). Literature denounces itself as fiction. But even when it operates in premodern contexts and remains within metaphysical ontologies or religious cosmologies, literature is a '*secular* scripture', because it is a narrative of the human adventure, the 'epic of the creature', humanity's 'vision of life as a quest' (Frye 1976b: 15). At the same time, and particularly in modernity, literature is a 'secular *scripture*', one that announces itself as resemblance to the sorts of profound reality formerly captured only through reference to revelatory visions. Influential narratives, Frye remarks drily, are not thought of as imaginative, or even of human origin, for very long:

> The difference between the mythical and the fabulous is a difference in authority and social function, not in structure. If we were concerned only with structural features, we should hardly be able to distinguish them at all. . . . There is no structural principle to prevent the fables of secular literature from also forming a mythology. Is it possible, then, to look at secular stories as a whole, and as forming a single integrated vision of the world, parallel to the Christian and biblical vision? (Frye 1976b: 8, 15)

The complicated apparatus of literary modes, plot typologies, speculative anthropology and schematic diagrams in Frye's *Anatomy of Criticism* make sense only against the background of this question. How does *all* literature contribute to the construction of an imaginative topocosm? How is the topocosm structured by social authorization? The key, for Frye, is the mode of Romance, which I think is best described as the Marvellous, a mode in which the protagonist is superior in degree (but not in kind) to other humans, and a master (but not a creator) of nature. The protagonist of a marvellous fiction is great because they work magic (or some correlate of magic, such as miracle, prophesy, technology or reincarnation). For Frye, all literature is derived from marvellous fictions, through a complicated process of declension marked by the increasing impact of the reality principle, and its rotation through a Frazerian anthropology designed to connect the idea of 'mastery of nature' to 'primitive rites' and thus to origins of religion. I do not intend to explicate the 'vegetal ceremonies' aspect of Frye's position, with its elaborate correlations between the four seasons and literary modes, because I cannot envisage a defensible construction emerging from it. Frye's theories of literary modes as a grammar of the topocosm and of plot typologies as its syntax, however, are extremely interesting, and I now want to reconstruct them in a somewhat modified form.

The utopian vision of Enlightenment humanism

According to Frye, there are four basic literary modes and four elementary plot typologies. These are presented in the 'theory of modes' and the 'theory of myths', respectively (Frye 2000: 33–70 and 141–239). Despite its apparent schematization, the derivation is logical, rather than metaphysical. There is also a 'theory of symbols' and a 'theory of genres', which I do not intend to discuss. Confusingly, Frye uses the term 'Romance' as both mode and type, so I will relabel this as the 'marvellous mode' and the 'adventure plot-type'. A mode is a power of action of the protagonist, with respect to society and nature. The degree of agency of the protagonist can be located on a continuum. In the Mythical, the protagonist is superhuman – superior in kind to humans and a creator of nature; a god, angel or demon. In the Marvellous, the protagonist is greater in degree than other humans and a master of nature; a magician, prophet or inventor. In the Mimetic, the protagonist is greater than or the same as other humans, but embedded in nature. Frye has several subdivisions of this category that do not need to derail this discussion. In the Ironic, the protagonist is lesser in degree than other humans and mastered by nature; the fool, the brute, the miserable. Meanwhile, a plot-type is a direction of movement of a sequence of causally enchained actions. Following Aristotle, plot-types involve a change in state, where the state is mis-/fortune: tragedy involves the transition from fortune to misfortune and comedy is its inverse. Frye notices that, logically speaking, it is possible to make a transition from fortune to fortune, or misfortune to misfortune, provided that the change in state is then defined in terms of knowledge and ignorance. In adventure, the fortune of the protagonist is revealed by the action, leading up to self-knowledge and its social recognition. In satire, the misfortune of the protagonist is revealed by the action, and their ignorance is socially recognized. It would be possible to schematize modern literature as a 4x4 matrix of modes and types (e.g. mimetic satire – *Don Quixote*; mimetic comedy – *Jane Eyre*; ironic satire – *The Trial*), but that would be a sterile exercise in classification, unless it were linked to a discussion of the significance of the resulting table that would go beyond the scope of the present book.

Now, Frye thinks that Romance (i.e. the marvellous mode) is the structural centre of all literature and that other modes are 'displacements', upwards into the celestial or downwards into nature. 'In Romance, essentially the whole human action depicted in the plot is ritualised action' (Frye 1976b: 56). The most important ritual actions represented in the marvellous mode are magical enchantments, which represent human symbolic action in a metaphysical universe. This connects with Frye's thesis that 'apocalyptic', 'analogical' and 'demonic' imagery is central to the meaning of literature in general and the marvellous mode in particular (Frye 1976b: 95–158; 2000: 141–57). Human symbolic action in a metaphysical universe (i.e. magic) is ceremonial wish-fulfilment, or it is the apotropaic invocation of anxieties; it is desire and dread, defining the 'idyllic' and the 'abhorrent', as well as the 'analogical' possibility that human beings might have to exist between the two extremes.

The marvellous mode, in other words, is the key to the definition and redefinition of the imaginative topocosm, including, fascinatingly, its modern version. Civilizations are founded through the elaboration of a body of socially authorized marvellous fictions that formulate, supplement, extended and sometimes modify the imaginative core of a civilization's literature (Frye 1976b: 15, 56). Then, the sceptical intellect sets in, 'displacing' the marvellous action downwards into nature, through mimetic treatments, until, eventually, a pervasive ironic consciousness effectively signifies the exhaustion of a civilizational vision. Frye explains this in terms of a theory of Viconian cycles that is indefensible in a post-metaphysical context. But the discussion of critique and disclosure in this book provides an alternative. Parallel to the religious dialectic of disenchantment and re-enchantment, there is a dynamic tension in modern literature. This is between tendencies towards increasing ironization, responding to rational critique, and counter-tendencies towards increasing mythologization, refreshing potential identification.

The modern, secular age is unique not only in its normative project, but also in its literary discourse. Although literature continues to signify its fictional status, the requirement that it denounce itself as a demonic parody of religious revelation has disintegrated, along with the sacred canopy that this practice supported. This is because the literary discourse of modernity departs not from a marvellous legend, but from realist fiction. Defoe, Fielding and Richardson, argues Ian Watt:

> were unprecedentedly independent of the literary conventions which might have interfered with their primary intentions, and they accepted the requirements of literal truth much more comprehensively. . . . [T]here

can be little doubt that the development of a narrative method capable of creating such an impression is the most conspicuous manifestation of that mutation of prose fiction which we call the novel; the historical importance of Defoe and Richardson therefore primarily depends on the suddenness and completeness with which they brought into being what may be regarded as the lowest common denominator of the novel genre as a whole, its formal realism. (Watt 1963: 32–3)

In the period of the democratic revolution, then, literature articulated a form of humanism that did not rely on supernatural support and that dealt, not with elevated, 'great' figures, but with a thief (*Moll Flanders*), a hypocrite (*Pamela*) and a fornicator (*Tom Jones*). In contrast with Frye's notion of a declension of literary forms downwards from a marvellous kernel, something applicable to the premodern world but not to the modern era, modern literary humanism begins from novel forms written in the mimetic mode. This is because it is articulated to kinds of modern humanism, both democratic and socialist, that have a non-metaphysical core. As Habermas notes, human dignity, conceptualized post-metaphysically as a substantive norm that articulates moral autonomy to legal equality, is an inference from mutual respect, rather than an essential nature to be historically realized. 'Human rights constitute a realistic utopia insofar as they no longer paint deceptive images of a social utopia that guarantees collective happiness, but anchor the ideal of a just society in the institutions of constitutional states themselves' (Habermas 2010: 467). There is a 'politically explosive force' of humanism, shorn of claims to the mastery of nature and no longer captive to an essentialist politics of the socially exemplary incarnation of universality in some particular (i.e. hegemonic) group. It can be the 'portal through which the egalitarian and universalistic substance of morality is imported into law', in the structural transformation of social formations (Habermas 2010: 469). It can also be the generative matrix for struggles for recognition that refuse exclusions from the universal and for the validation of human needs as possible and legitimate. Against this background, it is certainly possible for literature to be humanist and emancipatory without needing to rely on a metaphysical foundation.

The Enlightenment, however, held open a place for the mastery of nature, if not for the sort of mythic apotheosis of literary marvels that Frye discusses. From the Habermasian perspective, there most certainly is a mythology of specifically bourgeois humanism, once it becomes a form of ideological legitimation for social inequality. As Habermas notes, the Enlightenment philosophers dethroned God from the absolute locus of a transcendental being, only in order to situate human nature in the resulting empty place (Habermas 1992a: 40–2). This echoes Sartre:

In the philosophical atheism of the eighteenth century, the notion of God is suppressed, but not, for all that, the idea that essence is prior to existence;

something of that idea we still find everywhere, in Diderot, in Voltaire, and even in Kant. [Humanity] possesses a human nature; that 'human nature' which is the conception of the human being, is found in every [human]; which means that every [human] is a particular example of a universal conception, the conception of [Humanity]. (Sartre 1973: 27)

The radical separateness of humanity from nature – the *sui generis* status of human nature – can be summed up in the notion that the human being is the master of nature; this is the core of the Enlightenment humanism of the 'bourgeois implementation of the modern project'. Further, there is a partitioning of domains of realization of the human essence into the public citizen (concentrated on the nation), the private individual (centred on career) and personal intimacy (focused on romance), characteristic of nationalist ideology and 'civic-familial privatism'. In the terms just developed, that raft of ideas has the status of a myth of concern articulated in the marvellous mode. It would be possible to debate whether modern culture is adventurous or comic. But the one truly modern myth (i.e. a myth that has no ancient or medieval precedent) is the Faust myth, from Doctor Faustus to Viktor Frankenstein, which is a marvellous tragedy involving the dialectical destiny of the human capacity to master nature. Rotated into the adventure plot-type, this figure becomes a world-redeeming, technologically endowed wonder-worker of the James Bond variety. This mythic captivation of modern literature does not detract from its description of the human condition and its cultivation of humaneness, from its exploration of human needs and criticism of social arrangements, but it certainly does frame it historically as bound up with the ideological legitimation of bourgeois society.

10

The phoenix and the serpent

J. K. Rowling's Harry Potter series

Literature sparks debate. But it also changes lives. Reading for the vision is about the latter. It looks at how and why literature transforms its readers. It frames 'how?' in terms of processes of identification. How does the text seek to guide its readers towards its new vision? How, for instance, does it provide pathways and barriers to identification with characters? What kinds of ambivalence and ambiguity does it arouse? How might this facilitate opening up the reader's personality towards hitherto excluded motivations and orientations? It frames 'why?' in terms of the meanings that renovate society's imaginative topocosm. What is the text's conjecture about idyllic and abhorrent social possibilities? Why does the text present these as structures of desire and dread that promote human flourishing? What is the relationship between this imaginary map and the existing topocosm?

The difference between sparking debate and changing lives can be thought of in terms of the distinction between representation and presentation, as well as those between suspicion and retrieval. Literary critiques intervene in public debates about the reception of a fictional representation of the relation between individuals, society and nature, and such critiques are often suspicious that a deeper motivation is hidden beneath the surface of representations. By contrast, the hermeneutics of retrieval investigates the imaginary world that is presented, envisioned, by a narrative fiction, seeking to relate this to the collective myths that shape readers' expectations, and to the effects on readers of its patterns of identification. Reading for the vision, then, is not about switching off political judgement for an agnostic descriptivism that simply catalogues the textual repertoire and narrative strategies available to the ideal reader. In many ways, reading for the vision is about facing outwards, into the work's potential formation of a new readership community in the world, rather than inwards, into scholarly disagreements about the effectiveness of its intervention.

My test case for reading for the vision is J. K. Rowling's well-known Harry Potter series (hereafter, HPS). In what follows, I aim to describe the open locus that is the implied reader of the series, exploring it as the point of condensation for the construction of a (literary, cultural and social) repertoire, which supports the narrative strategies that solicit active reception (Iser 1974). I begin with the generic controls over the scope of reception and the way that their multiplication generates blanks, before describing the imaginary world of the HPS (the 'Potterverse') that results from the repertoire. Then, I turn to the narrative strategies whose voids, in the form of dramatic ironies, catalyse revisions of expectations, while supporting psychological identification with the main character.

The anti-fascist inspiration of J. K. Rowling

In the case of Rowling's series, which is a wildly popular, yet progressive, fantasy fiction, it is not necessary to guess whether it is influential. The series has been phenomenally successful, selling, according to *Fortune* magazine (26 June 2017), in excess of 400 million copies in more than 68 languages. But this success is not the direct result of a corporate campaign by a multinational media-entertainment giant. Even hostile critics have conceded the opposite – that the novel by a small UK publishing firm initially circulated on the basis of personal recommendations, before reaching that threshold at which news reporting transforms something into a bestseller, first in the UK, and then internationally (Blake 2002: 3–4). The literary success of the Harry Potter series has generated a series of highly successful movies and a massive merchandizing phenomenon. There is also an academic industry – with twenty-one critical works in the initial decade of its reception alone, plus numerous dissertations – and a highly loyal (and extremely large) fan base who continue to write Harry Potter spin-offs themselves, to buy Rowling's other books and so forth. And there is direct evidence that this changes lives. The Harry Potter Alliance is an independent and progressive activist community, located on every continent except Antarctica, whose 'chapters' campaign for an impressive list of causes (Blackwell et al. 2008). These include LGTBQ+ recognition, gender equality, racial justice, youth advocacy and addressing climate change. They state that they 'believe in joyful activism' and that 'heroes aren't born – they develop with practice and support', as well as that 'the weapon we have is love', as opposed to hate, all of which resonate with the motifs of the HPS. It is therefore highly plausible to suppose that the series has also changed the motivations and orientations of many others among its 400 million readers, even if they have not literalized this identification as membership of the Alliance.

Unlike the majority of cinematic blockbusters and literary bestsellers, the HPS is driven by emancipatory hopes and expresses progressive ideals. Inspired by the life of the communist journalist and anti-fascist campaigner Jessica Mitford, the HPS dramatizes a desperate struggle by contemporary anti-fascist forces against an apparently irresistible (neo-)fascist movement. The twist that made the series so successful is that it is set in an imaginary reality where magic is possible and where the oppression of magical species (such as elves and goblins) replaces racial hierarchy as the social principle of fascist domination. The protagonist of the series, the young wizard Harry Potter, confronts the terrifying power of the dark wizard, Lord Voldemort, and his followers, the Death Eaters, as these attempt a counter-revolution aimed at establishing a totalitarian order. Set mainly in the boarding school environment of Hogwarts School of Witchcraft and Wizardry, the seven books of Harry's quest trace out the growing solidarity of Harry's friends, including his close friends, Ron Weasley and Hermione Grainger, through the seven years of his school life. But they also detail the developmental crises of Harry's moral and emotional maturation, as he clashes repeatedly with representatives of social authority, most of whom turn out to be either deeply complicit with the emergence of fascism, or to have fatally limited ethical horizons when confronted with ultimate social questions. Accordingly, the books are not just anti-fascist, but also deeply anti-authoritarian, advocating moral autonomy, political engagement and a progressive civic agenda, along the lines of Mitford's own maxim, to 'do the right thing, not the easy thing' (Compson 2003: 21–2).

The scale of the impact of the HPS enters the territory where a narrative fiction begins to rival the *Bible*, the *Quran* and the *Analects*, something that deeply disturbs cultural conservatives around the globe. Religious fundamentalists, particularly in the United States, have made the HPS into the most banned books in the world (Miller 2013). The fundamentalists' ground is that the series actively solicits rebellion against established social authority, consistent with its engagement with 'permissive culture', 'sexual promiscuity' and active promotion of homosexuality (Jones 2002). This impressive agenda is apparently part of the series' 'promotion of the occult', something that supposedly belongs to anti-Christian contemporary mainstream culture (Abanes 2001; Wohlberg 2002). Although there is a vast body of such criticism, especially online, Christian fundamentalists have been challenged by conservative Christians. The main argument from the conservative position is that, in a confused and irresolute way, there do exist representations of 'moral realism', which basically means agreement with Christian values as unconditional absolutes. Matthew Dickerson and David O'Hara, for instance, provide conditional support to the series on these 'triumph of the good' grounds, while warning that it falls well short of the literary standards set by J. R. R. Tolkein and C. S. Lewis, let alone *Beowulf* and the *Bible* (Dickerson and O'Hara 2006: 227–52). Fundamentalist critics, however, will have none of that: Harry Potter is generally prepared to clash with institutionally legitimate authority, based on nothing more than his own moral judgement, rather than with reference to an absolute standard of ethical good (Jones 2002: 4–5). In short, they agree with Rowling's perspective, that the vision of the series is that 'you should question authority and you should not assume that the establishment tells you all of the truth' (A. Barrett 2007), but they think that this represents a pernicious influence.

The politics of reading for the vision

What makes a Habermasian analysis of the series potentially illuminating is that (highly surprisingly and somewhat depressingly) other left-wing readings of the series have mainly been hostile, even vituperative. I have already presented the Habermasian analysis of neoconservative ideology and technocratic rationality, in the context of increasing political authoritarianism, worsening global poverty and escalating environmental crisis. In the present context, then, it is only necessary to notice that Rowling's fiction about neo-fascist counter-revolution may turn out not to be a fantasy after all. The need for a united front against fascism is certainly something that can be imagined today. Last time, in Germany, the communists' ultra-left and sectarian policy of denouncing socialists and democrats as 'social-fascists' guaranteed defeat by dividing the resistance (Trotsky 1975). It would perhaps be a good idea not to repeat that mistake. Furthermore, it is difficult to imagine the development of a popular radical democratic movement that would not begin from moral autonomy, ego maturity, questioning authority and a politics that is fiercely opposed to all forms of discrimination and domination – exactly what the books promote.

The intemperate tone of some left-wing critiques is, I suspect, generated by the implications of the (excessively monolithic) culture industry thesis. Jack Zipes frames it perfectly: 'it is impossible to be [a] phenomenal [publishing success], without conforming to conventionality' (Zipes 2002: 172); the HPS is a phenomenal success – therefore it is conventional and conformist. Against this background, it is not surprising that, instead of elaborating on the work's anti-authoritarian impetus, important left-wing publisher Verso Press commissioned Andrew Blake to demolish the series. For Blake, Rowling's books provide a 'magical transformation' that turns political sloganeering into ideological conviction, because they whisk out of sight the politically marginalized and socially excluded, behind a joyful image of cultural and social renewal (Blake 2002: 25–6). The title for Blake's monograph, *The Irresistible Rise of Harry Potter*, echoes Brecht's *The Irresistible Rise of Arturo Ui* – which is a play about Mussolini! – and indeed, Blake adapts some aspects of Gramsci's analysis of the fascist 'passive revolution' to critique the HPS (Blake 2002: 17). The logic of interpreting the HPS as pro-fascist advocacy is exemplified in the following broadside against the series, from a scholarly collection whose tone is unremittingly hostile:

> The Harry Potter books feature images of nuclear families without the inclusion of representations of step, single, gay or lesbian, or adoptive foster families of our contemporary society. The books also reinforce cultural stereotypes of power and gender, consistently portraying women as secondary characters. In addition, there is little cultural diversity represented and, when it is represented, it is in the form of tokenism and colonialism. Racialized groups of wizards, giants and other creatures are presented in a hierarchical order in which racial difference creates one's place. Such normative messages about families, community, race and gender exemplify who is *not* part of the conversation by the exclusion of their representation in the texts. What appears to be represented in the Harry Potter books, then, is an aggregation of quintessential, hegemonic, hierarchical middle-class social and cultural values. The fact that the social normative messages in the Harry Potter texts are ones of exclusivity is bothersome and warrants critical attention, but there are additional inherent implications here. . . . [T]hose not represented in the texts, those not living the good life, those being oppressed, persecuted, abused, neglected, or simply left behind mainstream society must somehow be to blame. It is made inconceivable, from this perspective, that society might be to blame. (Turner-Vorbeck 2003: 20–1)

It would be disastrous were progressive criticism to degenerate into a 'police mentality', basically reducing criticism to a 'stop-and-search' routine which hunts through the text for incriminating evidence of ideological contraband, based on 'textual profiling'. In the HPS, as I will now discuss, it is *Voldemort's* programme to have 'racialized groups of wizards, giants and other creatures presented in a hierarchical order in which racial difference creates one's place', not Harry Potter's. Some progressive critics risk missing what it is about the series that irritates those conservative forces which authoritarian populists look to today, for support in their terribly real programmes for the restoration of hierarchical order.

The Order of the Phoenix

Before analysing the repertoire and strategy of the novels, I want to describe the series' arc and the role of my main focal text, book five. Not only is the story of each novel structured around the ordeal of magical combat characteristic of a marvellous adventure, but the trajectory of the series as a whole also features escalating powers of Harry's magical adversaries, culminating in a final battle against Voldemort himself. Combining elements of the marvellous quest from fantasy literature with novels of school days and the genre of identity formation and cultural education (*Bildungsroman*), each book of the HPS characteristically revolves around a confrontation between Harry and Voldemort's proxy. This is usually an infiltrator into Hogwarts, and typically, it is the Defense Against the Dark Arts teacher, who is (either consciously or unconsciously) complicit with Voldemort. As the series progresses, Harry learns that Voldemort murdered Harry's parents in his infancy and tried to kill Harry also, failing because of a spell placed on Harry by his mother that gravely disempowered Voldemort for a time. Voldemort now seeks to destroy Harry because he believes him to be the most important obstacle to recruitment to the Death Eaters, and to the dark wizard's return to power. Each novel traces a year in Harry's secondary education at Hogwarts, where, typically, after beginning the book with Harry's suffocatingly prejudiced, middle-class guardians, Harry escapes cultural conformity and industrial normality for school. Here, Harry discovers that the dark wizard has grown even more powerful than last year, a fresh plot to destroy him is afoot, and he and his friends must race to recover something magical (typically secreted in the school itself) before Voldemort gets it.

The intertwinement of different genres makes it possible to situate Harry's adolescent identity problems in a repertoire that includes ethical and emotional elements, as well as generic innovations in relation to school stories and popular fantasy. The repertoire also prominently includes social elements relevant to historical fascism and contemporary neo-fascism. The malice of Voldemort and his Death Eaters is compounded by the bureaucratic incompetence and sometimes corruption of the wizards' institution of governance, the Ministry of Magic, which, instead of prosecuting a vigorous campaign against Voldemort, prefers for most of the series to deny reality and persecute Harry and friends. That turns out to be hardly surprising, as the series gradually reveals that the wizarding world is characterized by hierarchies of 'pure' versus 'mixed' lineages, and is rife with prejudice and oppression. Eventually, Harry and friends discover that 'we wizards have mistreated and abused our fellow creatures for too long, and we are now reaping our reward' from the structures of domination and exclusion that are the foundation of society (5: 767). The wizarding world, with the Ministry of Magic at its centre, is, in other words, a colonial power regulating an exclusionary society, and the series presents a magical version of Aimé Césaire's insight that fascism is 'colonial procedures . . . applied to Europe' (Césaire 2000: 36). As Lana Whited has demonstrated, the dates 1492 and 1942 are crucial to the entwinement of colonialism and anti-Semitism in reality, and enslavement and prejudice in the series (Whited 2006). The defeat of Voldemort's precursor in 1945, introduced in the first book (1: 109), makes the relevance of the series to anti-fascism unmistakeable.

As treachery and selfishness swirl around Harry, the initial moral absolutes of a struggle against dark wizardry as a 'war against evil' blur into the difficulties of group loyalties and conflicting values, personal vendettas and private motivations, and the increasing problem of sorting out the right thing from what seems to be the good thing to do. In this fundamental dilemma, the adult characters who have seemed to provide clear moral positions – the wise Headmaster Albus Dumbledore, the hyper-intelligent professor Minerva McGonagall and the apparently sinister potions teacher Severus Snape – turn out to be far more complex, and limited, than Harry had dreamt of at the start. Meanwhile, Lord Voldemort, aka former Hogwarts student and magical prodigy (not unlike Harry himself) Tom Marvolo Riddle, who had seemed a vision of metaphysical evil, is revealed as an extremely damaged individual characterized by both psychological and spiritual fragmentation, whose moral maliciousness is indivisible from his pathological state. The highly original development in the series is that Voldemort's destruction requires, not Harry's triumph, but his death, for Harry is not alone 'the Chosen One', but only, in a complex way, the proxy for an entire alliance.

That alliance is the Order of the Phoenix – originally set up by the generation before Harry to oppose Voldemort's initial rise – and book five concerns the irruption of civil war between it and the Death Eaters, in the context of the Ministry of Magic's final effort to suppress the truth about Voldemort's return. 'I want to join', Harry announces, the moment that he learns that the Order has been revived: 'I want to fight' (5: 89). This expresses a combination of resolution and aggression that it is the task of the novel to separate. Harry's immature enthusiasm for instant confrontation is aggravated in the novel by prolonged frustration, as Defense Against the Dark Arts has been taken over by a Ministry appointee, Dolores Umbridge, who refuses to teach practical magic. Meanwhile, the Order refuses to inform Harry that it is secretly guarding a prophesy linking the reciprocally fatal destinies of 'the Chosen One' and Voldemort, on the assumption that although Harry *is* the Chosen One, he has a mysterious, and uncontrolled, telepathic connection to the dark wizard. Indeed, in his dreams, Harry inhabits Voldemort's monstrous serpentine servant, Nagini. Harry, meanwhile, rushes in, setting up 'Dumbledore's Army', a student equivalent of the Order of the Phoenix, which triggers a school rebellion against Umbridge's state-based tyranny. But this also results in the death of Harry's godfather, Sirius Black, following a dream magically sent by Voldemort, which is an elaborate trap laid by the dark wizard. The prophesy is found then lost; the students are outmatched by the Death Eaters; Sirius is killed by his own cousin, Bellatrix Lestrange; and Voldemort manifests in the heart of the Ministry of Magic, intent on the murder of Harry Potter. Dumbledore saves the day, of course, with some help from Harry, in a mighty magical confrontation that drives off the dark wizard while revealing his resurgence to the Ministry itself. In the aftermath, it is revealed that the recovered prophesy is ambiguous, for it might also concern the extraordinarily modest Neville Longbottom. Harry, however, abetted in this by Dumbledore, instantly misinterprets its declaration that 'neither can live while the other survives' (5: 774) as the injunction that he is the Chosen One who must kill Voldemort (5: 777). The remainder of the series is concerned with stripping away Harry's remaining parental proxy (Dumbledore is killed in the next book) before Harry must alone grasp the underlying reason why he survived Voldemort's initial attack, and its implication for the final confrontation. Harry has a fragment of Voldemort's tortured soul lodged in his own, lending a self-sacrificing inflection to book five's central idea, that 'there are some things worth dying for' (5: 444).

An inversion of the school days novel

Although many critics have noted that the HPS reactivates the tradition of the boarding school novel, whose canonical form is defined by Enid Blyton's *Malory Towers* series, few have noticed just how thoroughly Rowling reverses the expectations connected with this genre. As Iser notices, generic conventions strongly guide readers' anticipations, positioning the implied reader as a space where deviations from these expectations are highly significant (Iser 1980). But Blake speaks for many progressive critics in articulating the prefiguration of meaning that the genre provokes, as if it were the final perspective that the repertoire provides:

> Sitting between the lonely orphan and the quest, in all the Harry Potter books, are the public school story and the friends' adventure story. Some of the school stories – the classic is Thomas Hughes's *Tom Brown's Schooldays* – are versions of the story of manifest destiny. Our Hero survives (step)parental domination and underachievement at home, then in his early experiences at school also survives bullying and isolation from schoolmates. Finally – with the support of the older and wiser headmaster – he becomes the general hero of the day by helping to win a cricket match. Harry has friends who give important help in achieving his quests; his stories also owe something to . . . Enid Blyton . . . repackaged for contemporary readers. (Blake 2002: 19)

(It is worth remarking that Hogwarts is a selective-entry government school, not an elite fee-paying grammar.)

In the work of Thomas Hughes and Enid Blyton, the school environment is a scene of peer bonding and sporting success, where coping with school bullies (Hughes) or unconventional personalities (Blyton), authoritarian teachers and interpersonal rivalries is ultimately easy. This is because the student community is characterized by a cosy solidarity that is the result of the way in which the school environment provides a buffer against the outside world by homogenizing its social structure. Companionate friendship, facilitated by empathic identification and guided by that form of conventional morality known as interpersonal conformity, becomes the model for right conduct, which means that group loyalty is often the highest form of practical reasoning made available by the novels. Finally, there is generally a headmaster figure who represents benevolent authority and whose ethical values set the moral compass for the main characters, by seeing the potential in the hero/-ine while facilitating their difficult path towards wisdom.

The Harry Potter novels systematically falsify these expectations and reverse the ethical evaluations associated with this form of practical reasoning, presenting a direct contrast with the tradition of the boarding school novel. There are three aspects to this that I shall deal with in sequence: (1) the external social environment, characterized by status hierarchies and histories of species domination, turns out to be always-already within the school walls; (2) that fact inverts the apparent validity of group loyalty, exhibiting its potential to turn into stifling conformity and status oppression, so that belonging must ultimately spring from justice if it is to become true solidarity; (3) the transition from companionate friendship to social solidarity is a path of conflict with authority that culminates in a school rebellion, not in acceptance of the principal's wisdom, and of coming to terms with complexity and ambivalence that transcends group loyalty.

The fault lines of exclusion and domination that traverse the wizarding world do not magically stop at the borders of the school grounds, despite the assurances of the Ministry of Magic, as personified in book five by Dolores Umbridge. The members of the dark house Slytherin do not just bring their prejudices in through the front gates with them, for the structures that support the school itself are profoundly unjust. Rowling depicts a wizarding world rooted in violent oppression and systematic exploitation, emblematized not only by the syllabus of the History of Magic classes, but also by Umbridge's prejudices towards 'filthy half-breed [centaurs]' (5: 694) and Hermione's campaign to free the house elves (5: 146). The enslavement of house elves is an abomination condemned only by Hermione and Dumbledore, but it turns out to be something with momentous consequences in book five, for Dobby (a free elf) informs Harry about a space where Dumbledore's Army can train, while Kreacher (an unfree elf) informs Voldemort about Harry. At the same time, the centaurs are the key to the student rebellion against Umbridge, while Hagrid, the school's half-giant gamekeeper, provides desperately needed spectral flying horses to the rebels. The eventual alignment of Umbridge with Slytherin manifests the kinship between her prejudices and Voldemort's animosity towards 'mudbloods' (i.e. non-pure lineage wizards). Finally, book five spends time in the 'Noble House of Black', Harry's godfather's family home, which provides the reader with a vision of dark hatred fuelled by disintegrating privilege.

The competitive rivalry between elitist Slytherin and the other more egalitarian houses, Ravenclaw, Hufflepuff and Gryffindor, can easily distract from this, as can the ludic sequences involving the wizarding sport, Quidditch. By the time of book five, however, it is evident that wizarding sports and wizarding houses have the opposite function to their role in conventional school days novels, for the sports are increasingly the scene for tragic conflicts (rather than integrative successes) and the houses are increasingly the site for exclusion (rather than reconciliation). This escalates: in book four, the wizarding tournament turns out to be a murderous environment, while the Quidditch World Cup is interrupted by a Death Eater attack; in books five and six, Quidditch is simply divisive, first of Harry from the team, and then of Harry from his friends; by book seven, it is irrelevant, thus completing the inversion of the trope of sporting reconciliation. Interpersonal destructiveness within Gryffindor increases, too: in book four, Harry's select role in the wizard tournament causes resentment that isolates him; in book five, this turns into ostracism; in book six, Harry's loneliness and grievance sets him against his friends; by book seven, it is evident that the house system has failed entirely. Dumbledore's Army, inaugurated in book five, which is the closest thing in the series to an unequivocally valorized school community, involves students from across the school, not just from within Gryffindor. Crucially, its members are a roll-call of cultural undesirability and interpersonal marginalization: intellectual females (Hermione), working-class males (Ron), shy girls (Ginny Weasley), strange young women (Luna Lovegood), sensitive boys (Neville) and disruptive characters (the Weasley twins, George and Fred).

As I have already discussed the student rebellion, I will look at the way that justice, not group loyalty, mediates the transition from friendship to solidarity, by focusing on intergenerational divergences. As introduced in book three, Harry's friendship circle is a repetition-with-difference of his father's group at the school, James Potter, Sirius Black, Remus Lupin and Peter Pettigrew (who turns out to be a traitor). Harry strongly identifies with the first three, with Remus and Sirius acting implicitly and explicitly (respectively) as surrogate fathers. These 'Marauders' are rakish daredevils, student rebels, heroes of the resistance and so on, and, as books five and six reveal, either bullies (James) or accomplices (Sirius) – only Lupin, stigmatized by lycanthropy, comes out of the series without looking ambivalent. Meanwhile, Harry and friends in the final books confront decisions with respect to apparent enemies – Severus Snape, the head of Slytherin, and Draco Malfoy, school bully, both of whom are in the service of Voldemort – that so transcend group loyalty as to make it ultimately seem hopelessly flawed. Snape, the victim of James's bullying in the last generation, turns out to be a courageous double-agent working for the Order and possibly the most complex character in the series. His apparent murder of Dumbledore in book six is revealed in book seven as an assisted euthanasia whose end is deception of Voldemort (7: 556–61), while Harry's use of an illegitimate (if not forbidden) curse on Draco in book six (6: 434–5), while perhaps justified by self-defence and motivated by grievance, has disturbing resonances with his father's bullying of Snape. Neither Harry's nor James's generations resemble the cast of Malory Towers, despite the resonances with Blyton's series, and Hogwarts is the opposite of Blyton's schools.

Moral development and the novel of education

Crucial to the repertoire of the HPS as a whole, and of every book in the series, is the novel of education and formation, dealing with a young man's difficult transition from adolescence into adulthood, at a historical moment that foregrounds questions of right conduct and political engagement. As Lana Whited has shown in her research on the series, Harry's moral progress passes through a sequence of steps that closely resemble the six stages outlined in Lawrence Kohlberg's theory of moral development (Whited 2003). The transitions between stages are structured by a succession of developmental crises concerning affect regulation and moral development – and the relation between them – such that 'Harry's saga ultimately provides an effective illustration of Kohlberg's theory' (Whited 2003: 183).

Harry's basic developmental task is to advance to stage VI post-conventional moral reasoning, involving deontological considerations, where 'doing the right thing, not the easy thing' requires testing lines of conduct for their universal validity. He has to learn to deal with mortal anxiety, severe frustration and grievous loss, without aggression, while not only learning to reason post-conventionally, but also how to decide between competing consequentialist and deontological frameworks. The developmental crises that punctuate Harry's ascent through a sequence of moral stages are dramatized through an escalating series of confrontations with authority figures. Representatives of familial, educational and social authority are revealed, one by one, as custodians of fatally limited moral perspectives. These range from pre-conventional familial and house orientations, through the conventional 'law and order' perspective of the Ministry of Magic, to Dumbledore's post-conventional utilitarianism. This element of the repertoire foregrounds the HPS's status as young adult fiction with an educative role to play, and it is noteworthy that the moral reflection dramatized in the books shifts towards the post-conventional end of the spectrum as Harry himself ages (from 11 to 18).

In briefest compass, Voldemort, the Death Eaters and House Slytherin represent the pre-conventional reasoning of stages I and II (colloquially, the 'might makes right' and 'rewards & punishments' orientations), while Ron and House Gryffindor represent the conventional reasoning of stage III (interpersonal conformity and group loyalty). The stage III 'good boy/good girl' orientation is to pleasing authority figures by meeting their expectations. Hermione, most of the teachers and the Ministry represent the conventional reasoning of stage IV, 'social system and conscience maintenance', which is a 'law & order' orientation consisting in sticking to the rules because they are the rules, and embodying and enacting customary values as ethically good, simply because they are the values of the group, nation or collective. There are numerous examples in the series of group loyalty, law-abiding and customary value orientations as orientations that direct individuals towards moral wrong (from a post-conventional perspective) because their family, group, institution or community sits on the side of domination, not of liberation. When the Ministry decides 'to interfere in Hogwarts', it sends Dolores Umbridge, a rigid conformist to ministerial rules, to restore order in the school, something which not only objectively assists Voldemort's plots, but which also soon leads to her effectively torturing students to enforce the rules (book 5). Umbridge's cruel excesses are unchecked by the stage IV orientation, which exercises no controls over the substance of the rules. But the series raises wider questions about the law and order orientation and its potential relationship to judicial murder and legalized torture, with its insistent representations of the Ministry's use of terrifying spectral Dementors to guard the wizarding prison, Azkaban (book 3).

Most interesting, though, is the way that the series' exposure of the limitations of conventional morality impacts on ethically *good* values. It is easy to judge conventional moral reasoning as limited when the conventions are aligned with groups and rules that intend to cause suffering. But the HPS also brings into question the adequacy of conventional perspectives, even when these are in the service of humane values. The ambivalence of the House system in the school is the most evident case of a representation of conventional values as at once promoting group solidarity and being fatally limited, when confronting questions that affect all groups in society. As Whited notes, Ron Weasley is the representative throughout the novels of a conventional orientation to values of humaneness, fairness and decency, someone who almost always frames his decisions in terms of loyalty to friends, family, house and comrades. For this very reason, however, Ron cannot grasp why the enslavement of house elves is a moral wrong, why figures such as Dumbledore and Snape might have to make decisions that violate codes of loyalty, and why Harry struggles to know what the right thing to do is under circumstances that transcend the common good of the group. In book five, Harry experiences what typically happens in the real world, namely, that the conservative forces of social authority (such as ministry and media) turn to the suppression of dissent, rather than opposition to fascism. In this context, although House Gryffindor is also characterized by loyalty and courage, this quickly reverses into ostracism and provinciality once Harry confronts Voldemort directly. Meanwhile, Hermione acts as the representative throughout most of the series of a law and order orientation to codes, rules and laws that support mutual respect and political freedom. Hermione's orientation to fairness leads to her having a much more sophisticated grasp over social issues than Ron, but her understanding of the rules is not based on reasoning about the moral respect, legal rights, social equality and political liberty that the rules are meant to protect. Instead, most of the time, Hermione's orientation is to the rules as a good in themselves – she is a stickler for the rules, a swot and a goody-goody, a rigid partisan of order – which prevents her from making moral decisions that involve violating the rules when these no longer serve the interests of justice. Hermione follows her friends in breaking the rules, amusingly wracked by agonies of conscience, but cannot lead in this regard, until in the final three books she rather suddenly arrives at a deontological position via her house-elf campaign.

The main representative in the series of stage V, the stage of post-conventional moral reasoning described by Kohlberg as 'prior rights[1] and the social contract', is Dumbledore. This stage of post-conventional reasoning involves the insight that ethical conventions (group values, institutional rules, social laws) exist because of a social consensus on these conventions that aims at mutual benefit. Albus Dumbledore's version of the social contract is what is popularly called 'utilitarian' (i.e. in technical philosophical terms, consequentialist), based in a universal form of moral reasoning that judges the morality of an action based on its consequences for human welfare. Dumbledore happily advocates breaking the rules that he is supposed to enforce, not to mention the laws that he is supposed to obey, because these rules and laws become instruments for the promotion of suffering, not mutual benefit, when they stand in the way of opposition to Voldemort. Dumbledore acts catalytically to spark post-conventional moral reasoning among Harry and friends, because each book typically involves an adventure beyond the rules, which should result in expulsion from Hogwarts, but which has been actively encouraged by the headmaster and is then rewarded, rather than punished. 'I seem to remember telling you both that I would have to expel you if you broke any more school rules', Dumbledore tells Harry and Ron, 'which goes to show the best of us must sometimes eat our words' (2: 243). As Whited comments:

---

[1] What is meant by prior rights is the idea that a certain suite of rights simply exists by virtue of universal considerations of justice as the principle of fairness, and that individuals are entitled to exert and defend these rights. The limitation of the prior rights position is, of course, that rights are historically developed and politically enacted, which means that a form of moral reasoning higher than rights, one which determines rights and decides on the priority of different rights when these conflict, must exist and operate. As a matter of sociological fact, advocates of prior rights today typically defend established civil, legal and political rights, but oppose the development of social rights or the extension of existing rights to new groups; just as the same perspective yesterday defended the property franchise, argued against the extension of the vote to women, restricted legal rights and opposed the civil right of free assembly (Honneth 2014).

Albus Dumbledore, the man charged by the Ministry of Magic with the responsibility of enforcing Hogwarts' rules, not only allows Harry and Hermione to break a nearly inviolable precept but also tells them how to do it. His actions are guided by a motive not unlike Martin Luther King's, the notion that man-made laws can be broken if a higher moral law, such as justice, is at stake. (Whited 2003: 198)

The task of book five is to bring Harry from being prepared to violate a law and order orientation at the instigation of an authority figure, to beginning to legislate maxims guiding conduct himself from a post-conventional perspective. In book five, that development is mediated by identification with Sirius, who is a maverick outsider rather than a conventional authority, and whose conception of consequential reasoning is laced with impulsiveness and rebellion. In book six, with Sirius dead, Harry strongly identifies with Dumbledore's explicitly consequentialist thinking about social order and political resistance, becoming in the process much more self-disciplined than Sirius.

Nonetheless, Dumbledore's utilitarian calculations are not the final resting point for moral reasoning in the HPS. The alienation of Harry from Dumbledore dramatized in Order of the Phoenix is instigated by the headmaster's distance from the student, part of Dumbledore's efforts to prevent Voldemort from learning the plans of the Order. But Dumbledore's refusal to consult Harry is really only the tip of the manipulative iceberg, for all along, Dumbledore has calculated on Harry's potential to be the prophesied figure fated to defeat Voldemort. Across a whole range of crucial points in Harry's life (being left with the Dursleys, the instigation of the quests in most of the books, exposing Harry to bullying and harassment by Snape, selective exposure to elements of the riddle of Voldemort's identity), Dumbledore has again and again manipulated events to manufacture 'the Chosen One', the nemesis of Voldemort. Not only that: Dumbledore has also calculated that Harry must die in order to destroy the final piece of Voldemort's soul, lodged magically in Harry's psyche, but he has not let him know. As Harry eavesdrops on Snape's memories, Snape confronts Dumbledore with the accusation that 'you have kept [Harry] alive so that he can die at the right moment . . . you have been raising him like a pig for slaughter' (7: 561). Dumbledore does not disagree.

That Dumbledore's manipulations involve self-sacrifice for 'the greater good', in book six, is not in contradiction with the notion that utilitarianism has limitations. This is because its fundamental problem is that it is a moral framework that condones sacrificing and manipulating individuals when the consequences advance the good. Indeed, book seven spends four chapters exposing the nature of these limitations to an increasingly disillusioned Harry, who has to learn that Dumbledore was originally the best friend – perhaps the lover – of the *Ur*-Voldemort, the dark wizard Grindelwald, whose slogan for world domination was: 'the greater good'. 'We seize control *for the greater good*', Dumbledore wrote to Grindelwald, 'and from this it follows that where we meet resistance we must use only that force necessary and no more' (7: 291). Here, Dumbledore exhibits the play of identity and difference between himself and his eventual adversary. Grindelwald is an act-consequentialist (calculations maximizing the good are measured relative to individual acts), whose definition of the good is morally counterintuitive (i.e. he is a Hitlerian figure). Dumbledore, by contrast, is a rule-consequentialist (calculations maximizing the good are measured relative to the rules that generate individual acts), whose definition of the good is welfare-based. 'Where we meet resistance we must use only that force necessary and no more' is a rule intended to limit the morally counterintuitive acts that might be performed in advancing the greater good. The problem is that throughout the series, it has meant the systematic manipulation of Harry, as if he were not a moral subject, but merely a welfare-contributing object (towards whom Dumbledore is sentimentally inclined – as indeed, he is towards his own, ultimately expendable, self). Dumbledore's speech at the end of book four, where he declares that Voldemort has returned, that a key student has just been murdered by Voldemort, and that dark times are ahead, concludes with the injunction 'to make a choice between what is right and what is easy' (4: 724). This announces a development that Dumbledore himself cannot complete.

Fantasy quest with a *doppelgänger* twist

Superficially, every book in the series involves a quest for some supernatural item that may assist or prevent Voldemort's return to power, twinned with a proxy for Voldemort who is the magical adversary that Harry and friends must defeat in each novel. Because this element of the repertoire strongly conforms to the conventional expectations of the fantasy genre, it is easy to forget that the success of the series originated with its deviations from the dominant pattern in popular fantasy, set by J. R. R. Tolkein and his epigones. These all involve the 'return of the prince' and the restoration of order, based in an objective ethical system, where the good and evil poles typically spawn opposed characters (e.g. Frodo and Gollum), which lets the repertoire include a spectrum of existential and positional concerns despite the limitations of its binary settings. Not so the HPS. In the marvellous elements of its repertoire, the main feature is that revolutionary struggle and the mandate to transform the world spring from stages of moral reflection which implicate the protagonist as complicit and undermine any absolute framing of the threat posed by the antagonist. The repertoire of the series excludes any ethical binaries for a vision of moral complexity. Two signature examples of this are the destiny of Harry as the 'Chosen

One' and the presentation of Voldemort. Considerations of space mean that I can only mention the first of these. Book six is entitled *Harry Potter and the Half-Blood Prince*, and the narrative unfolds to raise the question of whether Harry's supposed election makes him a 'half-blood prince'. 'Is this a title you're thinking of adopting?' asks Lupin sarcastically; 'I should have thought being the "Chosen One" would be enough' (6: 280). But the half-blood prince turns out to be Snape, while Harry's 'predestination' is in actuality an opportunity to dramatize the paradoxical loop of identification (where successful anticipation retroactively transforms contingency into necessity). Harry is merely a figurehead for a collective, one whose 'destiny' is the result of a series of accidents: 'I didn't get through [it] because I was brilliant', Harry confesses to the other students; 'I got through it all because – because help came at the right time, or because I guessed right – but I just blundered through it all' (5: 304). Now I want to discuss Voldemort.

At first glance, Voldemort is the uncanny adversary, an ambassador of death whose intrusion into Harry's life marks it with grief and twists it towards thoughts of revenge, a representation of negativity connected to acts of violence whose trademark is a spectral skull with a hissing serpent. Voldemort's position in the magical ethos is indicated by his specialization in the 'forbidden curses', causing murder, torture and possession, as well as his expertise in necromancy and violation of the soul. By contrast, Harry and friends fight back with shielding spells and disarming hexes, shunning the forbidden curses and dark magic, and seeking to dispel Voldemort's baleful enchantments. A shadowy creature of disintegration who re-forms his material body using dark magic, Voldemort remains, for most of the characters throughout the series, nameless, 'He Who Shall Not be Named', or 'You Know Who'. As the series unfolds, it transpires that Lord Voldemort has named himself, for his magical name is an anagram of his real name, Tom Marvolo Riddle, and he is the product of magical possession of a normal human by his mother, a tragically desocialized and miserably oppressed female magician. He is, in other words, what he denigrates as a 'mudblood', and his ferocious racism is actually a strategic calculation about how best to gain violent followers, through manipulation of their prejudices. Strange and lonely, Tom is a figure of the isolated ego against the world who exhibits all of the characteristics of pathological narcissism, as Harry discovers in books five and six, through magical access to others' memories. Surrounded by a dreamlike ambience fretted with nightmarish scenes of confinement and coercion, then, Voldemort seems the opposite of Harry's buttered crumpets, adolescent romance and last-minute essays.

Yet a series of eerie parallels establish Voldemort as a classic figure of the supernatural double, the terrifying other who is an inversion of the self, locked in mortal rivalry but armed with an uncanny ability to anticipate every move of the protagonist.

In Otto Rank's psychoanalytic study of the double, he argues that the *doppelgänger*, like the soul, is the double of the ego, effectively the narcissistic component of the archaic ego that is the recipient of erotic cathexes from the id, as opposed to the mature component of the ego that is formed through identification and depends on desexualized cathexes. The ego is the seat where potential threats, emanating from excessive impulses arising from the id, are registered as anxiety and imagined as the death of the body and its disintegration. According to Rank (following Freud), the ego, as foremost a bodily image, makes no distinction between the desolation of narcissism, the deconstruction of the ego's architecture (and its potential reconstruction), and the destruction of the organism, so that anxiety is always represented as the spectacle of the disintegration of the self. In the literary representation of the double, Rank argues, what is being represented is the primitive ego defence of projection: unacceptable impulses, such as aggression, which the ego cannot cope with realistically, are projected outwards onto another person. The result is delusions of persecution and pre-emptive aggression against this other, for the alter ego is the site for all of the impulses that the ego experiences but cannot repress or sublimate, which accounts for the darkness of the double and the spiral towards mutual destruction that is always represented in the literature. As Rank says, 'the double, who personifies narcissistic self-love, becomes an unequivocal rival and sexual love; or else, originally created as a wishful defence against a threatened external destruction, he reappears in superstition as the messenger of death' (Rank 1971: 85–6).

In other words, the fantasy adventure properly speaking is a *doppelgänger* story about the uncanny resemblance between Tom Marvolo Riddle (aka Lord Voldemort), and Harry Potter. A complicated magical narrative 'explains' the mystical connection between them in terms of Voldemort's fragmentation of his soul, a part of which is lodged in Harry. But in terms of the actual mechanism of the narrative development, this is irrelevant: Tom and Harry are linked by a subterranean resemblance that it is the task of the story to disclose. Around this central conflict, the series arranges a sequence of quests where every book is structured by a race against a furtive, yet dangerous, enemy, in which some magical item or secret information that Voldemort must possess becomes the objective. Yet despite the apparent logic of an ascending series of magical stages, ratified by magical combat against increasingly powerful proxies for the main villain, it is the logic of the double that actually drives the fantasy plot. There is a developmental sequence at operative in the quest-romance strand, then, but it is not the standard fantasy motif of a narcissistic accumulation of powers of enchantment. Instead, the learning process at work is about affect regulation, and in the last three books of the series, this process reaches down into unconscious processes that have to do with mortal anxiety and the drive for self-preservation. The appearance of the double inevitably signals the death of the protagonist, for they are ultimately one, and in defeating their nemesis, the protagonist necessarily destroys themselves (Rank 1971), something that indeed happens in the final book of the series.

Triple elaboration

This threefold repertoire, with its evident relevance to the problem of fascism, creates 'blanks' for the implied reader, in the form of the question of what the connection is between these elements. It is the task of the narrative strategy to direct that towards a triple elaboration of the idea of the protagonist's journey as a learning process, centred on the problematic relation between moral autonomy and social authority. The learning processes are ethical-evaluative, normative and expressive-affective, concerning Harry's solidarity with others, his moral development and his capacity to regulate his feelings. Each strand of the threefold journey has its own crisis point and means of resolution, so that it is only as the narrative approaches its conclusion that they converge, and the reader notices that each learning process supports the others.

The division of labour among the story arcs supporting these learning processes is fairly stable. The narrative of education and formation is focused on Harry's relationship to authority figures and to the moral perspectives and political decisions that these social authorities represent and implement. Ultimately, as we have seen, Harry's journey to moral autonomy involves questions of post-conventional moral reasoning, to do with the difficult questions of whether it is right to act on consequentialist principles and how to deal with the anxiety-provoking fact that moral autonomy entails responsibility without certainty. Harry's clashes with his foster parents, then with school teachers, followed by the ministry's leadership, and finally, with beloved authorities, especially the headmaster, Dumbledore, are all centred on the question of what it is right to do. In the context of the rise of (magical) neo-fascism, normative issues of resistance or collaboration join existential problems to do with mortal threats, to sharpen the moral conflicts by lending them a 'life and death' urgency. Essentially, the learning process involved in the novel of education strand concerns the realization that there is a higher standard of justice than that provided by school rules and official institutions, as well as by venerated ideals and beloved figures.

In short, the boarding school narrative is all about entry into the forms of mutual recognition constitutive of ethical life, with their intensely conventional reciprocal expectations of social conduct and their strong solidaristic bonds. The solidarity between friends at the centre of this narrative arc acts as a force-multiplier on Harry's often questionable magical abilities, providing him with a loyal sidekick (Ron) and with the most intelligent character, a brilliant magician (Hermione). The school-days strand supports the moral development arc by progressively introducing post-conventional normative considerations into interpersonal conformity and group loyalties, so that eventually solidarity and justice are fully reciprocal. Effectively, that disintegrates cosy house-based environments and forces Harry to turn to collectives that are the result of social contracts (both Dumbledore's Army and the Order of the Phoenix require a binding oath to join), bringing post-conventional arrangements home. Additionally, the school story is the site for an exploration of the mundane aspects of any individual's relation to institutional authority, where the series clearly valorizes nonconformity and rebellion. Finally, there is a sprinkling of romantic *frisson*, which, although it is generally agreed that it is not well done by Rowling, provides another dimension that complicates group solidarity with interpersonal links.

Meanwhile, the fantasy adventure supports the arc of moral development by relating normative considerations to impulse control and affect regulation. Magic in the HPS responds to emotions in a way that is absolutely transparent; two instances will suffice to demonstrate this: '"Never used an unforgiveable curse before, have you, [Harry]?" [Bellatrix] yelled.... "You need to *mean* them Potter! You need to really want to cause pain – to enjoy it – righteous anger won't hurt me for long"' (5: 746). Likewise, the Patronus charm in book three, which protects against the soul-destroying Dementors, is, Lupin says, 'an incantation which will only work if you concentrate, with all your might, on a single, very happy memory' (3: 252). The suspect Latin names of the spells – *Expecto Patronum* – provide a symbolic inscription of emotional states that make it possible to render affects effective in the Potterverse as magical power. As might be expected, then, love is arrayed against hate, sympathy against anger, light magic against dark wizardry, and Harry must choose, because both are powerful currents within him, from the moment when the Sorting Hat tries to assign him to Slytherin (1: 130) onwards. The affective groundtone of Harry's frustrating and terrifying existence is not difficult to detect, for his main emotional problem is that he struggles to contain his rage when his designs are thwarted. Harry Potter, who lives in the cupboard under the stairs but has dreams of wizarding greatness, is not without strangeness, loneliness or ambitiousness; nor does he lack motivation to retaliate against those who seek to harm him, for he is, in his own words, full of anger, all the time. Many times in the series, Voldemort goads him to lash out against his foes: in book five, he uses the banned torture curse against one of his enemies (5: 746); in book six, he uses an unregulated vivisection curse on Malfoy (6: 435); more often, Harry has plentiful opportunities to resort to desperate measures in seeking to save himself and his friends from mortal peril. The plot arc of book five makes this parallel obvious, for it hinges upon the characters' efforts to recover an equivocal prophesy that 'neither [Harry nor Voldemort] may live while the other survives', a fate that, although it seems to indicate the rationality of pre-emptive violence, actually signals mutual destruction. It is only once

Harry overcomes his destructive rage and confronts Voldemort 'calmly', 'softly', in a whisper (7: 605, 607, 608), with confidence that love outsmarts fury, that he can triumph: Voldemort's final curse is murderous; Harry's is disarming (7: 608).

Accordingly, the books in the HPS combine the novel of education and formation (about moral development) with the boarding school novel (about friendship and solidarity) and the quest-romance (focused on the double motif). The solidaristic context provides a forum for testing Harry's moral development, while the affect regulation gained through conflict with the dark aspect of himself makes it possible for Harry to exercise autonomy constructively.

The ironization of Harry Potter

The strategy of triple elaboration reduces the blanks around the connection between inverted generic narrative strands, but this generates 'voids' in the strategy, to do with the selection of Harry's perspective as the main standpoint on the repertoire provided to the implied reader. What might it look like to others? The reader is solicited to an active investigation of this void in the narrative by the strategy itself, which subtly reminds the reader that Harry's development is a *via negativa*. In the HPS, then, the protagonist's journey is structured as a series of transcended stages, which the narrative strategy frames through a process of negative reinforcement, expressed through the dramatic ironization of Harry's perspective. Harry, in short, is constantly wrong about things, as well as being evidently the focus for identification in the series.

The series is narrated throughout by an anonymous narrating agency that relies almost exclusively on third-person figural narration, employing psycho-consonant narrative discourse, with Harry as the main focalizing character (Cohan and Shires 1988: 83–112). What this basically means is that the 'camera' is positioned over Harry's shoulder and it records the world more or less consonantly with how Harry perceives it, without explicitly foregrounding 'dissonant' details in conflict with his viewpoint. Here is a key example.

> 'So, you want me to say I'm not going to take part in the Defence group?' [Harry] muttered finally. 'Me? Certainly not!' said Sirius, looking surprised. 'I think it's an excellent idea!' 'You do?' said Harry, his heart lifting. 'Of course I do!' said Sirius. 'Do you think your father and I would've lain down and taken orders from Umbridge?' (5: 343)
>
> But he had to think . . . It was his fault Sirius had died, it was all his fault. If he, Harry, had not been stupid enough to fall for Voldemort's trick . . . if he had only opened his mind to the possibility that Voldemort

was, as Hermione had said, banking on Harry's love of playing the hero. (5: 755)

The narrating agency positions the reader to audit Harry's thoughts and feelings, framed as subjective states narratively, but expressed as perceptions of the world, not reported as external states (it is not: 'If he', Harry thought, 'had not been stupid enough to fall for Voldemort's trick'). By contrast, the thoughts and feelings of other characters are reported externally ('said Sirius, looking surprised'), whereas Harry's interpretation is expressed as a perception of the world, not as a reported state (it is not: said Sirius, and Harry thought he looked surprised).

The implication of this narrative strategy is that the implied reader is solicited to identification with Harry's perspective, including his thoughts and feelings about the world, as if it were always a true report on the imaginary world. The narrating agency never distances itself from this perspective explicitly, but – as the juxtaposed quotes above show – generally Harry discovers that his perception of the world was a distortion of the truth, caused mainly by a combination of a limited normative position with a failure of impulse control. If the implied reader is positioned to learn anything, it is because in every novel Harry almost fails, finally muddling through in a way that brokers sympathetic identification with the protagonist. As in the quote above, the most important perspectives that manifestly transcend Harry's are Hermione's and Dumbledore's, and the most interesting thing about the series is that although Dumbledore himself acknowledges that Harry has gone beyond the headmaster (7: 588), the implications of Hermione's standpoint are not unpacked by the story. The implied reader is thereby solicited *implicitly*, not explicitly, to transcend Harry's perspective, re-evaluating the imaginary world from a position independent of Harry's perceptions. This is something that the fan community does extensively, of course, with many fan fictions expressing standpoints based on Hermione's perspective, or that involve a highly critical evaluation of Dumbledore.

By soliciting identification with Harry but then ironizing his perspective, the strategy invites the implied reader to undertake the same journey as the protagonist, while catalysing reflection about how things might look from other perspectives and feel for other beings. Because the enchantments in the series are emotions that have been marvellously rendered materially effective through magic, the sympathetic elements of the protagonist's learning process are particularly available to the reader. But again, irony is the leitmotif of the series. Although the implied reader is repeatedly positioned to sympathize with Harry's justified fury and deep grievances, not to mention his resentment towards authority and hostility to Slytherin, when Harry lashes out it always turns out to be a bad idea, or to be morally ambivalent. An obvious example of this is the vivisection curse already mentioned, *Sectum Sempra*, which Harry employs on arch-rival and school bully, Draco Malfoy in book six:

> Harry slipped over as Malfoy, his face contorted, cried 'Cruci—'
> 'SECTUMSEMPRA!' bellowed Harry form the floor, waving his wand wildly. Blood spurted from Malfoy's face and chest as though he had been slashed with an invisible sword. He staggered backwards and collapsed onto the waterlogged floor with a great splash, his wand falling from his limp right hand. 'No –' gasped Harry.
> Slipping and staggering, Harry got to his feet and plunged towards Malfoy, whose face was now shining scarlet, white hands scrabbling at his blood-soaked chest. 'No – I didn't –' Harry didn't know what he was saying, he fell to his knees beside Malfoy, who was shaking uncontrollably in a pool of his own blood. (6: 435)

By the time this happens, the reader has endured six 500-page books of Draco's sneering and taunting, his derogatory expressions and his haughty entitlement, his scheming and plotting, his cruelty and his lying, and, in book six, his recruitment as a Death Eater with the mission to murder Dumbledore. All of this has been seen and felt from Harry's perspective, and Harry is righteously furious; moreover, in this moment, it is self-defence, and Harry does not know (but might have guessed) that the spell is that destructive. It is easy to ignore the fact that Malfoy is alone, crying in the bathroom (6: 434). The reader is primed for fury, perhaps, even, hate. Nonetheless, this scene is deliberately appalling, and Harry is horrified at what he has committed. Such cathartic moments, involving Harry's desire to play the hero, Harry's wish to punish his enemies, Harry's blind rage and desperate will to live, punctuate the identificatory process and its conceptual ironization with a series of emotional shocks, which seem calculated to bring the reader face to face with their own (and Harry's) desire.

Dialectic of enchantment

Perhaps the biggest void that the strategy raises is this question: what, ultimately, is the nature of desire? What does Harry Potter *want*? What is it that Voldemort wants? Harry, standing in front of the Mirror of Erised in book one, wants nothing more than to be reunited with his murdered parents, or, rather his heart's desire is that they live yet (1: 224). Voldemort, meanwhile, wants immortality, which is why he has magically fragmented his soul to preserve parts of it in 'horcruxes', a forbidden kind of resurrection bank that involves a sort of soul murder, or suicide into half-life (6: 415). But what is the connection?

In posing this question, the strategy insists on one thing: Harry is constantly in deadly danger. The HPS is fundamentally about death and particularly about coping with mortal anxiety – the acute anxiety caused by the imminence of death and the chronic terror of potential death that is built into human mortality. Death marks off the beginning and end of every novel in the series, for the series begins with the disclosure that Harry Potter is the 'boy who lived', the child who survived his parents' murder, and somebody dies at the end of each book. The changes in Harry (and friends) catalysed by this sequence of fatalities are cumulative and irreversible – he is touched by death, especially in books five and six, where, after witnessing the murder of Cedric Diggory in book four, he can suddenly see the spectral horses of death at the school, and then loses his godfather, Sirius, in magical combat against Voldemort's forces, before finally losing Dumbledore, apparently to Snape.

The confrontation with death is, of course, inscribed in the name of the antagonist (*vol-de-mort*), Lord Death Cheater, whose followers are those who defy death, the Death Eaters. Yet a central part of the learning process that constitutes the quest-romance strand is the dawning awareness that Voldemort's seeming thanatophilia, and his followers' empty bravado, actually springs from, and is a defence against, thanatophobia (even, perhaps, cowardice). In fact, the main arc of the series' narrative rests on the idea that Voldemort is terrified of death, wants to live forever and emblematizes, not the will-to-destruction, but the terror of death, driven by instinctual self-preservation. Voldemort's desire to cheat death is the root of his instrumentalization of others, which leads, via the standard Hobbesian calculus, to a perversion of the life instinct into pre-emptive violence.

The significance of Rank's discussion of the double for the HPS, however, is that the uncanny equivalence between Harry and Voldemort implies that 'Voldemort' is really a potential developmental endpoint for Harry, for Voldemort's anxiety about death is also Harry's anxiety, and Voldemort's retaliatory aggression is exactly the same as Harry's. Harry might become, but must not become, Voldemort. The connection between masculinity as a gender position in the field of romantic relations and masculinity as a cultural code involving aggressive self-assertion (in other words, masculine domination and sexual violence) is backgrounded by the series. Nonetheless, it is unquestionably present, for Harry must discover an alternative masculinity by rejecting the conventional responses that script Voldemort as a cultural possibility. That discovery, involving admissions of vulnerability, affirmation of collective solidarity, respect for others and empathy with human suffering, is exhibited most strikingly in Harry's gradually growing sympathy for Voldemort, who he comes to see as a pathetic, rather than terrifying, figure. The reconciliatory path of understanding that Harry must, with difficulty, follow is the same path that the reader must also follow, as the disturbing implications of premature identification with aggressive self-preservation finally become clear.

In the end, the vision of the HPS is remarkably similar to the one presented in *Dialectic of Enlightenment*. Mastery of nature, especially the quest for immortality driven by instinctual self-preservation, is the sorcerer's apprentice, which transforms the world into a scene of domination, only to turn upon the wielder and enchant them into enslavement. The *Harry Potter* books literalize this as a marvellous adventure stalked by a supernatural double, while inflecting reservations about metaphysical humanism in the direction of a doctrine of natural sympathy. To be sure, the series also gestures towards humanist Christianity as a possible alternative, and it deliberately curtails the development of the main female character, Hermione, while suppressing questions about the politics of romance with its ghastly, suburban Epilogue. But the main thing that the HPS does with its dialectic of enchantment is to refuse the bourgeois structures of civic (as opposed to familial) privatism: the series is notable in that there is no private career that does not have public significance; there are no individual decisions about normative questions that do not impact on collective life, solidarity and justice. Rowling's series is detested by conservatives because its vision for citizen engagement is framed by post-conventional moral thinking, so that the books' reservations about the Hobbesian society of self-interested self-preservation lead, not to the advocacy of religion as a social cement, but to activist resistance as a duty of democratic politics.

REFERENCES

Abanes, Richard (2001), *Harry Potter and the Bible: The Menace Behind the Magick* (Camp Hill, PA: Horizon Books).
Abromeit, John (2011), *Max Horkheimer and the Foundations of the Frankfurt School* (Cambridge; New York; Melbourne: Cambridge University Press).
Adorno, Theodor (1967a), *Prisms* (Cambridge, MA: MIT Press).
Adorno, Theodor (1967b), 'Sociology and Psychology (Part Two)', *New Left Review*, 1 (47), 79-97.
Adorno, Theodor (1973), *Negative Dialectics*, trans. E. B. Ashton (London: Routledge).
Adorno, Theodor (1976), *Introduction to the Sociology of Music*, trans. E. B. Ashton (New York: Seabury).
Adorno, Theodor (1981), *In Search of Wagner*, trans. Rodney Livingstone (London: Merlin).
Adorno, Theodor (1987), 'Late Capitalism or Industrial Society?', in Volker Meja, Dieter Misgeld, and Nico Stehr (eds), *Modern German Sociology* (New York: Columbia University Press), 33-56.
Adorno, Theodor (1999), *Sound Figures*, trans. Rodney Livingstone (Stanford, CA: Stanford University Press).
Adorno, Theodor (2002), *Essays on Music: Theodor W Adorno*, trans. Richard Leppert (Berkeley, CA; London: UCLA Press).
Adorno, Theodor (2003), 'Reflections on Class Theory', in Rolf Tiedemann (ed.), *Can One Live After Auschwitz?* (Stanford, CA: Stanford University Press), 93-110.
Adorno, Theodor (2005a), *Minima Moralia: Reflections on a Damaged Life*, trans. Edmund Jephcott (London; New York: Verso).
Adorno, Theodor (2005b), *Minima Moralia: Reflections from Damaged Life*, trans. Edmund Jephcott (London: Verso).
Adorno, Theodor (2007a), 'Commitment', in Fredric Jameson (ed.), *Aesthetics and Politics* (London; New York: Verso), 177-95.
Adorno, Theodor (2007b), *Philosophy of Modern Music*, trans. Anne Mitchell and Wesley Blomster (London; New York: Continuum).
Adorno, Theodor (2019), *Notes to Literature (Combined Edition)*, trans. Shierry Weber Nicholson (New York: Columbia University Press).
Adorno, Theodor and Horkheimer, Max (2002), *Dialectic of Enlightenment: Philosophical Fragments*, trans. Edmund Jephcott (Stanford, CA: Stanford University Press).
Adorno, Theodor, et al. (2019), *The Authoritarian Personality* (New York: Wiley).

Alford, C. Fred (1987), 'Habermas, Post-Freudian Psychoanalysis and the End of the Individual', *Theory, Culture & Society*, 4, 3-29.
Althusser, Louis (1971), *Lenin and Philosophy and Other Essays*, trans. Ben Brewster (London: New Left Books).
Antonio, Robert (1989), 'The Normative Foundations of Emancipatory Theory: Evolutionary Versus Pragmatic Perspectives', *American Journal of Sociology*, 94 (4), 721-48.
Arato, Andrew and Cohen, Jean (1992), *Civil Society and Political Theory* (London and Cambridge: MIT Press).
Barrett, Annie (2007), 'J. K. Rowling Outs Dumbledore!', *Popwatch*.
Barrett, Michèle (1993), 'Althusser's Marx, Althusser's Lacan', in E. Ann Kaplan and Michael Sprinker (eds), *The Althusserian Legacy* (London and New York: Verso), 169-81.
Beddow, Michael (1994), *Thomas Mann: Doctor Faustus (Landmarks of World Literature)* (Cambridge; New York: Cambridge University Press).
Benhabib, Seyla (1986), *Critique, Norm and Utopia: A Study of the Normative Foundations of Critical Theory* (New York: Columbia University Press).
Benhabib, Seyla (1992a), 'Communicative Ethics and Current Controversies in Practical Philosophy', in Seyla Benhabib and Fred Dallmayr (eds), *The Communicative Ethics Controversy* (Cambridge, MA; London: MIT Press), 330-69.
Benhabib, Seyla (1992b), *Situating the Self: Gender, Community and Postmodernism in Contemporary Ethics* (New York: Routledge).
Benhabib, Seyla (1995), 'The Debate Over Women in Moral Theory Revisited', in Johanna Meehan (ed.), *Feminists Read Habermas: Gendering the Subject of Discourse* (New York and London: Routledge).
Benhabib, Seyla (1996), 'Toward a Deliberative Model of Democratic Legitimation', in Seyla Benhabib (ed.), *Democracy and Difference: Contesting the Boundaries of the Political* (New Jersey: Princeton University Press), 67-94.
Benhabib, Seyla (2002), *The Claims of Culture: Equality and Diversity in the Global Era* (Princeton and Oxford: Princeton University Press).
Benjamin, Walter (1970), 'The Author as Producer', *New Left Review*, 1 (62), 83-96.
Benjamin, Walter (1973), 'The Work of Art in the Age of Mechanical Reproduction', in Hannah Arendt (ed.), *Illuminations* (London: Jonathan Cape), 219-54.
Bergsten, Gunilla (1969), *Thomas Mann's Doctor Faustus: Sources and Structure of the Novel*, trans. Krishna Winston (Chicago; London: University of Chcago Press).
Berman, Russell (1986), *The Rise of the Modern German Novel: Crisis and Charisma* (Cambridge, MA: Harvard University Press).
Bernstein, J. M. (1992), *The Fate of Art: Aesthetic Alienation from Kant to Derrida and Adorno* (University Park: Pennsylvania State University Press).
Bernstein, J. M. (1995), *Recovering Ethical Life: Jürgen Habermas and the Future of Critical Theory* (London; New York: Routledge).
Bernstein, J. M. (2001), *Adorno: Disenchantment and Ethics* (Cambridge: Cambridge University Press).

Blackwell, Taekia, et al. 'The Harry Potter Alliance'. https://www.thehpalliance.org/. (accessed 23 October 2020).
Blake, Andrew (2002), *The Irresistible Rise of Harry Potter* (London: Verso).
Böhm, Karl Werner (1990), 'Der Narziß Thomas Mann und die Pathologisierung seiner Homosexualität', *Psyche – Zeitschrift für Psychoanalyse*, 44 (4), 308-22.
Bohman, James (1994), 'World Disclosure and Radical Criticism', *Thesis Eleven*, 37, 82-97.
Bohman, James (1997), 'Two Versions of the Linguistic Turn', in Seyla Benhabib and Maurizio Passerin d'Entrèves (eds), *Habermas and the Unfinished Project of Modernity: Critical Essays on The Philosophical Discourse of Modernity* (Cambridge, MA: MIT Press), 197-220.
Bolz, Norbert (1979), *Geschichtsphilosophie des Ästhetischen: Hermeneutische Rekonstruction der 'Noten zur Literatur' Th. W. Adornos* (Hildesheim: Gerstenberg).
Booth, Wayne (1988), *The Company We Keep: An Ethics Of Fiction* (Berkeley: University of California Press).
Bradford, Richard (1994), *Roman Jakobson: Life, Language, Art* (London; New York: Routledge).
Buck-Morss, Susan (1977), *The Origin of Negative Dialectics: Theodor W. Adorno, Walter Benjamin and the Frankfurt Institute* (New York: The Free Press).
Bürger, Peter (1984), *Theory of the Avant-Garde* (Minneapolis: University of Minnesota Press).
Bürger, Peter (2010), 'Avant-Garde and Neo-Avant-Garde', *New Literary History*, 41, 696-715.
Castoriadis, Cornelius (1997), *The Imaginary Institution of Society*, trans. Kathleen Blamey (Cambridge, MA: MIT Press).
Cawelti, John (1976), *Adventure, Mystery and Romance: Formula Stories as Art and Popular Culture* (Chicago: University of Chicago Press).
Cerf, Steven (1981), 'Love in Thomas Mann's *Doktor Faustus* as an Imitatio Shakespeari', *Comparative Literature Studies*, 18 (4), 475-86.
Césaire, Aimé (2000), *Discourse on Colonialism*, trans. Joan Pinkham (New York: New York University Press; Monthly Review Press).
Chapelle, Daniel (1999), 'Nietzsche and Psychoanalysis', in Jacob Golomb, Weaver Santaniello, and Ronald Lehrer (eds), *Nietzsche and Depth Psychology* (Albany, NY: SUNY Press), 37-50.
Cheetham, Marcus, Hänggi, Jürgen, and Lutz, Jancke (2014), 'Identifying with Fictive Characters: Structural Brain Correlates of the Personality Trait "Fantasy"', *SCAN*, 9 (179), 1836-44.
Clarke, Simon (1980), 'Althusserian Marxism', in Simon Clarke (ed.), *One-Dimensional Marxism* (London: Alison & Busby), 5-102.
Claussen, Detlev (2008), *Theodor W. Adorno: One Last Genius*, trans. Rodney Livingstone (Cambridge, MA; London: Harvard University Press).
Cobley, Evelyn (2002a), 'Avant-Garde Aesthetics and Fascist Politics: Thomas Mann's Doctor Faustus and Theodor W. Adorno's "Philosophy of Modern Music"', *New German Critique*, 86, 43-70.
Cobley, Evelyn (2002b), *The Temptations of Faust: The Logic of Fascism and Postmodern Archaeologies of Modernity* (Toronto: University of Toronto Press).

Cohan, Steven and Shires, Linda (1988), *Telling Stories: A Theoretical Analysis of Narrative Fiction* (London; New York: Routledge).
Colclasure, David (2010), *Habermas and Literary Rationality* (London; New York: Routledge).
Colebrook, Claire (2004), *Irony (Kindle Edition)* (London; New York: Routledge).
Compson, William (2003), *J. K. Rowling* (New York: The Rosen Publishing Group).
Currie, Gregory (1986), 'Works of Fiction and Illocutionary Acts', *Philosophy and Literature*, 10 (2), 304–8.
Currie, Gregory (2008), *The Nature of Fiction* (Reprint) (Cambridge: Cambridge University Press).
Dahlhaus, Carl (1982), 'Fiktive Zwölftonmusik: Thomas Mann und Theodor W. Adorno', *Jahrbuch der Deutschen Akademie für Sprache und Dichtung*, 1, 33–49.
Dews, Peter (1995), 'The Truth of the Subject: Language, Validity and Transcendence in Lacan and Habermas', in Peter Dews (ed.), *The Limits of Disenchantment: Essays on Contemporary European Philosophy* (London and New York: Verso), 259–79.
Di Cesare, Donatella (2018), *Heidegger and the Jews: The Black Notebooks* (London; New York: Polity Press).
Dickerson, Matthew and O'Hara, David (2006), *From Homer to Harry Potter* (Grand Rapids, MI: Brazos Press).
Dollimore, Jonathan (2001), *Sex, Literature and Censorship* (Cambridge; Malden, MA: Polity Press).
Dollimore, Jonathan (2017), 'The Violence of Desire: Shakespeare, Nietzsche, Mann', in Tobias Döring and Ewan Fernie (eds), *Something Rich and Strange: Thomas Mann and Shakespeare* (London; New York: Bloomsbury Academic), 23–46.
Döring, Tobias and Fernie, Ewan, eds (2015), *Thomas Mann and Shakespeare: Something Rich and Strange* (London; New York: Bloomsbury Academic).
Duvenage, Pieter (2003), *Habermas and Aesthetics: The Limits of Communicative Reason* (Cambridge: Polity Press).
Duvenage, Pieter (2010), 'Communicative Reason and Religion: The Case of Habermas', *Sophia*, 49, 343–57.
Eberly, Rosa (2000), *Citizen Critics: Literary Public Spheres* (Urbana and Chicago: University of Illinois Press).
Ellenberger, Henri (1981), *The Discovery of the Unconscious: The History and Evolution of Dynamic Psychiatry*, 2nd edn (New York: Basic Books).
Erikson, Erik (1954), 'The Specimen Dream of Psychoanalysis', *Journal of the American Psychoanalytic Association*, 2, 5–56.
Erikson, Erik (1974), *Dimensions of a New Identity (Jefferson Lectures in the Humanities)* (New York: WW Norton & Co).
Erikson, Erik (1994), *Identity and the Life Cycle* (New York; London: WW Norton).
Felski, Rita (1989), *Beyond Feminist Aesthetics: Feminist Literature and Social Change* (Cambridge, MA: Harvard University Press).
Felski, Rita (2015), *The Limits of Critique* (Chicago: University of Chicago Press).

Felski, Rita and Anker, Elizabeth S. eds (2017), *Critique and Postcritique* (Durham: Duke University Press).

Ferrara, Alessandro (1998), *Reflective Authenticity: Rethinking the Project of Modernity* (London; New York: Routledge).

Fetzer, John (1991), 'Melos, Eros, Thanatos in Thomas Mann's Doctor Faustus', in Herbert Lehnert and Peter Pfeiffer (eds), *Thomas Mann's Doctor Faustus: A Novel at the Margins of Modernism* (Columbia: Camden House).

Fetzer, John (1996), *Changing Perceptions of Thomas Mann's Doctor Faustus: Criticism 1947-1992* (Columbia: Camden House).

Fialho, Olivia (2019), 'What is Literature For? The Role of Transformative Reading', *Cogent Arts and Humanities*, 6 (1).

Flynn, Bernard Charles (1985), 'Habermas Reading Freud', *Human Studies*, 8 (1), 57-76.

Fonagy, Peter (2015), 'The Effectiveness of Psychodynamic Psychotherapies: An Update', *World Psychiatry*, 14 (2), 137-50.

Forst, Rainer (2013), *Toleration in Conflict: Past and Present* (Cambridge: Cambridge University Press).

Fraser, Nancy (1992), 'Rethinking the Public Sphere: A Contribution to the Critique of Actually Existing Democracy', in Craig Calhoun (ed.), *Habermas and the Public Sphere* (Cambridge, MA: MIT Press), 109-42.

Fraser, Nancy (1995), 'What's Critical about Critical Theory?', in Johanna Meehan (ed.), *Feminists Read Habermas: Gendering the Subject of Discourse* (New York and London: Routledge), 21-55.

Fraser, Nancy (1997), *Justice Interruptus: Critical Reflections on the "Postsocialist" Condition* (London; New York: Routledge).

Fraser, Nancy and Honneth, Axel eds (2003), *Redistribution or Recognition? A Political-Philosophical Exchange* (London and New York: Verso).

Freud, Anna (1967), *The Ego and the Mechanisms of Defense: Revised Edition* (New York: International Universities Press).

Freud, Sigmund (1923), 'The Ego and the Id', in James Strachey (ed.), *The Standard Edition of the Complete Psychological Works of Sigmund Freud, Volume XIX (1923-1925): The Ego and the Id and Other Works* (London: The Hogarth Press), 1-66.

Freud, Sigmund (1924), 'The Dissolution of the Oedipus Complex', in James Strachey (ed.), *The Standard Edition of the Complete Psychological Works of Sigmund Freud, Volume XIX (1923-1925): The Ego and the Id and Other Works* (London: The Hogarth Press), 171-80.

Freud, Sigmund (1926), 'Inhibitions, Symptoms and Anxieties', in James Stracey (ed.), *The Standard Edition of the Complete Psychological Works of Sigmund Freud, Volume XX (1925-1926)* (London: The Hogarth Press), 75-175.

Freud, Sigmund (1930), 'Civilization and Its Discontents', in James Strachey (ed.), *The Standard Edition of the Complete Psychological Works of Sigmund Freud, Volume XXI (1927-1931): The Future of an Illusion, Civilization and its Discontents, and Other Works* (London: The Hogarth Press), 57-146.

Freud, Sigmund (1939), 'Moses and Monotheism', in James Strachey (ed.), *The Standard Edition of the Complete Psychological Works of Sigmund Freud, Volume XXIII (1937-1939)* (London: The Hogarth Press), 1-138.

Fromm, Erich (1991), 'Psychoanalytic Characterology and its Significance for Social Psychology', in Erich Fromm (ed.), *The Crisis of Psychoanalysis: Essays on Freud, Marx and Social Psychology* (New York: Holt & Reinhart), 161–80.
Fromm, Erich (1994), *Escape from Freedom* (New York: Holt Publishers).
Frow, John (1997), *Time and Commodity Culture: Essays in Cultural Theory and Postmodernity* (Oxford: Clarendon Press).
Frye, Northrop (1964), *The Educated Imagination* (Bloomington: Indiana University Press).
Frye, Northrop (1970), *The Stubborn Structure: Essays on Criticism and Society* (London: Methuen).
Frye, Northrop (1976a), *Spiritus Mundi: Essays on Literature, Myth and Society* (Bloomington: Indiana University Press).
Frye, Northrop (1976b), *The Secular Scripture: A Study of the Structure of Romance* (Cambridge, MA; London: Harvard University Press).
Frye, Northrop (2000), *Anatomy of Criticism: Four Essays (Fifteenth Edition with a New Foreword)* (Princeton; Oxford: Princeton University Press).
Genette, Gerard (1983), *Narrative Discourse: An Essay in Method* (Ithaca, NY: Cornell University Press).
Gerrig, Richard and Rapp, David (2004), 'Psychological Processes Underlying Literary Impact', *Poetics Today*, 25 (2), 265–81.
Gerrig, Richard J. (1993), *Experiencing Narrative Worlds: On the Psychological Activities of Reading* (New Haven: Yale University Press).
Green, Melanie and Donahue, John (2011), 'Persistence of Belief Change in the Face of Deception: The Effect of Factual Stories Revealed to Be False', *Media Psychology*, 14 (3), 312–31.
Green, Melanie and Brock, Timothy (2013), 'In the Mind's Eye: Transportation-imagery Model of Narrative Persuasion', in Melanie Green, Timothy Brock, and Jeffrey Strange (eds), *Narrative Impact: Social and Cognitive Foundations* (New York: Psychology Press), 315–41.
Green, Melanie, Brock, Timothy, and Kaufman, Geoff (2004), 'Understanding Media Enjoyment: The Role of Transportation Into Narrative Worlds', *Communication Theory*, 14 (4), 311–27.
Grünbaum, Adolph (1984), *The Foundations of Psychoanalysis: A Philosophical Critique* (Berkeley, CA: UCLA Press).
Habermas, Jürgen (1970a), 'Towards a Theory of Communicative Competence', *Inquiry*, 13 (1–4), 360–75.
Habermas, Jürgen (1970b), 'On Systematically Distorted Communication', *Inquiry*, 13 (1–4), 205–18.
Habermas, Jürgen (1970c), *Toward a Rational Society: Student Protest, Science and Politics*, trans. Jeremy Shapiro (Boston: Beacon Press).
Habermas, Jürgen (1975a), 'Towards a Reconstruction of Historical Materialism', *Theory and Society*, 2 (3), 287–300.
Habermas, Jürgen (1975b), *Legitimation Crisis* (Boston: Beacon Press).
Habermas, Jürgen (1976), 'A Positivistically Bisected Rationalism', in Theodor Adorno, et al. (eds), *The Positivism Dispute in German Sociology* (London: Heinemann), 198–225.
Habermas, Jürgen (1979a), 'Consciousness-Raising or Redemptive Criticism: The Contemporaneity of Walter Benjamin', *New German Critique*, 17, 30–59.

Habermas, Jürgen (1979b), *Communication and the Evolution of Society*, trans. Thomas McCarthy (London: Heinemann).

Habermas, Jürgen (1981), 'Modernity versus Postmodernity', *New German Critique*, (22), 3-14.

Habermas, Jürgen (1982), 'The Entwinement of Myth and Enlightenment: Re-Reading *Dialectic of Enlightenment*', *New German Critique*, 26, 13-30.

Habermas, Jürgen (1983), *Political-Philosophical Profiles* (London: Heinemann).

Habermas, Jürgen (1984), *The Theory of Communicative Action: Reason and the Rationalisation of Society*, trans. Thomas McCarthy, 2 vols. (1; Boston: Beacon Press).

Habermas, Jürgen (1985), 'Modernity - An Incomplete Project', in Hal Foster (ed.), *Postmodern Culture* (London: Pluto Press), 3-15.

Habermas, Jürgen (1987), *The Theory of Communicative Action: System and Lifeworld*, trans. Thomas McCarthy, 2 vols (2; Boston: Beacon Press).

Habermas, Jürgen (1988), *On The Logic of the Social Sciences*, trans. Shierry Weber Nicholson and Jerry Stark (Cambridge: Polity).

Habermas, Jürgen (1991a), 'A Reply', in Axel Honneth and Hans Joas (eds), *Communicative Action* (London: MIT Press), 214-64.

Habermas, Jürgen (1991b), *The Structural Transformation of the Public Sphere: An Inquiry into a Category of Bourgeois Society*, trans. Thomas Burger (Cambridge, MA: MIT Press).

Habermas, Jürgen (1992a), *Postmetaphysical Thinking: Philosophical Essays* (Cambridge: Polity Press).

Habermas, Jürgen (1992b), 'Concluding Remarks', in Craig Calhoun (ed.), *Habermas and the Public Sphere* (Cambridge, MA: MIT Press), 464-9.

Habermas, Jürgen (1992c), 'Further Reflections on the Public Sphere', in Craig Calhoun (ed.), *Habermas and the Public Sphere* (Cambridge, MA: MIT Press), 421-61.

Habermas, Jürgen (1996a), *The Habermas Reader: Edited by William Outhwaite* (Cambridge: Polity Press).

Habermas, Jürgen (1996b), *Between Facts and Norms: Contribution to a Discourse Theory of Law and Democracy*, trans. William Rehg (Cambridge, MA: MIT Press).

Habermas, Jürgen (1998a), *The Inclusion of the Other: Studies in Political Theory*, trans. Ciaran Cronin and Pablo de Greiff (Cambridge, MA: MIT Press).

Habermas, Jürgen (1998b), *On the Pragmatics of Communication*, trans. Maeve Cooke (Cambridge, MA: Polity Press).

Habermas, Jürgen (1999a), 'Questions and Counter-Questions', in Maeve Cooke (ed.), *On the Pragmatics of Communication* (Cambridge: Polity Press), 403-33.

Habermas, Jürgen (1999b), *Moral Consciousness and Communicative Action*, trans. Christian Lenhardt and Sherry Nicholsen (Cambridge: MIT Press).

Habermas, Jürgen (2001), *The Post-National Constellation: Political Essays*, trans. Max Pensky (Cambridge: Polity Press).

Habermas, Jürgen (2002), *Religion and Rationality: Essays on Reason, God and Modernity* (Cambridge, MA: MIT Press).

Habermas, Jürgen (2005), *Truth and Justification*, trans. Barbara Fultner (Cambridge, MA: MIT Press).

Habermas, Jürgen (2006), *The Divided West* (Cambridge: Polity Press).

Habermas, Jürgen (2008a), 'A Post-secular Society–What Does That Mean?', *Reset: Dialogues on Civilizations*, (16 September 2008).
Habermas, Jürgen (2008b), *Between Naturalism and Religion: Philosophical Essays*, trans. Ciaran Cronin (Cambridge: Polity Press).
Habermas, Jürgen (2008c), 'Notes on Post-secular Society', *NPQ*, (Fall, 2008), 1–14.
Habermas, Jürgen (2010), 'The Concept of Human Dignity and the Realistic Utopia of Human Rights', *Metaphilosophy*, 41 (4), 464–80.
Haug, Wolfgang (1986), *Critique of Commodity Aesthetics: Appearance, Sexuality and Advertising in Capitalist Society*, trans. Robert Bock (Cambridge: Polity Press).
Heidegger, Martin (2008), *Basic Writings* (New York: Harper Perennial).
Heim, Robert (1980), 'Lorenzer und/oder Lacan. Das Subjekt zwischen Sinn und Buchstabe', *Psyche: Zeitschrift für Psychoanalyse*, 34 (10), 910–44.
Held, David (1980), *Introduction to Critical Theory* (Berkeley: UCLA Press).
Hengen-Fox, Nicholas (2012), 'A Habermasian Literary Criticism', *New Literary History*, 43 (2), 235–54.
Hengen-Fox, Nicholas (2017), *Reading as Collective Action: Text as Tactics* (Iowa City: University of Iowa Press).
Herf, Jeffrey (1984), *Reactionary Modernism: Technology, Culture and Politics in Weimar and the Third Reich* (Cambridge; New York; Melbourne: Cambridge University Press).
Hoelzel, Alfred (1988), 'Leverkühn, the Mermaid, and Echo: A Tale of Faustian Incest', *Symposium: A Quarterly Journal in Modern Literatures*, 42 (1), 3–16.
Hohendahl, Peter Uwe (1997), *Prismatic Thought: Theodor W. Adorno* (Lincoln: University of Nebraska Press).
Honneth, Axel (2014), *Freedom's Right: The Social Foundations of Democratic Life*, trans. Joseph Ganahl (New York: Columbia University Press).
Honneth, Axel (1991), *The Critique of Power: Reflective Stages in a Critical Social Theory* (Cambridge, MA and London: MIT Press).
Honneth, Axel (1995), *The Struggle for Recognition: The Moral Grammar of Social Conflicts*, trans. Joel Anderson (Cambridge: Polity Press).
Honold, Alexander (2017), 'The Musical Development of Shakespeare's Comedy in Mann's Faustus', in Tobias Döring and Ewan Fernie (eds), *Something Rich and Strange: Thomas Mann and Shakespeare* (London; New York: Bloomsbury Academic), 70–94.
Horkheimer, Max (1973), 'The Authoritarian State', *Telos: A Quarterly Journal of Critical Thought*, 15 (2), 3–20.
Horkheimer, Max (1974), *Eclipse of Reason* (New York: Seabury Press).
Horkheimer, Max (1982), *Critical Theory: Selected Essays* (New York: Continuum).
Horkheimer, Max (1989), 'The Jews and Europe', in Stephen Eric Bronner and Douglas Kellner (eds), *Critical Theory and Society* (London; New York: Routledge), 77–94.
Hume, Kathryn (1984), *Fantasy and Mimesis: Responses to Reality in Western Literature* (London: Methuen).
Hunter, G. Frederick (1985), 'Commitment and Autonomy in Art: Antinomies of Frankfurt Esthetic Theory', *Berkeley Journal of Sociology*, 30, 41–64.

Hutcheon, Linda (1988), *A Poetics of Postmodernism: History, Theory, Fiction* (New York: Routledge).
Hutcheon, Linda (2013), *Narcissistic Narrative: The Metafictional Paradox; With a New Preface (Kindle Edition)* (Waterloo: Wilfrid Laurier University Press).
Huyssen, Andreas (1986), *After the Great Divide: Modernism, Mass Culture, Postmodernism* (Bloomington: Indiana University Press).
Ingram, David (1987), *Habermas and the Dialectic of Reason* (New Haven: Yale University Press).
Ingram, David (1991), 'Habermas on Aesthetics and Rationality: Completing the Project of Enlightenment', *New German Critique*, 53, 67–103.
Iser, Wolfgang (1974), *The Implied Reader* (Baltimore; London: Johns Hopkins University Press).
Iser, Wolfgang (1980), *The Act of Reading: A Theory of Aesthetic Response* (Baltimore; London: The Johns Hopkins University Press).
Jakobson, Roman (1987), *Language In Literature* (Pomorska, Krystyna Rudy, Stephen edn.; Cambridge, MA: Belknap Press).
Jameson, Fredric (1981), *The Political Unconscious: Narrative as a Socially Symbolic Act* (Ithaca: Cornell University Press).
Jameson, Fredric (1990), *Late Marxism: Adorno, Or, The Persistence of the Dialectic* (London and New York: Verso).
Jameson, Fredric (1991), *Postmodernism, Or, The Cultural Logic of Late Capitalism* (Durham: Duke University Press).
Jameson, Fredric (1992), *Signatures of the Visible* (London and New York: Routledge).
Jameson, Fredric (2005), *Archaeologies of the Future: The Desire called Utopia and Other Science Fictions* (London; New York: Verso).
Jarvis, Simon (1998), *Adorno: A Critical Introduction* (Cambridge: Polity Press).
Jauss, Hans Robert (1982a), *Towards an Aesthetic of Reception* (Minneapolis: University of Minnesota Press).
Jauss, Hans Robert (1982b), *Aesthetic Experience and Literary Hermeneutics* (Minneapolis: University of Minnesota Press).
Jay, Martin (1973), *The Dialectical Imagination* (Boston; Toronto: Little, Brown & Co.).
Jay, Martin (1977), 'The Concept of Totality in Lukács and Adorno', in Shlomo Avineri (ed.), *Varieties of Marxism* (The Hague: Martinus Nijhoff), 147–74.
Jay, Martin (1994), *Downcast Eyes: The Denigration of Vision in Twentieth-century French Thought* (Los Angeles: UCLA Press).
Jendreiek, Helmut (1977), *Thomas Mann: Der demokratische Roman* (Dusseldorf: Bagel).
Johnson, Pauline (1987), 'An Aesthetics of Negativity/An Aesthetics of Reception: Jauss's Dispute with Adorno', *New German Critique*, 42, 51–70.
Jones, E. Michael (2002), 'Education as Magic: Harry Potter and the Culture of Narcissism', *Culture Wars*.
Kandel, Eric R. (2005), *Psychiatry, psychoanalysis, and the new biology of mind* 1st edn (Washington, DC: American Psychiatric Pub.) xxvi, 414 p.
Kernberg, Otto F. (1975), *Borderline Conditions and Pathological Narcissism* (New York: Aronson).

Kline, Paul (2014), *Fact and Fantasy in Freudian Psychoanalysis* 2nd edn (London; New York: Methuen).
Kohlberg, Lawrence, Noam, Gil, and Snarey (1983), 'Ego Development in Perspective: Structural Stage, Functional Phase, and Cultural Age-period Models', *Developmental Review*, 3 (3), 303–38.
Kompridis, Nikolas (2006), *Critique and Disclosure: Critical Theory between Past and Future* (Cambridge, MA; London: MIT Press).
Koppe, Franz (2004), *Grundbegriffe der Ästhetik* (Paderborn: Mentis Verlag).
Lacan, Jacques (2006), *Écrits: The First Complete Edition in English*, trans. Bruce Fink and Russell Grigg (New York: Norton).
Lafont, Christina (1994), 'World-Disclosure and Reference', *Thesis Eleven*, 34, 46–65.
Lafont, Christina (2000), *Heidegger, Language and World-disclosure* (Cambridge: Cambridge University Press).
Lee, Frances (2007), *Overturning Dr Faustus: Rereading Thomas Mann's Novel in Light of Observations of a Nonpolitical Man* (Rochester, NY: Camden House).
Lefort, Claude (1986), *The Political Forms of Modern Society* (Cambridge: Polity Press).
Lefort, Claude (1988), *Democracy and Political Theory* (Cambridge: Polity Press).
Lesser, J. (1950), 'Of Thomas Mann's Renunciation (Part I)', *The Germanic Review: Literature, Culture, Theory*, 25 (4), 245–56.
Lesser, J. (1951), 'Of Thomas Mann's Renunciation (Part II)', *The Germanic Review: Literature, Culture, Theory*, 26 (1), 22–33.
Loevinger, Jane (1983), 'On Ego Development and the Structure of Personality', *Developmental Review*, 3 (3), 339–50.
Loevinger, Jane and Blassi, Augusto (1976), *Ego Development* (San Francisco: Jossey-Bass Publishers).
Lorenzer, Alfred (1970a), *Sprachzerstörung und Rekonstruktion: Vorarbeiten zu einer Metatheorieder Psychoanalyse* (Frankfurt am Main: Suhrkamp).
Lorenzer, Alfred (1970b), *Zur Kritik des psychoanalytischen Symbolbegriffs* (Frankfurt am Main: Suhrkamp).
Lorenzer, Alfred (1986), 'Tiefenhermeneutische Kulturanalyse', in Alfred Lorenzer (ed.), *KulturAnalysen: Psychoanalytische Studien zur Kultur* (Frankfurt am Main: Fischer Verlag), 11–98.
Lukács, Georg (1962), *The Historical Novel* (London: Merlin).
Lukács, Georg (1963), *Die Eigenart des Ästhetischen*, 2 vols (Neuwied: Luchterhand).
Lukács, Georg (1971), *History and Class Consciousness: Studies in Marxist Dialectics*, trans. Rodney Livingstone (London: Merlin).
Lukács, Georg (1980), *The Destruction of Reason* (London: Merlin Press).
Lukács, György (1964), *Essays on Thomas Mann* (London: Merlin).
Lukács, György (1975), *The Young Hegel: Studies in the Relations Between Dialectics and Economics*, trans. Rodney Livingstone (Cambridge: MIT Press).
Macherey, Pierre (1978), *A Theory of Literary Production*, trans. Geoffrey Wall (London: Routledge and Kegan Paul).
MacKendrick, Kenneth (2008), *Discourse, Desire and Fantasy in Jürgen Habermas's Critical Theory* (London; New York: Routledge).

MacPherson, C. B. (1962), *The Political Theory of Possessive Individualism: From Hobbes to Locke* (London: Oxford University Press).
Maltby, Paul (1991), *Dissident Postmodernists: Barthelme, Coover, Pynchon* (Philadelphia: University of Pennsylvania Press).
Mann, Thomas (1947a), 'The Suffering and Greatness of Richard Wagner', in H. T. Lowe-Porter (ed.), *Thomas Mann: Essays of Three Decades* (New York: Alfred Knopf), 332–61.
Mann, Thomas (1947b), 'Schopenhauer', in H. T. Lowe-Porter (ed.), *Thomas Mann: Essays of Three Decades* (New York: Alfred Knopf), 362–410.
Mann, Thomas (1947c), 'Freud and the Future', in H. T. Lowe-Porter (ed.), *Thomas Mann: Essays of Three Decades* (New York: Alfred Knopf), 411–28.
Mann, Thomas (1959), 'Nietzsche's Philosophy in the Light of Recent History', in Dorothy Lowe Porter (ed.), *Last Essays* (New York: Alfred Knopf), 141–77.
Mann, Thomas (1961), *The Story of a Novel: The Genesis of Doctor Faustus* (New York: Alfred A. Knopf).
Mann, Thomas (1973), 'Germany and the Germans', in Library of Congress (ed.), *Literary Lectures Presented at the Library of Congress* (Washington, DC: Library of Congress), 1–20.
Mann, Thomas (1988), 'Mario and the Magician', in Thomas Mann (ed.), *Mario and the Magician and Other Stories* (London: Vintage), 113–57.
Mann, Thomas (2001), 'Blood of the Walsungs', *Thomas Mann's Collected Stories* 2nd edn (London: Everyman's Library), 289–316.
Mann, Thomas (2008), *Death in Venice and Other Stories*, trans. David Luke (New York: Bantam Publishers).
Mannoni, Octave (2003), 'I Know Very Well, But All the Same ...', in Molly Anne Rothberg, Denis Foster, and Slavoj Žižek (eds), *Perversion and the Social Relation* (Durham: Duke University Press), 68–92.
Marcuse, Herbert (1968), *Negations: Essays in Critical Theory*, trans. Jeremy Shapiro (London: Penguin).
Marcuse, Herbert (1999), *Reason and Revolution* (Amherst, NY: Humanity Books).
Marsh, James L (1983), 'Adorno's Critique of Stravinsky', *New German Critique*, 28, 147–69.
Marx, Karl (1963), *Capital, Vol. 1* (Moscow: Progress Publishers).
Masling, Joseph and Bornstein, Robert eds, (1994–2005), *Empirical Studies of Psychoanalytic Theories* 11 vols (Washington, DC: American Psychological Association).
McCarthy, Thomas (1996), *The Critical Theory of Jürgen Habermas* (Cambridge, MA; London: MIT Press).
McMahon, Jennifer A. (2011), 'Aesthetic Autonomy and Praxis: Art and Language in Adorno and Habermas', *International Journal of Philosophical Studies*, 19 (2), 155–75.
Mendelson, Jack (1979), 'The Habermas-Gadamer Debate', *New German Critique*, 18, 44–73.
Mendieta, Eduardo (2000), 'Modernity's Religion: Habermas and the Linguistification of the Sacred', in Lewis Edward Hahn (ed.), *Perspectives on Habermas* (Chicago; La Salle, IL: Open Court), 123–38.

Menninger, Karl A. (1954a), 'Psychological Aspects Of The Organism Under Stress: Part I–The Homeostatic Regulatory Function Of The Ego', *Journal of the American Psychoanalytic Association*, 2 (1), 67–106.

Menninger, Karl A. (1954b), 'Psychological Aspects Of The Organism Under Stress: Part II–Regulatory Devices of the Ego Under Major Stress', *Journal of the American Psychoanalytic Association*, 2 (1), 280–310.

Metz, Christian (1982), *The Imaginary Signifier* (Bloomington: Indiana University Press).

Miller, Alyson (2013), *Haunted by Words: Scandalous Texts* (Bern: Peter Lang).

Müller, Harro and Gillespie, Susan (2009), 'Mimetic Rationality: Adorno's Project of a Language of Philosophy', *New German Critique*, 108, 85–108.

Mundt, Hanelore (2004), *Understanding Thomas Mann* (Columbia: University of South Carolina Press).

Nell, Victor (1988), *Lost in a Book: The Psychology of Reading for Pleasure* (New Haven: Yale University Press).

Nell, Victor (2013), 'Mythic Structures in Narrative: The Domestication of Immortality', in Melanie Green, Timothy Brock, and Jeffrey Strange (eds), *Narrative Impact: Social and Cognitive Foundations* (New York: Psychology Press), 17–38.

Noerr, Gunzelin Schmid (2002), 'Editor's Afterword', in Gunzelin Schmid Noerr (ed.), *Dialectic of Enlightenment: Philosophical Fragments* (Stanford, CA: Stanford University Press), 217–47.

Norris, Christopher (1987), *Derrida* (London and Cambridge: Harvard University Press).

Norris, Christopher (2001), *Against Relativism: Philosophy of Science, Deconstruction and Critical Theory* (Oxford: Blackwell).

Nussbaum, Martha (1997), *Poetic Justice: The Literary Imagination and Public Life* (Boston: Beacon Press).

O'Neill, John (1988), 'Religion and Postmodernism: The Durkheimian Bond in Bell and Jameson', *Theory, Culture and Society*, 5 (2–3), 493–508.

Oatley, Keith (1995), 'A Taxonomy of the Emotions of Literary Response and a Theory of Identification in Fictional Narrative', *Poetics*, 23 (1), 53–74.

Paddison, Max (1993), *Adorno's Aesthetics of Music* (Cambridge: Cambridge University Press).

Paddison, Max (2003), 'Stravinsky as the Devil: Adorno's Three Critiques', in Jonathan Cross (ed.), *The Cambridge Companion to Stravinsky* (Cambridge: Cambridge University Press), 192–202.

Pelikan-Strauss, Nina (1987), 'Why Must Everything Seem Like Its Own Parody? Thomas Mann's Parody of Sigmund Freud in *Doctor Faustus*', *Literature and Psychology*, 33 (3–4), 59–75.

Plass, Ulrich (2012), *Language and History in Adorno's Notes to Literature* (London; New York: Routledge).

Pollock, Friedrich (1985), 'State Capitalism: Its Possibilities and Limitations', in Andrew Arato and Eike Gephardt (eds), *The Essential Frankfurt School Reader* (New York: Continuum), 71–94.

Potter, Brett David (2014), 'A Word Not Our Own: Northrop Frye and Karl Barth on Revelation and Imagination', *Literature and Theology*, 28 (4), 438–56.

Pratt, Mary (1977), *Toward A Speech Act Theory Of Literary Discourse* (Bloomington, IN: Indiana University Press).
Rancière, Jacques (1999), *Disagreement*, trans. Julie Rose (Minneapolis: University of Minnesota Press).
Rank, Otto (1971), *The Double: A Psychoanalytic Study* (Chapel Hill: University of North Carolina Press).
Ricoeur, Paul (1970), *Freud and Philosophy: An Essay on Interpretation*, trans. Denis Savage (New Haven and London: Yale University Press).
Ricoeur, Paul (1984), *Time and Narrative, Volume One*, trans. Kathleen Blamey and David Pellauer, 3 vols. (1; Chicago and London: University of Chicago Press).
Ricoeur, Paul (1985), *Time and Narrative, Volume Two*, trans. Kathleen Blamey and David Pellauer, 3 vols. (2; Chicago and London: University of Chicago Press).
Rimmon-Kenan, Shlomith (1983), *Narrative Fiction: Contemporary Poetics* (London; New York: Methuen).
Rose, Gillian (2014), *The Melancholy Science: An Introduction to the Thought of Theodor W. Adorno (Verso Reprint)* (London; New York: Verso).
Russell, Matheson and Montin, Andrew (2015), 'The Rationality of Political Disagreement: Rancière's Critique of Habermas', *Constellations: An International Journal of Critical and Democratic Theory*, 22 (4), 543-54.
Sartre, Jean-Paul (1973), *Existentialism and Humanism*, trans. Pierre Mairet (London: Methuen).
Schiller, Herbert (1976), *Communication and Cultural Domination* (London: Routledge).
Schiller, Herbert (1991), *Culture Inc.: The Corporate Takeover of Public Expression* (Oxford: Oxford University Press).
Schmidt, James (2004), 'Mephistopheles in Hollywood: Adorno, Mann and Schönberg', in Thomas Huhn (ed.), *The Cambridge Companion to Adorno* (Cambridge: Cambridge University Press), 148-80.
Schönberg, Arnold (1975), *Style and Idea*, trans. Leo Black (Berkeley; Los Angeles: UCLA Press).
Schutz, Alfred (1970), *Reflections on the Problem of Relevance* (New Haven: Yale University Press).
Searle, John (1975), 'The Logical Status of Fictional Discourse', *New Literary History*, 6 (2), 319-32.
Seelow, David (2005), *Radical Modernism and Sexuality: Freud, Reich, D.H. Lawrence and Beyond* (New York: Palgrave Macmillan).
Sherratt, Yvonne (2002), *Adorno's Positive Dialectic* (Cambridge: Cambridge University Press).
Sitton, John (2003), *Habermas and Contemporary Society* (London; New York: Palgrave Macmillan).
Strange, Jeffrey (2013), 'How Fictional Tales Wag Real World Beliefs: Models and Mechanisms of Narrative Influence', in Melanie Green, Timothy Brock, and Jeffrey Strange (eds), *Narrative Impact: Social and Cognitive Foundations* (New York: Psychology Press), 263-86.
Sutrop, Margit (2000), *Fiction and Imagination: The Anthropological Function of Literature* (Paderborn: Mentis).

Taylor, Charles (1989), *Sources of the Self* (Cambridge, MA: Harvard University Press).
Taylor, Charles (1991), *The Ethics of Authenticity* (Cambridge, MA; London: Harvard University Press).
Taylor, Charles (1994), 'The Politics of Recognition', in Amy Gutmann (ed.), *Multiculturalism: Examining the Politics of Recognition* (Princeton: Princeton University Press).
Taylor, Charles (2003), *Modern Social Imaginaries* (Durham; Leeds: Duke University Press).
Taylor, Charles (2007), *A Secular Age* (Cambridge, MA: Belknap Press of Harvard University Press).
Therborn, Göran (1980), *The Power of Ideology and the Ideology of Power* (London: New Left Books).
Thompson, Michael J. (2016), *The Domestication of Critical Theory* (London; Lanham: Rowman & Littlefield).
Todorov, Tzvetan (1975), *The Fantastic: A Structural Approach to a Literary Genre* (Ithaca, NY: Cornell University Press).
Trotsky, Leon (1975), *The Struggle against Fascism in Germany* (Harmondsworth: Pelican).
Turner-Vorbeck, Tammy (2003), 'Pottermania: Good Clean Fun or Cultural Hegemony?', in Elizabeth Heilman (ed.), *Harry Potter's World: Multidisciplinary Critical Perspectives* (New York: Routledge-Falmer), 13-24.
Vaget, Hans Rudolf (2002), 'German Music and German Catastrophe: A Re-reading of Doktor Faustus', in Herbert Lehnert and Eva Wessell (eds), *A Companion to the Works of Thomas Mann* (London: Boydell & Brewer, Camden House), 221-44.
Vila-Matas, Enrique ed, (2012), *Thomas Mann and Theodor Adorno: An Exchange* (Berlin: Hatje Cantz Verlag).
Von Rohr Scaff, Susan (2002), 'Doctor Faustus', in Richie Robertson (ed.), *The Cambridge Companion to Thomas Mann* (Cambridge; New York: Cambridge University Press), 168-84.
Warner, Michael (2005), *Publics and Counterpublics* (New York: Zone Books).
Watt, Ian (1963), *The Rise of the Novel: Studies in Defoe, Richardson and Fielding* (Harmondsworth: Penguin).
Waugh, Linda (1980), 'The Poetic Function in the Theory of Roman Jakobson', *Poetics Today*, 2 (1a), 57-82.
Weber-Nicholsen, Sherry (1997), *Exact Imagination, Late Work: On Adorno's Aesthetics* (Cambridge, MA: MIT Press).
Weber, Max (1958), *The Rational and Social Foundations of Music* (Carbondale: Southern Illinois University Press).
Weber, Max (1968), *Economy and Society: An Outline of Interpretive Sociology*, 2 vols (1; Berkeley, CA: University of California Press).
Wellmer, Albrecht (1991), *The Persistence of Modernity: Essays on Aesthetics, Ethics and Postmodernism*, trans. David Midgley (Cambridge, MA and London: MIT Press).
Wellmer, Albrecht (1998), *Endgames: The Irreconcilable Nature of Modernity*, trans. David Midgley (Cambridge, MA and London: MIT Press).

Whitebook, Joel (1979), 'The Problem of Nature in Habermas', *Telos: A Quarterly Journal of Critical Thought*, 40, 41–69.
Whitebook, Joel (1995), *Perversion and Utopia: A Study in Psychoanalysis and Critical Theory* (Cambridge, MA: MIT Press).
Whited, Lana (2003), 'What Would Harry Do?', in Lana Whited (ed.), *The Ivory Tower and Harry Potter: Perspectives on a Literary Phenomenon* (Columbia: University of Missouri Press), 182–208.
Whited, Lana (2006), '1492, 1942, 1992: The Theme of Race in the Harry Potter Series', *The Looking Glass: New Perspectives on Children's Literature*, 10 (1).
Wiggershaus, Rolf (1994), *The Frankfurt School: Its History, Theories, and Political Significance*, trans. Michael Robertson (Cambridge: Polity).
Williams, Raymond (1974), *Television: Technology and Cultural Form* (London: Fontana).
Wohlberg, Steve (2002), *Hidden Dangers in Harry Potter* (Kindle Edition: Amazing Facts).
Zipes, Jack (2002), *Sticks and Stones: The Troublesome Success of Children's Literature from Slovenly Peter to Harry Potter* (London; New York: Routledge).
Žižek, Slavoj (1996), *The Indivisible Remainder: An Essay on Schelling and Related Matters* (London and New York: Verso).
Zuidervaart, Lambert (1991), *Adorno's Aesthetic Theory: The Redemption of Illusion* (Cambridge, MA: MIT Press).
Zuidervaart, Lambert (2004), *Artistic Truth: Aesthetics, Discourse and Imaginative Disclosure* (Cambridge, UK; New York: Cambridge University Press).

INDEX

Note: Page numbers followed by 'n' refer to notes.

action coordination   64, 65, 77, 113, 125, 195, 200, 201
The Act of Reading   108
Adorno, Theodor   2–4, 159. *See also individual entries*
  aesthetic theory   35–58
  Aesthetic Theory   13, 29, 32
  analysis of dialectical process   52
  Beckett, Samuel   56–8
  Beethoven: The Philosophy of Music   45
  conception   43
  critical social theory   15
  Dialectic of Enlightenment   4, 13–15, 20, 21, 28, 33, 159–60
  George, Stefan   54–6
  Habermas's critique of   30–3
  insights, retrieving   89–90
  Minima Moralia   29
  Missa Solemnis   45
  music theory   49
  Negative Dialectics   13, 32
  perspective   161, 168
  Philosophy of Modern Music   28, 39, 43, 160, 165
  'Reflections on Class Theory'   23
  Schönberg, Arnold   49–52
  social philosophy   13–33
  Stravinsky, Igor   52–4
aesthetic-expressive rationality   111, 112
aesthetic mimesis   13, 28–31, 33, 35–8, 42, 89, 90, 94
  antidote to instrumental rationality   28–30
aesthetic theory   8, 13, 16, 29, 30, 32, 35–58, 169, 170

authenticity *vs.* rationalization   39–41
avant-garde rupture and artistic truth   41–2
classicism, romanticism, modernism   45–7
content and form   42
creative praxis and artistic monads   37–9
historical dialectics, literary material   47–9
historical dialectics, musical material   43–5
import and impact   42–3
material and technique   42
affirmative culture   44, 46, 53, 88, 89, 98–102, 105, 106
allegorical interpretation   160–3, 165–8
Althusser, Louis   212–14
antinomies   22, 90, 91, 184, 185
antinomy, resolving   90–2
Antonio, Robert   81
anxiety   182, 183
argumentation   67, 112, 114, 116, 121, 122, 196, 198, 200, 201
art   38–9
artistic monads   37–9
artistic truth   41–2, 198, 199
artworks   25, 28–30, 35–9, 42, 43, 46, 91, 170
authenticity
  vs. rationalization   39–41
  Stefan George and   54–6
authentic literature   115–18
authoritarian personality   21, 26–8
authoritarian populism   1

Index

autonomous artworks 36–8
autonomous literature 8, 90, 94, 100
avant-garde rupture 41–2

baroque literature 102
Baudelaire, Charles 49
Beckett, Samuel 37, 57
   Endgame 57, 58
   and rationalization 56–8
Beddow, Michael 166
Beethoven, Ludwig van 44
Benhabib, Seyla 4, 82–3, 218–19
Benjamin, Walter 91
Berlioz, Louis-Hector 46
Berman, Russell 101, 102
   The Rise of the Modern German Novel: Crisis and Charisma 101
Bernstein, J. M. 30, 80
Bernstein, Richard 30
Bohman, James 198–9
Bolz, Norbert 37 n.1
bourgeois society 18, 22, 24, 45, 49, 60, 90, 96, 98, 104, 229
Buck-Morss, Susan 15, 17
Bürger, Peter 52

capitalism 35
civilizations 15, 26, 179, 182, 184, 190, 205, 224, 227
civil society 73, 214
classicism 45–7
Cobley, Evelyn 161
Colclasure, David 117
   Habermas and Literary Rationality 117
colonization 13
   of public sphere 76–9
commodity aesthetics 92
communicative action 8, 13, 14, 59, 64–8, 70, 74, 187, 188, 195, 200
communicative approach 2
communicative disturbances 73, 147, 151, 152, 154, 158
communicative intersubjectivity 15
communicative model 8, 123–4, 127, 128

communicative perspective 6, 11, 86, 98, 119, 133, 134, 151, 162, 184
communicative reading 184–5
communicative reason 5–7, 66–72, 89, 90, 105–7, 111–13, 187, 201
concretization 108, 109, 120, 134, 204
corporate colonization 76–9
counter-hegemony 102–4
creative praxis 37–9
crisis tendencies 5, 18, 59, 60, 62, 63, 70, 73
critical enlightenment 85, 89, 93
Critical Theory 3–5, 15–18, 79–81, 89, 90, 197–9
critique of surplus repression 143
cultural value spheres 67, 75, 90, 92, 113
culture industry 20, 22, 25, 27, 38, 39, 47, 48, 60, 62, 88, 89, 99, 100, 102

Dahlhaus, Carl 52
death 165, 167, 173–6, 182–5, 237, 246, 247, 253
decomposition 170, 174
defence mechanisms 150–4
democratic expectations 62–4
democratic politics 60–2
developmental psychology 113, 119, 140, 147, 148, 155
devil 159–85
dialectical reinscription 14
dialectical social programme 35
dialectical theory 47
dialectic of enlightenment 13
disavowal 151, 152, 154
disclosure
   category 189–91
   debate on 196–9
   hermeneutics of retrieval 203–4
   language and 191–4
   reciprocity of 199–202
   and truth-potential 194–6
discourse 65, 71, 113, 120, 121, 149, 151, 159, 187, 197
discourse ethics 3, 5, 66–72, 81, 155, 218

distorted communication 77, 78, 147
Döbert, Rainer 149
Döblin, Alfred 102
Dollimore, Jonathan 178
doppelgänger 245–8
dramaturgical actions 67, 116
Duvenage, Pieter 6, 107, 197, 200, 222–3

Eclipse of Reason 21
education 78, 95, 96, 99, 118, 241, 248, 250
education novel 241–5
ego 27–30, 135, 139, 140, 142, 144, 145, 148–52, 155, 182, 247
  deformations 150–4
  identity 131, 132, 142, 147–9, 155, 156, 189
  maturity 147–50
  psychology 147–9
Eichendorf, Joseph Freiherr von 48
emancipatory critique 60–2
emancipatory literature 9, 86, 93, 118, 135
emplotment 207–10
enlightenment 4, 13, 15, 19–24, 28, 32, 33, 80, 86, 87, 160
enlightenment humanism, utopian vision 226–9
equivocal reference 128–30, 204
Erikson, Erik 149, 150
ethical life 10, 11, 14, 24, 93, 94, 153–5, 209, 210, 214, 216–18
exclusive humanism, secular age 219–21
experimental literature 9
expressive institution 114, 118–20, 122
expressive rationality 113–15
expressive truthfulness 115–18
expressive validity claims 70, 113, 128, 200, 201

fantasy quest 245–8
fascist dictatorship 4
feelings 40, 41, 54, 55, 67, 68, 94, 113, 115–17, 120, 121, 131, 251
Felski, Rita 5, 81–2, 121

Ferrara, Alessandro 117, 138, 156, 157
Fontane, Theodor 101
Forst, Rainer 71
Foucault, Michel 198
  Discipline and Punish 198
Frankfurt School Marxism 5, 10, 17, 18, 30
Fraser, Nancy 4, 61, 81–2, 218
Freud, Anna 151
Freud, Sigmund 18, 19, 26, 27, 29, 79, 80, 137, 139, 141, 143, 151, 175, 181–3
  Civilization and Its Discontents 26, 182
Freytag, Gustav 101
Fromm, Erich 26, 27
Frye, Northrop 203–6, 223–8
functional systems 64, 65, 73, 74, 79, 218

gender 81, 82, 235
George, Stefan 37, 40, 54–6
Goethe, Johann Wolfgang von 48
group loyalty 237, 239–42, 249

Habermas, Jurgen (books)
  Between Facts and Norms 59
  Between Naturalism and Religion 59
  The Intervention of the Other 59
  Knowledge and Human Interests 137
  Legitimation Crisis 62
  The Philosophical Discourse of Modernity 32, 85, 125, 188, 196, 201
  The Structural Transformation of the Public Sphere 3, 4, 14, 160
  The Theory of Communicative Action 14, 31, 59, 66
Habermasian social theory 59–83
Handel, George Friedrich 44
Harry Potter series 231–54
  dialectic of enchantment 252–4
  doppelgänger twist 245–8
  education novel 241–5
  fantasy quest 245–8

ironization of Harry Potter   250–2
moral development   241–5
politics of reading   234–5
school days novel inversion
   238–41
triple elaboration   248–50
Hartmann, Heinz   148
Haydn, Joseph   44
Hegelian Marxism   18
Heine, Heinrich   37, 48
Hengen-Fox, Nicholas   5
Hermann, Georg   101
hibernation   13
hidden desires   137–58
historical dialectics   41
   of literary material   47–9
   of musical material   43–5
historical enlightenment   87
historical materialism   3, 18, 59, 60,
   62, 64
historical teleology   14, 16, 17
Hohendahl, Peter   37
Hölderlin, Friedrich   48
Honneth, Axel   4, 66, 73, 82,
   217–18, 243
hope   2
Horkheimer, Max   18, 19, 23, 27
   'The Authoritarian State'   23
   Dialectic of Enlightenment   4,
      13–15, 20, 21, 28, 33, 159–60
   'The Jews and Europe'   28
human interests   132, 137–40, 155–7
   literature and   157–8
   in subjective integration   155–7
humanism   161, 166, 183, 211, 212,
   214, 220, 221, 228
human nature   26, 138, 139, 228,
   229

ideological interpellation   212–14
ideology   11, 62, 77, 78, 147, 151,
   180, 213, 214
imaginative disclosure   187–210
imaginative topocosm   211, 212,
   223–5, 227, 231
immersion   29, 30, 206–10
Ingram, David   5–6, 100
institutionalization   95, 96, 114

instrumental rationality   3, 13, 20,
   21, 23, 28, 29, 32, 33, 36–8, 58,
   89, 90
instrumental reason   17–19
intersubjective dialogue   151–3
intimacy   61, 98–100, 103
Iser, Wolfgang   107–9

Jakobson, Roman   125, 126
Jameson, Fredric   105, 157–8,
   213, 224
Jauss, Hans-Robert   134, 135
Jay, Martin   15, 17, 190
Jendreieck, Helmut   165
Jünger, Ernst   102
juridification   77, 78, 111

Kafka, Franz   37, 55
   The Trial   55
Kant, Immanuel   22
Kantian morality   10
Kantian moral law   10
Kiefer, Anselm   7
knowledge   138–40
   human interests and   138–40
Kompridis, Nikolas   199

labour process   14, 19, 38, 60, 91, 97
Lafont, Christina   191
late modernism   102–4
learning processes   70, 95, 96,
   111, 113, 119, 120, 155, 247,
   248, 253
legitimation crises   62–4
life history   147–50
linguistification   137, 140–2, 145–7,
   154, 161, 222
   unconscious   140–3
literal model   112–13
   limits to   118–20
literary autonomy   93–5
literary communication   1, 86–9
literary-critical method   5
literary criticism   5, 6, 114, 118, 123,
   187, 188, 194, 195, 205, 224
literary critique nature   111–18
   ambiguity of reference   124–7
   communicative model   123–4

'Discourse' and 'Critique'   121–2
expressive rationality   113–15
expressive truthfulness and authentic literature   115–18
fictive utterances   124–7
literal model   112–13
literary innovation and symbolic coherence   133–5
literary interventions and equivocal reference   129–33
literary semblances   127–9
literature and therapy   118–20
rhetorical model   120
literary discourse, modernity   85–109
  Adorno's insights, retrieving   89–90
  affirmative culture   99–102
  antinomy, resolving   90–2
  communicative reason and postmodernism debate   105–7
  Habermas and   2–5
  late modernism and counter-hegemony   102–4
  literary communication and philosophical discourse   86–9
  literary institutions and socialization processes   95–7
  reception aesthetics   107–9
  republic of letters, structural transformation   97–9
  value enhancement and literary autonomy   93–5
literary identification   187–210, 212–14
literary innovation   133–5
literary inscription, imaginative topocosm   223–6
literary institutions   95–7
literary materials   47, 48, 123, 133
literary realism   94, 100–2, 158
literary semblances   127–9
literary visions   211–29
literary works   5–8, 90, 91, 94, 103, 106, 188, 189, 204, 205, 207, 210
Loevinger, Jane   113–15, 140, 148, 149
Lorenzer, Alfred   138, 144–8, 158

Lukács, Georg   14–17, 19, 128, 168
  History and Class Consciousness   15

McCarthy, Thomas   140
Macherey, Pierre   213
MacKendrick, Kenneth   143
Mann, Thomas   102, 159, 162, 167
  Apocalypsis cum figuris   167, 170–2
  Death in Venice   185
  Doctor Faustus   159
  'Freud in the twentieth century'   181–4
  Joseph Tetralogy   183
  The Lamentation of Doctor Faustus   167, 172–4
  and *The Man Shakespeare and His Tragic Life Story*   175
  The Story of a Novel   162, 167
  'Tristan'   184
Marcuse, Herbert   3, 31–2
market society   38, 87, 88, 217, 220
Marsh, James   52
Marx, Karl   26
Marxism   3
mass culture   99, 105–7
Mendieta, Eduardo   221–2
metaphor   126, 127, 130, 158
metonymy   126, 127, 130, 158
modernism   45–7, 88–90, 96, 100–6, 163, 165, 168, 169
modernist revolt   99–102
modernity   80, 85–9, 93, 111, 159–61, 187, 188, 211, 215, 223
  literary discourse of   85–109
'modernity *vs.* postmodernity'   100
modern literature   1, 6, 8, 9, 85, 88, 93, 97, 101, 227, 229
modern social imaginary   221–3
moral development   115, 132, 241–5, 248–50
moral formalism   22, 24, 26, 87
morality   10
moral orders   217–19
moral reasoning   10
moral universalizability   72
motivational development   133

motivations 10
Mozart, Wolfgang Amadeus 44
Mündt, Hannelore 168
musical form 44, 53, 170
musical material 43–7, 50, 52, 54, 170

natural environment 1, 17, 20, 67, 92, 94, 118, 123, 139, 143, 150
Nazism 4
negative dialectics 3
Nietzsche, Freidrich 33, 178–82
  The Genealogy of Morals 181–2
novelistic anamorphosis 168–70
Nunner-Winckler, Gertud 149
Nussbaum, Martha 209

Oedipal conflict 183
orientations 10, 11

Paddison, Max 36, 37, 46, 52
phoenix, order of 235–8
Plass, Ulrich 37 n.1
politics of reading 234–5
Pollock, Friedrich 23
post-metaphysical psychoanalysis 143–6, 150
post-metaphysical thinking 4, 5, 79–83
postmodernism 37, 105–7, 157
postmodernism debate 105–7
post-traditional need-interpretations 113, 115, 123, 130, 137, 149, 215
Pratt, Mary 125
  Towards a Speech Act Theory of Literary Discourse 125
psychoanalysis 8, 10, 26, 81, 119, 137–41, 144–7, 183
psychoanalytic theories 26, 121, 137, 140, 184
public communication 140, 141, 144, 146

Rancière, Jacques 71
rationalization 15, 19–21, 36, 39–43, 47, 49, 55–7

readerships 94, 100, 123, 130, 134, 135
realization, philosophy 35
reception aesthetics 107–9
recognition frameworks 10, 82, 217–19
reflexive authenticity 156
reification 15–21, 35, 36, 56, 57, 59, 161, 163, 173
  alienation plus rationalization 15–17
  plus repression 17–19
religion 221–3
re-naturalization of music 170
repertoire 108, 109, 204, 206, 209, 232, 235, 236, 238, 241, 245, 248, 250
repression 17, 18, 21, 26, 27, 89, 137, 140, 141, 151, 153, 154, 172, 177, 182
republic of letters 97–9
rhetorical model 120, 122–5, 127, 201
Ricoeur, Paul 6, 203–4
Rilke, Rainer Maria 49
Rohr Scaff, Susan von 168
Romantic critique 19, 87–9
romanticism 45–7
Rose, Gillian 16–17, 37
Rowling, J. K.
  anti-fascist inspiration of 232–4
  Death Eaters 233, 236, 237, 252, 253
  Harry Potter series 231–54

scenic representations 145
Schönberg, Arnold 37, 49–52, 159, 165, 168, 172–4
self-contradiction 152
self-realization 8, 117, 122
semblances 204–7
Shakespeare, William 175–8
  Love's Labour Lost 176
  Measure for Measure 154
Sherrat, Yvonne 29, 30, 37 n.1
silenced needs 137–58
single existential judgment 3

social action 16, 62, 65, 66, 74, 112, 126, 130, 216
social antithesis 37
social authority 138, 142, 153, 154, 233, 241, 242, 248
social democratization 5
social imaginary 211–17, 219–21, 223, 225, 227, 229
socialization processes 95–7
social labour 22, 36, 38, 94, 155, 205
social philosophy 2, 4, 8, 13–33, 59
    aesthetic judgement and culture industry, metacritique 25–6
    aesthetic mimesis 28–30
    alienation plus rationalization 15–17
    authoritarian personality 26–8
    dialectical critique, Kant 22
    dialectic of enlightenment 20–2
    instrumental reason 17–19
    practical (normative) reason and moral formalism, metacritique 24–5
    reification 15–17
    reification plus repression 17–19
    repression of nature 26–8
    theoretical (cognitive) reason and social labour, metacritique 22–3
social relations 17, 37, 42, 50, 76, 77, 99, 101
social theory 3, 4, 8, 11, 35, 36, 59–83, 87, 215, 217
    communicative action 64–6
    communicative reason and discourse ethics 66–72
    corporate colonization, public sphere 76–9
    democratic politics and emancipatory critique 60–2
    legitimation crises 62–4
    post-metaphysical thinking and utopian energies 79–83
    system vs. lifeworld 72–6
societal rationalization 75, 97
sociocultural subsystems 62–4, 66
sociocultural system 64, 66
Stalinism 3
state capitalism 23, 60
Stifter, Adalbert 101
Stravinsky, Igor 37, 52–4, 170–2
subjective integration 155–7
sublimation 29, 30, 117, 137, 151, 162, 173, 177, 182
superego 27, 28, 140–2, 144, 148, 150, 153, 154, 156, 182, 184
surplus repression 141, 143, 153, 156, 178, 184
symbolic coherence 133–5
symbolic conception 141, 143, 144

Taylor, Charles 191–2, 211–12, 214–21
theory of communicative action 13, 14, 59, 64, 66, 111–13, 118, 120, 124, 125, 138, 187, 188
Thompson, Michael 79
transportation 207–10
truthfulness 68, 70, 93, 94, 113, 116, 189, 196

utopian energies 79–83

value enhancement 93–5
value-rational actions 67
value rationality 16
values 93, 116, 117, 121–3, 154, 156, 179, 180, 237, 242
value standards 116, 121, 122

Wagner, Richard 46
Weber, Max 26
    The Rational and Social Foundations of Music 43
Weber-Nicholson, Shierry 37 n.1
Wellmer, Albrecht 4, 6, 37, 105–6, 127–8, 188, 195–6
Whitebook, Joel 30, 143–4
work of art 30, 54, 91, 104, 106, 116, 128, 195, 196
world-disclosure 125, 187, 188, 190, 191, 197

Žižek, Slavoj 154
Zuidervaart, Lambert 5, 37–8, 197–9

www.ingramcontent.com/pod-product-compliance
Lightning Source LLC
Chambersburg PA
CBHW052217300426
44115CB00011B/1726